Copyright Acknowledgments

Grateful acknowledgment is made to the following sources for permission to reprint material copyrighted or controlled by them:

"Chapter 13: Of the Natural Condition of Mankind as concerning their Felicity and Misery," by Thomas Hobbes, reprinted from *Leviathan* (1962).

Excerpt from "Second Treatise of Civil Government (1690)," by John Locke, reprinted from *Of Civil Government and Toleration* (1905).

"The Social Contract," by Jean Rousseau, reprinted from *The Social Contract* (1913).

"The Declaration of Independence," (1776).

"The Declaration of the Rights of Man and Citizen," (1789).

"The Declaration of the Rights of Woman, September 1791," by Olympe de Gouges (Marie Gouze), reprinted from *The French Revolution and Human Rights: A Brief Documentary History*, edited by Lynn Hunt (1996), by permission of Bedford/St. Martin's.

"The World We Have Lost," by Peter Laslett, reprinted from *The World We Have Lost* (1965), by permission of Prentice Hall, Inc.

Excerpts from: The Sadler Report; Minutes of Evidence, reprinted from *Sessional Papers* (1833).

"Exploitation," by E.P. Thompson, reprinted from *The Making of the English Working Class* (1963), by permission of Pantheon Books.

"On Liberty," by John Mills (1859).

"The Return of Karl Marx," by John Cassidy, reprinted from *The New Yorker* (October 20/29, 1997), by permission of the author.

"The New Nationalism and Racism," by Heinrich Treitschke, reprinted from *Main Currents of Western Thought: Readings in Western European Intellectual History from the Middle Ages to the Present* (1978), by permission of Yale University Press.

"Imperialism, the Latest Stage of Capitalism," by V.I. Lenin, (1916).

"The White Man's Burden," by Rudyard Kipling.

"On the Democratic Welfare of the State," by Franklin Roosevelt, reprinted from *The Public Papers and Addresses of Franklin D. Roosevelt* (1941), by permission of Georges Borchardt Literary Agency.

Contents

Commerce, Cities, and Capitalism

John McGrath

During the High Middle Ages, Europeans had envied the wealth and sophistication of Asian and Middle Eastern civilizations. Italian trade with the eastern Mediterranean, stimulated by the Crusades, had connected the European economy to the extensive Asian trade networks that stretched all the way to China. While this gave Europeans access to useful and valuable goods from the east, Europe was comparatively poor and its participation in such early international trade was relatively minor. Moreover, Europeans' understanding of these societies was limited, since they knew them mostly indirectly through travelers' tales and legends of questionable accuracy; as a result, their attitudes towards non-Christians were characterized by suspicion and fear.[1]

Europe's insularity began to wane during the thirteenth and fourteenth centuries, as Europeans took the initiative in expanding their interactions with the outside world. Trade, as it frequently has in history, provided much of the impetus. Despite the problems of the Late Middle Ages, advances in both maritime technology and financial practices made it easier for merchants to do business farther and farther afield. The rise of powerful Italian trading states such as Venice and Genoa created regular links with the Middle East and North Africa. Further north, the emergence of trade associations such as the Hanseatic League energized trade in the Baltic and Atlantic regions. In turn, the growth of complex financial enterprises, such as the Medici Bank, and the protection and sponsorship of royal governments facilitated such developments. The expansion of commerce promoted economic diversification and regional specialization, highlighting the role of towns and cities as commercial centers.

By the Renaissance era, such economic development had made much of Europe dependent on trade for even basic and necessary commodities. While Europe's cities had begun to produce finished goods, notably textiles, for export to markets in the Middle East and North Africa, their inhabitants were becoming reliant on interregional and international imports of goods that were unavailable locally, including spices and manufactured products such as cotton cloth, paper, and ceramics. Even in the countryside, complete economic self-sufficiency was becoming rarer as a monetary economy became more pronounced.

The Beginnings of a Global Economy

However, as the economy of Europe evolved to become more complex and reliant on commerce, certain critical external developments began to disrupt its operation. Of particular importance was the expansion of Muslim power in the Eastern Mediterranean, notably the rise of the Ottoman Empire, which made trade in this region more hazardous and expensive. Almost simultaneously, European merchants and monarchies alike had begun to suffer from a shortage of precious metals, especially gold, that placed them at a distinct trade disadvantage with societies to their south and east. Additionally, the ravages caused by the Black Death, as well as the wars and civil unrest of the Late Middle Ages, slowed economic activity even further.[2] Difficult access to the two critical commodities of gold and spices posed a problem for the continued growth of the European economy. A shortage of the former reduced the purchasing power of European merchants, while the latter, necessary for preserving and flavoring food, became more expensive as Muslims asserted control over Middle Eastern and North African marketplaces.

The urban bourgeoisie and the royal monarchies, the same two groups whose fortunes had risen during the Late Medieval era, cooperated to provide a solution to this problem. The merchant community, in Italy and elsewhere, was always eager and able to fund promising ventures that might bring a profit. Meanwhile, even by the beginning of the Renaissance, most European monarchs recognized that healthy economies contributed to the power and stability of their realms, and thus they too saw the value of finding easier access to gold and spices. The logical alternative was establishing more direct access to the regions further east where such goods originated, enabling them to bypass the Muslim-controlled areas.

This meant the exploration of the oceans and the creation of entirely new trade links, and by the fifteenth century, Europe possessed both the will and the means to carry out these goals. The economic motives coincided with others, such as a desire to spread Christianity, monarchies that were eager to expand, and the genuine geographical curiosity that Renaissance humanism was encouraging. Certain important technological advances in ship-building and navigation, the results of both investment-driven innovation and cultural borrowing, provided the means.[3]

Two relatively new kingdoms, Portugal and Spain, became the first to explore and trade out into the Atlantic Ocean and beyond. During the fifteenth century, Portuguese mariners relied on both government and merchant investment to sail south along the west coast of Africa. Gradually expanding their reach, they built coastal trading forts that gave them access to gold, ivory, and slaves for importation back to Europe, and this trade provided profits that could be invested in new ventures. The Portuguese continually refined their maritime technology and navigational abilities, while contributing a great deal of new geographical knowledge.

Before the end of the fifteenth century Portuguese vessels had rounded the tip of Southern Africa and established a direct maritime route to the wealthy commercial cities of India. During the decades that followed, large, heavily armed Portuguese fleets used superior naval firepower to almost literally blast their way into the middle of existing Asian trading networks.[4] Seizing control of certain strategic points, they set up a series of militarily protected trading posts that stretched around the edges of the Indian Ocean as far as Southeast Asia, China, and Japan. These outposts became the foundation of a direct and profitable Portuguese commerce in spices and other valuable Eastern cargo. This trade transformed a tiny kingdom of slightly more than a million people into a remarkably wealthy and powerful state; equally importantly, the Portuguese success demonstrated the advantages that might be gained from taking a more energetic role overseas.

Meanwhile, Portugal's rival, the newly-united kingdom of Spain, had been dispatching ships westward out into the Atlantic, colonizing the Canary Islands and trading in Northern Europe. **Christopher Columbus**, the son of a Genoese textile merchant, had established a successful career in Atlantic and Mediterranean seaborne commerce. While living in Lisbon, Portugal, he had become an expert in navigation and geography, and had heard sailors' reports of further islands that lay far to the west. Motivated by a complex combination of geographical theory, a hunger for gold, and Christian mysticism, Columbus developed a plan to reach "the Indies" by sailing west. Though he underestimated the circumference of the world, his previous experience sailing the Atlantic had revealed westward flowing currents and winds, which suggested to him he might reach the fabled kingdom of Japan after only a few weeks of sailing west from the Canary Islands.[5]

For more than a decade, various European monarchs rejected Columbus's appeals for financial support for his project. However, in 1492, Ferdinand and Isabella, the king and queen of Spain, who had previously turned him down, completed the conquest of the last Muslim city in the Iberian peninsula, and by then had also become anxious about the newly-found Portuguese route into the Indian Ocean. They provided Columbus with the means to outfit three ships for his momentous first voyage, and upon his return from the Caribbean, Ferdinand and Isabella made a formal claim to these territories. Even while uncertainties remained about the nature of this "New World," the Spanish crown began to sponsor permanent settlements, hoping to establish a trade in gold, spices, and other valuable goods. Before the end of the fifteenth century, both a papal decree and a diplomatic treaty formalized the division of the globe between Spain and Portugal, and both kingdoms were intensifying their overseas empire-building efforts.

The benefits in what soon became known as "America" were not as immediate as those enjoyed in the Indian Ocean. For almost thirty years, the Spanish outposts in the Caribbean remained largely unprofitable backwaters, but this changed suddenly in the 1520s and 1530s, when the conquests of Cortez and Pizarro, in Mexico and the South American Andes respectively, revealed wealthy societies and sources of precious metals. This energized both private and public interest, and the Spanish crown constructed a highly bureaucratized colonial system in order to control the territories it claimed. From the mid-sixteenth century onward, soldiers, adventurers, missionaries, administrators, and merchants—as well as African slaves—flooded into Spain's Central and South American colonies. Soon, fleets of heavily armed ships were hauling massive quantities of treasure, mostly silver, back to Spain to support the expanding Spanish European empire and pay for its frequent wars. Even by the 1570s, Spanish ships were sailing regularly across the Pacific Ocean to link the New World with Spanish possessions that had been established in the Philippines.[6]

Other European nations quickly recognized the advantages of overseas trade and colonization, and soon the English, French, and the Dutch were competing for a share of the presumed riches available around the globe. Even before the end of the seventeenth century, Europeans had conquered and/or established permanent outposts in virtually every latitude and longitude, including India, Brazil, Indonesia, East and West Africa, the Caribbean, the Persian Gulf, the Canadian Maritimes, and China. Sugar, cotton, tobacco, dyes, silks, spices, slaves, lumber, furs, and ceramics were just a few of the earliest commodities they imported back to Europe and sold in foreign marketplaces. Even as different European powers fought indigenous populations—and each other—to expand their overseas interests, Europe became the hub of a global maritime trade network that moved goods and people around the world. Though modest in scale at first, this marks the foundation of the first global economy, one that would become more dominant and complex over the next five centuries.

These first two colonizing nations, Portugal and Spain, established the European pattern of empire-building by creating powerful formal institutions to regulate and control the process. Through royal licenses and monopolies, private entities—usually banks and wealthy merchant companies, often of foreign origin—were encouraged to invest in profit-making ventures under government sponsorship. While such investors took the initiative and assumed much of the risk, the royal governments administered and directed this commerce for the benefit of their kingdoms, and often protected and promoted it with military force. Later, other European powers developed their own versions of these private/public partnerships as European control of the seas expanded.[7]

As mentioned above, there were many motives behind what has been called "The Age of Discoveries," and they varied both among the different participants and over time. These included the pursuit of profit, the desire to spread European culture and Christianity, diplomatic and strategic advantage, individual quests for adventure and fame, and genuine Renaissance inquisitiveness. But whatever the particular intentions and accomplishments of individuals such as Columbus, Magellan, or Hudson, they all added up to the creation of a network of ocean highways that connected, however tenuously, almost all of the settled parts of the earth that could be reached by sea.

"Spain's Century"

Although there were similarities in the ways that European states went about the process of overseas expansion, each did so under unique conditions, both at home and abroad, which affected their differing experiences with modernization. Spain provides a case in point. During the sixteenth century this kingdom emerged as the dominant power in Europe and had seemed to contemporaries to be the prime beneficiary of the "Age of Discovery." However, the Spanish experience demonstrates that the link between overseas dominion and economic development is not simple.

Charles V of the Habsburg dynasty became king of Spain in 1516, and by the 1520s he had inherited an enormous collection of territories that included Spain, Austria, present-day Belgium and the Netherlands, much of Italy, and several German states. In 1530, he was elected as Holy Roman Emperor, and the territories that he also ruled in America exceeded, in terms of land area, all of his European possessions put together. Thus, Charles controlled not only the lion's share of the wealthy parts of Europe, but by midcentury, when the export of New World silver to Spain began in earnest, the Spanish royal treasury had access to a seemingly unlimited supply of precious metals. Although Charles's abdication in 1556 resulted in the detachment of most of the central European Habsburg possessions, in 1580, Portugal and all of its overseas territories were joined to the Spanish dominions as the result of a dynastic struggle.

On paper, this made Spain the wealthiest and most powerful monarchy on the face of the earth. It seems remarkable, then, that by the late sixteenth century, the Spanish empire was facing financial collapse, which became a reality during the next century; after this time, Spain, bankrupt and impoverished, would never again be a major world power. How could this be, in a society that possessed almost unimaginable amounts of wealth? In hindsight, Spain's problems provide a useful lesson about the nature of economic growth.[8]

A main part of the answer has to do with the fate of the silver and gold that made its way into Seville every year aboard the royally-controlled "silver fleets." Having been formed into bars and ingots in the New World, most of this treasure passed into the hands of the financiers and merchants—many of whom were foreigners—whose loans had underwritten had the shipping, mining, ranching, settlement, and military activities that were instrumental in the development of New World resources. Much of what remained went to the merchants who possessed royal licenses—generally monopolistic—over different portions of the American economy, such as the cattle, silk, and wine trades. Finally, about 20% of the New World treasure went directly into the royal treasury as the so-called "king's fifth."

While the payouts received often amounted to enormous profits on investments, much of it left Spain almost immediately upon arrival. In particular, an increasing portion flowed into the coffers of German and Italian banks, especially the Fugger financial empire that served as the Habsburgs' bankers. Much of the rest was used for consumption, as the merchants and nobles who had privileged roles in the American trade spent their profits lavishly on the palaces, fine clothing, carriages, and artwork that they felt was necessary to display their status. However, most of these extravagances were neither made in Spain, nor made by Spaniards, because Italians, French, Dutch, and Germans dominated the luxury trades. What this meant was that as this American wealth arrived in Spain, much of it quickly departed again for other destinations. In this way, the economies outside of Spain wound up benefiting the most from all this American treasure.

It can be argued that the treasure retained by the Spanish crown had an even less constructive fate. The possession of such a huge empire meant that Spanish kings had to devote a tremendous amount of resources to defending it and keeping it under their control.[9] The menace presented by the Ottoman Turks in central Europe and the Mediterranean was only one threat that needed to be countered through enormous military expenditure. By the 1560s, the Reformation had also promoted conflicts in several Habsburg possessions, such as the wealthy Netherlands, while political and social disorder also plagued other Habsburg dominions. The result was that during the entire course of the sixteenth century, Spain was never truly at peace for a single moment; in fact, for most of the century, the kingdom was directly involved in at least two major wars. What this added up to was the unfortunate reality that, by the time the Spanish crown got its hands on its share of the American treasure, they already owed it all to bankers—in Germany, Italy, and the Netherlands—because they had been borrowing from them to equip their armies and navies. The kings of Spain were not the first rulers, nor would they be the last, to learn a fairly simple lesson: no matter the century, war is a horribly expensive undertaking.

What happened to the American treasure coming into Spain may have been wasteful enough, but what is equally important is what did *not* happen to it: neither the private nor public sector in Spain invested much of it into the domestic economy. The growth and administration of empire relied largely on foreign capital and skills, and largely as a result the Spanish economy had weak financial institutions and few opportunities for entrepreneurial business owners. Despite the massive imports of treasure, Spain remained a society with a small bourgeoisie, few homegrown businesses, little domestic manufacturing, and, especially after mid-century, an economic system that was utterly dependent on the more sophisticated economies of Europe. Spain became a society with a few tremendously wealthy people, and a great mass of impoverished, unskilled, and illiterate peasants, while their towns and cities experienced high levels of unemployment. The royal government itself was constantly on the edge of bankruptcy, and continued to raise taxes on subjects already staggered by a rising cost of living. In a sense, sixteenth century Spain was a kingdom that had access to a tremendous amount of money, yet it possessed very little real wealth. Ultimately, it was the bourgeoisie elsewhere who wound up with this treasure, and they were the ones who used it to create genuine economic development.

Capitalism and Economic Specialization

During the High Middle Ages Europe had played merely a relatively minor role in a long-established trans-Asian chain of trade. By the early seventeenth century, economic, political, and cultural developments had placed Europe at the center of a global economy. From headquarters in growing cities such as Antwerp, London, and Bordeaux, royal governments and powerful financial enterprises exerted an increasing level of control over this system and had a profound influence on the modernization of European society.

One of the most noticeable and important shifts was an acceleration of the regional economic specialization that had first begun to appear in the medieval era. The demographic crises of the Late Middle Ages had already greatly influenced Europe's economic structure, as larger, more capital intensive enterprises began to replace self-sufficient enterprises like the manor system and village artisans. As commerce and trade intensified between the fourteenth and seventeenth centuries, different regions in Western Europe began to focus even more on particular products and industries, varying according to available natural, human, and financial resources. This specialization, in turn, promoted the emergence of larger, more complex economic and financial entities that became the backbone of what was essentially a different sort of economy.

One particularly important change took place in the organization of manufacturing. Since the Middle Ages, textiles, especially woolen cloth, had been the foundation of Europe's manufacturing sector. By the sixteenth century, increased trade, investment, and innovation had allowed this industry to evolve into something far more complex. Different parts of Italy, England, the Low Countries and Northern France began to produce specialized types of textiles and textile products: cotton cloth, silk stockings, luxury tapestries, and many diverse wool products. These found markets both within and outside of Europe.

Much of this textile output was produced in a new arrangement, known as the "**putting-out system**," that emerged during the Late Middle Ages. Entrepreneurs with capital purchased raw materials, usually wool or cotton, and then paid workers to use their own home looms and equipment to perform different stages of the production process, such as spinning and dyeing, while retaining ownership of the materials.[10] In this method of production, there was a clear distinction between those who invested the money and those who performed the labor, and these early capitalists could sell the finished products and reinvest the profits that came from the difference between their expenses and their revenues. The putting-out system, also known as "cottage industry," relied on the availability of start-up capital, insurance, reliable transportation, and economic demand for such goods, each of which had been made possible by the evolution of the European economy over the previous centuries. Over the course of the Early Modern Period, such capital-intensive manufacturing became a powerful engine of economic growth, creating the conditions necessary for the Industrial Revolution.

Eventually, less developed areas both within and outside Europe were drawn into the expanding global economic network. For instance, the hinterlands of Spain and England, unable to compete with the towns in textile production, concentrated on sheep raising and wool production, which were less labor intensive than growing wheat and less capital intensive than manufacturing. Rural areas of the Mediterranean began to specialize in fruit growing, while the lumber industry in the Baltic region expanded. Large parts of central and Eastern Europe began to export wheat and cereals in large quantities to Western towns that had previously relied on their surrounding regions for such food staples. Meanwhile, products from overseas, such as sugar and cotton in the sixteenth century and many other commodities by the seventeenth, added to the diversity of the products purchased and consumed by Europeans. What this all meant was that, by the seventeenth century, few parts of Europe remained economically self-sufficient, while many other parts of the globe were becoming economically dependent on Europe. Traditional economies evolved to become specialized parts of a larger international economy, a process that continued into the Industrial Revolution and beyond.

Urban Growth and the Bourgeoisie

This internationalization of the European economy could not fail to have a massive impact on European life. One of the most important effects was that it intensified the ongoing process of urbanization that had begun during the medieval era. By the sixteenth century, and expanding beyond, European cities assumed a far greater role in economic life, in politics, and in Europe's cultural world. The populations of the biggest cities in Europe grew tremendously during the sixteenth century, transforming the importance and roles of regional capitals. Seville became the headquarters of New World commerce; Lisbon, and later Antwerp, controlled the international spice trade; while Paris and London evolved from agricultural marketplaces into centers of manufacturing, finance, politics, and culture. Such cities experienced tripling and quadrupling of their populations into the hundreds of thousands of residents.[11]

Some of this can be explained by a higher standard of living, especially cheaper food and more disposable income. But this accounts for only part of this population growth; an equally important cause was a new sort of immigration. While Medieval and Late Medieval towns had attracted new residents from the surrounding countryside, people came into these Early Modern cities and towns from further afield, from other parts of Europe and even from outside of Europe. These newcomers were responding to the economic demand for skilled workers and artisans, like metalsmiths, printers, and shipbuilders, as well as for educated professionals of all types, such as lawyers, officials, and entrepreneurs. They brought their skills, their new ideas, and their money with them, increasing the economic vitality of the growing cities. Because of more efficient monetary systems and financial institutions, capital flowed from one place to the next, stimulating employment, creating new inventions and business methods, and leading to more and more profits, for more and more people who were looking for new places where they might put their wealth.

Logically enough, this urban dynamism also had political and cultural effects. To expand and modernize, royal political administrations required educated officials and access to finance, which prompted many monarchies to relocate their administrations to urban areas. The schools and universities that educated such officials and other professionals expanded, while new ones were created. Meanwhile, in the largest European cities, the influx of educated and wealthy new residents representing different cultures and religious traditions broke down what remained of the traditional *gemeinschaft* culture. Inevitably, the mainstays of the earlier medieval system—the church, feudalism, and the manorial system—survived in the cities only as cultural relics. In such places, by the seventeenth century, capitalism, rationality, and individualism had established firm roots in a changing society that was increasingly dominated by a varied and upwardly mobile bourgeoisie. The modern world of industrialization and the nation-state would spring from these roots.

Capitalism, Protestantism, and Modernization

Another clearly identifiable pattern that emerged during the Early Modern Period was a shift in economic balance. The economies of the southern parts of Europe—notably Spain, Portugal, and Italy—began to decline in the late sixteenth and early seventeenth centuries. Meanwhile, the northern parts of Europe experienced significant economic growth, both in relative terms and in real terms, and this economic change would be accompanied by a similar shift in political and military power.

The observer might also notice that in the south Roman Catholicism remained, often literally, the law of the land; for various political and social reasons, the Protestant Reformation never got a foothold in Iberia and Italy. In contrast, many parts of the north, like England, Germany, the Netherlands and France, developed either multireligious societies or followed Protestantism. It was the latter places that took over the economic leadership of Europe during the sixteenth century and beyond.

For the German sociologist Max Weber, this development was no coincidence. He argued that the emergence of Protestantism helped to encourage certain new cultural values that affected economic behavior. Specifically, the new religious ideas contributed to a new ethos—what he called the "Protestant Ethic"—that promoted hard work, savings, personal integrity, and self-confidence. According to Weber, in the long run, during the late sixteenth century and beyond, these new economic behaviors stimulated the growth of capitalism as an economic system.[12]

Though his point appears logical, proving the cause and effect between capitalism and Protestantism is quite difficult. Since Weber's time, historians have argued about the nature of the relationship between these two important features of Early Modern Europe. Did Protestantism in fact encourage capitalism, and if so, how and why? Alternatively, as many Marxists have suggested, perhaps it was the other way around: that the rise of capitalism encouraged Protestant beliefs that were less critical of the accumulation of wealth than the Christian Paternalistic Ethic had been.

Whatever their perspectives, most historians would admit that, in reality, the relationship between these two elements of social change was rather more complicated than either of these prescriptions might suggest. This is because there were some other notable changes during the sixteenth century that also factored into the equation. One was the spread of literacy, promoted by the development of the **printing press** during the fifteenth century. By the early sixteenth century printing technology had become efficient enough to produce books by the thousands. This lowered their cost, and books became affordable to many more people than just the very elite classes. It has been persuasively argued that both the production and consumption of typographic material (that is, books and other typeset reading materials) made a vast contribution to social change. Though its impact was often subtle and long term, it affected both private and public life in different ways by promoting rationalism, bureaucracy, capitalism, tolerance, and social mobility. It greatly facilitated cultural diffusion by making it much easier for the public to gain access to new ideas in a permanent and consistent format. In the long run, printing and literacy affected practically every area of European life, serving as a powerful engine in the movement towards modernization.[13]

There can be little doubt that this increased literacy stimulated both Protestantism and capitalism. Luther, Calvin, and other early Protestant leaders based much of their reformed theology on their own studies of the Bible and the works of early Christian scholars. They argued that their own interpretations were superior to those presented by the Roman Church, which, they argued, had been distorted over the centuries, and they encouraged their followers to read the Scriptures for themselves. Luther's German Bible, for example, was designed to enable literate Germans to experience the word of God firsthand.

Meanwhile, the spread of increasingly complex record keeping and bureaucratic procedures frequently made literacy an absolute necessity for those engaged in both private and public enterprise. It can hardly be surprising, then, that those who already possessed the skill of literacy—and thus enjoyed more options in an increasingly modern society—were more likely to follow the suggestions of Protestant theologians who urged them to read the Holy Word for themselves. On the other hand, it is equally unsurprising that early converts to Protestantism had incentives to learn reading and writing, which in turn contributed to their own personal success in an increasingly capitalistic, competitive society. In other words, literacy was becoming more of a social norm than an exceptional skill, and both religious change and economic development contributed to its proliferation.

Yet another element of modernization, one discussed above, reinforced the links among literacy, Protestantism, and capitalism during the Early Modern period. This was the increasingly important role of cities, which provided an environment where each of these other three developments could flourish. As they had already done during the Middle Ages, but even more so, cities in the Early Modern era attracted concentrations of people with increasingly diverse backgrounds and ideas, while providing critical economic and cultural links with the wider world. As cities prospered, and these factors reinforced each other, they contributed a more vibrant and dynamic way of life throughout Europe.[14]

What all of this began to add up to was the realization of a critical legacy of the Renaissance, one that contradicted much traditional medieval thinking. Renaissance humanists had promoted the idea that human life could be worthwhile and even improved, while a corollary of this conviction was the idea that the lives of individual human beings mattered. As medieval towns grew into modern cities, a new social attitude developed: that freedom for the individual was beneficial, instead of a challenge to the Will of God. Before the end of the sixteenth century, there were even numerous people who were arguing—in print—that personal liberty was a God-given right. To point out what is probably obvious, most of these people were educated members of the urban bourgeoisie.

The sixteenth and seventeenth centuries saw an intensification of the process of modernization that had begun centuries earlier. Social change had brought capitalism, Protestantism, literacy, and urbanization to many parts of Western Europe. Even in strongly Catholic regions, the collective and fatalistic mentality promoted by the Christian Paternalistic Ethic was in retreat, especially in the burgeoning towns and cities. Individualism, perhaps the most critical element of modernization, and the one that binds the rest together, was for the first time becoming a widely accepted social norm. In this way, Western Europe became the first major civilization in world history to experience this change.

References and Suggested Readings:

Eisenstein, Elizabeth. *The Printing Press as an Agent of Change.* Cambridge UK: Cambridge University Press, 1979.

Elliott, J.H. *The Old World and the New, 1492-1650.* Cambridge: Cambridge University Press, 1992.

Fernández-Armesto. Felipe. *Before Columbus, Exploration and Colonisation from the Mediterranean to the Atlantic, 1229-1492.* Philadelphia: University of Pennsylvania Press, 1987.

Houston, R.A. "Colonies, Enterprises, and Wealth: The Economies of Europe and the Wider World in the Seventeenth Century," in *Early Modern Europe: An Oxford History*. Ewan Cameron, ed. Oxford: Oxford University Press, 1999.

Kamen, Henry. *Empire: How Spain Became a World Power, 1492-1763*. New York: Harper-Collins, 2003.

Koenigsberger, H.G., George L. Mosse, and G.Q. Bowler. *Europe in the Sixteenth Century*, 2nd Ed. London: Longman, 1989.

Newitt, Malyn. *A History of Portuguese Overseas Expansion 1400-1668*. London: Routledge, 2005.

Phillips, J.R.S. *The Medieval Expansion of Europe*. Oxford: Oxford University Press, 1988.

Phillips, William D. Jr., and Carla Rahn Phillips. *The Worlds of Christopher Columbus*. New York: Cambridge University Press, 1992.

Scammell, G.V. *The First Imperial Age: European Overseas Expansion, 1400-1715*. London: Unwin Hyman, 1989.

Vilches, Elvira. *New World Gold: Cultural Anxiety and Monetary Disorder in Early Modern Spain*. Chicago: Chicago University Press, 2010.

Vives, Jaime Vicens. *An Economic History of Spain*. Princeton: Princeton University Press, 1969.

Wallerstein, Immanuel. *The Modern World System I: Capitalist Agriculture and the Origins of the European World Economy in the Sixteenth Century*. New York: Academic Press, 1974.

Weber, Max. *The Protestant Ethic and the Spirit of Capitalism*. Translated by Talcott Parsons. Reprint Edition. London: Scribners, 1995.

Wiesner-Hanks, Merry, *Early Modern Europe, 1450-1789*. New York: Cambridge University Press, 2006.

Notes

1. A solidly researched and interesting view of Europe's relationship with the non-European world in the High and Late Middle Ages is J.R.S. Phillips' *The Medieval Expansion of Europe* (Oxford: Oxford University Press, 1988).

2. On late Medieval European society and the non-European world, see William D. Phillips, Jr., and Carla Rahn Phillips *The Worlds of Christopher Columbus*, (New York: Cambridge University Press, 1992). p. 1-81; and Felipe Fernández-Armesto. *Before Columbus, Exploration and Colonisation from the Mediterranean to the Atlantic, 1229-1492* (Philadelphia: University of Pennsylvania Press, 1987).

3. J. H. Elliott, *The Old World and the New, 1492-1650* (Cambridge: Cambridge University Press, 1992).

4. A useful modern study of Portuguese discoveries and empire building is Malyn Newitt, *A History of Portuguese Overseas Expansion 1400-1668* (London: Routledge, 2005).

5. On Columbus's career in its historical context see Phillips and Phillips, *The Worlds of Christopher Columbus*.

6. A reasonably concise account of the growth of the Spanish empire in the New World can be found in Henry Kamen, *Empire: How Spain Became a World Power, 1492-1763* (New York: Harper-Collins, 2003), p. 95-149.

7. A useful discussion of the process of empire building can be found in G.V. Scammell, *The First Imperial Age: European Overseas Expansion, 1400-1715* (London: Unwin Hyman, 1989)

8. Over the last eighty years there have been many interpretations of the problems of the sixteenth century Spanish economy, and some of the arguments are quite complicated. While causes and effects are controversial, there is unanimity that the failure of domestic capital investment was in the long run disastrous and prevented economic development. One fascinating new study is Elvira Vilches's *New World Gold: Cultural Anxiety and Monetary Disorder in Early Modern Spain* (Chicago: Chicago University Press, 2010); for a nuanced Marxist interpretation, see Immanuel Wallerstein, *The Modern World System I: Capitalist Agriculture and the Origins of the European World Economy in the Sixteenth Century* (New York: Academic Press, 1974), especially p. 164-221; Jaime Vicens Vives's, *An Economic History of Spain* (Princeton: Princeton University Press, 1969) remains a solid overview.

9. On the challenges Spain faced see Kamen, *Empire*, p. 285-329.

10. Wiesner-Hanks, Merry, *Early Modern Europe, 1450-1789* (New York: Cambridge University Press, 2006), p. 418-423.

11. H.G. Koenigsberger, George L. Mosse, and G.Q. Bowler, *Europe in the Sixteenth Century*, 2nd Ed. (London, 1989), 30-37; Wiesner-Hanks, *Early Modern Europe*, p. 243-249.

12. Weber's *The Protestant Ethic and the Spirit of Capitalism* was first published as a series of essays in 1904-1905, and has since appeared as a book in numerous editions.

13. The classic work on the impact of publishing on modernization remains Elizabeth Eisenstein's *The Printing Press as an Agent of Change* (Cambridge, UK: Cambridge University Press, 1979).

14. R.A. Houston, "Colonies, Enterprises, and Wealth: The Economies of Europe and the Wider World in the Seventeenth Century," in *Early Modern Europe: An Oxford History*. Ed, Euan Cameron (Oxford: Oxford University Press, 1999), p. 137-170.

The Centralization and Rationalization of the Political State

John McGrath

While long-term economic and social forces helped to redefine the role of government during the Early Modern Period, more immediate circumstances also spurred political change, reinforcing the movement towards more concentrated forms of authority. During the Reformation era, religious divisions within and among European states, often intensified by ethnic, social and economic differences, challenged even the most powerful monarchs to keep a firm grip on their subjects. This gave many European rulers another reason to increase the size, power, and efficiency of their administrations. The result was a new form and style of political organization known as **absolutism**.[1] Typically, absolutism "introduced standing armies, a permanent bureaucracy, national taxation, a codified law, and the beginnings of a unified market."[2] Together, these elements rationalized and centralized political authority and represent a significant step in the modernization of the political state.

These new structures and policies were justified on the basis of new ideologies that marked a distinct shift from the traditional medieval concept of authority. In contrast to the largely decentralized feudal system where successive levels of nobility ruled in accordance with local customs and practices, absolutist monarchies began to enjoy, at least in theory, total and absolute power over all of their subjects. Such power was often supported by the religious concept of "**Divine Right**," the idea that God had specially selected the royal family and endowed it with extraordinary qualities with which to lead their kingdoms. In this view, the machinery of absolutist government became merely the instruments through which such rulers exercised their supreme wills. Their subjects, who had grown increasingly impatient with the insecurity that had accompanied the Reformation, largely accepted this new arrangement, since it provided badly needed stability and order.

Absolutism as a Remedy for Instability: England and France

England and France had been two of the first kingdoms to create effective national monarchies during the High Middle Ages. In response to Reformation-era turmoil, the rulers of both kingdoms modified already relatively sophisticated political systems by steadily expanding and strengthening them over the course of the sixteenth century. In doing so, they created the first absolutist governments.

The end of the 100 Years' War saw England embroiled in a violent domestic power struggle among competing branches of the royal family, known as the **Wars of the Roses** (1455-1485). Ultimately, Henry Tudor emerged as the victor and took the throne as Henry VII. To prevent further instability and secure power for himself and his successors, he began a process that placed more power in the hands of the monarchy and replaced much local and customary authority.[3] His son Henry VIII's creation of the national Anglican Church can be seen as only one aspect of this process, which, as it developed over more than a century, involved the creation of new royal administrative, legal, and financial institutions and practices.

This process culminated under Henry VIII's youngest daughter, **Elizabeth I**, who took the throne in 1558, after the brief and divisive reigns of her two immediate predecessors. Faced with domestic religious conflict, financial difficulties, and foreign threats, Elizabeth's response had to be both firm and practical. She improved the efficiency of the government through internal reforms and by delegating authority to capable, trustworthy individuals. To minimize religious division, she implemented distinctly secular policies that balanced the more conservative supporters of the Anglican Church against the reform-minded "Puritans," English subjects who had converted to continental varieties of Protestantism. During her forty-five year reign, she vastly strengthened her subjects' loyalty to the kingdom and to herself through the cunning employment of imagery and propaganda. Although military expenditures strained her royal treasury, when she died in 1603 Elizabeth bequeathed to her successors, the Scottish Stuart dynasty, a stronger royal government that ruled over a more united populace. Unfortunately, this unity was not to last.

Meanwhile, in France, the reigns of three weak kings after 1559 had allowed almost forty years of intermittent but ferocious religious civil war between Catholics and Calvinists, known as the **French Wars of Religion**. The accession of King **Henri IV** in 1589 marked a turning point, as this Protestant prince was willing to convert to Catholicism in order to win the loyalty of his subjects, and subsequently proclaimed an official policy of religious toleration. He used his personal popularity and highly competent and dedicated ministers to return the kingdom of France to peace and prosperity before the end of the century.[4]

Though Henri's reign ended prematurely in 1610 with his assassination by a Catholic fanatic, his successors, Louis XIII and Louis XIV, followed up on his accomplishments. Louis XIII's chief minister, the Cardinal Armand-Jean du Plessis, known as **Cardinal Richelieu**, significantly reorganized the structure of royal government, creating a hierarchical system of bureaucratic authority that he could control from the top. He continued the steady growth of the size of the royal government; Royal courts, a centralized government treasury, and royally-appointed officials began to replace local and customary authority. Richelieu also created a network of spies and informants throughout the kingdom who kept him aware of developments throughout the entire kingdom, and who enabled him to identify those whose loyalty to the French crown was questionable. In foreign policy, he followed a pragmatic approach designed to weaken the power of France's traditional enemy, the Habsburg dynasty that ruled Spain, Austria, and the Netherlands.

The full accession of King **Louis XIV** in 1661 resulted in what many consider to have been the ultimate example of absolutist rule.[5] Determined to quell any possible resistance from quarreling noble factions, Louis expanded the power of his government by increasing the size of his government and army, supported by higher taxes. Notably, to manage his expanded state, Louis relied on the talents of educated bourgeoisie, instead of either churchmen or the nobility, as had been the usual practice. For example, his most powerful minister was Jean-Baptiste Colbert, a trained accountant who was the son of a clothier, who rose through the ranks of the royal state on merit, instead of through personal or political connections. Colbert directed French royal finances for two decades and immensely strengthened France's colonial interests and maritime capabilities. In doing so, he developed many of its **mercantilist** policies (discussed below), while gaining a reputation for financial wizardry. Louis XIV's reign represents the culmination of the growth of royal bureaucracy: from 1505 until 1664, the number of salaried employees of the French Crown increased almost sevenfold, from 12,000 to over 80,000.[6]

From the beginning of his reign, Louis XIV consciously cultivated a public image of himself as almost a semi-deity, and enjoyed popularity and even awe among the masses. To reinforce this image, he moved the center of his government outside Paris to the town of **Versailles**, where he constructed an enormous and spectacular chateau. Here he could both conduct affairs of state and keep an eye on the nobles, whose presence he required at his court, and whose power he was determined to minimize. Though he probably never uttered the widely cited quote "I am the state," he acted with a boldness and decisiveness in both domestic and foreign affairs that demonstrated an almost complete disregard for restraint.

Other European monarchies, such as Austria, the larger German states, and Spain, followed the lead of France by embracing absolutism during the seventeenth and eighteenth centuries. Each constructed a larger and more centralized political system, with variations according to circumstance, and adopted mercantilist economic policies. Increasingly, such governments relied on rational planning, instead of tradition, to create news laws, policies, and institutions that helped them maintain control and order. In each case, even in many Protestant states, they justified their power on the basis of "Divine Right."

By the end of the seventeenth century, the only two major states in Europe that had not adopted and intensified absolutism were the Netherlands and England. The former achieved independence from Spanish rule and became a federated republic that prospered mightily from overseas trade; rather uniquely, the Dutch government promoted commercial freedom and opposed mercantilist forms of state control. England, known as **Great Britain** after its formal union with Scotland in 1707, became a constitutional monarchy, as outlined below. Even so, the English national government increased its size and authority over the course of the seventeenth century, and mercantilist economic policies provided the foundations for Great Britain's growing overseas empire.

The Thirty Years' War

By the early seventeenth century, more than 300 separate, mostly German-speaking states, large and small, comprised the Holy Roman Empire that extended over much of central Europe. Since the Middle Ages, these states had exercised a significant measure of independence from their nominal and elected Catholic overlord, the Emperor. During the Reformation some of these states had became Lutheran or Calvinist, while others remained faithful to Rome. This religious diversity made political unity impossible while causing considerable tension and disorder. By 1618, these inflammatory conditions provoked the most destructive war yet seen on the European continent, known as the **Thirty Years' War**.[7]

This conflict began locally, when a religiously influenced rebellion against the authority of the Emperor erupted in the state of Bohemia, but soon other states within the Empire entered to support one side or the other. The war escalated further during the 1620s, as the leaders of practically every sovereign state in continental Europe eventually decided that their involvement might lead to some political or economic advantage, and it became a continent-wide conflagration. Though most of the fighting took place in central Europe, especially Germany, military campaigns of unprecedented size ravaged parts of Italy, the Low Countries, France, and the Baltic states.

Not only did the scale of the warfare expand, so too did the political complexity, and the original causes of the war were soon practically irrelevant. By the mid-1630s, it had become nearly impossible to construct a peace agreement that would satisfy each of the dozens of belligerents—so the armies continued to fight, even without any evident goal. Meanwhile, many of the participating governments had run out of money due to the ever-rising military costs, and their unpaid mercenary armies marauded virtually at random through the countryside. Besieging cities and burning villages, they left vast areas almost completely depopulated, while starvation and disease took a terrible toll on the civilian populations.

At long last, in 1648, a series of treaties ended the war for most of the combatants, and this marks the end of large-scale religious conflict between European states. From this point on, governments pursued largely secular foreign policies and engaged in what became known as "**balance of power**" diplomacy, by forming alliances with each other that would discourage enemies from starting hostilities. As well, the demands of conducting major military efforts had forced many of the participating monarchies to expand both their taxation and their political administrations; after the end of the war such kingdoms as France, Austria, Denmark, Sweden, and the rising German state of Brandenburg/Prussia, made these changes permanent. For these reasons, one can see the Thirty Years' War as contributing to the process of political modernization. Even so, the sheer destructiveness of this conflict provoked one historian to judge it as "morally subversive, economically destructive, socially degrading, devious in its course, futile in its result . . . (it is) the outstanding example in European history of meaningless conflict."[8]

State Finance and Mercantilism

The Thirty Years' War forced virtually every European state to increase the size and effectiveness of its standing (permanent) army, which required them to pay, transport, and supply larger numbers of troops. Moreover, the evolution of military technology also necessitated more expenditure per soldier; by the Thirty Years' War, warfare had become more capital intensive, relying on an array of gunpowder weapons as well as larger fortifications and ships. As a direct result, by the beginning of the eighteenth century, the percent of state revenues for the military ranged from 25% in peace up to more than 80% during wartime. In the words on one historian, the state "became, in effect, a military institution in its own right."[9]

As Early Modern governments became more powerful, they also increased their control over their kingdoms' economies. An important aspect of absolutism were economic policies known collectively as mercantilism, which gave the state a larger direct role in the economy in the interest of strengthening the overall kingdom.[10] It represents a move towards a command-style economy that maximized economy of scale, and undermined the role of tradition in European economies. As it did so, mercantilism helped protect and encourage the accumulation and investment of capital that was critical in promoting the economic growth that took place in the seventeenth and eighteenth centuries.

As a result, the size and responsibilities of the nonmilitary aspects of government also expanded. Added to the higher cost of military, the mushrooming royal bureaucracies, legal systems, and infrastructure expenses made it essential that government revenues expand as well. This, of course, required more and higher taxation. As absolutist states extended their power, they instituted all sorts of new taxes and fees, including sales taxes on essential materials such as salt, "head" and "hearth" taxes that amounted to per-capita charges, and even taxes on land ownership.

Necessarily, the process of tax collection itself became more bureaucratized and efficient, with the appearance of centralized royal treasuries and finance ministries. Under Cardinal Richelieu, the French government subcontracted tax collection by allowing private citizens to bid for contracts as "tax farmers." What this meant in essence was that in exchange for the payment of a fixed sum representing the taxes owed by a province or town, such individuals—who were usually financiers with access to large amounts of capital—received a royal license to collect as much as they were able, usually over and above the sum they had given the state. Tax farming became an investment, one that was often extremely lucrative for both the state and the investor.[11]

However, as the overall tax requirements rose, so too did the number of individuals exempted from taxes. While European nobles were traditionally immune to taxation, the growth of the royal state meant that an increasing number of ambitious individuals became members of the nobility and/or became royal officials, giving them tax privileges as well. This meant that the poorer members of society wound up shouldering most of this expanding tax burden. With better recordkeeping, an expanded bureaucracy, and more soldiers and police to quash peasants' and workers' revolts, tax officials were consistently able to increase the amounts they collected. But even so, the delicate balance between revenues and expenditures could be quickly upset by the outbreak of warfare, which happened frequently during the late seventeenth and the eighteenth century. Many absolutist states began selling bonds and borrowing from financiers to pay for their growing expenses, as the financial structures of royal governments continued to become more complex during the eighteenth century.

Much of the early development of mercantilism can be traced to the spread of overseas trade and empire-building, as discussed in the previous chapter. As early as the fifteenth century, monarchs and their ministers had started to measure their "wealth" in terms of the amount of precious metals, or bullion, circulating within the kingdom. This principle, known as **bullionism**, encouraged royal treasuries to find ways to reduce the flow of bullion out of the realm while increasing the amount that came into it; a widely held assumption was that the wealth of the kingdom could be measured by the amount of money in circulation within it.

One almost universal mercantilist policy was the taxation of imports, to discourage subjects from buying foreign goods and thus sending bullion outside the kingdom. Mercantilist policies guided the administration of colonial systems so that more "wealth" flowed towards the "home country" than towards the colony. For example, mercantilist governments usually forbade colonial subjects from buying foreign goods. In some cases they even prevented colonies from producing many needed commodities themselves, which forced them to buy manufactured goods from the "home country," often at monopoly prices. Such practices contributed not only to the sorts of dissatisfaction that spurred the American Revolution, but also established a pattern of uneven economic development that persists even today, long after the dissolution of European colonial empires.

Mercantilist policy also called for direct government support of certain industries considered critical to the economic, military, and political power of the state. To avoid a dependence on foreign goods, domestic businesses in key industries such as manufacturing, shipping, and armaments were often granted or sold licenses and monopolies to operate under royal directives, and sometimes enjoyed direct government investment. Such privileged enterprises generally benefited from both an economy of scale and a lack of competition, and these arrangements amounted to a monopoly partnership between the state and private business owners where both entities prospered. The profits that often accrued from this sort of mercantilist protection helped many businesses to accumulate capital that could be used for reinvestment and future expansion. In the long run, mercantilist policies can be credited with helping rising industries—especially technologically dependent manufacturing—become firmly established in many European countries. In these sorts of arrangements, mercantilism both provided opportunities for ambitious entrepreneurs and investors, especially the wealthiest members of the bourgeoisie, and also was directly promoted the long-term economic modernization that absolutist rulers desired for their states.

Stuart England

The only large European state to avoid major involvement in the Thirty Years' War was England, which experienced its own transformations over the course of the seventeenth century. Under the kings of the **Stuart Dynasty**, political, social, and religious divisions created a civil war, and its aftermath saw the emergence of the first modern constitutional monarchy.[12] The different path taken by England would have immense consequences for the future of Western development.

According to traditional law, English kings were required to call the institution of **Parliament** for approval of any new laws and taxes. However, by the 1600s, one of its two branches, the elected House of Commons, was dominated by wealthy, largely Calvinist, landowners, a social class known as the **landed gentry**. Members of the House of Commons found their interests increasingly at odds with those of the Scottish Stuart kings who had followed Elizabeth Tudor, and throughout the first part of the century, serious disagreements over religion, taxation, and military spending provided an obstacle to the continued expansion of royal power. In 1641, these issues came to a head with the outbreak of the **English Civil War**, between separate armies fighting on behalf of Crown and Parliament.

After several years of campaigning, the Parliamentary forces emerged victorious under the innovative military leadership of Parliamentarian **Oliver Cromwell**, and they even captured King Charles I, who was executed for treason in early 1649. However, little consensus emerged among the victors on how to manage affairs of state. An experiment with parliamentary rule created only government paralysis, followed by several years in the 1650s when Cromwell headed what has been called a "Puritan military dictatorship," but which was equally ineffective in solving England's mounting problems. One significant result of this troubled period was that its political frustrations fueled remarkably fertile debate, featuring the publication of many influential and often novel political arguments. Among the most significant of these was *Leviathan*, by **Thomas Hobbes**, former tutor to the king, who advocated a strong central government to ensure order and security. Notably, *Leviathan* was based on reason and logic, as opposed to the Divine Right argument that justified many continental absolutist monarchies.

Cromwell's death and the further deterioration of effective political leadership led to popular calls for a return to kingship. In the Restoration of 1660, the executed King's son, Charles II, returned from exile on the continent to take the throne, and for the most part, he worked constructively with Parliament. But when he was succeeded by his brother James II in 1685, the Calvinist-dominated Parliament recoiled from the new king's Catholicism and pro-French sympathies, mobilizing yet another rebellion against the monarchy. This time, though, events were carefully managed, and the nearly bloodless **Glorious Revolution** of 1688 forced James to flee and handed the kingship to William of Orange, ruler of the Netherlands, who was married to James' daughter Mary. However, Parliamentary leaders had attached a condition to the arrangement: William was required to sign the **English Bill of Rights**, which acknowledged the supremacy of Parliament in managing most domestic affairs.

One of the major figures involved in this transfer of power was the philosopher **John Locke**, whose ***Second Treatise of Government*** of 1689 provided a rebuttal to

Hobbes' Leviathan. In the *Second Treatise*, which is universally regarded as one of history's most important works of political philosophy, Locke argued that a division of powers between monarchy and an elected legislature was necessary to avoid the dangers of tyranny. Not coincidentally, the Glorious Revolution had just created such an arrangement, giving England a division of powers between the king and Parliament.

Early Modern Europe and the Absolutist Age

Historians often refer to the two and a half centuries between the Protestant Reformation and the French Revolution in 1789 as the **Early Modern Period** of European history. By the beginning of this era, the main elements of modernity had already been established in most parts of Western and Central Europe. Building on this foundation, monarchies employed increasingly efficient methods of securing their power and imposing order on their kingdoms; as they did so, the absolutist form of government helped to promote and even accelerate the further spread of modernity. In particular, it fostered the rationalism, political centralization, and bureaucratization that together provide a reasonably complete definition of what absolutism actually was. In addition, it enabled early modern governments to regulate and direct the increasingly complicated economic systems that became the foundations of a global economy.

For the most part, monarchs ruled such states with the active cooperation of some or all of the elite social classes, whether noble or bourgeoisie, who possessed the talents and resources needed for more modern and efficient governance. Such elites had evident positive incentives, material and otherwise, to attach themselves to the centers of power. As assemblies of notables, royal advisors, military officers, or government functionaries, the upper classes hardly needed to be bludgeoned or threatened into assuming their new roles as instruments of the royal will. Although occasional revolts and lesser types of resistance took place during the Early Modern period, these were more the exception than the rule. For the most part, during the absolutist age the interests of the highest social orders largely coincided with, instead of conflicting with, the interests of the expanding royal state, and this helped to maintain the social order that the crises of the Reformation era had disrupted.

This new arrangement necessarily extended throughout the social system, as persons of all ranks adjusted to living in a monarchy with more unified administrative, economic, and legal systems. As this happened over centuries, the medieval corporate ethos adjusted to become something significantly different: the acceptance of the monarchy as the rightful head of a distinctive entity, one that bound subjects together in a sense of mutual obligation. All subjects, inevitably, developed some sense of common interest with other subjects of that kingdom, and a self-identity based on a common loyalty to the crown.

Thus, during the sixteenth, seventeenth, and even eighteenth centuries, we can detect a broad pattern of mutually reinforcing developments. Despite significant variations from case to case, we can see the decisive establishment of European overseas trade and colonies, the formation of larger armies that were engaged in more frequent warfare, the growth of cities, and the increased specialization and monetization of the economy. Each of these important steps was connected as both cause and effect to the growth of absolutism and mercantilism. Whatever the particular ideological justification for absolutist rule, during the Early Modern Period, local and traditional authority steadily gave way to a more centralized legal/rational authority, reinforcing the mutual dependence of the ruler and those over whom he or she ruled.

While it would be anachronistic to call this "nationalism," we can consider it a type of "protonationalism" that set the stage for the age of the nation-state in the nineteenth century. Moreover, the relative stability and rationalization of government during the absolutist age laid a steady foundation for the economic, social, and intellectual growth that stimulated other elements of modernization during the eighteenth century and beyond.

References and Suggested Readings:

Anderson, Perry. *Lineages of the Absolutist State*. London: Verso, 1974.

Beik, William. *Absolutism and Society in Seventeenth Century France*. Cambridge: Cambridge University Press, 1985.

Coward, Barry. *The Stuart Age*, 3rd ed. London: Longman, 2003.

Gunn, Steven. "War, Religion, and the State." *Early Modern Europe: An Oxford History*. Editor Euan Cameron. London: Oxford University Press, 1999.

Guy, John. *Tudor England*. New York: Oxford University Press, 1990.

Heckscher, Eli. *Mercantilism*, 2nd ed. 2 vols. London: Bradford and Dickens, 1962.

Miller, John. *Absolutism in Seventeenth Century Europe*. London: Palgrave Macmillan, 1991.

Parker, Geoffrey. ed. *The Thirty Years' War*. 2nd ed. London: Routledge, 1997.

Parker, Geoffrey. *Europe in Crisis: 1598-1648*. New York: Wiley Blackwell, 2001.

Wallerstein, Immanuel, *The Modern World-System II: Mercantilism and the Consolidation of the European World-Economy, 1600-1750*. New York: Academic Press, 1980.

Wedgewood, C.V. *The Thirty Years War*. New York: Doubleday Anchor, 1961.

Wiesner-Hanks, Merry E. *Early Modern Europe, 1450-1789*. New York: Cambridge University Press, 2006.

Wilkinson, Rich. *Louis XIV*. New York: Routledge, 2007.

John B. Wolf, *Louis XIV*. New York, Norton, 1974.

Notes

1. A solid general study of absolutism is John Miller, *Absolutism in Seventeenth Century Europe* (London: Palgrave Macmillan, 1991). More concise explanations can be found in Geoffrey Parker, *Europe in Crisis: 1598-1648* (New York: Wiley Blackwell, 2001), p. 54-66, and Merry Wiesner-Hanks, *Early Modern*

Europe 1450-1789 (New York: Cambridge University Press, 2006), p. 285-325. Perry Anderson's *The Lineages of the Absolutist State* (London: Verso, 1974) remains the standard Marxist interpretation of absolutism.

2. Anderson, *Lineages*, p. 16.

3. Among the numerous studies of *Tudor England*, a very solid scholarly work is John Guy, Tudor England (New York: Oxford University Press, 1990). See also Wiesner-Hanks, *Early Modern Europe*, p. 303-309.

4. On developments in France under Henri IV and Louis XIII, see William Beik. *Absolutism and Society in Seventeenth Century France* (Cambridge: Cambridge University Press, 1985), Wiesner-Hanks, *Early Modern Europe*, p. 297-303, and Anderson, Lineages, p. 90-100.

5. Numerous excellent studies of the Sun King include John B. Wolf, *Louis XIV* (New York: Norton, 1974), a detailed and thorough work; and Rich Wilkinson, *Louis XIV* (New York: Routledge, 2007) which is shorter and more accessible, and contains numerous entertaining anecdotes.

6. Geoffrey Parker, *Europe in Crisis*, p. 44.

7. Now regarded as the standard work on this confusing war is Geoffrey Parker's *The Thirty Years War*, 2nd Ed. (London: Routledge, 1997), which has supplanted C.V. Wedgwood's *The Thirty Years War* (New York: Doubleday Anchor, 1961).

8. Wedgewood, *The Thirty Years War*, p. 506.

9. Parker, *Europe in Crisis 1598-1648* 72, Steven Gunn, "War, Religion, and the State" in *Early Modern Europe: An Oxford History*, Euan Cameron ed., (London: Oxford University Press, 1999), p. 110-119.

10. The classic work on mercantilism is Eli Heckscher, *Mercantilism*, 2 vols, (London: Bradford and Dicken, 1962). See also Immanuel Wallenstein, *The Modern World-System II: Mercantilism and the Consolidation of the European World-Economy, 1600-1750* (New York, 1980), and Anderson, *Lineages*, p. 35-42.

11. Beik, *Absolutism and Society in Seventeenth Century France*, p. 245-278.

12. In the crowded field of historical writing on the Stuart era, Barry Coward's *The Stuart Age*, 3rd ed. (London: Longman, 2003) is recommended.

From *Leviathan*

Thomas Hobbes

An Oxford educated mathematician, Hobbes (1588–1679) is best known for Leviathan, *one of the world's most influential works on political theory. This book, published in 1651 during an era of political and social turmoil, argued that rational persons could best attain order and security by agreeing to the formation of a social contract, a new and radical idea at the time. Under such an arrangement, he said, citizens would willingly surrender some of their freedom in exchange for the safety that a powerful sovereign ruler could give them.*

Of the Natural Condition of Mankind as Concerning Their Felicity and Misery

Men by nature equal. Nature hath made men so equal, in the faculties of the body, and mind; as that though there be found one man sometimes manifestly stronger in body, or of quicker mind than another; yet when all is reckoned together, the difference between man, and man, is not so considerable, as that one man can thereupon claim to himself any benefit, to which another may not pretend, as well as he. For as to the strength of body, the weakest has strength enough to kill the strongest, either by secret machination, or by confederacy with others, that are in the same danger with himself.

From equality proceeds diffidence. From this equality of ability, ariseth equality of hope in the attaining of our ends. And therefore if any two men desire the same thing, which nevertheless they cannot both enjoy, they become enemies and in the way to their end, which is principally their own conservation, and sometimes their delectation only, endeavour to destroy, or subdue one another. And from hence it comes to pass, that where an invader hath no more to fear, than another man's single power; if one plant, sow, build, or possess a convenient seat, others may probably be expected to come prepared with forces united, to dispossess, and deprive him, not only of the fruit of his labour, but also of his life, or liberty. And the invader again is in the like danger of another.

So that in the nature of man, we find three principal causes of quarrel. First, competition; secondly, diffidence; thirdly, glory.

The first, maketh men invade for gain; the second, for safety; and the third, for reputation. The first use violence, to make themselves masters of other men's persons, wives, children, and cattle; the second, to defend them; the third, for trifles, as a word, a smile, a different opinion, and any other sign of undervalue, either direct in their persons, or by reflection in their kindred, their friends, their nation, their profession, or their name.

Out of civil states, there is always war of every one against every one. Hereby it is manifest, that during the time men live without a common power to keep them all in awe, they are in that condition which is called war; and such a war, as is of every man, against every man. For WAR, consisteth not in battle only, or the act of fighting; but in a tract of time, wherein the will to contend by battle is sufficiently known: and therefore the notion of *time*, is to be considered in the nature of war; as it is in the nature of weather. For as the nature of foul weather, lieth not in a shower or two of rain; but in an inclination thereto of many days together: so the nature of war, consisteth not in actual fighting; but in the known disposition thereto, during all the time there is no assurance to the contrary. All other time is PEACE.

The incommodities of such a war. Whatsoever therefore is consequent to a time of war, where every man is enemy to every man; the same is consequent to the time, wherein men live without other security, than what their own strength, and their own invention shall furnish them withal. In such condition, there is no place for industry; because the fruit thereof is uncertain: and consequently no culture of the earth; no navigation, nor use of the commodities that may be imported by sea; no commodious building; no instruments of moving, and removing, such things as require much force; no knowledge of the face of the earth; no account of time; no arts; no letters; no society; and which is worst of all, continual fear, and danger of violent death; and the life of man, solitary, poor, nasty, brutish, and short.

Of the First and Second Natural Laws, and of Contracts

Right of nature what. The RIGHT OF NATURE, which writers commonly call *jus naturale*, is the liberty each man hath, to use his own power, as he will himself, for the preservation of his own nature; that is to say, of his own life; and consequently, of doing any thing, which in his own judgment, and reason, he shall conceive to be the aptest means thereunto.

Liberty what. By LIBERTY, is understood, according to the proper signification of the word, the absence of external impediments: which impediments, may oft take away part of a man's power to do what he would; but cannot hinder him from using the power left him, according as his judgment, and reason shall dictate to him.

A law of nature what. Difference of right and law. A LAW OF NATURE, *lex naturalis*, is a precept or general rule, found out by reason, by which a man is forbidden to do that, which is destructive of his life, or taketh away the means of preserving the same; and to omit that, by which he thinketh may be best preserved. For though they that speak of this subject, use to confound *jus*, and *lex*, *right* and *law*: yet they ought to be distinguished; because RIGHT, consisteth in liberty to do, or to forbear: whereas LAW, determineth, and bindeth to one of them: so that law, and right, differ as much, as obligation, and liberty; which in one and the same matter are inconsistent.

Naturally every man has right to every thing. The fundamental law of nature. And because the condition of man, as hath been declared in the precedent chapter, is a condition of war of every one against every one; in which case every one is governed by his own reason; and there is nothing he can make use of, that may not be a help unto him, in preserving his life against his enemies; it followeth, that in such a condition, every man has a right to every thing; even to one another's body. And therefore, as long as this natural right of every man to every thing endureth, there can be no security to any man, how strong or wise soever he be, of living out the time, which nature ordinarily alloweth men to live. And consequently it is a precept, or general rule of reason, *that every man, ought to endeavour peace, as far as he has hope of obtaining it; and when he cannot obtain it, that he may seek, and use, all helps, and advantages of war.* The first branch of which rule, containeth the first, and fundamental law of nature; which is, *to seek peace, and follow it.* The second, the sum of the right of nature; which is, *by all means we can, to defend ourselves.*

Of the Causes, Generation, and Definition of a Commonwealth

The end of commonwealth, particular security. The final cause, end, or design of men, who naturally love liberty, and dominion over others, in the introduction of that restraint upon themselves, in which we see them live in commonwealths, is the foresight of their own preservation, and of a more contented life thereby; that is to say, of getting themselves out from that miserable condition of war, which is necessarily consequent, as hath been shown (chapter 15), to the natural passions of men, when there is no visible power to keep them in awe, and tie them by fear of punishment to the performance of their covenants, and observation of those laws of nature set down in the fourteenth and fifteenth chapters.

Which is not to be had from the law of nature. For the laws of nature, as *justice, equity, modesty, mercy,* and, in sum, *doing to others, as we would be done to,* of themselves, without the terror of some power, to cause them to be observed, are contrary to our natural passions, that carry us to partiality, pride, revenge, and the like. And covenants, without the sword, are but words, and of no strength to secure a man at all. Therefore notwithstanding the laws of nature (which every one hath then kept, when he has the will to keep them, when he can do it safely) if there be no power erected, or not great enough for our security; every man will, and may lawfully rely on his own strength and art, for caution against all other men. And in all places, where men have lived by small families, to rob and spoil one another, has been a trade, and so far from being reputed against the law of nature, that the greater spoils they gained, the greater was their honour; and men observed no other laws therein but the laws of honour; that is, to abstain from cruelty, leaving to men their lives, and instruments of husbandry. And as small families did then; so now do cities and kingdoms which are but greater families, for their own security, enlarge their dominions, upon all pretences of danger, and fear of invasion, or assistance that may be given to invaders, and endeavour as much as they can, to subdue, or weaken their neighbours, by open force, and secret arts, for want of other caution, justly; and are remembered for it in after ages with honour.

For if we could suppose a great multitude of men to consent in the observation of justice, and other laws of nature, without a common power to keep them all in awe; we might as well suppose all mankind to do the same; and then there neither would be, nor need to be any civil government, or commonwealth at all; because there would be peace without subjection.

The generation of a commonwealth. The definition of commonwealth. The only way to erect such a common power, as may be able to defend them from the invasion of foreigners, and the injuries of one another, and thereby to secure them in such sort, as that by their own industry, and by the fruits of the earth, they may nourish themselves and live contentedly; is, to confer all their power and strength upon one man, or upon one assembly of men, that may reduce all their wills, by plurality of voices, unto one will; which is as much as to say, to appoint one man, or assembly of men, to bear their person; and every one to own, and acknowledge himself to be author of whatsoever he that so beareth their person, shall act, or cause to be acted, in those things which concern the common peace and safety; and therein to submit their wills, every one to his will, and their judgments, to his judgment. This is more than consent, or concord; it is a real unity of them all, in one and the same person, made by covenant of every man with every man, in such manner, as if every man should say to every man, *I authorize and give up my right of governing myself, to this man, or to this assembly of men, on this condition, that thou give up thy right to him, and authorize all his actions in like manner.* This done, the multitude so united in one person, is called a COMMONWEALTH, in Latin CIVITAS. This is the generation of that great LEVIATHAN, or rather, to speak more reverently, of that *mortal god,* to which we owe under the *immortal God,* our peace and defence. For by this authority, given him by every particular man in the commonwealth, he hath the use of so much power and strength conferred on him, that by terror thereof, he is enabled to form the wills of them all, to peace at home, and mutual aid against their enemies abroad. And in him consisteth the essence of the commonwealth; which, to define it, is *one person, of whose acts a great multitude, by mutual covenants one with another, have made themselves every one the author, to the end he may use the strength and means of them all, as he shall think expedient, for their peace and common defence.*

Sovereign, and subject, what. And he that carrieth this person is called SOVEREIGN, and said to have *sovereign power;* and every one besides, his SUBJECT.

The attaining to this sovereign power, is by two ways. One by natural force; as when a man maketh his children, to submit themselves, and their children to his government, as being able to destroy them if they refuse; or by war subdueth his enemies to his will, giving them their lives on that condition. The other, is when men agree amongst themselves, to submit to some man, or assembly of men, voluntarily, on confidence to be protected by him against all others. This latter, may be called a political commonwealth, or commonwealth by *institution;* and the former, a commonwealth by *acquisition.* And first, I shall speak of a commonwealth by institution.

The Enlightenment

John McGrath

The Enlightenment was a period of European intellectual and cultural development that began in the late seventeenth century and lasted through the eighteenth century. Building on the foundations established by the Renaissance and Scientific Revolution, the Enlightenment encouraged Europeans to view their world from a more rational, goal-oriented perspective, setting the stage for much of the massive social change that took place in the late eighteenth and nineteenth centuries. People during the Enlightenment often referred to their era as "The Age of Reason."

Science and Reason

The **Scientific Revolution** that had begun in the late sixteenth century was a critical stage in the modernization of Europe, since it emphasized the systematic study and observation of natural phenomena. This allowed scholars like Descartes and Galileo to develop theories and "natural laws" that could be applied universally. Because of the printing press, such ideas could be compared and debated, but although their discoveries were important in the history of scientific inquiry, early scientists comprised a somewhat isolated intellectual community. In comparison, the Enlightenment featured wider participation by the rapidly growing community of literate and educated people of all sorts, who were pursuing a much wider spectrum of topics that included education, philosophy, technology, politics, criminology, music, literature, and even the beginnings of sociology and economics.

The Scientific Revolution had helped to discredit the narrow Christian explanations of the nature of humanity, the earth, and the cosmos. Instead, it promoted the sense that some sort of rational benevolent force had created the world, a perspective that is often called **deism**, which became an essential foundation of the Enlightenment approach to the pursuit of knowledge.[1] A frequent analogy demonstrating the concept of deism is "God as clockmaker"; many scholars held the conviction that had God created the universe as an entity that operated somewhat like a machine, according to rationally designed principles of cause and effect. Enlightenment scholars largely devoted their efforts to uncovering these principles and applying them in ways that would benefit humanity.

On the whole, the Enlightenment demolished the blind acceptance of tradition as a guiding principle of life. In marked contrast to the medieval era, with its emphasis on faith and obedience, many Europeans began to question customary methods, institutions, and authorities of all sorts. As one historian expressed it,

> Armed with science, reason, and empirical facts, the Enlightenment saw itself as engaged in a noble struggle against the constricting medieval darkness of Church dogma and popular superstition, tied to a backward and tyrannical political structure of corrupt privilege.[2]

Optimism, Knowledge and Skepticism

Many historians would consider the first major Enlightenment figure to be the Englishman **John Locke**, because of his more optimistic view of human capabilities compared to common previous outlooks. Convinced that an individual's thinking and behavior were shaped by experience, instead of determined by birth, Locke promoted the influential idea that people could use reason to educate themselves and improve their societies.[3] In 1689, the year after England's Glorious Revolution, he published his *Two Treatises on Government*, which judged absolutism to be an irrational way of organizing a political state, and even a dangerous one, since it could so easily turn into tyranny. In the *Second Treatise*, Locke constructed a supremely rational argument in favor of a separation of powers in government, where an elected legislature could act as a check on monarchy, and he further asserted that the prime responsibility of political power was the protection of the God-given rights of life, liberty, and property.

Locke's ideas, and those of other early Enlightenment figures, stimulated the next generations of educated Europeans to follow the path of reason. As the eighteenth century progressed, the movement grew and spread, as Enlightenment-inspired thinking began to dominate intellectual discourse throughout the western world, including France, Holland, Italy, Scandinavia, Spain, Germany, and even the British colonies in America. By this time, technological improvements in printing had enabled the publication of more affordable books, pamphlets, and magazines on a wide variety of subjects, for an increasingly educated and literate population. Throughout Europe, cafes, bookstores, private clubs, and scientific societies provided environments where educated people could mingle to debate ideas.[4]

During the eighteenth century, the kingdom of France soon achieved recognition as the cultural capital of Europe. There, leading intellectual figures known as ***philosophes*** ("lovers of learning") achieved celebrity status.[5] Especially in Paris, a "salon culture" evolved where Enlightenment scholars of many backgrounds gathered regularly in the houses of wealthy sponsors, especially noble women. One of the most influential early *philosophes* was a French aristocrat, the Baron de la Brède et de **Montesquieu**, who was among the first to examine the dynamics of human societies from a comparative perspective. He recognized that each society had unique needs and resources available to it, and he investigated how these factors could influence the development of distinctive cultures, laws and institutions. Montesquieu's 1748 *Spirit of the Laws* has been described as the first serious study of political science and sociology; in this important work, he followed and expanded upon Locke's argument in favor of a balance of differing political powers.[6]

Undoubtedly the most famous and influential of the philosophes was the Frenchman François-Marie Arouet, known by his pen name of **Voltaire**.[7] Starting in the 1730s, until his death in 1778, he authored hundreds of separate works in various genres, including poetry, social history, essays, and fiction. For most of his career, Voltaire lived in exile from France, due to his attacks on privileged interests such as organized religion and monarchical governments. Younger Enlightenment figures practically worshipped Voltaire, to the point where he has often been called "the Grandfather of the Enlightenment."

Voltaire urged his readers to look objectively at their societies, and to be skeptical of what traditional authority defined as proper and right. He considered the abuse of power to be a particular problem, and he became a champion of tolerance of all sorts. While he was more socially and politically conservative than many other Enlightenment figures--such as Jean-Jacques Rousseau, with whom he quarreled bitterly—he possessed an optimism that with some effort, people's lives could be made better. Yet at the same time he warned against overly idealistic expectations. The novel *Candide*, written in 1759, illustrates nearly all of Voltaire's main criticisms of society.[8] As the title character journeys through a world featuring a seemingly endless number of cruelties, he wonders why human beings seem to insist on creating such avoidable evils as war, persecution, and slavery. As in many of his other works, Voltaire employs satire and irreverence in *Candide* to make his points, poking fun at practically everything, including the Enlightenment itself.

Probably the most ambitious project of the Enlightenment was the ***Encyclopedia***, edited by the multitalented *philosophes* Denis Diderot and Jean d'Alembert.[9] Envisioned as a collection of all the world's knowledge, it eventually appeared in 28 volumes between 1751 and 1772, and its almost 72,000 total articles were authored by the leading intellectual figures of Europe, including Voltaire (anonymously) on religion and other topics, Montesquieu on politics, and Rousseau on music and political economy. While the *Encyclopedia* proclaimed itself objective and neutral, all of its contributors were favorable to the principles of intellectual freedom, and the articles tended to be critical of both monarchy and organized religion. Though it was officially banned in France by royal decree in 1759, it continued, in large part because it had many supporters at the royal court, and, in fact, the wives of some of the king's ministers regularly hosted the *Encyclopedia* editors in their salons.

A Diversity of Viewpoints: Rousseau and Smith

Despite such attempts to consolidate the new learning, as time went on the Enlightenment promoted an ever greater diversity of ideas, promoting more and more argument and debate, some of it quite serious and profound. A good illustration of the difficulty in generalizing about Enlightenment thinking can be seen in comparing the contributions of two eighteenth century figures, the Frenchman **Jean-Jacques Rousseau** and the Scotsman **Adam Smith**. While they shared certain fundamental assumptions concerning the rationality of human beings and the possibility of progress, they arrived at quite different conclusions about what should be done.

Rousseau, a largely self taught intellectual from a rather humble background, saw a just and moral society as the highest aspiration of humanity, but lamented that artificial "civilization," with its emphasis on private property, encouraged greed and inequality.[10] He possessed a great optimism that people could do better, arguing that for real enlightenment to be achieved, people must recognize their dependence on each other. A society that could encourage sympathy for one's fellows and make the common welfare the highest priority, would be, by his definition, a virtuous one. He lamented the greed and abuse of power that he saw in eighteenth century France, which he believed retarded social progress towards a more "enlightened" society. Rousseau's view of human nature and his emphasis on virtue, as expressed in his works *Discourse on Inequality* (1754) and *The Social Contract* (1762), made him a transitional figure between the Enlightenment and the Romantic era that took root in the late eighteenth century. After his death, during the French Revolution, his ideas energized such revolutionary leaders as Jean-Paul Marat and Maximilien Robespierre to undertake massive changes in French society.

Smith, a Professor of Moral Philosophy in Glasgow, Scotland, was likewise concerned with human nature. However, Smith believed that people were most effectively motivated by "enlightened self-interest," which, he argued, could be a powerful instrument for creating a more humane and happier society.[11] His most famous work, **The Wealth of Nations** (1776) argues that restraints on economic competition posed by mercantilist controls and the emergence of monopolies retarded economic growth. Individuals were motivated by a rational desire to compete with one another in order to better their economic standing, and if the political state would allow the "Invisible Hand" of supply and demand to operate with a minimum of interference, the result would be increased productivity and material progress. Both his view of human nature as essentially rational and his explanation of cause and effect on a society-wide level demonstrate important elements of the Enlightenment approach to understanding the world. Smith's thinking reflects many of Locke's convictions about human capabilities, as well as providing much of the foundation for the ideology of Classical Liberalism that would emerge in the next century.

In a sense, Smith promoted a principle that was the complete opposite of Rousseau's: he argued that if individuals could work towards their own self-interests, the result would be an improvement in the common welfare. In contrast, Rousseau had contended that citizens who put the common welfare ahead of their own selfish desires would personally benefit from their membership in a virtuous society. While this may not seem like a major difference, it has great implications for the sorts of laws, institutions and social structures that each thought would work the best.

A Rational Ethos

It is difficult in a brief space to do justice to all of the accomplishments achieved by Enlightenment thinkers, in various parts of Europe, over a span of more than a century. Different places, such as Italy, Germany, Scotland, Spain, and Holland developed distinctive Enlightenment themes and approaches that often clashed in substance and style, and provoked a constant give and take of ideas. Perhaps the single unifying element is best expressed through the frequent assertion that the Enlightenment was "not so much a specific set of opinions or beliefs as an attitude of mind."[12] Encouraging lofty scholars and casual readers alike to question conventional wisdom, this attitude became firmly entrenched in the western cultural outlook and played a major role in promoting social change in all areas of life.

One does not have to look very hard to see that, even in the eighteenth century, Enlightenment ideas directly contributed to material improvement in many European societies. In many absolutist states, including some of the most backward and repressive, these new perspectives were used to reform some of the more counterproductive elements of absolutist and traditional societies; such efforts have sometimes been called "**enlightened absolutism**" or "enlightened despotism." Additionally, Enlightenment thinking motivated people to come up with new and useful ideas in all sorts of fields, from politics to education to science to literature, helping to make European society more innovative and dynamic.

Elsewhere, the impact of the Enlightenment was significant in another way. While new ideas promoted optimism, they also helped to undermine the traditions, customs, and social norms that had helped bind the society together, and the Enlightenment unleashed changes that were difficult to rein in. Beginning in the late eighteenth century, the Enlightenment's encouragement of skepticism played a central role in the profound political and social upheavals that occurred in North America, Europe, and Latin America.[13] During this critical era, for the first time, a critical mass of people had started to believe that, by making the best use of their abilities, they could shape the destinies of their societies as never before. Though was often fierce disagreement about what direction to take, this, too, was an important step in the creation of modern society.

References and Suggested Readings:

Artz, Frederick B. *The Enlightenment in France*. Kent, OH: Kent State University Press, 1968.

Gay, Peter. *The Enlightenment: The Rise of Modern Paganism*. New York: Norton, 1965.

Hampson, Norman. "The Enlightenment," in *Early Modern Europe: An Oxford History*, Euan Cameron ed., Oxford: Oxford University Press, 1999.

Heilbroner, Robert L. *The Worldly Philosophers*, 7th Ed. New York: Touchstone, 1999.

Osborne, Roger. *Civilization: A New History of the Western World*. New York: Pegasus, 2006.

Tarnas, Richard. *The Passion of the Western Mind*. New York: Ballantine, 1991.

Notes

1. Norman Hampson, "The Enlightenment," in *Early Modern Europe: An Oxford History*, ed. Euan Cameron (Oxford: Oxford University Press, 1999), p. 269-274.

2. Richard Tarnas, *The Passion of the Western Mind* (New York: Ballantine, 1991), p. 312.

3. Ibid., p. 333-336.

4. Roger Osborne, *Civilization: A New History of the Western World* (New York: Pegasus, 2006), p. 306-311.

5. A good brief study of the central role of France and Paris is Frederick B. Artz, *The Enlightenment in France* (Kent, OH: Kent State University Press, 1968).

6. Ibid., p. 57-65.

7. Ibid., p. 66-82.

8. On *Candide*, see Peter Gay, *The Enlightenment: The Rise of Modern Paganism* (New York: Norton, 1965), p. 197-203.

9. Artz, *Enlightenment in France*, p. 88-98; Osborne, *Civilization*, p. 311.

10. Artz, *Enlightenment in France*, p. 130-150.

11. On Smith, see Robert L. Heilbroner, *The Worldly Philosophers*, 7th Ed. (New York: Touchstone, 1999), p. 42-74.

12. Hampson, "The Enlightenment," p. 289.

13. Gay, *The Enlightenment*, p. 127-207.

From *Second Treatise of Civil Government*

John Locke

John Locke is regarded by many as both the first major Enlightenment figure and as the father of modern democracy. An ardent supporter of William of Orange, who became king of England in 1688 during the Glorious Revolution, Locke published The Second Treatise *shortly after William's accession to the throne. In it, he outlined the case for a more rational, responsive type of monarchy—a constitutional monarchy—that was designed to protect the "natural rights" of citizens as its primary responsibility. In this work, Locke directly rebuts many of the earlier ideas of Thomas Hobbes.*

I think it may not be amiss to set down what I take to be political power; that the power of a magistrate over a subject may be distinguished from that of a father over his children, a master over his servants, a husband over his wife, and a lord over his slave. All which distinct powers happening sometimes together in the same man, if he be considered under these different relations, it may help us to distinguish these powers one from another, and show the difference betwixt a ruler of a commonwealth, a father of a family, and a captain of a galley.

Political power, then, I take to be a right of making laws with penalties of death and, consequently, all less penalties for the regulating and preserving of property, and of employing the force of the community in the execution of such laws, and in the defence of the commonwealth from foreign injury, and all this only for the public good.

Of the State of Nature

To understand political power right, and derive it from its original, we must consider what state all men are naturally in, and that is a state of perfect freedom to order their actions and dispose of their possessions and persons as they think fit, within the bounds of the law of nature, without asking leave or depending upon the will of any other man.

A state also of equality, wherein all the power and jurisdiction is reciprocal, no one having more than another; there being nothing more evident than that creatures of the same species and rank, promiscuously born to all the same advantages of nature and the use of the same faculties, should also be equal one amongst another without subordination or subjection. . . .

But though this be a state of liberty, yet it is not a state of license. . . . The state of nature has a law of nature to govern it which obliges every one; and reason, which is that law, teaches all mankind who will but consult it that, being all equal and independent, no one ought to harm another in his life, health, liberty, or possessions; for men being all the workmanship of one omnipotent and infinitely wise Maker—all the servants of one sovereign master, sent into the world by his order, and about his business—they are his property whose workmanship they are, made to last during his, not one another's, pleasure; and being furnished with like faculties, sharing all in one community of nature, there cannot be supposed any such subordination among us that may authorize us to destroy another, as if we were made for one another's uses as the inferior ranks of creatures are for ours. . . .

Of Property

Whether we consider natural reason, which tells us that men, being once born, have a right to their preservation, and consequently to meat and drink and such other things as nature affords for their subsistence; or revelation, which gives us an account of those grants God made of the world to Adam, and to Noah and his sons; it is very clear that God, as King David says (Psal. cxv. 16), "has given the earth to the children of men," given it to mankind in common. . . . But this being supposed, it seems to some a very great difficulty how any one should ever come to have a property in anything. . . .

Though the earth and all inferior creatures be common to all men, yet every man has a property in his own person; this nobody has any right to but himself. The labour of his body and the work of his hands, we may say, are properly his. Whatsoever then he removes out of the state that nature hath provided and left it in, he hath mixed his labour with, and joined to it something that is his own, and thereby makes it his property. . . . Thus this law of reason makes the deer that Indian's who hath killed it; it is allowed to be his goods who hath bestowed his labour upon it, though before it was the common right of every one. . . . As much land as a man tills, plants, improves, cultivates, and can use the product of, so much is his property. . . . God gave the world to men in common; but since he gave it them for their benefit and the greatest conveniences of life they were capable to draw from it, it cannot be supposed he meant it should always remain common and uncultivated. He gave it to the use of the industrious and rational—and labour was to be his title to it—not to the fancy or covetousness of the quarrelsome and contentious.

Of the Beginning of Political Societies

Men being, as has been said, by nature all free, equal, and independent, no one can be put out of this estate and subjected to the political power of another without his own consent. The only way whereby any one divests himself of his natural liberty, and puts on the bonds of civil society, is by agreeing with other men to join and unite into a community for their comfortable, safe, and peaceable living one amongst another, in a secure enjoyment of their properties and a greater security against any that are not of it. This any number of men may do, because it injures not the freedom of the rest; they are left as they were in the liberty of the state of nature. When any number of men have so consented to make one community or government, they are thereby presently incorporated and make one body politic wherein the majority have a right to act and conclude the rest. . . .

Of the Ends of Political Society and Government

If man in the state of nature be so free, as has been said, if he be absolute lord of his own person and possessions, equal to the greatest, and subject to nobody, why will he part with his freedom, why will he give up his empire and subject himself to the dominion and control of any other power? To which it is obvious to answer that though in the state of nature he hath such a right, yet the enjoyment of it is very uncertain and constantly exposed to the invasion of others; for all being kings as much as he, every man his equal, and the greater part no strict observers of equity and justice, the enjoyment of the property he had in this state is very unsafe, very unsecure. This makes him willing to quit a condition which, however free, is full of tears and continual dangers; and it is not without reason that he seeks out and is willing to join in society with others who are already united, or have a mind to unite, for the mutual preservation of their lives, liberties, and estates, which I call by the general name "property."

The great and chief end, therefore, of men's uniting into commonwealths and putting themselves under government is the preservation of their property.

Of the Dissolution of Government

The reason why men enter into society is the preservation of their property; and the end why they choose and authorize a legislative is that there may be laws made and rules set as guards and fences to the properties of all the members of the society, to limit the power and moderate the dominion of every part and member of the society; for since it can never be supposed to be the will of the society that the legislative should have a power to destroy that which every one designs to secure by entering into society, and for which the people submitted themselves to legislators of their own making, whenever the legislators endeavour to take away and destroy the property of the people, or to reduce them to slavery under arbitrary power, they put themselves into a state of war with the people who are thereupon absolved from any further obedience, and are left to the common refuge which God hath provided for all men against force and violence. Whensoever, therefore, the legislative shall transgress this fundamental rule of society, and either by ambition, fear, folly, or corruption, endeavour to grasp themselves, or put into the hands of any other, an absolute power over the lives, liberties, and estates of the people, by this breach of trust they forfeit the power the people had put into their hands for quite contrary ends, and it devolves to the people who have a right to resume their original liberty, and by the establishment of a new legislative, such as they shall think fit, provide for their own safety and security, which is the end for which they are in society.

The Social Contract

Jean Jacques Rousseau

Jean-Jacques Rousseau (1712–1778) was a Genevan-born Frenchman who first attained fame as an essayist in Paris, and who quarreled bitterly and publicly with many other leading French Enlightenment figures. During the French Revolution, the ideas contained in his Social Contract *became wildly popular and greatly influenced revolutionary leaders, especially Jacobin leaders such as Maximilien Robespierre.*

Book 1: Chapter 1: Subject of the First Book

Man is born free; and everywhere he is in chains. One thinks himself the master of others, and still remains a greater slave than they. How did this change come about? I do not know. What can make it legitimate? That question I think I can answer. If I took into account only force, and the effects derived from it, I should say: "As long as a people is compelled to obey, and obeys, it does well: as soon as it can shake off the yoke, and shakes it off, it does still better; for, regaining its liberty by the same right as took it away, either it is justified in resuming it, or there was no justification for those who took it away." But the social order is a sacred right which is the basis of all other rights. Nevertheless, this right does not come from nature, and must therefore be founded on conventions. Before coming to that, I have to prove what I have just asserted. . . .

Book 1: Chapter 3: The Right of the Strongest

The strongest is never strong enough to be always the master, unless he transforms strength into right, and obedience into duty. Hence the right of the strongest, which, though to all seeming meant ironically, is really laid down as a fundamental principle. But are we never to have an explanation of this phrase? Force is a physical power, and I fail to see what moral effect it can have. To yield to force is an act of necessity, not of will—at the most, an act of prudence. In what sense can it be a duty?

Suppose for a moment that this so-called "right" exists. I maintain that the sole result is a mass of inexplicable nonsense. For, if force creates right, the effect changes with the cause: every force that is greater than the first succeeds to its right. As soon as it is possible to disobey with impunity, disobedience is legitimate; and, the strongest being always in the right, the only thing that matters is to act so as to become the strongest. But what kind of right is that which perishes when force fails? If we must obey perforce, there is no need to obey because we ought; and if we are not forced to obey, we are under no obligation to do so. Clearly, the word "right" adds nothing to force: in this connection, it means absolutely nothing.

Obey the powers that be. If this means yield to force, it is a good precept, but superfluous: I can answer for its never being violated. All power comes from God, I admit; but so does all sickness: does that mean that we are forbidden to call in the doctor? A brigand surprises me at the edge of a wood: must I not merely surrender my purse on compulsion; but, even if I could withhold it, am I in conscience bound to give it up? For certainly the pistol he holds is also a power.

Let us then admit that force does not create right, and that we are obliged to obey only legitimate powers. In that case, my original question recurs.

Book 1: Chapter 4: Against Slavery

... To renounce liberty is to renounce being a man, to surrender the rights of humanity and even its duties. For him who renounces everything no indemnity is possible. Such a renunciation is incompatible with man's nature; to remove all liberty from his will is to remove all morality from his acts. Finally, it is an empty and contradictory convention that sets up, on the one side, absolute authority, and, on the other, unlimited obedience. Is it not clear that we can be under no obligation to a person from whom we have the right to exact everything? Does not this condition alone, in the absence of equivalence or exchange, in itself involve the nullity of the act? For what right can my slave have against me, when all that he has belongs to me, and, his right being mine, this right of mine against myself is a phrase devoid of meaning?

Grotius and the rest find in war another origin for the so-called right of slavery. The victor having, as they hold, the right of killing the vanquished, the latter can buy back his life at the price of his liberty; and this convention is the more legitimate because it is to the advantage of both parties. But it is clear that this supposed right to kill the conquered is by no means deducible from the state of war. Men, from the mere fact that, while they are living in their primitive independence, they have no mutual relations stable enough to constitute either the state of peace or the state of war, cannot be naturally enemies. War is constituted by a relation between things, and not between persons; and, as the state of war cannot arise out of simple personal relations, but only out of real relation, private war, or war of man with man, can exist neither in the state of nature, where there is no constant property, nor in the social state, where everything is under the authority of the laws.

Individual combats, duels and encounters, are acts which cannot constitute a state; while the private wars, authorized by the Establishments of Louis IX, King of France, and suspended by the Peace of God, are abuses of feudalism, in itself an absurd system if ever there was one, and contrary to the principles of natural right and to all good polity.

War then is a relation, not between man and man, but between State and State, and individuals are enemies only accidentally, not as men, nor ever as citizens, but as soldiers; not as members of their country, but as its defenders. Finally, each State can have for enemies only other States, and not men; for between things disparate in nature there can be no real relation. . . .

Book 1: Chapter 6: The Social Contract

I suppose men to have reached the point at which the obstacles in the way of their preservation in the state of nature show their power of resistance to be greater than the resources at the disposal of each individual for his maintenance in that state. That primitive condition can then subsist no longer; and the human race would perish unless it changed its manner of existence.

But, as men cannot engender new forces, but only unite and direct existing ones, they have no other means of preserving themselves than the formation, by aggregation, of a sum of forces great enough to overcome the resistance. These they have to bring into play by means of a single motive power, and cause to act in concert.

This sum of forces can arise only where several persons come together: but, as the force and liberty of each man are the chief instruments of his self-preservation, how can he pledge them without harming his own interests, and neglecting the care he owes to himself? This difficulty, in its bearing on my present subject, may be stated in the following terms:

"The problem is to find a form of association which will defend and protect with the whole common force the person and goods of each associate, and in which each, while uniting himself with all, may still obey himself alone, and remain as free as before." This is the fundamental problem of which the Social Contract provides the solution.

The clauses of this contract are so determined by the nature of the act that the slightest modification would make them vain and ineffective; so that, although they have perhaps never been formally set forth, they are everywhere the same and everywhere tacitly admitted and recognized, until, on the violation of the social compact, each regains his original rights and resumes his natural liberty, while losing the conventional liberty in favor of which he renounced it.

These clauses, properly understood, may be reduced to one—the total alienation of each associate, together with all his rights, to the whole community; for, in the first place, as each gives himself absolutely, the conditions are the same for all; and, this being so, no one has any interest in making them burdensome to others.

Moreover, the alienation being without reserve, the union is as perfect as it can be, and no associate has anything more to demand: for, if the individuals retained certain rights, as there would be no common superior to decide between them and the public, each, being on one point his own judge, would ask to be so on all; the state of nature would thus continue, and the association would necessarily become inoperative or tyrannical.

Finally, each man, in giving himself to all, gives himself to nobody: and as there is no associate over whom he does not acquire the same right as he yields others over himself, he gains an equivalent for everything he loses, and an increase of force for the preservation of what he has.

If then we discard from the social compact what is not of its essence, we shall find that it reduces itself to the following terms—

"Each of us puts his person and all his power in a common agreement under the supreme direction of the general will, and, in our corporate capacity, we receive each member as an indivisible part of the whole."

At once, in place of the individual personality of each contracting party, this act of association creates a moral and collective body, composed of as many members as the assembly contains votes, and receiving from this act its unity, its common indemnity, its life and its will. This public person, so formed by the union of all other persons formerly took the name of city, and now takes that of Republic or body politic; it is called by its members State when passive, Sovereign when active, and Power when compared with others like itself. Those who are associated in it take collectively the name of people, and severally are called citizens, as sharing in the sovereign power, and subject, as being under the laws of the State. But these terms are often confused and taken one for another: it is enough to know how to distinguish them when they are being used with precision.

Book 1: Chapter 7: The Sovereign

This formula shows us that the act of association comprises a mutual undertaking between the public and the individuals, and that each individual, in making a contract, as we may say, with himself, is bound in a double capacity; as a member of the Sovereign, he is bound to the individuals, and as a member of the State to the Sovereign. But the maxim of civil law that no one is bound by undertakings made to himself, does not apply in this case; for there is a great difference between incurring an obligation to yourself and incurring one to a whole of which you form a part.

Attention must further be called to the fact the public deliberation, while competent to bind all the subjects to the Sovereign, because of the two different capacities in which each of them may be regarded, cannot, for the opposite reason, bind the Sovereign to itself; and that it is consequently against the nature of the body politic for the Sovereign to impose on itself a law which it cannot infringe. Being able to regard itself in only one capacity, it is in the position of an individual who makes a contract with himself; and this makes it clear that there neither is nor can be any kind of fundamental law binding on the body of the people—not even the social contract itself. This does not mean that the body politic cannot enter into undertakings with others, provided the contract is not infringed by them; for in relation to what is external to it, it becomes a simple being, an individual.

But the body politic or the Sovereign, drawing its being wholly from the sanctity of the contract, can never bind itself, even to an outsider, to do anything derogatory to the original act, for instance to alienate any part of itself, or to submit to another Sovereign. Violation of the act by which it exists would be self-annihilation; and that which is itself nothing can create nothing.

As soon as this multitude is so united in one body, it is impossible to offend against one of the members without attacking the body, and still more to offend against the body without the members resenting it. Duty and interest therefore equally oblige the two contracting parties to give each other help; and the same men should seek to combine, in their double capacity, all the advantages dependent upon that capacity.

Again, the Sovereign, being formed wholly of the individuals who compose it, neither has nor can have any interest contrary to theirs; and consequently the sovereign power need give no guarantee to its subject, because it is impossible for the body to wish to hurt all its members. We shall also see later on that it cannot hurt any in particular. The Sovereign, merely by virtue of what it is, is always what it should be.

This, however, is not the case with the relation of the subjects to the Sovereign, which, despite the common interest, would have no security that they would fulfill their undertakings, unless it found means to assure itself of their fidelity.

In fact, each individual, as a man, may have a particular will contrary or dissimilar to the general will which he has as a citizen. His particular interest may speak to him quite differently from the common interest: his absolute and naturally independent existence may make him look upon what he owes to the common cause as a gratuitous contribution, the loss of which will do less harm to others than the payment of it is burdensome to himself; and, regarding the moral person which constitutes the State as a *persona ficta*, because to a man, he may wish to enjoy the rights of citizenship without being ready to fulfill the duties of a subject. The continuance of such an injustice could not but prove the undoing of the body politic.

In order then that the social compact may not be an empty formula, it tacitly includes the undertaking, which alone can give force to the rest, that whoever refuses to obey the general will shall be compelled to do so by the whole body. This means nothing less than that he will be forced to be free; for this is the condition which, by giving each citizen to his country, secures him against all personal dependence. In this lies the key to the working of the political machine; this alone legitimizes civil undertakings, which, without it, would be absurd, tyrannical, and liable to the most frightful abuses.

Book 1: Chapter 8: The Civil State

The passage from the state of nature to the civil state produces a very remarkable change in man, by substituting justice for instinct in his conduct, and giving his actions the morality they formerly lacked. Then only, when the voice of duty takes the place of physical impulses and right of appetite, does man, who so far had considered only himself, find that he is forced to act on different principles, and to consult his reason before listening to his inclinations. Although, in this state, he deprives himself of some advantages which he got from nature, he gains in return others so great, his faculties are so stimulated and developed, his ideas so extended, his feelings so ennobled, and his whole soul so uplifted, that, did not the abuses of this new condition often degrade him below that which he left, he would be bound to bless continually the happy moment which took him from it for ever, and, instead of a stupid and unimaginative animal, made him an intelligent being and a man.

Let us draw up the whole account in terms easily commensurable. What man loses by the social contract is his natural liberty and an unlimited right to everything he tries to get and succeeds in getting; what he gains is civil liberty and the proprietorship of all he possesses. If we are to avoid mistake in weighing one against the other, we must clearly distinguish natural liberty, which is bounded only by the strength of the individual, from civil liberty, which is limited by the general will; and possession, which is merely the effect of force or the right of the first occupier, from property which can be founded only on a positive title.

We might, over and above all this, add, to what man acquires in the civil state, moral liberty, which alone makes him truly master of himself; for the mere impulse of appetite is slavery, while obedience to a law which we prescribe to ourselves is liberty. But I have already said too much on this head, and the philosophical meaning of the word liberty does not now concern us.

Book 1: Chapter 9: Real Property

... I shall end ... this book by remarking on a fact on which the whole social system should rest: i.e. that, instead of destroying natural inequality, the fundamental compact substitutes, for such physical inequality as nature may have set up between men, an equality that is moral and legitimate, and that men, who may be unequal in strength or intelligence, become every one equal by convention and legal right.

Book 2: Chapter 1: The Sovereignty Is Inalienable

The first and most important deduction from the principles we have so far laid down is that the general will alone can direct the State according to the object for which it was instituted, i.e., the common good: for if the clashing of particular interests made the establishment of societies necessary, the agreement of these very interests made it possible. The common element in these different interests is what forms the social tie; and, were there no point of agreement between them all, no society could exist. It is solely on the basis of this common interest that every society should be governed.

I hold then that Sovereignty, being nothing less than the exercise of the general will, can never be alienated, and that the Sovereign, who is no less than a collective being, cannot be represented except by himself: the power indeed may be transmitted, but not the will.

In reality, if it is not impossible for a particular will to agree on some point with the general will, it is at least impossible for the agreement to be lasting and constant; for the particular will tends, by its very nature, to partiality, while the general will tends to equality. It is even more impossible to have any guarantee of this agreement for ever if it should always exist, it would be the effect not of art, but of chance. The Sovereign may indeed say: "I now will actually what this man wills, or at least what he says he wills"; but it cannot say: "What he wills tomorrow, I too shall will" because it is absurd for the will to bind itself for the future, nor is it incumbent on any will to consent to anything that is not for the good of the being who wills. If then the people promises simply to obey, by that very act it dissolves itself and loses what makes it a people; the moment a master exists, there is no longer a Sovereign, and from that moment the body politic has ceased to exist.

This does not mean that the commands of the rulers cannot pass for general wills, so long as the Sovereign, being free to oppose them, offers no opposition. In such a case, universal silence is taken to imply the consent of the people. This will be explained later on.

Book 2: Chapter 2: The Sovereignty Is Indivisible

Sovereignty, for the same reason as makes it inalienable, is indivisible; for will either is, or is not, general; it is the will neither of the body of the people, nor only of a part of it. In the first case, the will, when declared, is an act of Sovereignty and constitutes law: in the second, it is merely a particular will, or act of magistracy—at the most a decree.

But our political theorists, unable to divide Sovereignty in principle, divide it according to its object: into force and will; into legislative power and executive power; into rights of taxation, justice and war; into internal administration and power of foreign treaty. Sometimes they confuse all these sections, and sometimes they distinguish them; they turn the Sovereign into a fantastic being composed of several connected pieces: it is as if they were making man of several bodies, one with eyes, one with arms, another with feet, and each with nothing besides. We are told that the jugglers of Japan dismember a child before the eyes of the spectators; then they throw all the members into the air one after another, and the child falls down alive and whole. The conjuring tricks of our political theorists are very like that; they first dismember the body politic by an illusion worthy of a fair, and then join it together again we know not how.

This error is due to a lack of exact notions concerning the Sovereign authority, and to taking for parts of it what are only emanations from it. Thus, for example, the acts of declaring war and making peace have been regarded as acts of Sovereignty; but this is not the case, as these acts do not constitute law, merely the application of a law, a particular act which decides how the law applies, as we shall see clearly when the idea attached to the word law has been defined. . . .

Book 2: Chapter 3: Whether the General Will Is Fallible

It follows from what has gone before that the general will is always right and tends to the public advantage; but it does not follow that the deliberation of the people are always equally correct. Our will is always for our own good, but we do not always see what that is; the people is never corrupted, but is often deceived, and on such occasions only does it seem to will what is bad.

There is often a great deal of difference between the will of all and the general will; the latter considers only the common interest, while the former takes private interest into account, and is not more than a sum of particular wills: but take away from these same wills the pluses and minuses that cancel one another, and the general will remains as the sum of the differences.

If, when the people, being furnished with adequate information, held its deliberations, the citizens had no communication one with another, the grand total of the small differences would always give the general will, and the decision would always be good. But when fractions arise, and partial associations are formed at the expense of the great association, the will of each of these associations becomes general in relation to its members, while it remains particular in relation to the State: it may then be said that there are no longer as many votes as there are men, but only as many as there are associations. The differences become less numerous and give a less general result. Lastly, when one of these associations is so great as to prevail over all the rest, the result is no longer a sum of small differences, but a single difference; in this case there is no longer a general will, and the opinion which prevails is purely particular.

It is therefore essential, if the general will is to be able to express itself, that there should be no partial society within the State, and that each citizen should think only his own thought which was indeed the sublime and unique system established by the great Lycurgus. But if there are partial societies, it is best to have as many possible and to prevent them from being unequal, as was done by Solon, Numa and Servius. These precautions are the only ones that can guarantee that the general will shall be always enlightened, and that the people shall in no way deceive itself.

Book 2: Chapter 4: The Limits of the Sovereign Power

If the state is a moral person whose life is in the union of its members, and if the most important of its cares is the care of its own preservation, it must have a universal and compelling force, in order to move and dispose each part as may be most advantageous to the whole. As nature gives each man absolute power over all his members, the social compact gives the body politic absolute power over all its members also; and it is this power which, under the direction of the general will, bears, as I have said, the name of Sovereignty.

But, besides the public person, we have to consider the private persons composing it, whose life and liberty are naturally independent of it. We are bound then to distinguish clearly between the respective rights of the citizens and the Sovereign, and between the duties the former have to fulfill as subjects, and the natural rights they should enjoy as men.

Each man alienates, I admit, by the social compact, only such part of his powers, goods and liberty as it is important for the community to control; but it must also be granted that the Sovereign is sole judge of what is important.

Every service a citizen can render the State he ought to render as soon as the Sovereign demands it; but the Sovereign, for its part, cannot impose upon its subjects any fetters that are useless to the community, nor can it ever wish to do so; for no more by the law of reason than by the law of nature can anything occur without a cause.

The undertakings which bind us to the social body are obligatory only because they are mutual; and their nature is such that in fulfilling them we cannot work for others without working for ourselves. Why is it that the general will is always in the right, and that all continually will the happiness of each one, unless it is because there is not a man who does not think of "each" as meaning him, and consider himself in voting for all? This proves that equality of rights and the idea of justice which such equality creates originate in the preference each man gives to himself, and accordingly in the very nature of man. It proves that the general will, to be really such, must be general in its object as well as its essence; that it must both come from all and apply to all; and that it loses its natural rectitude when it is directed to some particular and determinate object, because in such a case we are judging of something foreign to us, and have no true principle of equity to guide us.

Indeed, as soon as a question of particular fact or right arises on a point not previously regulated by a general convention, the matter becomes contentious. It is a case in which the individuals concerned are one party, and the public the other, but in which I can see neither the law that ought to be followed nor the judge who ought to give the decision. In such a case, it would be absurd to propose to refer the question to an express decision of the general will, which can be only the conclusion reached by one of the parties and in consequence will be, for the other party, merely an external and particular will, inclined on this occasion to injustice and subject to error. Thus, just as a particular will cannot stand off for the general will, the general will, in turn, changes its nature, when its object is particular, and, as general, cannot pronounce on a man or a fact. When, for instance, the people of Athens nominated or displaced its rulers, decreed honors to one, and imposed penalties on another, and, by a multitude of particular decrees, exercised all the functions of government indiscriminately, it had in such cases no longer a general will in the strict sense; it was acting no longer as Sovereign, but as magistrate. This will seem contrary to current views; but I must be given time to expound my own.

It should be seen from the foregoing that what makes the will general is less the number of voters than the common interest uniting them; for, under this system, each necessarily submits to the conditions he imposes on others: and this admirable agreement between interest and justice gives to the common deliberations an equitable character which at once vanishes when any particular question is discussed, in the absence of a common interest to unite and identify the ruling of the judge with that of the party.

From whatever side we approach our principle, we reach the same conclusion, that the social compact sets up among the citizens an equality of such a kind, that they all bind themselves to observe the same conditions and should therefore all enjoy the same rights. Thus, from the very nature of the compact, every act of Sovereignty, i.e. every authentic act of the general will, binds or favors all the citizens equally; so that the Sovereign recognizes only the body of the nation, and draws no distinctions between those of whom it is made up. What, then strictly speaking, is an act of Sovereignty? It is not a convention between the body and each of its members. It is legitimate, because based on the social contract, and equitable, because common to all; useful, because it can have no other object than the general good, and stable, because guaranteed by the public force and the supreme power. So long as the subjects have to submit only to conventions of this sort, they obey no one but their own will; and to ask how far the respective rights of the Sovereign and the citizens extend, is to ask up to what point the latter can enter into undertakings with themselves, each with all, and all with each.

We can see from this that the sovereign power, absolute, sacred and inviolable as it is, does not and cannot exceed the limits of general conventions, and that every man may dispose at will of such goods and liberty as these conventions leave him; so that the Sovereign never has a right to lay more charges on one subject than on another, because, in that case, the question becomes particular, and ceases to be within its competency.

When these distinctions have once been admitted, it is seen to be so untrue that there is, in the social contract, any real renunciation on the part of the individuals, that the position in which they find themselves as a result of the contract is really preferable to that in which they were before. Instead of a renunciation, they have made an advantageous exchange: instead of an uncertain and precarious way of living they have got one that is better and more secure; instead of natural independence they have got liberty, instead of power to harm others' security for themselves, and instead of their strength, which others might overcome, a right which social union makes invincible. Their very life, which they have devoted to the State, is by it constantly protected; and when they risk it in the State's defence, what more are they doing than giving back what they have received from it? What are they doing that they would not do more often and with greater danger in the state of nature, in which they would inevitably have to fight battles at the peril of their lives in defence of that which is the means of their preservation? All have indeed to fight when their country needs them; but then no one has ever to fight for himself. Do we not gain something by running, on behalf of what gives us our security, only some of the risks we should have to run for ourselves, as soon as we lost it?

Book 2: Chapter 6: Law

I . . . give the name "Republic" to every State that is governed by laws, no matter what the form of its administration may be: for only in such a case does the public interest govern, and the *res publica* rank a reality. Every legitimate government is republican; what government is I will explain later on.

Laws are, properly speaking, only the conditions of civil association. The people, being subject to the laws, ought to be their author: the conditions of the society ought to be regulated solely by those who come together to form it. But how are they to regulate them? Is it to be by common agreement by a sudden inspiration? Has the body politic an organ to declare its will? Who can give it the foresight to formulate and announce its acts in advance? Or how is it to announce them in the hour of need? How can a blind multitude, which often does not know what it wills, because it rarely knows what is good for it, carry out for itself so great and difficult an enterprise as a system of legislation? Of itself the people wills always the good, but of itself it by no means always sees it. The general will is always in the right, but the judgement which guides it is not always enlightened. It must be got to see objects as they are, and sometimes as they ought to appear to it; it must be shown the good road it is in search of, secured from the seductive influences of individual wills, taught to see times and spaces as a series, and made to weigh the attractions of present and sensible advantages against the danger of distant and hidden evils. The individuals see the good they reject; the public wills the good it does not see. All stand equally in need of guidance. The former must be compelled to bring their wills into conformity with their reason; the latter must be taught to know what it wills. If that is done, public enlightenment leads to the union of understanding and will in the social body: the parts are made to work exactly together, and the whole is raised to its highest power. This makes a legislator necessary.

The French Revolution

John McGrath

July 14, 1789

At about ten o'clock on a warm summer morning, about nine hundred residents of Paris, mostly men from the nearby working class St. Antoine district, congregated in the shadow of the venerable fortress known as the Bastille. Two officials from the Paris Town Hall had just gone inside, to discuss the fate of the large quantity of gunpowder that had recently been moved there.

The crowd was hungry and nervous. In recent days, there had been unsettling reports from the royal palace at Versailles, where the newly elected body known as the Estates General was trying to resolve the kingdom's financial problems. King Louis XVI had removed the popular Minister of Finance, Jacques Necker, and in Paris, where civil disorder had already been common for several months, this news had provoked several violent clashes between royal troops and local residents. Many Parisians now believed that Louis was intent on reasserting his control of the city, perhaps by ordering foreign mercenary troops to seize it. Hastily organized into militias under the command of city officials, they were becoming desperate to find the means to defend Paris from a possible attack by their own king. Although they possessed cannon, muskets, and ammunition, they lacked gunpowder, and they knew that more than 250 barrels now lay within the massive walls of the fortress.[1]

In the minds of many, the Bastille was a hated symbol of royal despotism, having served as a prison for numerous enemies of the absolutist state. As the situation in Paris had deteriorated in recent weeks, it remained a defiant outpost of the king's power. While the city officials inside pressed for the release of the gunpowder, the hours passed, the heat rose, and the crowd waiting outside grew more restless. At half-past one, several men, apparently acting independently, climbed on top of a perfume shop next to the fortress's front gate and from there cut the chains that held up the drawbridge. Without warning the massive platform slammed down with an ear-splitting crash, killing a man standing below it.

Like many other pivotal events in history, what happened next was fueled by misperception and confusion. The members of the crowd, taken by surprise, experienced a few minutes of uncertainty before assuming—wrongly—that the Bastille's commander had ordered the gate to be lowered as a means of inviting them inside. And so, with enthusiastic shouts, men began streaming across the bridge. They were largely unarmed.

However, the royal troops inside the courtyard were equally confused. They could only conclude the worst: that the members of the approaching mob were forcing their way in. Vastly outnumbered, but with muskets and cannon already loaded, the soldiers opened fire with a deadly hail of projectiles that halted the approaching surge of cheering men.

Faced with such unexpected, withering, fire, it did not take long for the onrushing men to come to an ugly, though again erroneous, conclusion: that this had been a trap carefully crafted by the treacherous King Louis. Now enraged, they set about besieging the fortress, reinforced by Paris militiamen and deserting royal troops who had rushed to the scene. By three-thirty, after about ninety of their number had been killed, the attackers had maneuvered cannon opposite the Bastille's main gate, which forced the defenders to surrender.

The capitulation failed to quench the mob's fury. Men swarmed through the fortress, looking for gunpowder, more weapons, and rumored political prisoners they were determined to liberate. (Of the last, they were sorely disappointed, as only seven prisoners were being held there, and all of them were either petty criminals or insane.) By late afternoon, the Bastille's commander was marched to the nearby Town Hall, where the disorderly crowd killed and decapitated him and another official. Their heads were placed on pikes, which were carried at the head of an impromptu parade. As the procession moved through the streets of Paris, throngs of celebrating civilians joined in, along with various units of soldiers and police. Near the front marched the seven liberated prisoners, who included one elderly man who believed that he was Julius Caesar.

News of the episode—often wildly inaccurate and exaggerated—raced through Paris, from neighborhood to neighborhood, from house to house, and from shop to shop. Except for a few members of the privileged classes, almost all of the city's residents took to the streets to cheer or join the grisly procession, which lasted well into the night.

Paris was now in open rebellion against royal authority. The French Revolution had begun.

Social Change and Revolution

Literally thousands of books have been written about the French Revolution, which attests not only to its importance, but also to its complexity. From the summer of 1789 through the final defeat of Napoleon at Waterloo in 1815, French society underwent transformations that defy easy generalizations. A nation of close to thirty million people had thrown off the yoke of absolute monarchy and plunged into unknown territory, and as unexpected events seemed to provoke further unexpected events, the Revolution attained a life of its own. The French Revolution is one of the defining events in the emergence of what we call the "modern world." What, then, were the conditions that created it?

A useful way to answer this is by examining this episode in a context of social change and modernization. In France, the eighteenth century had been a time of long-term, gradual internal and external change, punctuated by sudden crises, which had disrupted familiar ways of life and created insecurity and uneasiness for many people within the kingdom. To many men and women in the kingdom, conventional solutions to their problems appeared inadequate, and indeed, as time went on and the sense of dissatisfaction deepened, the conventional solutions often seemed to be part of the problem itself. By July, 1789, a sequence of emergencies had pushed France's population beyond the breaking point, encouraging confused, angry, and fearful people to violently reject traditional authority. In all of the chaos and uncertainty that ensued, leaders emerged who offered new solutions, which themselves created new problems, and gave rise to other leaders who offered yet more new ideas. The result was incessant conflict, both within and outside of France, and the French Revolution continued until it had run its bloody course and overwhelmed most of a continent. It left in its wake new structures and ideas that remain essential parts of the modern world as we know it.

A Society in Transition

A hundred years before the fall of the Bastille, France had seemed the epitome of stability under King Louis XIV, the "Sun King," who ruled from his palace at Versailles with the iron hand provided by a relatively efficient absolutist political state. Though heavy taxes and warfare were constant burdens on the French people, the machinery of government succeeded in providing the political control that it had been designed for. King Louis dealt effectively with the occasional revolt by peasants, dissident nobles, or Protestants, and could even boast of great public support. However, when he died in 1715, he bequeathed to his great-grandson, Louis XV, a state that was already weakened by diplomatic isolation, financial problems, and the abuse of power.

During Louis XV's long reign (1715–1774), the royal government became even more complex, inefficient and corrupt, which dramatically magnified the longstanding problem of how to make tax revenues support royal spending. But despite the fact that his government was constantly on the edge of financial insolvency, Louis XV tried only halfhearted reforms of government structure and policies, and he accomplished nothing positive or lasting. Meanwhile, the society around him continued to change, becoming more diverse and unstable.

One main force of this change was the economic development that took place in the eighteenth century, which, though impressive by some measurements, had been quite uneven. While the average standard of living in France rose steadily, not everyone benefited equally. Mercantilist policies had helped many French cities, such as Bordeaux, Lyons, and Rouen, to become world class industrial and commercial centers. However, agriculture, long the backbone of the French economy, lagged behind, hindered by a confusing array of local laws and customs. Despite an occasional attempt by the royal government to centralize and rationalize the state and its economy, most of rural France stubbornly maintained traditional ways. Some historians speak of the existence of two different French economies, one tradition-bound and stagnant, and the other dynamic and innovative.[2]

The absolutist state, arising as a solution to the turbulence of the Reformation era, had been designed to provide stability. Yet, somewhat ironically, its success in doing so encouraged the economic growth that fueled this destabilizing social change, and the eighteenth century saw rising economic and social complexity in France that continued to evolve at an accelerating rate. This change wreaked havoc on the social stratification system, and inevitably, many came to resent their perceived victimization by other groups. By 1789, the sense of collective purpose that had been fostered by the absolutist state had largely evaporated, as different social groups saw themselves in competition with other groups for wealth, power, and status.[3]

Historically, the first two estates, the clergy and the nobility, enjoyed privileges that included access to political power and exemption from most taxes. The uneven modernization of the eighteenth century complicated that picture. Doctrinal and political disagreements paralyzed the Catholic Church as many people within France viewed it as the possessor of undeserved privileges and wealth. Meanwhile, a new nobility of state officials and bureaucrats, whose origins were bourgeois, had gained noble titles through royal favor, strategic marriages, or even monetary purchase, which blurred the distinctions at the high end of the stratification system. As a group, the nobility became much more diverse, with great differences among them in financial status, political power, and values. As the elite orders struggled for privilege, this created a great deal of social tension and animosity at the top levels of society.[4]

Economic change had brought similar changes to the rest of the social system, as well. Many bourgeoisie had amassed great wealth, through the manufacturing and finance that mercantilism had stimulated, while the fortunes of others declined in the face of foreign competition. While French cities provided great opportunities for the ambitious, they also became home to a growing mass of unskilled, impoverished commoners. The French working class came to include many different sorts of workers, with various levels of skills and incomes, ranging from self-employed artisans, to workers in huge factories, to domestic servants, to indentured laborers. In the meantime, the social situation in rural areas—where a large majority of the population still resided—was also in transition. Even peasant farmers had become a quite diverse group, varying from well-off independent landowners to laborers whose conditions approximated medieval serfdom, depending largely on the province and its local laws and customs. Throughout the kingdom, taxes fell disproportionately upon the poorest of the king's subjects, while tax collectors, known as tax farmers, were among the wealthiest people in France.

Since the age of the Sun King, a great deal had changed in popular attitudes, as well. The Enlightenment was spreading deeply and broadly through Western Europe, and in many respects, its nerve center was the city of Paris. Despite French government censorship, new voices emerged that called for the public to reexamine the nature of their society, and to consider new solutions for a changing world. Such new ideas reached many more people than ever before; in France, literacy rates had almost doubled between 1715 and 1789, so that perhaps 40% of the total population was literate by the outbreak of the Revolution. This meant that in French cities such as Paris, a majority of the adult population, including many working class people, could and did read, and also that literate peasants could be found even in the most backward rural areas. People at all levels of the social ladder were becoming receptive to the new ways of thinking—based on logic and reason, instead of tradition—promoted by the Enlightenment.[5]

It was not just the most popular Enlightenment literature, such as the *Encyclopedia* or the best-selling works of Voltaire, that altered the outlooks of the king's subjects. Late eighteenth century France also witnessed a virtual explosion of printed newspapers, pamphlets and leaflets that stimulated public interest in news and current issues. While some of this literary output was learned and informative, much was not. By the reign of Louis XVI, starting in 1775, the publication of pamphlets and broadsides, published in violation of censorship laws, were increasingly effective in promoting skepticism and even hostility towards the government.[6] Especially popular were cheaply printed pieces that crudely attacked members of the royal family; scandalous literature that depicted Queen Marie Antoinette as a sexually insatiable imbecile comprised almost an industry in itself. As one scholar put it, the scurrilous publications that became so popular and widespread during the 1780s "severed the sense of decency that bound the public to its rulers," through "a common denominator of irreligion, immorality, and uncivility."[7] Thus, written material, in addition to "enlightening" the French population, also contributed to a pervasive cynicism that undermined respect for authority.

Under the absolutist system of Louis XIV, people had largely understood what was expected of those in their social rank, and whatever their status, they had shared a respect for the king as his obedient subjects. But by the late eighteenth century the social realities had changed so dramatically that it was hard to determine even what ranks existed, never mind what their appropriate behaviors were. Moreover, any sense of belonging to a collective whole with a common purpose was disintegrating. Contempt for their king had become one of the only unifying factors among the diverse people of this fast-changing society.

Even by the time he wrote *Candide*, forty years earlier, Voltaire had hardly been exaggerating the antagonisms that existed in France when he wrote:

> Except during supper, when people are relatively gay and accommodating, the rest of the time is spent in trivial quarrels: Jansenists against Molinists, men of *parlement* against men of the Church, men of letters against men of letters, courtiers against courtiers, financiers against the people, wives against their husbands, relatives against relatives; it is an eternal war.[8]

Probably not even Voltaire understood just how literally true this would turn out to be.

The Crisis of the Monarchy

When Louis XV's son inherited the throne, as Louis XVI, he possessed some evident intentions to improve the situation. But he soon found that this was no easy task, as his efforts to restore order to royal finances with Enlightenment-inspired reforms failed for a variety of political and economic reasons. Initiatives to modernize the tax system met with firm opposition from powerful interest groups, including the king's own ministers and the law courts, who saw their authority threatened by the proposed changes. Meanwhile, France's military support for the American war of independence had forced the crown to take on huge levels of unmanageable debt.

Louis XVI also inherited an unwinnable situation regarding the price of bread, which, due to the fact that its cost made up about half of the total expenditure of most French households, was the most inflammatory political issue during the second half of the century.[9] Traditionally, the crown enforced a certain maximum price on bread as a way of serving the welfare of its subjects; however, during the eighteenth century, while the French population grew, the level of grain production stagnated, both because of a reliance on traditional farming practices and the fact that the maximum prices took away farmers' incentives to innovate and invest in agriculture. As time went on, urban populations often complained that the prices were too high, while rural farmers complained that prices were too low; whatever price the royal government decided on, it angered one group or the other, and often both at the same time. Inevitably, production diminished, while bread prices crept upward due to scarcity. One important longterm consequence of this state of affairs was that it spurred public anger against the already-mistrusted royal government and its officials, who were widely believed—perhaps with some justification—to be conspiring to profit from the situation. Worse, when a series of bad harvests occurred in the 1780s, an already difficult political and economic problem became a genuine crisis, as actual starvation appeared in some cities when there was no bread available at any price.

Meanwhile, the expenses of military spending, government salaries, and the costs of maintaining the royal household continued to rise, necessitating more and more tax revenue to pay for it. However, traditional privilege had given immunity from taxation to the first two estates, the Church and the nobility, while many of the wealthiest members of the bourgeoisie had been buying offices and noble titles that gave them immunity as well. All of these groups resisted any suggestions that they should pay a share of taxes, which only embittered the less privileged classes.[10] However, aside from expanding the tax base, the only other way that the royal government could meet its financial obligations was through borrowing from wealthy financiers and foreign banks. This provided only short term relief, and in the long run proved disastrous, because as the total debts of the royal government rose, so too did the interest rates that the crown had to pay.[11] Even five years into Louis XVI's reign, the expansion of government debt had grown beyond all practical levels, and as privileged interest groups blocked all attempts at reforming the financial system, it appeared that a declaration of royal bankruptcy was the only possible option.

By the mid-1780s, the crisis had become serious enough, and widely recognized enough, that Louis was persuaded by his advisors to summon a meeting of the **Estates-General**, an ancient institution that in past centuries had served as an advisory body to the king. The intention was to come up with government reforms, especially of taxation, that would solve the financial crisis and at the same time gather public support for further reforms.[12] As representatives of the three estates of the clergy, nobles, and commoners—chosen by elections held throughout France—assembled at Versailles in early 1789, the economy was on the brink of disaster. Meanwhile, bad weather and resulting food shortages were causing breakdowns of civil order in the cities, including Paris, just a dozen miles from Versailles.

However, before the pertinent issues even came up for consideration, the Estates-General found itself in serious disagreement about procedural issues, especially voting, a situation made worse by the king's contradictory statements concerning how much authority he would allow the assembly to have. In mid-June, out of anger and frustration, the 600 representatives of the Third Estate, joined by a few members of the clergy, proclaimed themselves the legitimate authority in France as the **National Assembly**. Defying the King's orders to disperse, they asserted their intention to transform the absolute monarchy into a constitutional monarchy with a division of powers. In order to prevent the clergy and nobility from completely losing influence, Louis ordered the representatives of the first two estates to join those of the third, and by the end of the month, a 1200-member National Assembly was in place at Versailles.[13] Yet both the extent of this new body's power and the king's intentions were anything but clear. Such were the immediate circumstances that preceded the seizure of the Bastille.

The Great Fear, the Declaration of Rights of Man and Citizen, and the October Days

The violent uprising in Paris on July 14 created widespread uncertainty throughout the entire kingdom as to who or what controlled the country. While the National Assembly at Versailles claimed to represent legitimate authority, many suspected that the king was plotting to destroy it by force of arms. In Paris, city officials defiantly rejected royal commands, but their relationship with the National Assembly remained problematic. In most parts of France, it was a legitimate question as to who was directing various administrative, military and police bodies. Rumors abounded of conspiracy, revolt, invasion, and persecution.

The period of confusion that followed was aptly referred to as "**The Great Fear**," since no one could be sure of what was happening around them and widespread panic was often the consequence. In an age where the timely transmission of reliable news was impossible, rumors and misperceptions spurred violence and civil unrest, especially in rural areas, during late July and August of 1789. In particular, a persistent belief that the nobles were arming groups of criminals to attack local villages provoked peasants in many places to rise against noble landowners. Large parts of France approached anarchy.

The National Assembly, somewhat legitimized by the king's halfhearted and probably insincere recognition, devoted its efforts to coming up with a set of principles to guide the creation of a reformed government. With significant input from the Marquis de Lafayette, a hero of the American Revolution who was in charge of the Paris militia, and from Thomas Jefferson, the American ambassador to France, a subcommittee composed the **Declaration of Rights of Man and Citizen**, a manifesto of principles that were intended to be the basis for a full constitution. Relying on the Enlightenment ideas of Locke and Rousseau, the product that emerged in August was rather vague, but it was dedicated, as its title suggests, to the principle of individual rights and freedoms. It was immediately printed and distributed widely, and become a symbol of the transformation that had taken place. By then, the word "revolution" had gained wide currency throughout France, but what it meant was not yet clear.[14]

A constitutional monarchy would require cooperation between an elected assembly and the king, but it was difficult to know what limitations on his power Louis would accept. In recent months he had demonstrated a talent for changing his mind unexpectedly, and as the weeks went along the situation remained tense. By October, high bread prices provoked an angry demonstration by Parisian women, who marched on Versailles, accompanied by Lafayette's militia. After a brief and bloody confrontation with the king's guards, they forced the king and the rest of the royal family to move to Paris, with the National Assembly following shortly thereafter. After these so-called "**October Days**," events in Paris largely dictated the course of the Revolution.

The Constitutional Monarchy

From Paris, the Assembly—now known as the Constituent Assembly—tried to make constitutional monarchy into a reality. Through the Declaration, it had already legally limited the king's power, abolished privileges of birth, and asserted the right of the people to determine their own form of government. By the end of the year, the Assembly had began to focus on more immediate, less theoretical issues, and initiated a number of significant administrative reforms concerning elections, justice, taxation, finance, commerce, and government structure.[15]

One particularly divisive issue—which would remain so throughout the Revolution—was the future role of the Catholic Church. The overwhelming majority of the French population was Catholic, including many deeply conservative believers, but the Church's traditional privileges made it an obvious target for reform-minded politicians. As early as the fall of 1789, the Assembly began to limit Church income and confiscate its property, culminating in July of 1790 with comprehensive legislation known as the **Civil Constitution of the Clergy**, which essentially made the Church a department of the political administration. These initiatives deeply offended many loyal Catholics, especially in the provinces, and the Assembly's perceived attack on religion provided the basis of the first widespread resistance to the new government.[16]

Even during the first year of existence, the early optimism of the Constituent Assembly began to wane. Since it was composed of members, known as deputies, from all three estates and from every part of the country, there were vastly different perspectives and it was never easy to gain consensus about any issue. As the Assembly made a determined effort to carry out its self-appointed tasks, there were already deep political factions among the representatives, largely based on different interpretations of the proper role of the Assembly itself and the amount of power the king would retain in any future constitutional arrangement.

Such political divisions were fueled, moreover, by the freedom of the press guaranteed by the Declaration, which had ended government censorship and promoted a tremendous expansion of political literature and a rapid politicization of the reading public. Related to this was the formation of formal and informal political clubs, where educated people met to debate issues, develop lobbying strategies, and compose political literature to influence public opinion. Inevitably, these clubs came to represent different interest groups and viewpoints, and they maintained important ties to political groups in the provinces. Even by 1790, such clubs, which included the reform-minded **Jacobins**, had begun to serve as power bases for active and aspiring politicians. The first factions that emerged within the Assembly reflected affiliations with these clubs, which evolved into *de facto* political parties.[17]

From late 1789 into 1791, the Constituent Assembly soldiered on with the burdens of maintaining order while working on a constitution. Yet even their undeniable accomplishments could not provide political and social tranquility. Unlike the case of England's Glorious Revolution in 1688, the events of 1789 had not achieved a popular acceptance of a new *status quo*. Disagreement, mistrust, and antagonism remained, and were even intensifying, among the people of France.

Civil Society Disintegrates

By early 1791, the most immediate threats to stability came from the conservative elements intent on defending the privileges of the Church, nobility, and monarchy. Since the summer of 1789, the king had generally cooperated with the Assembly, but within a year he had begun to publically express his displeasure with the actions it had taken in regard to the Church. Meanwhile, some local leaders in the provinces, often in alliance with the clergy, were actively undermining the Paris government's authority by refusing to obey it. And angry nobles, both those who had fled to neighboring countries and those who had remained, were vowing to raise armies to reverse the Revolution.

In particular, rumors abounded that the queen's Austrian relatives and their allies might provide military forces to help the king and conservative factions regain political power. The truth to these rumors seemed to be confirmed when, in June of 1791, Louis and his family attempted to secretly flee Paris, evidently with the intention of meeting up with Austrian troops at the border of the Netherlands. Largely due to their own sheer incompetence, they were caught, returned to Paris under heavy guard, and reinstalled in their palace there as virtual prisoners.

The "**flight to Varennes**," as it became known, convinced many people that the king was a potential counter-revolutionary who could not be trusted. This increased the power of the factions in the Assembly who advocated the creation of a republican form of government, that is, an elected legislature operating without a king at all. Protests against Louis and his supporters took place, including an episode in Paris where the National Guard, controlled by moderates, massacred republican demonstrators. Meanwhile, the rulers of several European nations, including Austria, were enraged by the treatment of the royal family after their failed escape. Even those foreign leaders who had little sympathy for the king feared instability in France, and diplomatic relations between the Assembly and its neighbors rapidly deteriorated.

To make matters even worse, 1791 had been another year of disappointing harvests, which increased turmoil in the cities even further. Working class wage earners, with jobs scarce and prices high, resented the fact that the Revolution had done little to benefit them, and had complained that it had just replaced one group of privileged elites with another; after all, the principles outlined in the Declaration, such as freedoms of assembly and expression, meant little to people who lacked enough to eat. In Paris, working people known as *sans-culottes*—referring to their lack of the stylish knee-length trousers worn by the wealthy—began to organize their own neighbor-hood political associations and emerged as an influential and unpredictable political factor. Gathering outside the Assembly's meeting hall on a daily basis, they pressured the Assembly towards more radical actions by threatening the deputies as they entered and departed, swayed by the exhortations of extremist leaders known as **enragés** ("the mad ones"). While some members of the Assembly despised the *sans-culottes* as a dangerous mob, others were more sympathetic, and advocated reforms that were designed to help the poorer members of society who felt overlooked by the Revolution.

With France seemingly threatened by conservative reaction from both within and without, the Jacobins both gained more power and became fiercely republican in their aims, gaining political and popular support at the expense of the Girondin faction that had sponsored many of the reforms of the previous year. The Jacobin leadership included some of the most influential and well-known personalities of the Revolution. Among them were **Georges Danton**, the headstrong and outspoken Assembly leader who rejected compromise and directed his efforts towards turning France into a republic. **Jean-Paul Marat**, a many talented firebrand, used his newspaper *The Friend of the People* to advocate increasingly harsh penalties against anyone sympathetic to the privileged classes; Marat's dramatic and inspiring prose transformed him, in the minds of many people, into the living voice of the Revolution. Meanwhile, **Maximilien Robespierre**, a lawyer by training and disciple of Jean-Jacques Rousseau's philosophy, emerged as the chief strategist of Jacobin policies.

The leadership of such men was largely responsible for a polarization of opinion that put moderate politicians into an uncomfortable position between pro-republican factions and supporters of a return to monarchy. Even though the king was persuaded to approve the long-awaited Constitution at the end of the summer of 1791, the political middle ground was fast disappearing. According to the procedures outlined by this Constitution, a new, somewhat smaller assembly known as the **Legislative Assembly** was elected, and it was largely dominated by the Jacobins. The Jacobins' resistance to compromise grew more pronounced as the *sans-culottes* became more influential, and reports of foreign threats raised public fears.[18]

War, Republic and Terror

In early 1792, two and a half years after the outbreak of Revolution and only a few months after the birth of the Legislative Assembly, all of these problems seemed to collide and hurl France towards even further extremes. In April, ongoing diplomatic hostility with neighboring monarchies resulted in a French declaration of war against Austria. However, the French army was underprepared, especially because many of its noble officers had fled the country, and the beginning of the conflict went badly. As war hysteria gripped the nation, the radical **Paris Commune** seized power in the capital with the support of the Jacobins and the *sans-culottes*, demanding not just political equality, but equality of wealth as well. As crowd violence in Paris surged out of control, the Commune set up revolutionary tribunals to seek out traitors, and began employing the **guillotine** for carrying out sentences of death. In August, when French armies failed to prevent Austrian troops from entering France, an angry demonstration against the king's possible support for the enemy led to a bloody confrontation at the royal palace where hundreds were killed. With public sentiment in Paris, if not necessarily elsewhere, now firmly in favor of a republic, the Legislative Assembly removed the king from any remaining political role and called for the election of a new republican legislature, the **National Convention**, to cope with the emergencies of warfare.[19]

Even as this new body was being created through another round of elections, further French military defeats in September of 1792 sent Paris crowds into an uncontrollable frenzy, leading to the cold-blooded massacre of 1300 imprisoned clergymen and other supposed counter-revolutionaries in Paris. By December, the king was brought to trial for his apparent complicity with foreign armies, and he was found guilty of treason. He and his queen went to the guillotine in 1793, which shocked and angered conservatives both inside and outside the country. By then, even though the fortunes of war were improving, paranoia was widespread, and violence of all sorts had become the social norm in many, and perhaps most, parts of France.[20]

The National Convention intended to develop a new republican constitution, but until that was accomplished, it claimed the right to act without restraint. The Jacobins, benefiting from an appeal to patriotism and the support of the *sans-culottes*, attained a near-monopoly on power. To deal with the threats surrounding them, they instituted a command wartime economy, created a military draft, and also established the **Committee of Public Safety**, an appointed twelve-member body designed to provide more efficient executive power. By late 1793, Robespierre largely controlled the Committee, and used it and the revolutionary tribunals to hunt out all whose loyalties were suspect, according to his standards of moral purity. Robespierre believed that he and the Jacobins were upholding the general will of the people in the struggle against forces of counterrevolution, and saw those who hesitated to fully support their cause as enemies of the Republic.[21]

By that time, however, there were many groups who had serious disagreements with the Jacobins, including dissatisfied *sans-culottes*, radical *enragés*, moderate deputies, former royal officials, army officers, provincial leaders, and loyal Catholics. With the war effort being the obvious priority, the Jacobins took severe steps against these "enemies of the Revolution," and their methods—often referred to as the **Reign of Terror**—provoked equally determined resistance. Revolts against the Convention's power broke out both in large cities and rural areas, often encouraged and even supported by foreign enemies. The most notable uprising took place in the **Vendée** region of western France, where Catholic peasants, aided by dissident nobles, fought a guerrilla war that was ultimately crushed by the Revolutionary Army. Out of a total population of around 800,000 in the Vendée, it is conservatively estimated that 200,000 civilians died during the fighting, and close to the same number of soldiers, before the region was "pacified."[22]

The Jacobins and the leaders of the National Convention were not satisfied with simply eliminating enemies. Inspired by Rousseau's ideas, they also undertook to change the cultural landscape of France by eliminating traces of the feudal past.[23] They instituted a revolutionary calendar that had new months and a Year One beginning in September 1792, as well as introducing the metric system as the basis of a new system of keeping time. A "de-Christianization" campaign abolished Church holidays, encouraged worship of the "Goddess of Liberty," and created a "Festival of the Supreme Being" as a major public celebration. The political leadership even formally legislated changes to speech, such as requiring people to address each other as "citizen," instead of the less democratic term "monsieur" ("my lord"). These efforts often approached the absurd, such as changing the rules of checkers to forbid the practice of "kinging" pieces that reached the last row. The Jacobins' attempt to erase the "corrupt" past and replace it with "correct" revolutionary thinking seems an eerie precursor to Mao's Chinese Cultural Revolution almost two centuries later.

As French military victories increased and the fear of invasion lessened during the summer of 1794, public support for the Jacobins' extreme policies weakened. In July (the revolutionary month of Thermidor), leaders in the Convention, in what was probably a pre-emptive strike designed to save themselves from charges of treason, denounced Robespierre and some of his closest allies. By then, because of Robespierre's uncompromising methods—which included the execution of his friend and colleague Danton—not even the *sans-culottes* or the Paris Commune was willing to protect him, and he and several of his associates went to the guillotine. This ended the Reign of Terror, as the Convention not only dismantled the revolutionary tribunals and stopped the mass executions, but also purged the remaining Jacobin leadership and dealt severely with *sans-culotte* agitation.[24]

This **Thermidorean Reaction** left the government as a republic, and in 1795 a new constitution provided for a two-chamber legislature and most executive power in the hands of a rotating five-member committee known as the **Directory**. In effect, power passed back to the propertied bourgeoisie, who concentrated their efforts on conducting the war, a task that they carried out reasonably competently for the next four years with relatively little internal opposition.[25]

Revolutionary War and Napoleon

A number of factors can explain the success of the French armies that began in late 1792.[26] For one thing, their officer corps had matured and benefited from a more democratic policy of advancement by merit, regardless of social class, instead of reserving the highest ranks for nobles. The Jacobins' military draft, moreover, greatly expanded the size of the army, and after 1792 French forces began to overwhelm smaller opponents on the basis of sheer numbers. Their opponents, meanwhile, were hampered by both a tendency to underestimate French military capabilities and a lack of coordination among their own various forces.

Perhaps the most important reason for French success, though, was that both officers and enlisted men in the Revolutionary Army had started to believe that they were fighting for an important cause. Initially, the troops fought desperately to save their homeland from foreign enemies of the Revolution, which gave them a sense of united purpose, and most historians would agree that the French Revolutionary Wars provided the forge out of which was fashioned a powerful new phenomenon known as **nationalism**. Because of this, their morale and effectiveness was considerably higher than that of the largely mercenary armies against whom they were fighting. Yet this advantage carried over even after the safety of French borders was assured, as the French troops began to see themselves as liberators who were spreading revolution and democracy to less enlightened parts of the continent. As time went on, at least part of the French military success can be attributed to the fact that, in many of the territories they invaded, local populations were won over by the rhetoric of liberation, and often aided the French armies against their own rulers.

Even as early as 1795, the young Corsican general **Napoleon Bonaparte** won public acclaim through his battlefield victories. Employing aggressive, innovative strategies and tactics, he gave the French people the young, energetic, and charismatic hero that they needed. Napoleon was also calculating and ambitious, and used his political connections to seize his opportunities while he negotiated the political minefields of revolutionary France.[27] Leading his armies against changing coalitions of European opponents, he never lost a major battle between 1795 and 1812, and positioned himself brilliantly by helping a new, more concentrated form of government known as the **Consulate** seize power from the Directory in 1799. By manipulating politicians and crowds alike, Napoleon emerged as a virtual dictator, and in 1804, had himself crowned Emperor, precisely a thousand years to the day after the coronation of Charlemagne as the first Holy Roman Emperor.

The years of struggle had made the French people especially vulnerable to Napoleon's charisma, and few leaders in history have been more successful in dazzling the masses with promises of glory and empire. Although Napoleon gained much support from his claim to be the defender of Revolutionary principles, his most important priorities were domestic stability and foreign conquest. He preserved most of the Enlightenment-inspired reforms that had taken place, and even added to these, with broad initiatives in banking, industry, and national education. Perhaps his most impressive accomplishment was the creation of the **Napoleonic Code**, the first truly unified and egalitarian legal system in Europe, which formalized and rationalized an unprecedented number of aspects of life. He also healed the rift between the Revolutionary government and the Church, a masterful move that cemented popular support for his regime.

During the era of the Empire, almost all of continental Europe came under the direct or indirect rule of France. In conquered areas, French armies brought elements of liberation, including social and legal equality, limited political democracy, and rational bureaucracies. Unwittingly, they also unleashed the forces of nationalism, which eventually energized numerous conquered peoples to remove the French. After his disastrous invasion of Russia in 1812, where his "Grande Armée" was nearly annihilated by starvation, disease, and freezing weather, Napoleon was unable to maintain his control over the rest of his European conquests. By 1815 he was defeated for the final time at Waterloo in today's Belgium.

The Legacy of the French Revolution

Although France's victorious opponents returned France to a monarchy in 1815, the Revolution and its wars had fatally wounded absolutism as a form of government, and the legitimacy of kingship would be on the defensive, in France and elsewhere in Europe, throughout the nineteenth century. This tumultuous era had transformed "liberty, equality and fraternity" from revolutionary slogans into cherished principles of civic life, and ever since we have struggled to implement them in a practical way.

We can see the French Revolution as an essential step in the development of the modern state, giving us a remarkable array of new ideologies, forms of political organization, and types of government power. Together with the economic transformations brought about by the Industrial Revolution, the entire structure of European society would change dramatically during the nineteenth century.

One of the most enduring effects of the Revolution was more abstract: its effect on how individuals saw themselves in relation to the larger society. The French Revolution encouraged people to believe that they no longer had to patiently accept the hand that they had been dealt at birth, as the idea emerged that people could—and even must—control their own destinies. To a much greater extent than ever before, people of all walks of life started to feel that they could question the *status quo*, and this more skeptical and less passive outlook has become an essential part of modern living.

Though the French Revolution has inspired generations of people throughout the world to make their world freer and more equitable, it also provides some cautionary lessons. As Martin Luther had discovered, and countless other revolutionaries have learned since, it is one thing to tear down an existing system, but quite another to agree on what to put in its place. In France, it may have been true that the destruction of the Old Regime in France was inevitable, and many have even argued that it was admirable. But once this process was underway, the people of France found themselves at odds with each other about what direction to take next, and after 1789, the course of events was largely determined by elements of chance and opportunistic leaders. This is what one historian meant when he wrote "the French Revolution had not been made by revolutionaries. It would be truer to say that the revolutionaries had been created by the Revolution."[28]

It is only in hindsight that we can impose some sort of order on the course of the French Revolution. Social change inevitably creates new realities and new ideas, which themselves promote more change, and the French Revolution opened up entirely new possibilities, both for France and for societies everywhere. Though 1789 remains a largely symbolic date, there is a great deal of validity to the assertion that the "modern era" began with the French Revolution.

Works Cited

Asprey, Robert B. *The Rise and Fall of Napoleon Bonaparte.* 2 Volumes. Boston: Little, Brown, 2000, 2002.

Bosher, J. F. *French Finances 1770–1795: From Business to Bureaucracy.* Cambridge: Cambridge University Press, 2008.

Darnton, Robert. *The Literary Underground of the Old Regime.* Cambridge: Harvard University Press, 1982.

Doyle, William. *Origins of the French Revolution.* Second Edition. Oxford: Oxford University Press, 1988.

Kaplan, Steven. *Bread, Politics, and Political Economy in the Reign of Louis XV.* 2 Vols. The Hague: Martinus Nijhoff, 1976.

Neely, Silvia. *A Concise History of the French Revolution.* Lanham: Rowman & Littlefield, 2008.

Popkin, Jeremy D. *A Short History of the French Revolution.* Third Edition. Upper Saddle River, 2002.

Schama, Simon. *Citizens: A Chronicle of the French Revolution.* New York: Knopf, 1991.

Scurr, Ruth. *Fatal Purity: Robespierre and the French Revolution.* New York: Metropolitan Books, 2006.

Voltaire. *Candide*, trans. & ed. Daniel Gordon. Boston: Bedford/St. Martin's, 1999.

Notes

1. The most complete historical rendering of the fall of the Bastille is found in Simon Schama, *Citizens: A Chronicle of the French Revolution* (New York, 1991), 363–406.

2. Schama, *Citizens*, 183–199; William Doyle, *Origins of the French Revolution*, 2nd ed. (Oxford, 1991), 31–32.

3. Jeremy D. Popkin, *A Short History of the French Revolution*, 3rd ed. (Saddle River, 2002), 11–15, Schama, *Citizens*, 112–121.

4. Popkin, *Short History*, 8–9; Doyle, *Origins*, 16–25.

5. Doyle, *Origins*, 78.

6. Robert Darnton, *The Literary Underground of the Old Regime* (Cambridge, 1982), 199–209.

7. Ibid., 204, 207.

8. Voltaire, *Candide*, trans. & ed. Daniel Gordon, (Boston, 1999) 94–95.

9. The monumental work of Steven Kaplan, including *Bread, Politics, and Political Economy in the Reign of Louis XV* (The Hague, 1976), is the most thorough on this critically important though often neglected topic.

10. Sylvia Neely, *A Concise History of the French Revolution*, (Lanham, 2008) 55–56; Popkin, *Short History*, 8–9.

11. J. F. Bosher's *French Finances 1770–1795: From Business to Bureaucracy* (Cambridge, 2008), building on his own earlier research and many new discoveries, contributes major insights on the often messy subject of French government debt and taxation.

12. Popkin, *Short History*, 22–23.

13. A nice explanation of the often confusing sequence of events that led to the establishment of the National Assembly is provided by Neely, *Concise History*, 55–69.

14. Popkin, *Short History*, 36–43; Schama, *Citizens*, 442–443.

15. Neely, *Concise History*, 95–101.

16. Popkin, *Short History*, 51–52.

17. Neely, *Concise History*, 120-124; Popkin, *Short History*, 53–54.

18. Popkin, *Short History*, 44–45.

19. Neely, *Concise History*, 155–162.

20. Ibid, 164–173.

21. Ruth Scurr's *Fatal Purity: Robespierre and the French Revolution*, (New York, 2006) is an excellent recent work that captures Robespierre's influences and outlook exceptionally well.

22. Neely, *Concise History*, 206.

23. Popkin *Short History*, 86–87; Neely, *Concise History*, 197–203.

24. Popkin, *Short History*, 97–105.

25. Neely, *Concise History*, 221–230.

26. Ibid., 233.

27. On Bonaparte and the Empire, a useful summary can be found in Neely, *Concise History*, 241–248; of the many excellent studies on Napoleon's career, Robert B. Asprey's two volume *The Rise and Fall of Napoleon Bonaparte* (Boston, 2000, 2002) is recommended.

28. Doyle, *Origins*, 213.

The Declaration of Independence

(As it reads in the parchment copy)

The Unanimous Declaration of the Thirteen United States of America

When in the Course of human events, it becomes necessary for one people to dissolve the political bands, which have connected them with another, and to assume among the powers of the earth, the separate and equal station to which the Laws of Nature and of Nature's God entitle them, a decent respect to the opinions of mankind requires that they should declare the causes which impel them to the separation. We hold these truths to be self-evident, that all men are created equal, that they are endowed by their Creator with certain unalienable Rights, that among these are Life, Liberty and the pursuit of Happiness. That to secure these rights, Governments are instituted among Men, deriving their just powers from the consent of the governed. That whenever any Form of Government becomes destructive of these ends, it is the Right of the People to alter or to abolish it, and to institute new Government, laying its foundation on such principles and organizing its powers in such form, as to them shall seem most likely to effect their Safety and Happiness. Prudence, indeed, will dictate that Governments long established should not be changed for light and transient causes; and accordingly all experience hath shewn, that mankind are more disposed to suffer, while evils are sufferable, than to right themselves by abolishing the forms to which they are accustomed. But when a long train of abuses and usurpations, pursuing invariably the same Object evinces a design to reduce them under absolute Despotism, it is their right, it is their duty, to throw off such Government, and to provide new Guards for their future security. Such has been the patient sufferance of these Colonies; and such is now the necessity which constrains them to alter their former Systems of Government. The history of the present King of Great Britain is a history of repeated injuries and usurpations, all having in direct object the establishment of an absolute Tyranny over these States. To prove this, let Facts be submitted to a candid world. He has refused his Assent to Laws, the most wholesome and necessary for the public good. He has forbidden his Governors to pass Laws of immediate and pressing importance, unless suspended in their operation till his Assent should be obtained; and when so suspended, he has utterly neglected to attend to them. He has refused to pass other Laws for the accommodation of large districts of people, unless those people would relinquish the right of Representation in the Legislature, a right inestimable to them and formidable to tyrants only. He has called together legislative bodies at places unusual, uncomfortable, and distant from the depository of their public Records, for the sole purpose of fatiguing them into compliance with his measures. He has dissolved Representative Houses repeatedly, for opposing with manly firmness his invasions on the rights of the people. He has refused for a long time, after such dissolutions, to cause others to be elected; whereby the Legislative powers, incapable of Annihilation, have returned to the People at large for their exercise; the State remaining in the meantime exposed to all the dangers of invasion from without, and convulsions within. He has endeavoured to prevent the population of these States; for that purpose obstructing the Laws for Naturization of Foreigners; refusing to pass others to encourage their migrations hither, and raising the condition of new appropriations of Lands. He has obstructed the Administration of Justice, by refusing his Assent to Laws for establishing Judiciary powers. He has made Judges dependent on his Will alone, for the tenure of their offices, and the amount and payment of their salaries. He has erected a multitude of New Offices, and sent hither swarms of Officers to harass our people, and eat out their substance. He has kept among us, in times of peace, Standing Armies without the Consent of our legislatures. He has affected to render the Military independent of and superior to the Civil power. He has combined with others to subject us to a jurisdiction foreign to our constitution, and unacknowledged by our laws; giving his Assent to their Acts of pretended Legislation. For quartering large bodies of armed troops among us: For protecting them, by a mock Trial, from punishment for any Murders which they should commit on the Inhabitants of these States: For cutting off our Trade with all parts of the world: For imposing Taxes on us without our Consent: For depriving us in many cases, of the benefits of Trial by Jury: For transporting us beyond Seas to be tried for pretended offenses: For abolishing the free System of English Laws in a neighboring Province, establishing therein an Arbitrary government, and enlarging its Boundaries so as to render it at once an example and fit instrument for introducing the same absolute rule into these Colonies: For taking away our Charters, abolishing our most valuable Laws, and altering fundamentally the Forms of our Governments: For suspending our own Legislatures, and declaring themselves invested with power to legislate for us in all cases whatsoever. He has abdicated Government here, by declaring us out of his Protection and waging War against us. He has plundered our seas, ravaged our Coasts, burnt our towns, and destroyed the lives of our people. He is at this time transporting large Armies of foreign Mercenaries to compleat the works of death, desolation and tyranny, already begun with circumstances of Cruelty & perfidy scarcely paralleled in the most barbarous ages, and totally unworthy of the Head of a civilized nation. He has constrained our fellow Citizens taken Captive on the high Seas to bear Arms against their Country, to become the executioners of their friends and Brethren, or to fall themselves by their hands. He has excited domestic insurrections amongst us, and has endeavoured to bring on the inhabitants of our frontiers, the merciless Indian Savages, whose known rule of warfare, is an undistinguished destruction of all ages, sexes and conditions. In every stage of these Oppressions We have Petitioned for Redress in the most humble terms: Our repeated Petitions have been answered only by repeated injury. A Prince whose character is thus marked by every act which may define a Tyrant, is unfit to be the ruler of a free people. Nor have We been wanting in attentions to our British brethren. We have warned them from time to time of attempts by their legislature to extend an unwarrantable jurisdiction over us; We have reminded them of the circumstances of our emigration and settlement here. We have appealed to their native justice and magnanimity, and we have conjured them by the ties of our common kindred to disavow these usurpations, which would inevitably interrupt our connections and correspondence. They too have been deaf to the voice of justice and of consanguinity. We must, therefore, acquiesce in the necessity, which denounces our Separation, and hold them, as we hold the rest of mankind, Enemies in War, in Peace Friends.

We, therefore, the Representatives of the united States of America, in General Congress, Assembled, appealing to the Supreme Judge of the world for the rectitude of our intentions do, in the Name, and by the Authority of the good People of these Colonies, solemnly publish and declare, That these United Colonies are, and of Right ought to be Free and Independent States; that they are Absolved from all Allegiance to the British Crown, and that all political connection between them and the State of Great Britain, is and ought to be totally dissolved; and that as Free and Independent States, they have full Power to levy War, conclude Peace, contract Alliances, establish Commerce, and to do all other Acts and things which Independent States may of right do. And for the support of this Declaration, with a firm reliance on the protection of divine Providence, we mutually pledge to each other our lives, our Fortunes and our sacred Honor.

The Declaration of the Rights of Man and Citizen

Originally drafted by a committee of five, this historic document was approved by the French National Assembly in August of 1789. It later served as preamble to the 1791 Constitution, which allowed Louis XVI to continue ruling as a constitutional monarch.

Some have argued that Thomas Jefferson, who was then American ambassador at the French court, influenced the wording of the draft document. In any case, the Declaration of the Rights of Man and the American Declaration of Independence both embodied the universalistic themes of the Age of Enlightenment, the ideas of Montesquieu, Rousseau, and Voltaire.

The representatives of the French people, constituted in National Assembly, considering that the ignorance, neglect, and contempt of the Rights of Man, are the sole causes of public misfortunes and the corruption of governments, have resolved to expose, in solemn Declaration, the natural, inalienable, and sacred Rights of Man, in order that this Declaration, constantly remind them of their rights and duties; in order that the acts of the legislative power and those of the executive power, liable at any moment to be compared with the aims of all political institutions, may be the more respected; in order that the appeals of citizens, founded henceforth on simple and incontestable principles, may always tend to maintain the Constitution and the happiness of all men.

In consequence, the National Assembly recognizes and declares, in the presence and under the auspices of the Supreme Being, the following Rights of Man and of the Citizen:

1. Men are born, and remain, free and equal before the law. Social distinctions can be founded only on public utility.

2. The aim of all political associations is the conservation of the natural and imprescriptible rights of man. These rights are liberty, property, security, and resistance to oppression.

3. The principle of all sovereignty resides in the Nation. No body, no individual, can exercise authority which does not emanate expressly therefrom.

4. Liberty consists in being able to do whatever does not injure another. Thus the exercise of every man's natural rights is limited only by those which assure the other members of society of these same rights. These limits can be determined only by law.

5. The law has the right to prohibit only those actions which are harmful to society. All that is not prohibited by law cannot be hindered; and no one can be compelled to do what the law does not require.

6. The law is the expression of the general will. All citizens have the right to take part in person or through their representatives in its formulation. It must be the same for all, whether it protects or whether it punishes. All citizens being equal in the eyes of the law are equally eligible to all honors, offices, and public employments, according to their abilities and without other distinction than that of their virtues and talents.

7. No man can be accused, arrested, or detained except in cases determined by the law and according to the forms prescribed thereby. Those who solicit, promote, execute, or cause to be executed arbitrary orders shall be punished; but a citizen summoned or seized by virtue of the law must obey immediately: he becomes guilty if he resists.

8. The law must establish only those penalties which are strictly and evidently necessary; and no person can be punished except by virtue of law that has been established and promulgated before the offense, and is legally applied.

9. Since every man is presumed to be innocent until he has been pronounced guilty, if it is judged indispensable to arrest him, all rigorous measures not necessary to secure his person ought to be severely repressed by law.

10. No man is to be molested on account of his opinions, even his religious opinions, provided that their manifestation does not disturb the public order established by law.

11. The free communication of thoughts and opinions is one of man's most precious rights. Every citizen may therefore speak, write, and publish freely; except that he shall be responsible for the abuse of that freedom in cases determined by law.

12. The guarantee of the Rights of Man and of the Citizen makes necessary a public force. This force is therefore instituted for the advantage of all, and not for the particular use of those to whom it is confided.

13. For the maintenance of public force and the expenses of administration, a common contribution is indispensable. It must be equally apportioned among all citizens according to their abilities.

14. All citizens have the right to determine, themselves or through their representatives, the necessity of public contributions; to consent to them freely; to watch over the use thereof; and to fix their amount, assessment, collection, and duration.

15. Society has the right to ask an accounting from all public agents of their administration.

16. Any society in which the guarantee of Rights is not assured, nor the separation of Powers determined, has no Constitution.

17. Since property is an inviolable and sacred right, no man may be deprived of it except when public necessity, lawfully constituted, evidently requires it; and on condition that a just indemnity be paid in advance.

The Declaration of the Rights of Woman

September 1791

Olympe de Gouges

Marie Gouze (1748–1793) was a self-educated butcher's daughter from the south of France who, under the name Olympe de Gouges, wrote pamphlets and plays on a variety of issues, including slavery, which she attacked as based on greed and blind prejudice. In this pamphlet she provides a declaration of the rights of women to parallel the one for men, thus criticizing the deputies for having forgotten women. She addressed the pamphlet to the queen, Marie Antoinette, although she also warned the queen that she must work for the Revolution or risk destroying the monarchy altogether. In her postscript she denounced the customary treatment of women as objects easily abandoned. She appended to the declaration a sample form for a marriage contract that called for communal sharing of property. De Gouges went to the guillotine in 1793, condemned as a counterrevolutionary and denounced as an "unnatural" woman.

To be decreed by the National Assembly in its last session or by the next legislature.

Preamble

Mothers, daughters, sisters, female representatives of the nation ask to be constituted as a national assembly. Considering that ignorance, neglect, or contempt for the rights of woman are the sole causes of public misfortunes and governmental corruption, they have resolved to set forth in a solemn declaration the natural, inalienable, and sacred rights of woman: so that by being constantly present to all the members of the social body this declaration may always remind them of their rights and duties; so that by being liable at every moment to comparison with the aim of any and all political institutions the acts of women's and men's powers may be the more fully respected; and so that by being founded henceforward on simple and incontestable principles the demands of the citizenesses may always tend toward maintaining the constitution, good morals, and the general welfare.

In consequence, the sex that is superior in beauty as in courage, needed in maternal sufferings, recognizes and declares, in the presence and under the auspices of the Supreme Being, the following rights of woman and the citizeness.

1. Woman is born free and remains equal to man in rights. Social distinctions may be based only on common utility.

2. The purpose of all political association is the preservation of the natural and imprescriptible rights of woman and man. These rights are liberty, property, security, and especially resistance to oppression.

3. The principle of all sovereignty rests essentially in the nation, which is but the reuniting of woman and man. No body and no individual may exercise authority which does not emanate expressly from the nation.

4. Liberty and justice consist in restoring all that belongs to another; hence the exercise of the natural rights of woman has no other limits than those that the perpetual tyranny of man opposes to them; these limits must be reformed according to the laws of nature and reason.

5. The laws of nature and reason prohibit all actions which are injurious to society. No hindrance should be put in the way of anything not prohibited by these wise and divine laws, nor may anyone be forced to do what they do not require.

6. The law should be the expression of the general will. All citizenesses and citizens should take part, in person or by their representatives, in its formation. It must be the same for everyone. All citizenesses and citizens, being equal in its eyes, should be equally admissible to all public dignities, offices, and employments, according to their ability, and with no other distinction than that of their virtues and talents.

7. No woman is exempted; she is indicted, arrested, and detained in the cases determined by the law. Women like men obey this rigorous law.

8. Only strictly and obviously necessary punishments should be established by the law, and no one may be punished except by virtue of a law established and promulgated before the time of the offense, and legally applied to women.

9. Any woman being declared guilty, all rigor is exercised by the law.

10. No one should be disturbed for his fundamental opinions; woman has the right to mount the scaffold, so she should have the right equally to mount the tribune, provided that these manifestations do not trouble public order as established by law.

11. The free communication of thoughts and opinions is one of the most precious of the rights of woman, since this liberty assures the recognition of children by their fathers. Every citizeness may therefore say freely, I am the mother of your child; a barbarous prejudice [against unmarried women having children] should not force her to hide the

truth, so long as responsibility is accepted for any abuse of this liberty in cases determined by the law [women are not allowed to lie about the paternity of their children].

12. The safeguard of the rights of woman and citizeness requires public powers. These powers are instituted for the advantage of all and not for the private benefit of those to whom they are entrusted.

13. For maintenance of public authority and for expenses of administration, taxation of women and men is equal; she takes part in all forced labor service, in all painful tasks; she must therefore have the same proportion in the distribution of places, employments, offices, dignities, and in industry.

14. The citizenesses and citizens have the right, by themselves or through their representatives, to have demonstrated to them the necessity of public taxes. The citizenesses can only agree to them upon admission of an equal division, not only in wealth, but also in the public administration, and to determine the means of apportionment, assessment, and collection, and the duration of the taxes.

15. The mass of women, joining with men in paying taxes, have the right to hold accountable every public agent of the administration.

16. Any society in which the guarantee of rights is not assured or the separation of powers not settled has no constitution. The constitution is null and void if the majority of individuals composing the nation has not cooperated in its drafting.

17. Property belongs to both sexes whether united or separated; it is for each of them an inviolable and sacred right, and no one may be deprived of it as a true patrimony of nature, except when public necessity, certified by law, obviously requires it, and then on condition of a just compensation in advance.

Postscript

Women, wake up; the tocsin of reason sounds throughout the universe; recognize your rights. The powerful empire of nature is no longer surrounded by prejudice, fanaticism, superstition, and lies. The torch of truth has dispersed all the clouds of folly and usurpation. Enslaved man has multiplied his force and needs yours to break his chains. Having become free, he has become unjust toward his companion. Oh women! Women, when will you cease to be blind? What advantages have you gathered in the revolution? A scorn more marked, a disdain more conspicuous. During the centuries of corruption you only reigned over the weakness of men. Your empire is destroyed; what is left to you then? Firm belief in the injustices of men. The reclaiming of your patrimony founded on the wise decrees of nature; why should you fear such a beautiful enterprise? . . . Whatever the barriers set up against you, it is in your power to overcome them; you only have to want it. Let us pass now to the appalling account of what you have been in society; and since national education is an issue at this moment, let us see if our wise legislators will think sanely about the education of women.

Women have done more harm than good. Constraint and dissimulation have been their lot. What force has taken from them, ruse returned to them; they have had recourse to all the resources of their charms, and the most irreproachable man has not resisted them. Poison, the sword, women controlled everything; they ordered up crimes as much as virtues. For centuries, the French government, especially, depended on the nocturnal administration of women; officials kept no secrets from their indiscretion; ambassadorial posts, military commands, the ministry, the presidency [of a court], the papacy, the college of cardinals, in short everything that characterizes the folly of men, profane and sacred, has been submitted to the cupidity and ambition of this sex formerly considered despicable and respected, and since the revolution, respectable and despised. . . .

Under the former regime, everyone was vicious, everyone guilty. . . . A woman only had to be beautiful and amiable; when she possessed these two advantages, she saw a hundred fortunes at her feet. . . . The most indecent woman could make herself respectable with gold; the commerce in women was a kind of industry amongst the highest classes, which henceforth will enjoy no more credit. If it still did, the revolution would be lost, and in the new situation we would still be corrupted. Can reason hide the fact that every other road to fortune is closed to a woman bought by a man, bought like a slave from the coasts of Africa? The difference between them is great; this is known. The slave [that is, the woman] commands her master, but if the master gives her her freedom without compensation and at an age when the slave has lost all her charms, what does this unfortunate woman become? The plaything of disdain; even the doors of charity are closed to her; she is poor and old, they say; why did she not know how to make her fortune?

Other examples even more touching can be provided to reason. A young woman without experience, seduced by the man she loves, abandons her parents to follow him; the ingrate leaves her after a few years and the older she will have grown with him, the more his inconstancy will be inhuman. If she has children, he will still abandon her. If he is rich, he will believe himself excused from sharing his fortune with his noble victims. If some engagement ties him to his duties, he will violate it while counting on support from the law. If he is married, every other obligation loses its force. What laws then remain to be passed that would eradicate vice down to its roots? That of equally dividing [family] fortunes between men and women and of public administration of their goods. It is easy to imagine that a woman born of a rich family would gain much from the equal division of property [between children]. But what about the woman born in a poor family with merit and virtues; what is her lot? Poverty and opprobrium. If she does not excel in music or painting, she cannot be admitted to any public function, even if she is fully qualified. . . .

Marriage is the tomb of confidence and love. A married woman can give bastards to her husband with impunity, and even the family fortune which does not belong to them. An unmarried woman has only a feeble right: ancient and inhuman laws refuse her the right to the name and goods of her children's father; no new laws have been made in this matter. If giving my sex an honorable and just consistency is considered to be at this time paradoxical on my part and an attempt at the impossible, I leave to future men the glory of dealing with this matter; but while waiting, we can prepare the way with national education, with the restoration of morals and with conjugal agreements.

Form for a Social Contract Between Man and Woman

We, _____ and _____, moved by our own will, unite for the length of our lives and for the duration of our mutual inclinations under the following conditions: We intend and wish to make our wealth communal property, while reserving the right to divide it in favor of our children and of those for whom we might have a special inclination, mutually recognizing that our goods belong directly to our children, from whatever bed they come [legitimate or not], and that all of them without distinction have the right to bear the name of the fathers and mothers who have acknowledged them, and we impose on ourselves the obligation of subscribing to the law that punishes any rejection of one's own blood [refusing to acknowledge an illegitimate child]. We likewise obligate ourselves, in the case of a separation, to divide our fortune equally and to set aside the portion the law designates for our children. In the case of a perfect union, the one who dies first will give up half his property in favor of the children; and if there are no children, the survivor will inherit by right, unless the dying person has disposed of his half of the common property in favor of someone he judges appropriate. [She then goes on to defend her contract against the inevitable objections of "hypocrites, prudes, the clergy, and all the hellish gang."]

Justification of the Use of Terror

Maximilien Robespierre

Maximilien Robespierre (1758–1794) was the leader of the twelve–man Committee of Public Safety elected by the National Convention, which effectively governed France at the height of the radical phase of the revolution. He had once been a fairly straightforward liberal thinker—reputedly he slept with a copy of Rousseau's Social Contract *at his side. But his own purity of belief led him to impatience with others.*

The committee was among the most creative executive bodies ever seen—and rapidly put into effect policies which stabilized the French economy and began the formation of the very successful French army. It also directed its energies against counter-revolutionary uprisings, especially in the south and west of France. In doing so it unleashed the reign of terror. *Here Robespierre, in his speech of February 5, 1794, from which excerpts are given here, discussed this issue. The figures behind this speech indicate that in the five months from September, 1793, to February 5, 1794, the revolutionary tribunal in Paris convicted and executed 238 men and 31 women and acquitted 190 persons, and that on February 5 there were 5,434 individuals in the prisons in Paris awaiting trial.*

Robespierre was frustrated with the progress of the revolution. After issuing threats to the National Convention, he himself was arrested in July 1794. He tried to shoot himself but missed, and spent his last few hours with his jaw hanging off. He was guillotined, as a victim of the terror, on July 28, 1794.

But, to found and consolidate democracy, to achieve the peaceable reign of the constitutional laws, we must end the war of liberty against tyranny and pass safely across the storms of the revolution: such is the aim of the revolutionary system that you have enacted. Your conduct, then, ought also to be regulated by the stormy circumstances in which the republic is placed; and the plan of your administration must result from the spirit of the revolutionary government combined with the general principles of democracy.

Now, what is the fundamental principle of the democratic or popular government—that is, the essential spring which makes it move? It is virtue; I am speaking of the public virtue which effected so many prodigies in Greece and Rome and which ought to produce much more surprising ones in republican France; of that virtue which is nothing other than the love of country and of its laws.

But as the essence of the republic or of democracy is equality, it follows that the love of country necessarily includes the love of equality.

It is also true that this sublime sentiment assumes a preference for the public interest over every particular interest; hence the love of country presupposes or produces all the virtues: for what are they other than that spiritual strength which renders one capable of those sacrifices? And how could the slave of avarice or ambition, for example, sacrifice his idol to his country?

Not only is virtue the soul of democracy; it can exist only in that government. . . .

Republican virtue can be considered in relation to the people and in relation to the government; it is necessary in both. When only the government lacks virtue, there remains a resource in the people's virtue; but when the people itself is corrupted, liberty is already lost.

Fortunately virtue is natural to the people, notwithstanding aristocratic prejudices. A nation is truly corrupted when, having by degrees lost its character and its liberty, it passes from democracy to aristocracy or to monarchy; that is the decrepitude and death of the body politic. . . .

But when, by prodigious efforts of courage and reason, a people breaks the chains of despotism to make them into trophies of liberty; when by the force of its moral temperament it comes, as it were, out of the arms of the death, to recapture all the vigor of youth; when by turns it is sensitive and proud, intrepid and docile, and can be stopped neither by impregnable ramparts nor by the innumerable armies of the tyrants armed against it, but stops of itself upon confronting the law's image; then if it does not climb rapidly to the summit of its destinies, this can only be the fault of those who govern it.

From all this let us deduce a great truth: the characteristic of popular government is confidence in the people and severity towards itself.

The whole development of our theory would end here if you had only to pilot the vessel of the Republic through calm waters; but the tempest roars, and the revolution imposes on you another task.

This great purity of the French revolution's basis, the very sublimity of its objective, is precisely what causes both our strength and our weakness. Our strength, because it gives to us truth's ascendancy over imposture, and the rights of the public interest over private interests; our weakness, because it rallies all vicious men against us, all those who in their hearts contemplated despoiling the people and all those who intend to let it be despoiled with impunity, both those who have rejected freedom as a personal calamity and those who have embraced the revolution as a career and the Republic as prey. Hence the defection of so many ambitious or greedy men who since the point of departure have abandoned us along the way because they did not begin the journey with the same destination in view. The two opposing spirits that have been represented in a struggle to rule nature might be said to be fighting in this great period of human history to fix irrevocably the world's destinies, and France is the scene of this fearful combat. Without, all the tyrants encircle you; within, all tyranny's friends conspire; they will conspire until hope is wrested from crime. We must smother the internal and external enemies of the Republic or perish with it; now in this situation, the first maxim of your policy ought to be to lead the people by reason and the people's enemies by terror.

If the spring of popular government in time of peace is virtue, the springs of popular government in revolution are at once *virtue and terror:* virtue, without which terror is fatal; terror, without which virtue is powerless. Terror is nothing other than justice, prompt, severe, inflexible; it is therefore an emanation of virtue; it is not so much a special principle as it is a consequence of the general principle of democracy applied to our country's most urgent needs.

It has been said that terror is the principle of despotic government. Does your government therefore resemble despotism? Yes, as the sword that gleams in the hands of the heroes of liberty resembles that with which the henchmen of tyranny are armed. Let the despot govern by terror his brutalized subjects; he is right, as a despot. Subdue by terror the enemies of liberty, and you will be right, as founders of the Republic. The government of the revolution is liberty's despotism against tyranny. Is force made only to protect crime? And is the thunderbolt not destined to strike the heads of the proud?

. . . Indulgence for the royalists, cry certain men, mercy for the villains! No! mercy for the innocent, mercy for the weak, mercy for the unfortunate, mercy for humanity.

Society owes protection only to peaceable citizens; the only citizens in the Republic are the republicans. For it, the royalists, the conspirators are only strangers or, rather, enemies. This terrible war waged by liberty against tyranny—is it not indivisible? Are the enemies within not the allies of the enemies without? The assassins who tear our country apart, the intriguers who buy the consciences that hold the people's mandate; the traitors who sell them; the mercenary pamphleteers hired to dishonor the people's cause, to kill public virtue, to stir up the fire of civil discord, and to prepare political counterrevolution by moral counterrevolution—are all those men less guilty or less dangerous than the tyrants whom they serve?

The Industrial Revolution

John W. Mackey

Perhaps no other historical development has had such massive and far-reaching effects as the Industrial Revolution. It introduced new methods of production and an array of new products; it changed the nature of work for vast numbers of people; it created new social classes and vast new fortunes; instigated a rapid increase in urbanization; it greatly enhanced the speed of transportation and communication; it altered the relationship between the west and the non-western world; it created new, deadlier tools and methods of warfare; and it transformed our environment in profound ways.

The **Industrial Revolution** is described by economists Robert L. Heilbroner and William Milberg as "*a great turning period* in history, during which manufacturing and industrial activity became primary forms of social production."[1] Historians generally agree that this great turn toward industry and the factory system had its origins in the mid to late eighteenth century, and was in full force by the mid-nineteenth century. A later period, between about 1870 and the eve of the First World War, is often described as the **Second Industrial Revolution**, and it was marked by the development of electricity, new types of engines, and new chemicals and industrial materials.

This revolution began in Great Britain, matured there rather rapidly, and spread to Western Europe and the United States throughout the course of the nineteenth century. While it is impossible to pinpoint the exact factors that caused the Industrial Revolution, there were a number of conditions present in eighteenth-century Britain that made this transformation possible.

The Origins of the Industrial Revolution in Britain

After a tumultuous seventeenth century, Great Britain enjoyed relative stability and prosperity in the eighteenth century, when the beginnings of the industrial revolution took hold. Britain had comparatively stable and effective government institutions, a growing economy aided by a system of **banking and credit**, and a developing **market economy**.[2] As a result, the economic and political conditions for the accumulation of capital and economic development were in place. In addition, British institutions like the Royal Society, founded in 1660 to propagate science, and especially the Royal Society for the encouragement of Arts, Manufactures, and Commerce, founded in 1754, promoted **experimentation and innovation** in technology and production. Thus, Britain provided a more hospitable environment for economic change and invention than most nations in the eighteenth century.

Britain also had an available and relatively mobile **labor supply** in the eighteenth century. Britain, like much of Europe, was marked by a **population explosion** in the eighteenth century. Several factors, including an increasing food supply created by the rise of new, more efficient agricultural techniques help explain this population growth. Indeed, Britain, and much of Europe generally, is said to have experienced an **agricultural revolution** in the eighteenth century, in which more sophisticated crop rotation, enclosure, new animal breeding techniques, and improved farming equipment greatly increased yields. In addition to a growing food supply, a decrease in diseases like the plague and smallpox and earlier marriages may also have been significant contributors to population growth.

The available supply of labor in Britain was not only growing in eighteenth-century Britain, but relatively mobile, as well. Under the manorial system, peasants were tied to the land in a form of un-free labor that was highly exploitative, but stable. By the eighteenth century, however, the **enclosure movement** left many farm laborers seeking whatever employment they could find, without ties to a manor or lord. Enclosures were efforts by landowners to privatize and enclose their land, eliminating traditional common lands, and gearing agriculture toward the market rather than local family and village production. Therefore, eighteenth-century Britain had both a growing population and a significant number of landless laborers seeking a living. These factors meant that a ready supply of mobile and cheap labor would be available to work the factories, mills, and mines of the Industrial Revolution.

Britain also benefited from geographical factors that helped make industrialization possible. Transportation networks were strong, as Britain had a relatively developed canal and road system, in addition to many port cities and a long history of seafaring trade. This helped facilitate the movement of goods, people, and raw materials necessary for industrial growth. Britain also had large deposits of both **iron ore** and **coal**, two of the key ingredients in the mechanization of production. Iron was used to make machinery, and, especially after the 1850s, transformed into steel, which was crucial to the construction of railroads, cities, factories, and countless other structures of the industrializing world. Coal, along with **coke**, which is a substance made from super-heated coal, were the fuels most responsible for firing the steam engines and blast furnaces of the industrial revolution.

Most of the characteristics stated in the previous paragraphs were not unique to Great Britain. But the combination of these factors helped create the conditions under which significant economic and technological changes could occur. Taken together, these changes are what we call the Industrial Revolution.

The Nature of the Industrial Revolution

Perhaps the simplest way to distinguish the pre-industrial world from the industrialized world is by looking at common, everyday products; before the industrial revolution they were made by human hands, and ever since, they have increasingly been made by machines. This is of course somewhat over-simplified, but it illustrates the pervasiveness of the changes wrought by industrialization. In a pre-industrial age, the mast majority of average people would have owned or had access only to products—clothing, a few tools, some cooking implements—that were made by hand, and probably made locally, and perhaps even made by someone they knew. But the products a middle-class westerner might own today—a computer, a car, clothes, a cell phone, a television, sporting goods, furniture—were likely all made by machines, in factories run by people the purchaser of the products will never know, perhaps thousands of miles away. Such is the legacy of the mechanization of production and the global expansion of industrial capitalism.

The Mechanization of Production and Transportation

Mechanization involves at first enhancing, and then largely replacing the power of nature (human bodies, animals, wind, and water) with the power of machines. These changes greatly increased the speed and efficiency of production. Several inventions in the eighteenth century (the spinning jenny, the spinning mule) increased the productivity of the textile industry in Britain, by multiplying the power of humans, water, or animals. And as textile producers came to see that it was more efficient to bring large numbers of workers together in the same place to operate machinery than to rely on production by individuals in their homes, the **factory system** was born.

Even more striking changes to the production process accompanied the widespread use of the **steam engine** during the nineteenth century. **James Watt**, a Scottish engineer, is credited with making the necessary improvements to steam engines that eventually made them widely applicable for industrial uses. Watt patented his new steam engine in 1769, and by the early to mid-nineteenth century, advanced steam engines were in extensive use in industry and transportation.

Machines powered by coal or wood-fired steam power no longer relied as much on human muscle, and did not need to be located near water sources. As engine-powered mechanization grew, production grew ever faster, larger in scale, and cheaper. Therefore, industrialists whose factories were most technologically advanced and efficient enjoyed a **comparative advantage** in the growing capitalist marketplace. Cottage industries and small handcrafters could not compete with the power of the mechanized textile industry and its growing factories. The mechanization process and the factory system that largely started in the textile industry would also transform the production of countless other products, and the addition of steam power helped to create a massive, indeed revolutionary change in human societies.

Just as steam power transformed the speed of production, it greatly increased the speed at which people and their cargoes could travel, creating a **transportation revolution**. Industrialization and transportation also enhanced each other; new industrial technologies and materials led to faster, more widespread transportation networks, which in turn helped move products to new markets more quickly, fueling industrial growth. Before the use of steam engines, a land traveler and his or her cargo could move only as fast as a horse could pull a carriage or rail car. The creation of steam-powered locomotives, however, spectacularly transformed the speed and efficiency of travel and the distribution of freight. Thus, one of the hallmarks of the industrial age was the construction of extensive railroad networks in Europe, the United States, and numerous regions of the world that had been colonized by Europeans.

Like land travel, boat and ship transportation was also revolutionized by the steam engine. Before the industrial revolution, natural forces—the strength of people, horses, or winds—limited the speed and consistency of water transport. But steam-powered boats, equipped with a power source independent of such natural forces, greatly enhanced the movement of goods and people. Rapid industrialization in the United States, for example was aided by the **steamboats** that carried people and cargo on its rivers in the early to mid-nineteenth century. Practical and effective oceangoing steamships took longer to develop, but by the late nineteenth century, steam travel on the seas became much more rapid, effective and commonplace. **Steamships** were vital in transporting goods and raw materials over vast distances as the Industrial Revolution became more and more global, and more intertwined with European Empires.

The Second Industrial Revolution (cir. 1870-1914)

A number of important economic and technological developments in the late nineteenth and early twentieth centuries cause many historians to see this period as a Second Industrial Revolution. This revolution is perhaps best seen not as a separate event, but as an expansion the technological changes of the Industrial Revolution into new directions. New inventions, new fuel power sources, and new materials differentiate this later period from the earlier decades of the industrial revolution.

For example, while coal and iron were crucial to the early industrial revolution, **oil** and **steel** came to be more important in the later period, and would continue to be basic components of industrial societies in the twentieth century. While an advanced process for making steel, a strong and highly useful alloy consisting primarily of iron ore, was developed before this later period, steel production became increasingly crucial in the late nineteenth century. It became a key component in the construction of cities, factories, military hardware, and transport systems. Similarly, the invention of the **internal combustion engine**, along with the development of commercial drilling made oil a crucial fuel of industrialization. And in addition to more widespread construction railroad networks, the Second Industrial Revolution contributed the automobile and the airplane, as well as oceangoing steamships, to the revolution in transportation.

The era between about 1870 and 1914 was also marked by the development of **electricity**, the **wireless telegraph**, and the **chemical industry**, as well as by changes in the nature of industrial capitalism. While **heavy industries** (iron, steel, machines, etc.) dominated much of the nineteenth century, and continued to be crucial to industrial societies, **consumer capitalism** became more widespread near the turn of the twentieth century. Britain, in particular, began to gear more of its production toward **consumer products**—products designed to be bought by everyday people— than ever before. As a result, department stores and mail-order catalogs proliferated in this period, and businesses came to realize that there was great profit in catering to the consumptive desires of the middle class and skilled workers.

The Impact on the Class System

The traditional European class system, rooted in feudalism and manorialism, did not disappear overnight, but wherever the Industrial Revolution took hold, it transformed the social class system. Two new classes were created by industrial capitalism—the property-owning bourgeoisie or "middle" class, and the proletariat, or working class. For economists like Karl Marx, the development of these two new classes was the leading development of the nineteenth century. In industrial society, Marx argued, one's class position is determined by one's "relationship to the means of production;" members of the bourgeoisie own and/or control the means of production, while the members of the proletariat do not. An individual proletarian, who owns no capital, has only his labor to sell, and subsists on hourly wages.

The European bourgeoisie was not entirely new during the nineteenth century, of course (see chapter 7). But a new, *industrial* bourgeoisie was on the rise. During the industrial revolution, fortunes were increasingly linked to the factory system, the raw materials and fuel that supported it, and the financial capital that allowed it to expand. As a result, the industrial bourgeoisie emerged as the dominant class of the nineteenth century, flush with the profits of a rapidly expanding industrial economy. The richest members of the bourgeoisie did not entirely *replace* the aristocracy, however; in many cases, they *merged* with it through marriage. A marriage between a son of aristocratic lineage and the heiress to an industrial fortune, for example, could be beneficial to both parties, as the aristocratic family could gain the financial benefits of industry, while the bourgeois family could acquire the gentility of aristocratic title.

The industrial revolution also altered the lives of the laboring classes. As industrialization spread and grew, the industrial proletariat began to replace the peasantry as the class whose labor created the wealth of nations. As the rural, agricultural society of Europe was transformed into a more urban, industrial one, the majority of manual labor was increasingly performed in factories and mines by a new working class.[3]

Thus, the old estate system of Europe, and the manorial and feudal ties that bound it together, was being supplanted by a new, more individualistic social system. Traditional rural and village life, arguably based on what German sociologist Ferdinand Toennies called *gemeinschaft*, or "community," was marked by its smaller scale, an emphasis on primary relationships, and an orientation toward the needs of the group. By contrast, the social class system and mass society that accompanied industrial capitalism created what Toennies called *gesellschaft*, or "society." The new society was larger in scale, less personal, based more on secondary or transactional relationships, competitive, dominated by the money economy, and marked by a much more complex division of labor.

The Changing Nature of Work

As the bourgeoisie began to supplant the aristocracy as the wealthiest, most economically dynamic class in industrializing Europe, it changed the nature of ruling-class life. The aristocracy was a class whose authority and power were rooted in land ownership and an ancestry with a martial past, but it was in large part a class of leisure. An aristocrat, as a gentleman of leisure, was largely defined by what he did *not* do—

work. The industrial bourgeoisie was a different sort of class, defined not be leisure but by commercial or professional achievement. Bourgeois values of hard work, thrift, efficiency, self-discipline, and innovation were the hallmarks of the "new men" who emerged at the top of the economic ladder in the nineteenth century.[4] The culture of the industrial bourgeoisie was also marked by a distinct, male-dominated gender code, sometimes referred to as **separate spheres**.[5] The public sphere of business, politics, and property ownership was said to be a male domain, while women were expected to remain largely confined to the home, or domestic sphere.

The work of the laboring classes changed drastically as a result of industrialization. For centuries the majority of European society was made up of a toiling peasantry, landless and overworked. In addition to the peasants, European villages were home to small handcrafters, who produced the products of everyday life in their modest shops. As industrialization spread, the lives of the working class were still grindingly difficult, but in new ways. Instead of plowing and sowing, or cobbling and hand-weaving, the new industrial working class increasingly labored in mechanized factories and mines.

Industrial working conditions, especially before the late nineteenth century, were generally brutal. Factories were often crowded, hot, loud, poorly ventilated, and dangerous. Working hours were long, breaks were few, and child labor was common, as factory owners and managers in a competitive environment emphasized profit far above worker comfort and safety. In the coal mines, which quite literally fueled the industrial revolution, conditions were even worse. The lack of industrial regulation regarding safety, working hours, and job conditions meant that early industrial workers often risked their health, or even their lives, every day on the job.

Many members of the new industrial proletariat found the changing nature of work disturbing. Handcrafters, accustomed to traditional forms of production, the guild system, and a certain degree of personal control over their labor, found themselves driven out of business by faster, more efficient factories. Unlike the world of small, familial handcraft shops, the new industrial economy was based on an increasingly complex **division of labor**, which required workers to complete specific, repetitive tasks that left them feeling like anonymous cogs, alienated from the products of their labor. The new industrial workplace was less personal, more subject to change, and less rooted in familiar tradition than its pre-industrial counterpart.[6]

Some workers, angered by the threat of industrialization to their traditional forms of production and their livelihoods, attempted to fight back. Famously, textile workers in England, known as the **Luddites**, formed a secret society dedicated to putting a stop to the sweeping changes in the textile industry in the early nineteenth century. They issued demands to mill owners and sometimes destroyed machinery, but were ultimately unable to stop the changes that accompanied the mechanization of cloth production.

Industrial workers who came to the factory from an agrarian background also found life in the new mills and mines unsettling. Centuries of folk traditions were ingrained in rural life, and these traditions, like work itself, followed the rhythms of nature. The work of peasants and small farmers followed familiar cues—sunlight and darkness, the changing of seasons, weather conditions, and the like. Conversely, industrial life was governed by factory discipline. Rather than the needs of crops and livestock, workers now had to respond to dictates of the time-clock and the factory boss.[7] Both former craftspeople and former agricultural workers found the highly regimented demands of industrial work discipline unfamiliar and oppressive.

The nature of the industrial workplace led to the development of the modern **labor movement**, and eventually to the associated rise socialist and labor-oriented political parties. British workers who saw their traditional livelihoods threatened and believed themselves to be exploited attempted to form **unions** in the late eighteenth century. Property owners, capitalists, and the British government feared these "combinations" of workers would promote instability, violence, and social revolution. Thus, Britain passed the **Combination Acts** from 1799 to 1800, which made workers' unions illegal.

Unions operated secretly, outside the law, until the Combination Acts were repealed in 1825 (though full legal recognition for unions did not exist until workers won the right to strike in the 1870s). After repeal, trade and labor union organization grew in Britain, as well as in other industrializing regions and nations. Unions operated under the premise that while individual workers were powerless against exploitative capitalists, a unified front of workers could bargain for higher wages, more reasonable working hours, and better working conditions. And in industries and regions where union organization was strong, wages and working conditions did improve over time. But even after the legalization of unions, the organization of labor remained beset by challenges. Throughout the nineteenth century, business owners harassed union organizers, employed strike breakers, and sometimes took illegal actions to break unions or to prevent them from forming.

While wages of the working class remained pitifully low throughout the early decades of industrialization, their lot eventually improved somewhat. Debates about living standards of early industrial workers continue amongst historians, but it is clear that in the second half of the nineteenth century, wages and living standards of average industrial workers in Britain improved significantly.[8] Unskilled and semi-skilled laborers still remained near the bottom of a still highly stratified society, however, as the top twenty percent of people in industrialized societies earned over half of their nation's incomes during much of the nineteenth century.

In addition to the hard-won benefits gained by labor unions, reform and state regulation of the industrial economy gradually helped curb some of the worst abuses of the industrial workplace. For example, the **Factory Acts** were a series of laws regulating factories in Britain passed at various points, starting in 1802 and continuing over more than a century. However, in many cases, the provisions contained in these acts may seem modest at best. The Factories Act of 1847, for example (the long-awaited Ten Hours Act), established a maximum working day in textile factories of ten hours for women and for children between ages 13 and 18. To the extent that working-class life improved as industrial societies matured, it was government intervention and labor organization—not the invisible hand—that played the major role.

Urbanization and Environmental Impact

Just as industrialization transformed production, transportation, the class system, and the nature of work, it profoundly altered our natural and human-made environments.

As industrialization grew, it brought with it a great wave of **urbanization**. From the late eighteenth century on, enormous numbers of people migrated from small villages and rural areas into rapidly growing cities. The migrants were drawn by the possibility of finding factory work, which was increasingly located in urban areas. Before the invention of the steam engine, mills were generally dependent on water power, and were thus restricted to locations that provided appropriate river access. But steam-powered machinery allowed factory owners to build their facilities in cities, taking advantage of the concentration of people (to provide labor and possibly markets), better transportation and supply networks, and closer proximity to other businesses.

European cities had a long history as religious, cultural, commercial, and political centers. But the growth of the factory system created something new—industrial cities. The new urban centers were often almost entirely dependent upon industry, and in some cases, a single industry. Whereas London, for example, had long been a market town, a religious center, a bastion of culture, and the seat of royal authority, the cotton-producing city of Manchester, in northern England, owed its rise to prominence entirely to the rapid growth of the textile industry. Elsewhere, other cities grew rapidly around their industries; in the United States, the location of Pittsburgh, Pennsylvania near coal fields and supplies of ore that fueled iron foundries and steel mills, helped it grow rapidly from a tiny village into a mighty industrial center.

The pace and scale of urbanization in cities like Manchester and Pittsburgh, to name just two, was astounding. Manchester's modest population of about 20,000 in the 1770s exploded to over 300,000 by about the mid-nineteenth century. Pittsburgh was an insignificant settlement around a military fort in 1800, claiming a population of only about 1,500 people. By 1900, the "Steel City" was one of the world's great heavy industrial cities, and its population had grown by over 320,000. Industrialization caused some other cities to grow even faster. Between 1840 and 1890, the American city of Chicago, Illinois grew from small town of fewer than 5,000 people to a giant urban center of over 1 million inhabitants. And throughout the course of the nineteenth century, the percentage of the population in industrializing nations living in urban areas more than tripled.

As the populations of industrializing cities grew, so did their problems. Simply put, nineteenth-century industrial cities were crowded, filthy, and unsanitary in the extreme. Cities were unable to handle the rapid influx of new inhabitants, who were often forced to live in quickly and shoddily-constructed row houses that were crowded, poorly ventilated, and featuring only shared outhouses as facilities. A lack of public provision for sewage and sanitation meant that city streets were often filled with the stench of human and animal waste and rotting garbage. And the conditions of industrial cities were more than just unpleasant; in the 1830s and 1840s, for example, thousands died in **cholera** epidemics in British cities from contaminated water. The shocking conditions of cities led to a **public health movement** in industrialized countries, which convinced governments to act. By the second half of the nineteenth century, government initiatives helped supply more acceptable drinking water, sanitation, and sewage systems in industrial cities. While the conditions of urban areas gradually became less deadly, they still tended to be crowded and dirty places.

It was not only urban environments that were effected by industrialization. The Industrial Revolution represents nothing less than a turning point in the human relationship to our environment, as it was built upon massive alterations to our land, air, and water. Two of the main components of industrialization were tremendous quantities of coal and iron ore. In other words, factory production and the transportation revolution both relied on **extractive industries** for fuel and basic materials. Extractive industries, like coal or iron ore mining, involve *extracting* these elements from the ground, which causes tremendous impacts on both the land and water.

Not only the mining of coal, but also the burning of huge quantities of coal in factories, mills, locomotives, steamships, residences, and other buildings also led to significant environmental damage. Industrial cities were often thick with coal smoke; indeed the famous "London fog" of legend was a product not just of weather, but of the smokestacks and chimneys that filled the city's skyline. **Industrial pollution** of the air and water, along with destruction of the land from extraction are among the lasting legacies of industrialization.

Globalization and Western Dominance

The Industrial Revolution caused a veritable re-ordering of the global economic system. Western nations, especially those that industrialized earliest and most thoroughly, became far wealthier relative to the rest of the world than they had ever been. When Europe was still a pre-industrial, agricultural region, there was little global economic stratification *between* nations—virtually every nation in the world had a relatively poor majority, and a small, wealthy elite. Thus, the largest differences in wealth in the pre-industrial world were between the rich and poor *within* any given nation. But the massive profits of industrialization caused Europe and the United States to become the wealthiest societies to that point in history, many times wealthier than non-industrialized areas of Asia, Africa, and Latin America. The global legacies of this **uneven development** are still in place.

Industrialization coincided with the massive expansion of European empires and the imperialists of the nineteenth century were determined to make their colonies profitable. Various regions of the non-western world were viewed as potential sources of raw materials, and as captive markets. Since Britain controlled India, for example, it could force its products on the Indian market, prevent India from erecting any kind of protective tariff, and eventually drive many its manufacturers out of business. It was not only the speed and efficiency of industrial production that caused western nations to profit greatly during this period; European imperialists were also in a position to "rig the system" in their favor.

Between about 1840 and 1914, Europeans also produced two exports in huge quantities—people and capital. A **great migration**, the largest movement of people in history to that point, resulted from the rising population and changing economies of Europe. Rising populations in the nineteenth century meant increased competition for jobs and scarce land resources, and the efficiency of industrial production rendered the skills of numerous craftspeople obsolete. As a result, millions of small landholders and craftspeople emigrated from Europe to the Americas, Asiatic Russia, Australia, and New Zealand.

And during the period roughly corresponding with the Second Industrial Revolution, Europeans sent not only their people but their investments abroad as well. **Foreign investment** increased dramatically during this period, as western capitalists sought higher profit margins in as-yet undeveloped regions of the world. Higher rates of return on investment insured that continued to flow out of industrialized Europe until the world economy was devastated by World War I.

The industrialization that started in the textile mills of northern England spread rapidly across Europe and North America, and eventually transformed the non-western regions, too. Comparing the world in 1800 with the world in 1900, after about a century of industrialization (a very short period in human history), the immense transformation of the world becomes apparent. In industrialized regions the size and nature of cities changed dramatically, a new class system was established, new forms of production predominated, machines became a crucial part of life, the nature of work for the majority of people changed, new products and inventions were everywhere, transportation was revolutionized, and the environment was altered dramatically. And taking a wider perspective, a new kind of profound global inequality resulted from the fortunes compiled by the western nations.

The Industrial Revolution occurred during a time of great competition, not only between capitalists, but between European nations, as well. The nineteenth century was marked not only by economic changes, but by ideological ones, too. Thus, fueled by economic aspirations, but also by nationalist ideologies and imperialist ambitions, European nations created a competitive international environment that would lead to massive war by 1914. And, thanks to the technological advancements of industrialization, new kinds of weapons would make that war bloodier and more disastrous than any before.

Notes

1. Robert L. Heilbroner and William Milberg, *The Making of Economic Society* (Upper Saddle River, NJ, 2002), p. 100

2. Some historians have also suggested that a lack of regulation and interference in the economy by the British government also helped fuel the innovation that led to industrialization. Periods of rapid industrialization in nations like Germany and China, however, suggest that *laissez-faire* policies are not a necessary precondition for industrialization.

3. E.P. Thompson, *The Making of the English Working Class* (New York, 1964).

4. Anthony Weiner, *English Culture and the Decline of the Industrial Spirit, 1850-1980* (Cambridge, 1981).

5. See Lenore Davidoff and Catherine Hall, *Family Fortunes: Men and Women of the English Middle Class, 1780-1850* (Chicago, 1987).

6. A renowned study of the changing nature of work is Peter Laslett, *The World We Have Lost* (New York, 1965).

7. For a classic study of the transformation of time and work discipline that accompanied the industrial revolution, see E.P. Thompson, "Time, Work-Discipline, and Industrial Capitalism," *Past and Present* 104 (1967).

8. E.J Hobsbawm, "The Standard of Living During the Industrial Revolution: A Discussion," *Economic History Review* Vol 16 No. 1 (1963) 119-134.

References and Suggested Readings:

Briggs, Asa. *The Age of Improvement, 1783-1867*. London: Longman, 1965.

Davidoff, Lenore, and Catherine Hall. *Family Fortunes: Men and Women of the English Middle Class, 1780-1850*. Chicago: University of Chicago Press, 1987.

Heilbroner, Robert L. and William Milberg. *The Making of Economic Society*, 7th ed. Upper Saddle River, NJ: Prentice Hall, 2002.

Hobsbawm, E.J. *The Age of Capital, 1848-1975*. New York: Scribner, 1975.

Hobsbawm, E.J. "The Standard of Living During the Industrial Revolution: A Discussion," *Economic History Review* Vol 16 No. 1 (1963) 119-134.

Kemp, Tom. *Industrialization in Nineteenth-Century Europe*. New York: Longman, 1985.

Laslett, Peter. *The World We Have Lost*. New York: Scribner, 1965.

Thompson, E.P. *The Making of the English Working Class*. New York: Pantheon, 1964.

Thompson, E.P. "Time, Work Discipline, and Industrial Capitalism." *Past and Present* (104), 1967.

Thompson, F.M.L., ed. *The Cambridge Social History of Britain*, 1750-1950, 3 vols. Cambridge: Cambridge University Press, 1990.

Wiener, Martin J. English *Culture and the Decline of the Industrial Spirit, 1850-1980*. Cambridge: Cambridge University Press, 1981.

The World We Have Lost

Peter Laslett

The following has been excerpted from the 1965 book The World We Have Lost. *Laslett (1915–2001) was a cultural and intellectual historian at Cambridge University, whose work exploded numerous misperceptions about early modern English society.*

In the year 1619 the bakers of London applied to the authorities for an increase in the price of bread. They sent in support of their claims a complete description of a bakery and an account of its weekly costs. There were thirteen or fourteen people in such an establishment: the baker and his wife, four paid employees who were called journeymen, two apprentices, two maid-servants and the three or four children of the master baker himself. Six pounds ten shillings a week was reckoned to be the outgoings of this establishment of which only eleven shillings and eight-pence went for wages: half a crown a week for each of the journeymen and ten-pence for each of the maids. Far and away the greatest cost was food: two pounds nine shillings out of the six pounds ten shillings, at five shillings a head for the baker and his wife, four shillings a head for their helpers and two shillings for their children. It cost much more in food to keep a journeyman than it cost in money; four times as much to keep a maid. Clothing was charged up too, not only for the man, wife and children, but for the apprentices as well. Even school fees were claimed as a justifiable charge on the price of bread for sale, and it cost sixpence a week for the teaching and clothing of a baker's child.

A London bakery was undoubtedly what we should call a commercial or even an industrial undertaking, turning out loaves by the thousand. Yet the business was carried on in the house of the baker himself. There was probably a *shop* as part of the house, *shop* as in work*shop* and not as meaning a retail establishment. Loaves were not ordinarily sold over the counter: they had to be carried to the open-air market and displayed on stalls. There was a garner behind the house, for which the baker paid two shillings a week in rent, and where he kept his wheat, his *seacoal* for the fire and his store of salt. The house itself was one of those high, half-timbered overhanging structures on the narrow London street which we always think of when we remember the scene in which Shakespeare, Pepys or even Christopher Wren lived. Most of it was taken up with the living-quarters of the dozen people who worked there.

It is obvious that all these people ate in the house since the cost of their food helped to determine the production cost of the bread. Except for the journeymen they were all obliged to sleep in the house at night and live together as a family.

The only word used at that time to describe such a group of people was "family." The man at the head of the group, the entrepreneur, the employer, or the manager, was then known as the master or head of the family. He was father to some of its members and in place of father to the rest. There was no sharp distinction between his domestic and his economic functions. His wife was both his partner and his subordinate, a partner because she ran the family, took charge of the food and managed the women-servants, a subordinate because she was woman and wife, mother and in place of mother to the rest.

The paid servants of both sexes had their specified and familiar position in the family, as much part of it as the children but not quite in the same position. At that time the family was not one society only but three societies fused together: the society of man and wife, of parents and children and of master and servant. But when they were young, and servants were, for the most part, young, unmarried people, they were very close to children in their status and their function. Here is the agreement made between the parents of a boy about to become an apprentice and his future master. The boy covenants to dwell as an apprentice with his master for seven years, to keep his secrets and to obey his commandments.

> Taverns and alehouses he shall not haunt, dice, cards or any other unlawful games he shall not use, fornication with any woman he shall not commit, matrimony with any woman he shall not contract. He shall not absent himself by night or by day without his master's leave but be a true and faithful servant.

On his side, the master undertakes to teach his apprentice his art, science or occupation with moderate correction.

> Finding and allowing unto his said servant meat, drink, apparel, washing, lodging and all other things during the said term of seven years, and to give unto his said apprentice at the end of the said term double apparel, to wit, one suit for holydays and one suit for worken days.

Apprentices, therefore, were workers who were also children, extra sons or extra daughters (for girls could be apprenticed too), clothed and educated as well as fed, obliged to obedience and forbidden to marry, unpaid and absolutely dependent until the age of twenty-one. If apprentices were workers in the position of sons and daughters, the sons and daughters of the house were workers too. John Locke laid it down in 1697 that the children of the poor must work for some part of the day when they reached the age of three. The sons and daughters of a London baker were not free to go to school for many years of their young lives, or even to play as they wished when they came back home. Soon they would find themselves doing what they could in *bolting*, that is sieving flour, or in helping the maidservant with her panniers of loaves on the way to the market stall, or in playing their small parts in preparing the never-ending succession of meals for the whole household.

We may see at once, therefore, that the world we have lost, as I have chosen to call it, was no paradise or golden age of equality, tolerance or loving kindness. It is so important that I should not be misunderstood on this point that I will say at once that the coming of industry cannot be shown to have brought economic oppression and exploitation along with it. It was there already. The patriarchal arrangements which we have begun to explore were not new in the England of Shakespeare and Elizabeth. They were as old as the Greeks, as old as European history, and not confined to Europe. And it may well be that they abused and enslaved people quite as remorselessly as the economic arrangements which had replaced them in the England of Blake and Victoria. When people could expect to live for only thirty years in all, how must a man have felt when he realized that so much of his adult life, perhaps all, must go in working for his keep and very little more in someone else's family?

But people do not recognize facts of this sort, and no one is content to expect to live as long as the majority in fact will live. Every servant in the old social world was probably quite confident that he or she would some day get married and be at the head of a new family, keeping others in subordination. If it is legitimate to use the words exploitation and oppression in thinking of the economic arrangements of the pre-industrial world, there are nevertheless differences in the manner of oppressing and exploiting. The ancient order of society was felt to be eternal and unchangeable by those who supported, enjoyed and endured it. There was no expectation of reform. How could there be when economic organization was domestic organization, and relationships were rigidly regulated by the social system, by the content of Christianity itself?

Here is a vivid contrast with social expectation in Victorian England, or in industrial countries everywhere today. Every relationship in our world which can be seen to affect our economic life is open to change, is expected indeed to change of itself, or if it does not, to *be* changed, made better, by an omnicompetent authority. This makes for a less stable social world, though it is only one of the features of our society which impels us all in that direction. All industrial societies, we may suppose, are far less stable than their predecessors. They lack the extraordinarily cohesive influence which familial relationships carry with them, that power of reconciling the frustrated and the discontented by emotional means. Social revolution, meaning an irreversible changing of the pattern of social relationships, never happened in traditional, patriarchal, pre-industrial human society. It was almost impossible to contemplate.

Almost, but not quite. Sir Thomas More, in the reign of Henry VIII, could follow Plato in imagining a life where children would not know their parents and where promiscuity could be a political institution. Sir William Petty, 150 years later, one of the very first of the political sociologists, could speculate about polygamy; and the England of the Tudors and the Stuarts already knew of social structures and sexual arrangements, existing in the newly discovered world, which were alarmingly different from their own. But it must have been an impossible effort of the imagination to suppose that they were anything like as satisfactory.

It will be noticed that the roles we have allotted to all the members of the capacious family of the master-baker of London in the year 1619 are, emotionally, all highly symbolic and highly satisfactory. We may feel that in a whole society organized like this, in spite of all the subordination, the exploitation and the obliteration of those who were young, or feminine, or in service, everyone belonged in a group, a family group. Everyone had his circle of affection: every relationship could be seen as a love-relationship.

Not so with us. Who could love the name of a limited company or of a government department as an apprentice could love his superbly satisfactory father-figure master, even if he were a bully and a beater, a usurer and a hypocrite? But if a family is a circle of affection, it can also be the scene of hatred. The worst tyrants among human beings, the murderers and the villains, are jealous husbands and resentful wives, possessive partners and deprived children. In the traditional, patriarchal society of Europe, where practically everyone lived out his whole life within the family, often within one family only, tension like this must have been incessant and unrelieved, incapable of release except in crisis. Men, women and children have to be very close together for a very long time to generate the emotional power which can give rise to a tragedy of Sophocles, or Shakespeare, or Racine. Conflict in such a society was between individual people, on the personal scale. Except when the Christians fought with the infidels, or Protestants fought with Catholics, clashes between masses of persons did not often arise. There could never be a situation such as that which makes our own time, as some men say, the scene of perpetual revolution.

All this is true to history only if the little knot of people making bread in Stuart London was indeed the typical social unit of the old world in its size, composition and scale. There are reasons why a baker's household might have been a little out of the ordinary, for baking was a highly traditional occupation in a society increasingly subject to economic change. We shall see, in due course, that a family of thirteen people, which was also a unit of production of thirteen, less the children quite incapable of work, was quite large for English society at that time. Only the families of the really important, the nobility and the gentry, the aldermen and the successful merchants, were ordinarily as large as this. In fact, we can take the bakery to represent the upper limit in size and scale of the group in which ordinary people lived and worked. Among the great mass of society which cultivated the land, and which will be the major preoccupation of this essay, the family group was smaller than a London craftsman's entourage. . . . One reason for feeling puzzled by our own industrial society is that the historian has never set out to tell us what society was like before industry came and seems to assume that everyone knows.

We shall have much more to say about the movement of servants from farmhouse to farmhouse in the old world, and shall return to the problem of understanding ourselves in time, in contrast with our ancestors. Let us emphasize again the scale of life in the working family of the London baker. Few persons in the old world ever found themselves in groups larger than family groups, and there were few families of more than a dozen members. The largest household so far known to us, apart from the royal court and the establishments of the nobility, lay and spiritual, is that of Sir Richard Newdigate, Baronet, in his house of Arbury, within his parish of Chilvers Coton in Warwickshire, in the year 1684. There were thirty-seven people in Sir Richard's family: himself; Lady Mary Newdigate his wife; seven daughters, all under the age of sixteen; and twenty-eight servants, seventeen men and boys and eleven women and girls. This was still a family, not an institution, a staff, an office or a firm.

Everything physical was on the human scale, for the commercial worker in London, and the miner who lived and toiled in Newdigate's village of Chilvers Coton. No object in England was larger than London Bridge or St. Paul's Cathedral, no structure in the Western World to stand comparison with the Colosseum in Rome.

Everything temporal was tied to the human life-span, too. The death of the master baker, head of the family, ordinarily meant the end of the bakery. Of course there might be a son to succeed, but the master's surviving children would be young if he himself had lived only as long as most men. Or an apprentice might fulfill the final function of apprenticehood, substitute sonship, that is to say, and marry his master's daughter, or even his widow. Surprisingly often, the widow, if she could, would herself carry on the trade. . . .

We may pause here to point out that our argument is not complete. There was an organization in the social structure of Europe before the coming of industry which enormously exceeded the family in size and endurance. This was the Christian church. It is true to say that the ordinary person, especially the female, never went to a gathering larger than could assemble in an ordinary house except when going to church. When we look at the aristocracy and the church from the point of view of the scale of life and the impermanence of all man-made institutions, we can see that their functions were such as make very little sense in an industrial society like our own. Complicated arrangements then existed, and still exist in England now, which were intended to make it easier for the noble family to give the impression that it had indeed always persisted. Such, for example, were those intricate rules of succession which permitted a cousin, however distant, to succeed to the title and to the headship, provided only he was in the male line. Such was the final remedy in the power of the Crown, the fountain of honour, to declare that an anomalous succession should take place. Nobility was forever.

But the symbolic provision of permanence is only the beginning of the social functions of the church. At a time when the ability to read with understanding and to write much more than a personal letter was confined for the most part to the ruling minority, in a society which was otherwise oral in its communications, the preaching parson was the great link between the illiterate mass and the political, technical and educated world. Sitting in the 10,000 parish churches of England every Sunday morning, in groups of 20, 50, 100 or 200, the illiterate mass of the people were not only taking part in the single group activity which they ordinarily shared with others outside their own families. They were informing themselves in the only way open to them of what went on in England, Europe, and the world as a whole. The priesthood was indispensable to the religious activity of the old world, at a time when religion was still of primary interest and importance. But the priesthood was also indispensable because of its functions in social communication.

Not only did the scale of their work and the size of the group which was engaged make them exceptional, the constitution of the group did too. In the baking household we have chosen as our standard, sex and age were mingled together. Fortunate children might go out to school, but adults did not usually go out to work. There was nothing to correspond to the thousands of young men on the assembly line, the hundreds of young women in the offices, the lonely lives of housekeeping wives which we now know only too well. We shall see that those who survived to old age in the much less favourable conditions for survival which then were prevalent, were surprisingly often left to live and die alone, in their tiny cottages or sometimes in the almshouses which were being built so widely in the England of the Tudors and the Stuarts. Poor-law establishments, parochial in purpose and in size, had begun their melancholy chapter in the history of the English people. But institutional life was otherwise almost unknown. There were no hotels, hostels, or blocks of flats for single persons, very few hospitals and none of the kind we are familiar with, almost no young men and women living on their own. The family group where so great a majority lived was what we should undoubtedly call a "balanced" and "healthy" group.

When we turn from the hand-made city of London to the hand-moulded immensity of rural England, we may carry the same sentimental prejudice along with us. To every farm there was a family, which spread itself over its portion of the village lands as the family of the master-craftsman filled out his manufactory. When a holding was small, and most were small as are the tiny holdings of European peasants today, a man tilled it with the help of his wife and his children. No single man, we must remember, would usually take charge of the land, any more than a single man would often be found at the head of a workshop in the city. The master of a family was expected to be a householder, whether he was a butcher, a baker, a candlestick maker or simply a husbandman, which was the universal name for one whose skill was in working the land. Marriage we must insist, and it is one of the rules which gave its character to the society of our ancestors, was the entry to full membership, in the enfolding countryside, as well as in the scattered urban centres.

But there was a difference in scale and organization of work on the land and in the town. The necessities of rural life did require recurrent groupings of households for common economic purposes, occasionally something like a crowd of men, women and children working together for days on end. Where the ground was still being tilled as open fields, and each household had a number of strips scattered all over the whole open area and not a compact collection of enclosures, ploughing was cooperative, as were many other operations, above all harvesting, and this continued even after enclosure. We do not yet know how important this element of enforced common activity was in the life of the English rural community on the eve of industrialization, or how much difference enclosure made in this respect. But whatever the situation was, the economic transformation of the eighteenth and nineteenth centuries destroyed communality altogether in English rural life. The group of men from several farmsteads working the heavy plough in springtime, the bevy of harvesters from every house in the village wading into the high standing grass to begin the cutting of the hay, had no successors in large-scale economic activity. For the arrangement of these groups was entirely different in principle from the arrangement of a factory, or a firm, or even of a collective farm.

Both before and after enclosure, some peasants did well: their crops were heavier and they had more land to till. To provide the extra labour needed then, the farming householder, like the successful craftsman, would extend his working family by taking on young men and women as servants to live with him and work the fields. This he would have to do, even if the land which he was farming was not his own but rented from the great family in the manor house. Sometimes, we have found, he would prefer to send out his own children as servants and bring in other children and young men to do the work. This is one of the few glimpses we can get into the quality of the emotional life of the family at this time, for it shows that parents may have been unwilling to submit children of their own to the discipline of work at home. It meant, too, that servants were not simply the perquisites of wealth and position. A quarter, or a third, of all the families in the country contained servants in Stuart times, and this meant that very humble people had them as well as the titled and the wealthy. Most of the servants, moreover, male or female, in the great house and in the small, were engaged in working the land.

The boys and the men would do the ploughing, hedging, carting and the heavy, skilled work of the harvest. The women and the girls would keep the house, prepare the meals, make the butter and the cheese, the bread and the beer, and would also look after the cattle and take the fruit to market. At harvest-time, from June to October, every hand was occupied and every back was bent. These were the decisive months for the whole population in our damp northern climate, with its one harvest in a season and reliance on one or two standard crops. So critical was the winning of the grain for bread that the first rule of gentility (a gentleman never worked with his hands for his living) might be abrogated. . . .

The factory won its victory by outproducing the working family, taking away the market for the products of hand-labour and cutting prices to the point where the craftsman had either to starve or take a job under factory discipline himself. It was no sudden, complete and final triumph, for the seamstresses were working in the garrets right up to the twentieth century, and the horrors of sweated labour which so alarmed our grandfathers took place amongst the out-workers, not on the factory floor. It was not a transformation which affected only commerce, industry and the town, for the handwork of the cottages disappeared entirely, till, by the year 1920, rural England was an agrarian remnant, an almost lifeless shell. The process was not English alone, at any points in its development, and its effects on the Continent of Europe were in some ways more obviously devastating than ever they were amongst our people. But ours was the society which first ventured into the industrial era, and English men and women were the first who had to try to find a home for themselves in a world where family and household seemed to have no place.

But Marx and the historians who have followed him were surely wrong to call this process by the simple name of the triumph of capitalism, the rise and victory of the bourgeoisie. The presence of capital, we have seen, was the very circumstance which made it possible in earlier times for the working family to preserve its independence both on the land and in the cities, linking together the scattered households of the workers in such a way that no one had to make the daily double journey from home to workshop, from suburb to office and factory. Capitalism, however defined, did not begin at the time when the working household was endangered by the beginnings of the factory system, and economic inequality was not the product of the social transformation which so quickly followed after. Though the enormous, insolent wealth of the new commercial and industrial fortunes emphasized the iniquity of the division between rich and poor, it is doubtful whether Victorian England was any worse in this respect than the England of the Tudors and the Stuarts. It was not the fact of capitalism alone, not simply the concentration of the means of production in the hands of the few and the reduction of the rest to a position of dependence which opened wide the social gulf, though the writers of the eighteenth and nineteenth centuries give us ample evidence that this was observed and was resented—by the dispossessed peasantry in England especially. More important, it is suggested, far more likely a source for the feeling that there is a world which once we all possessed, a world now passed away, is the fact of the transformation of the family life of everyone which industrialism brought with it.

In the vague and difficult verbiage of our own generation, we can say that the removal of the economic functions from the patriarchal family at the point of industrialization created a mass society. It turned the people who worked into a mass of undifferentiated equals, working in a factory or scattered between the factories and mines, bereft forever of the feeling that work, a family affair, carried with it. The Marxist historical sociology presents this as the growth of class consciousness amongst the proletariat, and this is an important historical truth. But because it belongs with the large-scale class model for all social change it can also be misleading, as we shall hope to show. Moreover it has tended to divert attention from the structural function of the family in the preindustrial world, and made impossible up till now a proper, informed contrast between our world and the lost world we have to analyze. . . .

European society is of the patriarchal type, and with some variations, of which the feudal went the furthest, it remained patriarchal in its institutions right up to the coming of the factories, the offices and the rest. European patriarchalism, we may notice, was of a rather surprising kind, for it was marked by the independence of the nuclear family, man, wife and children, not by the extended family of relatives living together in a group of several generations under the same patriarchal head. Yet society was patriarchal, nevertheless, right up to the time of industrial transformation: it can now no longer be said to be patriarchal at all, except vestigially and in its emotional predisposition. The time has now come to divide our European past in a simpler way with industrialization as the point of critical change.

The word alienation is part of the cant of the mid-twentieth century and it began as an attempt to describe the separation of the worker from his world of work. We need not accept all that this expression has come to convey in order to recognize that it does point to something vital to us all in relation to our past. Time was when the whole of life went forward in the family, in a circle of loved, familiar faces, known and fondled objects, all to human size. That time has gone forever. It makes us very different from our ancestors. . . .

In every one of the village communities too, the families of craftsmen, labourers and paupers tended to be smaller than the families of yeomen, and those of the gentry to be largest. The traffic in children from the humbler to the more successful families shows up in the relative numbers in the various groups. Poverty, in our day, or, at least, in the very recent past, was associated with large numbers of children, but . . . in the seventeenth century exactly the reverse was true. The richer you were, the more children you had in your household. In [the village of Goodnestone] in 1676, the gentry with children had an average of 3.5 in their families, the yeomen 2.9, the tradesmen 2.3, the labourers 2.1 and the paupers 1.8.

These figures from Goodnestone are too good to be true and it is common enough to find humble families with many children at home, too many for the meager resources of the wage-earner and a promise of destitution for his widow if he should die too soon. Nevertheless, the association of few children with modest position and resources is almost as marked a feature of social structure in the traditional world as the association of smaller families generally with the poor. It was not simply a matter of the poor offering up their children to the rich as servants; they probably also had fewer children born to them, and of those which were born, fewer survived. It is likely that works on the expectation of life and size of the biological family will confirm what early impressions seem to show, which is that poor men and their wives could not expect to live together long enough to have as many offspring as the rich. This loss of potential labour-power was a matter of consequence, for it always must be remembered that the actual work on most of the plots of land was done by the working family, the man, his wife and children.

At harvest-time, of course, there was a difference: the individual farming family could no longer cope with the work. From the making of the hay in June until the winning of the corn and pease in late September, every able-bodied person in the village community was at work on everyone's land. How much cooperation there was is difficult to say, but when the crisis of the agricultural year came round, right up to the time of mechanized farming, the village acted as a community. When all was in, there was harvest home.

> It is usual, in most places, after they get all the pease pulled or the last grain down, to invite all the workfolks and their wives (that helped them that harvest) to supper, and then they have puddings, bacon, or boiled beef, flesh or apple pies, and then cream brought in platters, and every one a spoon; then after all they have hot cakes and ale; for they bake cakes and send for ale against that time: some will cut their cake and put it into the cream, and this feast is called cream-pot, or cream-kit; for on the morning that they get all done the workfolks will ask their dames if they have good store of cream and say they must have the cream-kit anon.

This was the Yorkshire custom in the 1640s when it was necessary, at harvest-time, to go even beyond the carpenters, the wheelwrights and the millers, in order to bring in the sheaves off the fields. The richer men had to make a home in the barns during harvest for folk, pastoral in their ways, who came down from the wild moor-land. Migration of labour at harvest was common enough in the eighteenth century, but eating and drinking together was a universal characteristic of rural life at all times. Whatever the church-wardens or the overseers of the poor did, when the church-bell was rung in celebration, or the churchyard mowed, there was an entry in the ill-written accounts for ale drunk on the occasion. . . . The meticulous, unpopular Rector of Clayworth in the last quarter of the seventeenth century, entertained the *husbandry* of the two settlements in his parish separately to dinner every year.

When the curate of Goodnestone returned the names of all his parishioners in April, 1676, "according to their families, according to the quality and according to their religion," he did as he was bid and told his lordship, the bishop, how many of them had been to holy communion that Eastertide. Apart from sixteen exceptions every person in the community known by their priest to be qualified for the sacrament had actually taken it at some time during the festival, which fell in that year between March 19th and 26th: 128 people communicated, that is to say, out of a population of 281. Even the defaulters had promised to make amends at Whitsuntide, all but the one family in the village which was nonconformist. But William Wanstall, senior, one of the absentees, was given no such grace; he had been "excluded the Holy

Sacrament for his notorious drunkenness, but since hath promised reformation." Francis Nicholson, the priest-in-charge, was evidently a devoted pastor, for he could give an account of every one of the absentees. Mrs. Elizabeth Richards, the widowed head of one of the households of gentry, was excused as "melancholy," and Barbara Pain since she was "under a dismal calamity, the unnatural death of her husband," who had left her at the head of a yeoman family, three children and two servants.

This . . . draws attention to a feature of the village community and of the whole of the world we have not half-forgotten which has scarcely been mentioned so far. All our ancestors were literal Christian believers, all of the time. Not only zealous priests, such as Francis Nicholson, not only serious-minded laymen, but also the intellectuals and the publicly responsible looked on the Christian religion as the explanation of life, and on religious service as its proper end. Not everyone was equally devout, of course, and it would be simple-minded to suppose that none of these villagers ever had their doubts. Much of their devotion must have been formal, and some of it mere conformity. But their world was a Christian world and their religious activity was spontaneous, not forced on them from above. When Francis Nicholson refused the cup to William Wanstall, in March, 1676, the scores of other people in the church that morning no doubt approved of what he did, as no doubt Wanstall deserved this very public rebuke. When William Sampson, the formidable Rector of Clayworth, did exactly the same thing in April, 1679, to Ralph Meers and Anne Fenton "upon a common fame that they lived and lodged together, not being married," he also had the community behind him. He knew what he was doing too, for Anne Fenton's first baby was christened two months later, only a week or two, presumably, after she had married Ralph Meers.

It has been shown only very recently how it came about that the mass of the English people lost their Christian belief, and how religion came to be a middle-class matter. When the arrival of industry created huge societies of persons in the towns with an entirely different outlook from these Stuart villagers, practically no one went to church, not if he was working class and was left untouched by religious emotion. Christianity was no longer in the social air which everyone breathed together, rich and poor, gentleman, husbandman, artificer, labourer and pauper. So much has been written about the abuses of the clergy, in earlier times, so much about the controversies and doubts, about the revivals, especially the Wesleyan revival, that the religious attitude of common folk has been lost sight of. Perhaps the twelve labourers who lived at Goodnestone in 1767 did not know very clearly what Our Lord's Supper meant, and perhaps they felt that it would displease Squire Hales if they stayed away, but every single one of them took communion. Their descendants in the slums of London in the 1830s, '40s and '50s did not do so: they already looked on Christianity as belonging to the rural world which they had lost. It was something for their employers, something for the respectable, which, perhaps, they might go in for if ever they attained respectability and comfort. This was not true of the hard-working, needy, half-starved labourers of pre-industrial times.

From *The Sadler Report*

Minutes of Evidence
Jovis, 12 die Aprilis, 1832

In the early 1830s, the British Parliament commissioned an official study to investigate factory working conditions. The following is an excerpt from the thousands of pages of testimony that were collected and later published as The Sadler Report. *This investigation ultimately led to some of the first government labor reforms in history, limiting working hours and improving worker safety.*

Michael Thomas Sadler, Esquire in the chair.
William Cooper called in; and Examined.

What is your business?—I follow the cloth-dressing at present.

What is your age?—I was eight-and-twenty last February.

When did you first begin to working in mills or factories?—When I was about 10 years of age.

With whom did you first work?—At Mr. Benyon's flax mills, in Meadow's lane, Leeds.

What were your usual hours of working?—We began at five, and gave over at nine; at five o'clock in the morning.

And you gave over at nine o'clock?—At nine at night.

At what distance might you have lived from the mill?—About a mile and a half.

At what time had you to get up in the morning to attend to your labour?—I had to be up soon after four o'clock.

Every morning?—Every morning.

What intermissions had you for meals?—When we began at five in the morning. We went on until noon, and then we had 40 minutes for dinner.

Had you no time for breakfast?—No, we got it as we could, while we were working.

Had you any time for an afternoon refreshment, or what is called in Yorkshire your "drinking"?—No; when we began at noon, we went till night; there was only one stoppage, the 40 minutes for dinner.

Then as you had to get your breakfast, and what is called "drinking" in that manner, you had to put it on one side?—Yes, we had to put it on one side; and when we got our frames doffed, we ate two or three mouthfuls, and then put it by again.

Is there not considerable dust in a flax mill?—A flax mill is very dusty indeed.

Was not your food therefore frequently spoiled?—Yes, at times with the dust; sometimes we could not eat it, when it had got a lot of dust on.

What were you when you were ten years old?—What is called a bobbin-doffer; when the frames are quite full, we have to doff them.

Then as you lived so far from home, you took your dinner to the mill?—We took all our meals with us, living so far off.

During the 40 minutes which you were allowed for dinner, had you ever to employ that time in your turn in cleaning the machinery?—At times we had to stop to clean the machinery, and then we got our dinner as well as we could; they paid us for that.

At these times you had no resting at all?—No.

How much had you for cleaning the machinery?—I cannot exactly say what they gave us, as I never took any notice of it.

Did you ever work even later than the time you have mentioned?—I cannot say that I worked later there. I had a sister who worked upstairs, and she worked till 11 at night, in what they call the card-room.

At what time in the morning did she begin to work?—At the same time as myself.

And they kept her there till 11 at night?—Till 11 at night.

You say that your sister was in the card-room?—Yes.

Is not that a very dusty department?—Yes, very dusty indeed.

She had to be at the mill at five, and was kept at work till eleven at night?—Yes.

During the whole time she was there?—During the whole time; there was only 40 minutes allowed at dinner out of that.

To keep you at your work for such a length of time, and especially toward the termination of such a day's labour as that, what means were taken to keep you awake and attentive?—They strapped us at times, when we were not quite ready to be doffing the frame when it was full.

Were you frequently strapped?—At times we were frequently strapped.

What sort of strap was it?—About this length [*describing it*].

What was it made of?—Of leather.

Were you occasionally very considerably hurt with the strap?—Sometimes it hurt us very much, and sometimes they did not lay on so hard as they did at others.

Were the girls strapped in that sort of way?—They did not strap what they called the grown-up women.

Were any of the female children strapped?—Yes; they were strapped in the same way as the lesser boys.

What were your wages at 10 years old at Mr. Benyon's?—I think it was 4 *s.* a week.

When you left Mr. Benyon, to what mill did you then go?—To Mr. Clayton's; that was a flax mill.

What age were you when you went there?—I was at Mr. Benyon's nearly a year and a half.

Then you were eleven years and a half old?—Yes.

What were your hours of work at Mr. Clayton's?—We started at five in the morning, and worked till ten minutes past eight at night.

That is 15 hours and 10 minutes?—Yes; and we had only 40 minutes out of that for dinner.

You assembled at five in the morning?—From five in the morning until ten minutes past eight at night.

Had you any time allowed for breakfast or drinking at that mill?—No, it was just the same as the other, with only 40 minutes for dinner.

So that, in point of fact, you had to be attending to your work on your legs for that length of time, with the short intermission of 40 minutes?—Yes, we had to get our meals as we could get them, all out our dinner.

Were your punishments the same in that mill as in the other?—Yes, they used the strap the same there.

How long did you work in that mill?—Five years.

And how did it agree with your health?—I was sometimes well, and sometimes not very well.

Did it affect your breathing at all?—Yes, sometimes we were stuffed.

When your hours were so long, you had not any time to attend to a day-school?—We had no time to go to a day-school, only to a Sunday-school; and then with working such long hours we wanted to have a bit of rest, so that I slept till the afternoon, sometimes till dinner, and sometimes after.

Did you attend a place of worship?—I should have gone to a place of worship many times, but I was in the habit of falling asleep, and that kept me away; I did not like to go for fear of being asleep.

Do you mean that you could not prevent yourself from falling asleep, in consequence of the fatigue of the preceding week?—Yes.

Did you work in any other flax mill?—In no other flax mill.

Did you afterwards work in a woollen mill?—I worked in what they call a cloth-dressing mill.

In whose mill did you next work?—I went to Mr. Pearson's.

What were your hours there?—I think it was from six to eight.

What time was allowed there for meals?—Half an hour for breakfast, an hour at dinner, and half an hour at drinking.

That was 12 hours at the woollen mill?—Yes.

When you left that mill, where did you go to next?—I went to Mr. Wilks's, in Meadow's-lane; that is a cloth mill.

Were your hours the same there?—No; there were short hours there.

Did you find the short hours working suit your health better?—It did a great deal better with me.

Where did you go to then?—To Mr. Giles, in Bowman-lane; that is a cloth mill.

What hours did you work there?—From six to eight, and from six to nine.

With the same intermissions?—Yes, with the same intermissions.

What was the next mill you worked at?—Then I went to Mr. Chorley's.

Were your hours the same there?—Not quite so long there; they were from six to seven.

With the same intervals for meals?—Yes.

You have already stated that your health was better when the labour was shorter?—It was a deal better when only working these hours.

Where did you go then?—To Mr. James Brown's.

What were you at Mr. James Brown's?—I was a gigger and a boiler.

When did you go there?—I should think I must be about 20 years of age when I went there.

Were you a gigger and a boiler when you first went to Mr. Brown's?—I was a gigger when I went to Mr. Brown's; I was a boiler a good while after.

State what was your usual work when you were only a gigger.—When I was only a gigger I went at five o'clock on a Monday morning, and had half an hour at breakfast and an hour at dinner, and half an hour at drinking; then went on till nine on Monday evening, and stopped half an hour; then went on to twelve at midnight, and stopped an hour; then went on to half-past four on Tuesday morning, and stopped half an hour; then went on again from five to eight, and stopped half an hour; then went on till twelve, and stopped an hour; then went on again from one to five, and stopped half an hour; then went on again to nine o'clock at night, when we went home.

What did you do on the Wednesday?—Went again at five o'clock in the morning.

What time did you close at night?—At nine.

What did you do on the Thursday?—Went again on Thursday morning at five, and returned at nine at night. On Friday morning we went at five; worked all Friday, Friday night, and till Saturday evening at five, with the same time for meals as before.

When you became a boiler, will you state the number of hours you had to labour at the same mill?—When I was a boiler, I began work at one o'clock on the Monday morning; went on till five, and stopped half an hour; then went on to eight, and stopped half an hour; then went on to twelve, and stopped an hour; then went on to five, and stopped half an hour; then went on to nine, and stopped half an hour; then went on to twelve, and stopped an hour; then began again, and went on to half-past four on Tuesday morning, and stopped half an hour; then went on to eight, and stopped half an hour; then went on to twelve, and stopped an hour; then went on to five, and stopped half an hour; then went on to nine, and then gave over on the Tuesday night. On Wednesday morning we went at five, and stopped half an hour at breakfast; then went on to twelve, and stopped an hour; then went on to five, and stopped half an hour; then went on to nine, and then gave over. Thursday was the same as Wednesday. On Friday morning we went at five, and stopped half an hour at breakfast; then we went on to twelve, and stopped an hour; then we went on to five, and stopped half an hour; then we went on to nine, and stopped half an hour; then we went on to twelve at midnight, and stopped an hour; then we went on to half-past four, and stopped half an hour; then we went on to eight, and stopped half an hour; then we went on to twelve, and stopped an hour; then we went on to five o'clock on Saturday night, and gave over.

Then in the whole week you had only four nights' rest, exclusive of Sunday night?—No.

And that rest was after nine o'clock, and before five?—Yes.

As I calculate, you laboured as a boiler 44 hours running, from Monday morning till Tuesday night, having 10 intervals, amounting altogether to only six hours and a half; and never going to bed?—You cannot go to bed.

And 36 hours of labour from Friday morning till you were let loose on Saturday evening, including five hours and an half for meals?—Yes.

On Wednesday and Thursday you had, from five till nine, 16 hours of labour, including meals?—Yes.

Then on Monday and Friday nights you had no rest?—No rest.

What was the effect of this excessive labour upon you?—We all felt unwell, and were stiff, and could not make proper use of our limbs till we had worked a little, when it went off.

Had this a serious effect on your health?—Yes, it had a great deal of effect on our health.

But as to yourself personally?—Yes.

After working at a mill to this excess, how did you find your health at last?—I found it very bad indeed; I found illness coming on me a long time before I fell down.

Did you at length become so ill as to be unable to pursue your work?—I was obliged to give it up entirely.

How long were you ill?—For six months.

Who attended?—Mr. Metcalf and Mr. Freeman.

What were you told by your medical attendants was the reason of your illness?—Nothing but hard labour, and working long hours; and they gave me up, and said no good could be done for me, that I must go into the country.

Did this excessive labour not only weaken you but destroy your appetite?—It destroyed the appetite, and I became so feeble that I could not cross the floor unless I had a stick to go with; I was in great pain, and could find ease in no posture.

You could drink in the meantime, if you could not eat?—Yes, I could drink.

But you found that [did] not improve your health?—No.

Has it been remarked that your excessive labour from early life has greatly diminished your growth?—A number of persons have said that such was the case, and that I was the same as if I had been made of iron or stone.

What height are you?—About five feet. It is that that has hindered me of my growth.

When you were somewhat recovered, did you apply for labour?—I applied for my work again, but the overlooker said I was not fit to work; he was sure of that, and he would not let me have it. I was then obliged to throw myself on the parish.

Have you subsisted on the parish ever since?—Yes.

Have you been always willing and anxious to work?—I was always willing and anxious to work from my infancy.

Have you been on the parish since your severe illness?—Yes.

When did you first begin to receive wages yourself?—Ever since I began to work; I gave them to my parents.

How old were you then?—Ten years.

How soon did you begin to work in your own account and make your own bargain with your master for wages?—I always bargained for my wages ever since I began to work for wages; always; my parents never bargained for me. I always bargained for myself.

Not when you were 10 years old?—Yes.

Do you know anything, of your own knowledge, of the hours of working at present in Mr. Benyon's and Mr. Clayton's flax-mills?—Mr. Clayton's flax-mill is not going; Mr. Benyon's is going, but I do not know what hours they are working now.

Is not trade rather slack in that part of the country just now?—It is very slack at present.

While you were with Mr. Pearson, Mr. Giles and Mr. Chorley, you were in a better state of health?—Yes.

How old were you when you became a boiler in Mr. Brown's mill?—I believe I was about 20 years of age when I went to Mr. Brown.

You said you were a gigger at first?—That is, what I mean, when I became a boiler, I was somewhere about between 25 and 26.

You received 18 *s.* a week wages?—Yes.

Was that the regular wages without the extra hours, or did you receive more than 18 *s.* a week when you worked all these extra hours?—Yes.

How much did you ever receive?—I received 18: *s.* and over-hours, about 26 *s.* or 27 *s.* and sometimes 28 *s.*

At a regular charge of 3 *d.* an hour?—No, at 18 *s.* a week; it is 3-1/2 *d.* for all the hours over.

If you had not wasted these over-hours, you would not have been kept in your employment?—No, I should not have been kept in employ if I had not worked them.

Did not you and others choose to undergo this excessive labor, rather than incur the disgrace of throwing yourselves on the parish?—Yes.

You attended at the mill at five in the morning; was that both winter and summer?—It has been, for two years back, winter and summer, working at Mr. Brown's.

Were you able to be punctual in your attendance at five o'clock?—I was always there at five o'clock; if we were too late they took us off what we call bating; if we were a quarter of an hour too late in the morning they took off a penny.

Are they ever turned away for being too late?—If they are what is called "bad comers," they turn them off and get fresh ones.

Are they ever strapped for being too late?—They did not strap them at the room that I was in.

How did you contrive to be awake so soon in the morning?—My father always used to call me up.

Did he get up so early as that for his own business?—He got up on purpose to call me.

How many hours did he work in a day at his own business?—Sometimes from five in the morning till eight at night.

You say he was a shoemaker?—Yes.

Then, according to this, he worked more hours than you did?—I think not so long.

Did your father take his regular intervals for his meals?—I should think so.

And walked about to market for his family; had he not many pauses in his labour?—He worked at home, and therefore could do as he pleased.

After you worked a month at these long hours, could you not get back into lighter employment?—I do not know whether you could get back or not.

You said that you were about 17 when you first went from the flax-spinning mills into the cloth-mills?—Yes.

Was that before the Act of Parliament made to regulate the hours?—I know nothing about that.

How often did these extra hours come about?—Very often.

Describe to us a period in which you have worked the greatest possible number of hours; how many weeks running have you worked?—I have gone on for a year round.

Working all the Monday night and Friday night?—Yes; always working long hours.

Is your sister older or younger than yourself?—There is a year and a half between us; I am the elder.

Has your health improved since you left off working long hours?—I am a deal better than I was; but I believe that if I could have got work, and have had something to support me, I should have recruited my health better. I have been very poorly kept for these last six months, having been out of work. I have only half a crown a week allowed from the parish for my wife and myself.

When you were working the long hours, were there any people in the same employment, when you were a gigger, for instance, who were working the short hours?—Yes; some mills were working short hours in the same line; there were none in the same room that worked less hours than I did.

[*Joseph Hebergam examined.*] What particular department of the mill had you to attend to?—I attended what are called the throstle machines.

How long did you continue in that mill?—I attended the throstles two years and a half, and then I went to the steam looms for half a year.

Were there many children in that mill?—Yes, I believe there were about fifty, of about the same age that I was.

State to the Committee how this excessive labour agreed with the health of these children so employed?—They were often sick and poorly; there were always, perhaps, half a dozen regularly that were ill.

From excessive labour?—Yes.

Did you consider the work to be hard work?—It was not very hard, but having to work so very many hours made it worse; it was rather hard of itself, but it would have been better if we had not had so long to stand.

Did you not become very drowsy and sleepy towards the end of the day, and feel much fatigued?—Yes; that began about 3 o'clock, and grew worse and worse, and it came to be very bad towards 6 and 7.

And still you had to labour on?—Yes.

What means were taken to keep you at your work so long?—There were three overlookers; there was a head overlooker, and then there was one man kept to grease the machines, and then there was one kept on purpose to strap.

Was the main business of one of the overlookers that of strapping the children up to this excessive labour?—Yes, the same as strapping an old restive horse that has fallen down and will not get up.

Was that the constant practice?—Yes, day by day.

Were there straps regularly provided for that purpose?—Yes, he is continually walking up and down with it in his hand.

And his office is to strap you on to your labour?—Yes.

Do you think the children could be kept so long to labour as you have stated, if they were not so treated?—No, they could not; they are obliged to do it.

Was it not reckoned by the children to be very bad usage, and did they not conceive themselves to be very unfortunate in being subject to such a course of labour as this?—Yes; and towards the end of the day the flies of the machines would burst their knuckles.

Did you meet with frequent accidents?—Yes.

So that you were not capable of performing the labour that was exacted from you without this perpetual cruelty?—No.

Had you any brothers or sisters similarly occupied?—I had at that time a brother and a sister; they called him John, and my sister Charlotte.

What ages were they when they began working at the mills?—I cannot say how old my sister Charlotte was, but my brother John was 7.

How did it suit their health?—It did not suit it at all; they were often sick.

Where is your brother John working now?—He died three years ago.

What age was he when he died?—Sixteen years and eight months.

To what was his death attributed by your mother and the medical attendants?—It was attributed to this, that he died from working such long hours, and that it had been brought on by the factory. They have to stop the flies with their knees, because they go so swift they cannot stop them with their hands; he got a bruise on the shin by a spindle-board, and it went on to that degree that it burst; the surgeon cured that, then he was better; then he went to work again; but when he had worked about two months more his spine became affected, and he died.

Exploitation

E. P. Thompson

E. P. Thompson (1924–1993) was a prominent British historian, socialist leader, and peace advocate. His The Making of the English Working Class *(1963), from which this is an excerpt, has been hailed as a classic work of social history, and is still regarded as an authoritative work on the impact of industrialization on the British class system.*

For most working people the crucial experience of the Industrial Revolution was felt in terms of changes in the nature and intensity of exploitation. Nor is this some anachronistic notion, imposed upon the evidence. We may describe some parts of the exploitive process as they appeared to one remarkable cotton operative in 1818—the year in which Marx was born. The account—an Address to the public of strike-bound Manchester by "A Journeyman Cotton Spinner"—commences by describing the employers and the workers as "two distinct classes of persons":

"First, then, as to the employers: with very few exceptions, they are a set of men who have sprung from the cotton-shop without education or address, except so much as they have acquired by their intercourse with the little world of merchants on the exchange at Manchester; but to counterbalance that deficiency, they give you enough of appearances by an ostentatious display of elegant mansions, equipages, liveries, parks, hunters, hounds, etc., which they take care to shew off to the merchant stranger in the most pompous manner. Indeed their houses are gorgeous palaces, far surpassing in bulk and extent the neat charming retreats you see round London . . . but the chaste observer of the beauties of nature and art combined will observe a woeful deficiency of taste. They bring up their families at the most costly schools, determined to give their offspring a double portion of what they were so deficient in themselves. Thus with scarcely a second idea in their heads, they are literally petty monarchs, absolute and despotic, in their own particular districts; and to support all this, their whole time is occupied in contriving how to get the greatest quantity of work turned off with the least expense. . . . In short, I will venture to say, without fear of contradiction, that there is a greater distance observed between the master there and the spinner, than there is between the first merchant in London and his lowest servant or the lowest artisan. Indeed there is no comparison. I know it to be a fact, that the greater part of the master spinners are anxious to keep wages low for the purpose of keeping the spinners indigent and spiritless . . . as for the purpose of taking the surplus to their own pockets."

"The master spinners are a class of men unlike all other master tradesmen in the kingdom. They are ignorant, proud, and tyrannical. What then must be the men or rather beings who are the instruments of such masters? Why, they have been for a series of years, with their wives and their families, patience itself—bondmen and bondwomen to their duel taskmasters. It is in vain to insult our common understandings with the observation that such men are free; that the law protects the rich and poor alike, and that a spinner can leave his master if he does not like the wages. True; so he can: but where must he go? why to another, to be sure. Well: he goes; he is asked where did you work last: 'Did he discharge you?' No; we could not agree about wages. Well I shall not employ you nor anyone who leaves his master in that manner. Why is this? Because there is an abominable *combination existing amongst the masters*, first established at Stockport in 1802, and it has since become so general, as to embrace all the great masters for a circuit of many miles round Manchester, though not the little masters: they are excluded. They are the most obnoxious beings to the great ones that can be imagined. . . . When the combination first took place, one of their first articles was, that no master should take on a man until he had first ascertained whether his last master had discharged him. What then is the man to do? If he goes to the parish, that grave of all independence, he is there told—We shall not relieve you; if you dispute with your master, and don't support your family, we will send you to prison; so that the man is bound, by a combination of circumstances, to submit to his master. He cannot travel and get work in any town like a shoe-maker, joiner, or taylor; he is confined to the district."

"The workmen in general are an inoffensive, unassuming, set of well-informed men, though how they acquire their information is almost a mystery to me. They are docile and tractable, if not goaded too much; but this is not to be wondered at, when we consider that they are trained to work from six years old from five in a morning to eight and nine at night. Let one of the advocates for obedience to his master take his stand in an avenue leading to a factory a little before five o'clock in the morning, and observe the squalid appearance of the little infants and their parents taken from their beds at so early an hour in all kinds of weather; let him examine the miserable pittance of food, chiefly composed of water gruel and oatcake broken into it, a little salt, and sometimes colored with a little milk, together with a few potatoes, and a bit of bacon or fat for dinner; would a London mechanic eat this? There they are, (and if late a few minutes, a quarter of a day is stopped in wages) locked up until night in rooms heated above the hottest days we have had this summer, and allowed no time, except three-quarters of an hour at dinner in the whole day: whatever they eat at any other time must be as they are at work. The negro slave in the West Indies, if he works under a scorching sun, has probably a little breeze of air sometimes to fan him: he has a space of ground, and time allowed to cultivate it. The English spinner slave has no enjoyment of the open atmosphere and breezes of heaven. Locked up in factories eight stories high, he has no relaxation till the ponderous engine stops, and then he goes home to get refreshed for the next day; no time for sweet association with his family; they are all alike fatigued and exhausted. This is no over-drawn picture: it is literally true. I ask again, would the mechanics in the South of England submit to this?"

"When the spinning of cotton was in its infancy, and before those terrible machines for superseding the necessity of human labour, called steam engines, came into use, there were a great number of what were then called *little masters*; men who with a small capital, could procure a few machines, and employ a few hands, men and boys (say to twenty or thirty), the produce of whose labour was all taken to Manchester central mart, and put into the hands of brokers. . . . The brokers sold it to the merchants, by which means the master spinner was enabled to stay at home and work and attend to his workmen. The cotton was then always given out in its raw state from the bale to the wives of the spinners at home, when they heat and cleansed it ready for the spinners in the factory. By this they could earn eight, ten, or twelve shillings a week, and cook and attend to their families. But none are thus employed now; for all the cotton is broke up by a machine, turned by the steam engine, called a devil: so that the spinners' wives have no employment, except they go to work in the factory all day at what can be done by children for a few shillings, four or five per week. If a man then could not agree with his master, he left him, and could get employed elsewhere. A few years, however, changed the face of things. Steam engines came into use, to purchase which, and to erect buildings sufficient to contain them and six or seven hundred hands, required a great capital. The engine power produced a more marketable (though not a better) article than the little master could at the same price. The consequence was their ruin in a short time; and the overgrown capitalists triumphed in their fall; for they were the only obstacle that stood between them and the complete control of the workmen."

"Various disputes then originated between the workmen and masters as to the fineness of the work, the workmen being paid according to the number of hanks or yards of thread he produce from a given quantity of cotton, which was always to be proved by the overlooker, whose interest made it imperative on him to lean to his master, and call the material coarser than it was. If the workman would not submit *he must summon his employer before a magistrate*; the whole of the acting magistrates in that district, with the exception of two worthy clergymen, being gentlemen who have sprung from the *same* source with the master cotton spinners. The employer generally contented himself with sending his overlooker to answer any such summons, thinking it beneath him to meet his servant. The magistrate's decision was generally in favour of the master, though on the statement of the overlooker only. The workman dared not appeal to the sessions on account of the expense . . ."

"These evils to the men have arisen from that dreadful monopoly which exists in those districts where wealth and power are got into the hands of the few, who, in the pride of their hearts, think themselves the lords of the universe."[1]

This reading of the facts, in its remarkable cogency, is as much an *ex parte* statement as is the "political economy" of Lord Brougham. But the "Journeyman Cotton Spinner" was describing facts of a different order. We need not concern ourselves with the soundness of all his judgements. What his address does is to itemize one after another the grievances felt by working people as to changes in the character of capitalist exploitation: the rise of a master-class without traditional authority or obligations: the growing distance between master and man: the transparency of the exploitation at the source of their new wealth and power: the loss of status and above all of independence for the worker, his reduction to total dependence on the master's instruments of production: the partiality of the law: the disruption of the traditional family economy: the discipline, monotony, hours and conditions of work: loss of leisure and amenities: the reduction of the man to the status of an "instrument."

That working people felt these grievances at all—and felt them passionately—is itself a sufficient fact to merit our attention. And it reminds us forcibly that some of the most bitter conflicts of these years turned on issues which are not encompassed by cost-of-living series. The issues which provoked the most intensity of feeling were very often ones in which such values as traditional customs, "justice," "independence," security, or family-economy were at stake, rather than straight-forward bread-and-butter issues. The early years of the 1830s are aflame with agitations which turned on issues in which wages were of secondary importance; by the potters, against the Truck System; by the textile workers, for the 10-Hour Bill; by the building workers, for cooperative direct action; by all groups of workers, for the right to join trade unions. The great strike in the north-east coalfield in 1831 turned on security of employment, "tommy shops," child labour.

The exploitive relationship is more than the sum of grievances and mutual antagonisms. It is a relationship which can be seen to take distinct forms in different historical contexts, forms which are related to corresponding forms of ownership and State power. The classic exploitive relationship of the Industrial Revolution is depersonalized, in the sense that no lingering obligations of mutuality—of paternalism or deference, or of the interests of "the Trade"—are admitted. There is no whisper of the "just" price, or of a wage justified in relation to social or moral sanctions, as opposed to the operation of free market forces. Antagonism is accepted as intrinsic to the relations of production. Managerial or supervisory functions demand the repression of all attributes except those which further the expropriation of the maximum surplus value from labour. This is the political economy which Marx anatomized in *Das Kapital*. The worker has become an "instrument," or an entry among other items of cost.

In fact, no complex industrial enterprise could be conducted according to such a philosophy. The need for industrial peace, for a stable labour-force, and for a body of skilled and experienced workers, necessitated the modification of managerial techniques—and, indeed, the growth of new forms of paternalism—in the cotton-mills by the 1830s. But in the overstocked outwork industries, where there was always a sufficiency of unorganized "hands" competing for employment, these considerations did not operate. Here, as old customs were eroded, and old paternalism was set aside, the exploitive relationship emerged supreme. . . .

These larger considerations have been, for some years, overlaid by the academic exercise (through which all students must march and counter-march) known as the "standard-of-living controversy." Did the living standards of the bulk of the people rise or fall between 1780 and 1830—or 1800 and 1850?[2]. . .

In fact, so far as the period 1790–1830 goes, there is very little in it. The condition of the majority was bad in 1790: it remained bad in 1830 (and forty years is a long time) but there is some disagreement as to the size of the relative groups within the working class. And matters are little clearer in the next decade. There were undoubted increases in real wages among organized workers during the burst of trade union activity between 1832–4: but the period of good trade between 1833 and 1837 was accompanied by the smashing of the trade unions by the concerted efforts of

Government, magistrates, and employers; while 1837–42 are depression years. So that it is indeed at "some unspecified date between the drafting of the People's Charter and the Great Exhibition" that the tide begins to turn; let us say, with the railway boom in 1843. Moreover, even in the mid-40s the plight of very large groups of workers remains desperate, while the railway crash led to the depression years of 1847–8. This does not look very much like a "success story"; in half a century of the fullest development of industrialism, the standard-of-living still remained—for very large but indeterminate groups—at the point of subsistence. . . .

The controversy falls into two parts. There is, first, the very real difficulty of constructing wage-series, price-series, and statistical indices from the abundant but patchy evidence. We shall examine some of the difficulties in interpreting such evidence when we come to the artisans. But at this point a further series of difficulties begins, since the term standard leads us from date amenable to statistical measurement (wages or articles of consumption) to those satisfactions which are sometimes described by statisticians as "imponderables." From food we are led to homes, from homes to health, from health to family life, and thence to leisure, work-discipline, education and play, intensity of labour, and so on. From standard-of-life we pass to way-of-life. But the two are not the same. The first is a measurement of quantities: the second a description (and sometimes an evaluation) of qualities. Where statistical evidence is appropriate to the first, we must rely largely upon "literary evidence" as to the second. A major source of confusion arises from the drawing of conclusions as to one from evidence appropriate only to the other. It is at times as if statisticians have been arguing: "the indices reveal an increased *per capita* consumption of tea, sugar, meat and soap, *therefore* the working class was happier," while social historians have replied: "the literary sources show that people were unhappy, *therefore* their standard-of-living must have deteriorated."

This is to simplify. But simple points must be made. It is quite possible for statistical averages and human experiences to run in opposite directions. A *per capita* increase in quantitative factors may take place at the same time as a great qualitative disturbance in people's way of life, traditional relationships, and sanctions. People may consume more goods and become less happy or less free at the same time. Next to the agricultural workers the largest single group of working people during the whole period of the Industrial Revolution were the domestic servants. Very many of them were household servants, living-in with the employing family, sharing cramped quarters, working excessive hours, for a few shillings' reward. Nevertheless, we may confidently list them among the more favoured groups whose standards (or consumption of food and dress) improved on average slightly during the Industrial Revolution. But the handloom weaver and his wife, on the edge of starvation, still regarded their status as being superior to that of "flunkey." Or again, we might cite those trades, such as coal-mining, in which real wages advanced between 1790 and 1840, but at the cost of longer hours and a greater intensity of labour, so that the breadwinner was "worn out" before the age of forty. In statistical terms, this reveals an upward curve. To the families concerned it might feel like immiseration.

Thus it is perfectly possible to maintain two propositions which, on a casual view, appear to be contradictory. Over the period 1790–1840 there was a slight improvement in average material standards. Over the same period there was intensified exploitation, greater insecurity, and increasing human misery. By 1840 most people were "better off" than their forerunners had been fifty years before, but they had suffered and continued to suffer this slight improvement as a catastrophic experience.

Notes

1. *Black Dwarf*, 30 September 1818.
2. The futility of one part of this discussion is shown by the fact that if different datum-lines are taken, different answers may come up. 1780–1830 favours the "pessimists"; 1800–1850 favours the "optimists."

Classical Liberalism and the Bourgeois State

Kathleen Callanan Martin

Writing in 1911, prominent English liberal L.T. Hobhouse proclaimed that liberalism is "saturated with the conviction that the unfettered action of the individual is the mainspring of all progress."[1] This is the underlying principle uniting a set of apparently diverse political and economic ideas that began to evolve in the eighteenth century and became the most influential ideology in the Western world during much of the nineteenth: the fervent belief that "The more the individual receives free scope for the play of his faculties, the more rapidly will society as a whole advance."[2] This ideology, which differs in significant ways from the liberalism known to Americans in the twentieth-first century, is customarily called **Classical Liberalism**.

Europe in the late seventeenth century was a significantly different culture from medieval Europe, and many of the changes that had taken place raised the status of the individual as opposed to the group. Protestant theology emphasized the responsibility of the individual for his own salvation, while the breakdown of manorial agriculture and then of the guild system increasingly made each man an independent economic actor as well. The Scientific Revolution of the seventeenth century had offered dramatic proof that man could use his faculties to understand the world around him and thereby gain more control over it. If Newton could understand the movement of heavenly bodies and Harvey the circulation of blood, might not mankind be able to solve the riddles of human interaction and find optimal ways to govern its affairs? The great thinkers of the Enlightenment certainly thought that this was possible, and they tried to lead the way. Most important of all, perhaps, was the Enlightenment's optimistic view of human nature. A political philosopher who sees man as a hopeless sinner, or as person likely to behave as badly as he can, will believe that it takes a very strong and vigilant government to prevent crimes, lawlessness, and even general chaos. Man must be closely governed for his own good. A political philosopher who sees man as inclined to good behavior, or at least not inclined to bad behavior, can imagine a world in which government can often leave people alone without dire consequences. This view of government — the liberal view—is one that the Enlightenment made possible.

A New View of Government

The most important contributors to liberal political thought agreed with each other in all of the most fundamental matters. Each had his own contributions to make, but their differences were largely differences of emphasis, rather than of basis premises. **John Locke** (1632-1704) advanced the idea that government can only be based on the consent of the governed, must protect the rights of the individual, and should be so organized as to divide power among several branches, rather than concentrating it in one person or institution, which would inevitably lead to abuse. His political writings, in particular his *Second Treatise of Civil Government*, built upon the experience of the English Civil War and Interregnum to advocate a constitutional monarchy responsible to a representative government. It is important to keep in mind that representative government and democracy are not the same thing. Democracy means, "rule by the people." In a democracy, every citizen would be entitled to have a voice in every decision. This would be extremely cumbersome in a large country, probably impossible. **Representative government** is not democracy; it is a system in which citizens elect legislators to represent them in making decisions. Locke was certainly no democrat. He expressly disapproved of democracy, not only for practical reasons, but because he felt that only people with a fair amount of property should take part in government.[3] Locke, in fact, placed a great deal of emphasis on property as the most important right that government must protect, along with freedom of worship, publication, and speech. He looked forward to a world in which social and economic progress would result from the energies of free people, unfettered by arbitrary government. His ideas had a tremendous influence on European political thought, and that influence was undoubtedly increased by the success of the American Revolution, whose founding documents everywhere reflect Locke's influence.

The French political thinkers Montesquieu and Tocqueville further developed these ideas of liberty and representative government. Both of them were born into aristocratic families, but they preferred limited representative government in the English tradition to the absolutist monarchy of France. Certainly they shared Locke's concern for property rights and freedom of opinion. In his most famous work, *The Spirit of the Laws* (1748), **Montesquieu** made a strong case for constitutional government based on the idea of the **separation of powers**, the deliberate division of governmental powers among several bodies so as to prevent too much power from falling into the hands of any one person or institution, thus threatening liberty. (This is why the US Constitution provides for executive, legislative, and judicial branches.) While Locke had assumed the virtues of this arrangement, which was characteristic of the British government tradition, Montesquieu made a strong theoretical argument for its importance in any type of government seriously committed to the preservation of freedom. **Alexis de Tocqueville** vehemently agreed with this idea but was concerned that representative government was no guarantee of freedom for the individual, even with carefully separated powers. Like Locke, he felt that it would be inappropriate for uneducated men of no property to be involved in government, and he worried that too much emphasis on equality might be a threat to liberty.

Democracy in America, published in two volumes in the 1830s, is a chronicle of Tocqueville's travels in the newly formed United States and his reactions to his experiences there. He admired much of what he saw, but he felt that too much democracy inhibited, rather than advanced, liberty. "I know of no country," he wrote, "in which there is so little independence of mind and real freedom of discussion as in America."[4] This was due to what he called "the **tyranny of the majority**" — the force of public opinion in a polity where sovereignty rests with the people. While in the unreformed absolutist regimes of continental Europe it was a repressive government that inhibited freedom of thought and speech, in egalitarian America unwillingness to be different from one's fellows had the same effect, possibly to a greater degree. In any system of government, therefore, there must be some kind of limit to what can be demanded from the citizen if freedom is to be preserved. "Unlimited power is in itself a bad and dangerous thing. Human beings are not competent to exercise it with discretion."[5] The logic of Tocqueville's argument suggests that government must be limited by some kind of inviolable guarantee of individual rights, one of the most fundamental political concepts in the liberal tradition. It also suggests that quick decisions based on outbursts of vehement public opinion should always be suspect in a society that values the rights of the individual. Democracy and freedom, in this view, are somewhat incompatible.

Another influential source of ideas on social improvement somewhat at odds with the Lockean tradition came from the great English eccentric **Jeremy Bentham** (1748-1832), who founded the school of thought known as **Utilitarianism**. A perfect exemplar of Enlightenment skepticism, he was by nature disinclined to adhere to any idea or practice simply because of its antiquity. Utility means usefulness. In Bentham's view, only policies that work well and are conducive to human progress and happiness are useful, and therefore worth pursuing. While he shared the reluctance of Locke to coerce people or to tell them what to think, Bentham tended to stress the public good, rather than individual rights, in his social thought. The best way to assess the desirability of any given policy or law was to assess its utility: it must be workable in practice and must give the most possible benefit to the greatest possible number of people. Otherwise it was an unjustified intrusion on the activities of individuals and probably would not achieve its purpose.

These, then, are the most important political ideas of Classical Liberalism: it sought reform in the interests of limited, constitutional government that is representative in nature and respects the rights of the individual, guarding against abusive office holders as well as against "the tyranny of the majority" in order to secure the public welfare in the least coercive way possible.

With the success of the American and French Revolutions, the political ideas of Classical Liberalism came to be more and more widely discussed by educated Europeans. People who felt oppressed by the old order came to hope (as people who felt attached to the old order came to fear) that liberal reforms were the wave of the future, that they would inevitably sweep across Europe bringing progress (or mob rule) to even the least Enlightened areas. Among the strongest supporters of Classical Liberalism were members of the bourgeoisie, professionals and businessmen who had no political role in the absolutist monarchies and who wanted recognition of their rights to think, worship, and conduct business as they saw fit, free from the restrictions of censorship, established religion, and mercantilist economic regulation.

Political Economy

The fundamental economic ideas of Classical Liberalism derive, for the most part, from the work of **Adam Smith** (1723-90). Smith, too, shared the optimistic Enlightenment view that mankind could use reason to understand and improve the world. Just as Newton had changed the way educated Europeans thought of the solar system, postulating that it was a self-regulating mechanism rather than an unfathomable mystery, Smith intended to show that there were natural laws dictating the action of the economy as well. Understanding those laws, and acting in accordance with them, could yield a higher standard of living than unnecessary and inefficient mercantilist interference in the economy could ever provide. Like liberal political ideas, Smith's preferred economic policies are designed to set the individual free to achieve what he can in life, unencumbered by unnecessary government supervision or regulation. In *The Wealth of Nations*, published in the very year of the American Revolution (1776), Smith extolled the virtues of a market economy in which economic activity is motivated by individual self-interest and regulated, not by the government, but by competition. In such an economy the natural ebb and flow of market forces will determine outcomes, as self-interested individuals do what seems best in the pursuit of profit. This freedom would not, Smith argued, benefit greedy individuals at the expense of the society as a whole. "Every individual is continually exerting himself to find out the most advantageous employment for whatever capital he can command. It is his own advantage, indeed, and not that of the society, which he has in view. But the study of his own advantage naturally, or rather necessarily, leads him to prefer that employment which is most advantageous to the society."[6] The impartial forces of the market reconcile all interests.

Much of Smith's great book is a protest against what he saw as the arbitrariness, economic ignorance, and general ineffectiveness of mercantilist economic policies. Smith did not deny that governments should care about the economic wellbeing of their people. He merely asserted that mercantilist policies did more harm than good. Protected monopolies did not provide consumers with the best goods at the best prices; they shielded incompetence and actually raised prices, since firms with no competition can charge whatever they like for their products. Why shield domestic producers from competition with foreign producers who make a better or cheaper product? Why not let people follow their own inclination to make money and let competition sort out the rest?

As Smith wrote, England was in the early stages of industrialization. The entrepreneurs who were driving this process were frustrated by government rules and regulations that they saw as burdensome, and indignant at the privileged status of licensed traders like the British East India Company, who enjoyed the sole right to import goods from South and East Asia into Britain. For obvious reasons, they found Smith's ideas very appealing. (In assessing the popularity of these ideas, it is important to bear in mind that Britain was the first country to industrialize and therefore was in a very strong position to compete with its trade rivals. Classical Liberalism was always more popular in the English-speaking world than elsewhere, and with good reason.) As the business sector of the British economy grew, more and more people came to favor Adam Smith's preferred policy of **free trade** unencumbered by taxes, monopolies, or restrictions on imports and exports. This "system of perfect liberty," as Smith called it, would stimulate economic growth and deliver the best goods at the best prices for consumers, while allowing individual businessmen and consumers to do as they pleased.[7] Manufacturers campaigned in particular against the so-called Corn Laws, which aimed to protect British farmers by placing a tariff on imported grain, thus keeping the price of bread artificially high. The manufacturers were acting, as good disciples of Smith, in their own self-interest rather than out of concern for the poor, since it is not possible to pay workers less than the cost of survival. High bread prices necessarily meant high wages. The repeal of the Corn Laws by Parliament in 1846 represented a significant victory for liberal economic thought.

As more and more parts of Europe came under the sway of market economies, and as the tide of industrialization swept across Europe and North America, the economic ideas of Classical Liberalism gained more adherents among businessmen and professionals outside Britain. Just as the success of the American and French Revolutions seemed to make a good case for political liberalism, the growing economic success of Britain and the United States seemed to make a good case for economic liberalism. Like liberal political thought, liberal economic thought offered members of the bourgeoisie more freedom from governmental restraint and an enhanced position in society as the agents of progress. They could make a new, better world for everyone (and considerable profits for themselves) if only the government would stand back and let them do it.

Smith's description of free trade as the "system of perfect liberty" highlights the close connection between the political and economic ideas of Classical Liberalism. They work very well together and form a coherent ideology because they all place a strong emphasis on the freedom of the individual to do whatever he feels is in his own best interests. In political terms, this means representative government and respect for individual rights. In economic terms it means a policy of ***laissez-faire***, or of leaving people alone to pursue their own self-interest. Both sets of ideas imply that the best government is the least government; government should intervene in the activities of the individual only when there is a compelling public reason to do so.

This insistence that the government had best leave well enough alone and keep its hands off the economy became axiomatic in the emerging discipline of Political Economy, as economics was called in the early period of its existence. Adam Smith is rightfully known as the father of economics, but the political economists who followed his lead made their own contributions to this school of thought. **David Ricardo** (1772-1823) argued that since the division of labor and specialization yield higher productivity, international specialization should be seen as desirable, not as a source of anxiety about foreign competition. In Britain, for example, the climate would make production of oranges or tea prohibitively expensive; in the production of these commodities Spain and China have a **comparative advantage** over the British. On the other hand, industrializing Britain could now produce large quantities of cotton cloth much cheaper than either Spain or China because of the capital investments that British firms had made in new technology. Why not let each country's economy do what it does best? This idea, of course, greatly enhanced the perceived advantages of free trade. **Thomas Malthus** (1766-1834) is best known for his *Essay on the Principle of Population*, which asserted that population will always expand to use (and overtax) the resources available. On this basis Malthus argued that attempts by the state to help the poor were, while well intended, counterproductive, because by helping the poor to survive they encouraged the growth of population. Only so much food could be produced; beyond this limit, starvation would result. Even if this were not true, as more people chased the same number of jobs, market forces would cause wages to decline, making the lot of the poor worse rather than better. Therefore liberals opposed relief for the poor on principle.

The logic of Classical Liberalism (and arguably the economic self-interest of its adherents as well) prompted nineteenth-century liberals to take many political positions that come as a surprise to contemporary Americans accustomed to contemporary American liberalism. In the nineteenth century, liberals vehemently opposed legislation intended to reform the appalling working conditions of the early factories. They fought hard against the legalization of labor unions, prohibition of child labor, attempts to shorten the very long work day, and efforts to make factory work less dangerous, all in the name of *laissez-faire*. These laws would inhibit freedom of contract between the employer and the employee, they argued, unjustifiably interfere with the economy, and put manufacturers at a disadvantage relative to their foreign competitors. On the same grounds they opposed slum clearance, building codes, and regulation of the purity of food and drugs. For most of the nineteenth century, British liberals opposed campaigns to widen the franchise, giving the vote to more than the small minority of propertied people (all of them male) who were eligible to vote at the start of the century. Because they shared Tocqueville's fear of mob rule, and because they knew that factory employees were less enthusiastic about the supremacy of *laissez-faire* policies than their employers were, liberals favored restricting the right to vote to men of property. It is for these reasons that it was always the Conservatives, rather than the Liberals, who granted successive enlargements of the British parliamentary franchise, and that the first establishment of health insurance and unemployment compensation in Europe came in distinctly conservative Germany rather than in liberal Britain.

John Stuart Mill

The harmony of the political and economic ideas of Classical Liberalism is most evident in the person of economist and political philosopher John Stuart Mill, undoubtedly its most eloquent spokesman. **John Stuart Mill** (1806-73) was the son of Jeremy Bentham's friend and disciple James Mill and, as a child, knew Bentham personally. Well educated at home by his demanding father, Mill undoubtedly read more widely and thought more penetratingly than most men of his or any other time. After a nervous breakdown early in life, Mill carefully re-examined all of his most cherished views and was never inclined to take any idea on authority or by custom. (Unlike most of his contemporary male liberals, for example, Mill argued forcefully for the right of women to be accepted as full adults and given the vote. Otherwise sympathetic observers attributed this eccentric view to his marriage to feminist Harriet Taylor.) For the ideas that did pass his intense scrutiny he was an ardent and effective advocate. In his *Principles of Political Economy* (1848) he clearly explained the concepts of *laissez-faire* economics, making a strong case for this approach to economic policy as the foundation of liberty itself, relying as it does on the achievements and energies of the unrestrained individual. *On Liberty* (1859) still ranks today as the finest argument ever made for allowing the fullest possible personal freedom to each and every individual. Infringing on the natural right of the individual to worship as he wishes, to read, say, and publish whatever he likes, and in general to do whatever he wants to do cannot be tolerated, Mill says, on grounds of unpopularity, perceived immorality, or even of possible harm to the individual himself. (In this last instance, of course, Mill permits exceptions for children and the insane, but only for them. Man has a right to risk harm to himself if he wishes to do so.) Only harm to others can make a valid excuse for encroachments on liberty. True to his Utilitarian upbringing, Mill does not rest his case on the natural rights of the individual alone. Society itself, he argues, is better off if all ideas can be heard and discussed, whether they are right or wrong. The greatest good of the greatest number demands the free play of the marketplace of ideas. In the end, the best ideas will triumph, provided people have sufficient practice in sifting through the available arguments so as to find the ones that legitimately convince. Even bad ideas and falsehoods, therefore, have utility and must be tolerated. "That mankind are not infallible; that their truths, for the most part, are only half-truths; that unity of opinion, unless resulting from the fullest and freest comparison of opposite opinions, is not desirable, and diversity not an evil, but a good, until mankind are much more capable than at present of recognizing all sides of the truth, are principles applicable to men's modes of action, not less than to their opinions."[8]

Clearly Mill did take seriously the idea of the tyranny of the majority. He argued that toleration of unpopular, even obnoxious opinion is essential to a free society and that its absence indicates a society that does not value freedom sufficiently. But he had faith in education and the free flow of ideas to create a safe climate for full participation by the many, rather than merely by the few. Liberty and democracy, perhaps, need not be at odds after all.

At the mid-point of the nineteenth century, the political and economic ideas of Classical Liberalism seemed to a growing number of people, particularly to middle-class people in Europe and America, to be an inevitable force that would bring progress to the entire world. Hobhouse summarized this vision superbly when he described liberalism as "a movement of liberation, a clearance of obstructions, an opening of channels for the flow of free spontaneous vital activity."[9] Yet by the end of the century Classical Liberalism was an ideology under siege. Even some of its most ardent supporters, Mill included, had begun to wonder if freedom without substantial equality is truly possible, since the poor must take whatever terms the rich choose to offer them. Capitalism, it seemed, was surpassingly good at production, but at distribution it seemed considerably less successful. To the right, the growing forces of militant nationalism opposed liberal views, to the left, the growing forces of socialist and communist movements. Even in Britain, the land of its birth, by the start of World War I the standard of the future appeared to many to have passed into other hands.

References and Suggested Readings:

Briggs, Asa. *Victorian People: A Reassessment of Persons and Themes 1851-1867.* Chicago: University of Chicago Press, 1970.

Heilbroner, Robert L. *The Worldly Philosophers: The Lives, Times and Ideas of the Great Economic Thinkers.* New York: Touchstone, 1999.

Hobhouse, L.T. *Liberalism.* London: Oxford University Press, [1911] 1964.

Mill, John Stuart. *On Liberty.* [1859]

—*The Subjection of Women.* [1869]

— *Utilitarianism.* [1861]

Smith, Adam. *The Wealth of Nations.* [1776]

Tocqueville, Alexis de. *Democracy in America.* 2 vols. [1835, 1840]

Notes

1. L.T. Hobhouse, *Liberalism* (London: Oxford University Press, [1911] 1964), p. 44.

2. Ibid., p. 34.

3. Christopher Hill, *The Century of Revolution* 1603-1714 (New York: W.W. Norton & Co., 1980), p. 255.

4. Alexis de Tocqueville, *Democracy in America* (New York: Alfred A. Knopf, Inc., [1835] 1945), p. 273. In any standard edition of this work, the discussion of the "tyranny of the majority" is to be found in Volume I, Chapter XVI.

5. Tocqueville, p. 270.

6. Adam Smith, *The Wealth of Nations* (New York: Bantam Dell, [1776] 2003), p. 569-70. In any full edition, this discussion is to be found in Book IV, Chapter II.

7. Smith, p. 770. In any full edition, this can be found in Book IV, Chapter VII, Part III.

8. John Stuart Mill, *The Basic Writings of John Stuart Mill: On Liberty, The Subjection of Women and Utilitarianism* (New York: Classic Books of America, [1859] 2009), p. 62-3. This passage comes from *On Liberty*, Chapter 3.

9. Hobhouse, p. 28

On Liberty

John Stuart Mill

Mill's On Liberty *(1859) is perhaps the most influential and persuasive explication of the principles of Classical Liberalism. His impassioned arguments concerning the extent and limitations of individual freedom, and the importance of free expression, are still considered essential components of most modern democratic governments.*

Chapter I: Introductory

. . . The struggle between Liberty and Authority is the most conspicuous feature in the portions of history with which we are earliest familiar, particularly in that of Greece, Rome, and England. But in old times this contest was between subjects, or some classes of subjects, and the Government. By liberty was meant protection against the tyranny of the political rulers. The rulers were conceived (except in some of the popular governments of Greece) as in a necessarily antagonistic position to the people whom they ruled. . . .

A time, however, came in the progress of human affairs when men ceased to think it a necessity of nature that their governors should be an independent power, opposed in interest to themselves. It appeared to them much better that the various magistrates of the State should be their tenants or delegates, revocable at their pleasure. In that way alone, it seemed, could they have complete security that the powers of government would never be abused to their disadvantage. By degrees this new demand for elective and temporary rulers became the prominent object of the exertions of the popular party, wherever any such party existed; and superseded to a considerable extent, the previous efforts to limit the power of rulers. As the struggle proceeded for making the ruling power emanate from the periodical choice of the ruled, some persons began to think that too much importance had been attached to the limitation of the power itself. That (it might seem) was a resource against rulers whose interests were habitually opposed to those of the people. What was now wanted was, that the rulers should be identified with the people; that their interest and will should be in the interest and will of the nation. The nation did not need to be protected against its own will. There was no fear of its tyrannizing over itself. Let the rulers be effectually responsible to it, promptly removable by it, and it could afford to trust them with power of which it could itself dictate the use to be made. Their power was but the nation's own power, concentrated, and in a form convenient for exercise. This mode of thought, or rather perhaps of feeling, was common among the last generation of European Liberalism, in the Continental section of which it still apparently predominates. Those who admit any limit to what a government may do, except in the case of such governments as they think ought not to exist, stand out as brilliant exceptions among the political thinkers of the Continent. A similar tone of sentiment might by this time have been prevalent in our own country, if the circumstances which for a time encouraged it had continued unaltered.

But, in political and philosophical theories, as well as in persons, success discloses faults and infirmities which failure might have concealed from observation. The notion, that the people have no need to limit their power over themselves, might seem axiomatic when popular government was a thing only dreamed about, or read of as having existed at some distant period of the past. Neither was that notion necessarily disturbed by such temporary aberrations as those of the French Revolution, the worst of which were the work of an usurping few, and which, in any case, belonged not to the permanent working of popular institutions, but to a sudden and convulsive outbreak against monarchical and aristocratic despotism. In time, however, a democratic republic came to occupy a large portion of the earth's surface, and made itself felt as one of the most powerful members of the community of nations; and elective and responsible government became subject to the observations and criticisms which wait upon a great existing fact. It was now perceived that such phrases as "self-government," and "the power of the people over themselves," do not express the true state of the case. The "people" who exercise the power are not always the same people with those over whom it is exercised; and the "self-government" spoken of is not the government of each by himself, but of each by all the rest. The will of the people, moreover, practically means the will of the most numerous or the most active part of the people; the majority, or those who succeed in making themselves accepted as the majority; the people, consequently, may desire to oppress a part of their number, and precautions are as much needed against any other abuse of power. The limitation, therefore, of the power of government over individuals loses none of its importance when the holders of power are regularly accountable to the community, that is, to the strongest party therein. This view of things, recommending itself equally to the intelligence of thinkers and to the inclination of those important classes in European society to whose real or supposed interests democracy is adverse, has had no difficulty in establishing itself; and in political speculations "the tyranny of the majority" is now generally included among the evils against which society requires to be on its guard. . . .

Chapter II: Of the Liberty of Thought and Discussion

The time, it is to be hoped, is gone by, when any defense would be necessary of the "liberty of the press" as one of the securities against corrupt or tyrannical government. No argument, we may suppose, can now be needed, against permitting a legislature or an executive, not identified in interest with the people, to prescribe opinions to them, and determine what doctrines or what arguments, they shall be allowed to hear . . . Let us suppose, therefore, that the government is entirely at one with the people, and never thinks of exerting any power of coercion unless in agreement with what it conceives to be their voice. But I deny the right of the people to exercise such coercion, either by themselves or by their government. The power itself is illegitimate. The best government has no more title to it than the worst. It is as noxious, or more noxious, when exerted in accordance with public opinion, than when in opposition to it. If all mankind minus one, were of one opinion, and only one person were of the contrary opinion, mankind would be no more justified in silencing that one person, than he, if he had the power, would be justified in silencing mankind. Were an opinion a personal possession of no value except to the owner; if to be obstructed in the enjoyment of it were simply a private injury, it would make some difference whether the injury was inflicted only on a few persons or on many. But the peculiar evil of silencing the expression of an opinion is that it is robbing the human race; posterity as well as the existing generation; those who dissent from the opinion, still more than those who hold it. If the opinion is right, they are deprived of the opportunity of exchanging error for truth: if wrong, they lose, what is almost as great a benefit, the clearer perception and livelier impression of truth, produced by its collision with error.

It is necessary to consider separately these two hypotheses, each of which has a distinct branch of the argument corresponding to it. We can never be sure that the opinion we are endeavoring to stifle is false opinion; and if we were sure, stifling it would be an evil still . . .

We have recognized the necessity to the mental well-being of mankind (on which all their other well-being depends) of freedom of opinion, and freedom of the expression of opinion, on four distinct grounds; which we will now briefly recapitulate.

First, if any opinion is compelled to silence, that opinion may, for aught we can certainly know, be true. To deny this is to assume our own infallibility.

Secondly, though the silenced opinion be an error, it may, and very commonly does, contain a portion of truth; and since the general or prevailing opinion on any subject is rarely or never the whole truth, it is only by the collision of adverse opinions that the remainder of the truth has any chance of being supplied.

Thirdly, even if the received opinion be not only true, but the whole truth; unless it is suffered to be, and actually is, vigorously and earnestly contested, it will, by most of those who receive it, be held in the manner of a prejudice, with little comprehension or feeling of its rational grounds. And not only this, but, fourthly, the meaning of the doctrine itself will be in danger of being lost, or enfeebled, and deprived of its vital effect on the character and conduct: the dogma becoming a mere formal profession, inefficacious for good, but cumbering the ground, and preventing the growth of any real and heartfelt conviction, from reason or personal experience . . .

Chapter III: Of Individuality, As One of the Elements of Well Being

Such being the reasons which make it imperative that human beings should be free to form opinions, and to express their opinions without reserve; and such the baneful consequences to the intellectual, and through that to the moral nature of man, unless this liberty is either conceded, or asserted in spite of prohibition; let us next examine whether the same reasons do not require that men should be free to act upon their opinions—to carry these out in their lives, without hindrance, either physical or moral, from their fellow men, so long as it is at their own risk and peril. This last proviso is, of course, indispensable. No one pretends that actions should be as free as opinions. On the contrary, even opinions lose their immunity, when the circumstances in which they are expressed are such as to constitute their expression a positive instigation to some mischievous act. An opinion that corn dealers are starvers of the poor, or that private property is robbery, ought to be unmolested when simply circulated through the press, but may justly incur punishment when delivered orally to an excited mob assembled before the house of a corn dealer, or when handed about among the same mob in the form of a placard. Acts, of whatever kind, which, without justifiable cause, do harm to others, may be, and in the more important cases absolutely require to be, controlled by the unfavorable sentiments, and, when needful, by the active interference of mankind. The liberty of the individual must be thus far limited; he must not make himself a nuisance to other people. But if he refrains from molesting others in what concerns them, and merely acts according to his own inclination and judgment in things which concern himself, the same reasons which show that opinion should be free, prove also that he should be allowed, without molestation, to carry his opinions into practice at his own cost. That mankind are not infallible; that their truths, for the most part, are only half-truths; that opposite opinions, are not desirable, and diversity not an evil, but a good, until mankind are much more capable than at present of recognizing all sides of the truth, are principles applicable to men's modes of action, not less than to their opinions. As it is useful that while mankind are imperfect there should be different opinions, so is it that there should be different experiments of living; that free scope should be given varieties of character, short of injury to others; and that the worth of different modes of life should be proved practically, when any one thinks fit to try them. It is desirable, in short, that in things which do not primarily concern others, individuality should assert itself. Where, not the person's own character, but the traditions or customs of other people are the rule of conduct, there is wanting one of the principal ingredients of human happiness, and quite the chief ingredient of individual and social progress . . . No one's idea of excellence in conduct is that people should do absolutely nothing but copy one another. No one would assert that people ought not to put into their mode of life, and into the conduct of their concerns, any impress whatever of their own judgment, or of their own individual character. On the other hand, it would be absurd to pretend that people ought to live as if nothing whatever had been known in the world before they came into it; as if experience had as yet done nothing towards showing that one mode of existence, or of conduct, is preferable to another. Nobody denies that people should be so taught and trained in youth, as to know and benefit by the ascertained results of human experience. But it is the privilege and proper condition of a human being, arrived at the maturity of his faculties, to use and interpret experience in his own way. It is for him to find out what part of recorded experience is properly applicable to his own circumstances and character. The traditions and customs of other people are, to certain extent, evidence of what their experience has taught them; presumptive evidence, and as such, have a claim to his deference; but, in the first place, their experience may be too narrow; or they may not have interpreted it rightly. Secondly, their interpretation of experience may be correct, but unsuitable to him. Customs are made for customary circumstances, and customary characters; and his circumstances or his character may be uncustomary. Thirdly, though the customs be both good as customs, and suitable to him, yet to conform to custom, merely as custom, does not educate or develop in him any of the qualities which are the distinctive endowment of a human being. The human faculties of perception, judgment, discriminative feeling, mental activity, and even moral preference, are exercised only in making a choice. He who does anything because it is the custom, makes no choice. He gains no practice either in discerning or in desiring what is best. The mental and moral, like the muscular powers, are improved only by being used. The faculties are called into no exercise by doing a thing merely because others do it, no more than by believing a thing only because others believe it. If the groups of opinion are not conclusive to the person's own reason, his reason cannot be strengthened, but is likely to be weakened, by his adopting it: and if the inducements to an act are not such as are consentaneous to his own feelings and character (where affection, or the rights of others, are not concerned) it is so much done towards rendering his feelings and character inert and torpid, instead of active and energetic . . .

Chapter V: Applications

. . . I offer not so much applications as specimens of application; which may serve to bring into greater clearness the meaning and limits of the two maxims which together form the entire doctrine of the Essay, and to assist the judgment in holding the balance between them, in the cases where it appears doubtful which of them is applicable to the case.

The maxims are, first, that the individual is not accountable to society for his actions, in so far as these concern the interests of no person but himself. Advice, instruction, persuasion, and avoidance by other people of thought necessary by them for their own good, are the only measures by which society can justifiably express its dislike or disapprobation of his conduct. Secondly, that for such actions as are prejudicial to the interests of others, the individual is accountable, and may be subjected either to social or to legal punishment, if society is of opinion that the one or the other is requisite for its protection.

In the first place, it must by no means be supposed, because damage, or probability of damage, to the interests of others, can alone justify the interference of society, that therefore it always does justify such interference. In many cases, an individual, in pursuing a legitimate object, necessarily and therefore legitimately causes pain or loss to others, or intercepts a good which they have a reasonable hope of obtaining. Such oppositions of interest between individuals often arise from bad social institutions, but are unavoidable while those institutions last; and some would be unavoidable under any institutions. Whoever succeeds in an over-crowded profession, or in a competitive examination; whoever is preferred to another in any contest for an object which both desire, reaps benefit from the loss of others, from their wasted exertion and their disappointment. But it is, by common admission, better for the general interest of mankind, that persons should pursue their objects undeterred by this sort of consequence. In other words, society admits no right, either legal or moral, in the disappointed competitors, to immunity from this kind of suffering; and feels called on to interfere, only when means of success have been employed which it is contrary to the general interest to permit—namely, fraud or treachery, and force.

Again, trade is a social act. Whoever undertakes to sell any description of goods to the public, does what affects the interest of other persons, and of society in general; and thus his conduct, in principle comes within the jurisdiction of society: accordingly, it was once held to be the duty of governments, in all cases which were considered of importance, to fix prices, and regulate the processes of manufacture. But it is now recognized, though not till after a long struggle, that both the cheapness and the good quality of commodities are most effectually provided for by leaving the producers and sellers perfectly free, under the sole check of equal freedom to the buyers for supplying themselves elsewhere. This is the so-called doctrine of Free Trade, which rests on grounds different from, though equally solid with, the principle of individual liberty asserted in this essay. Restrictions on trade, or on production for purposes of trade, are indeed restraints; and all restraint, *quo* restraint, is an evil: but the restraints in question affect only the part of conduct which society is competent to restrain, and are wrong solely because they do not really produce the results which it is desired to produce by them. . . . It is one of the undisputed functions of government to take precautions against crime before it has been committed, as well as to detect and punish it afterwards. The preventive function of government, however, is far more liable to be abused, to the prejudice of liberty, than the punitory function; for there is hardly any part of the legitimate freedom of action of a human being which would not admit of being represented, and fairly too, as increasing the facilities for some form or other of delinquency. Nevertheless, if a public authority, or even a private person, sees anyone evidently preparing to commit a crime, they are not bound to look on inactive until the crime is committed, but may interfere to prevent it. If poisons were never bought or used for any purpose except the commission of murder it would be right to prohibit their manufacture and sale. They may, however, be wanted not only for innocent but for useful purposes, and restrictions cannot be imposed in the one case without operating in the other. Again, it is a proper office of public authority to guard against accidents. If either a public officer or anyone else saw a person attempting to cross a bridge which had been ascertained to be unsafe, and there were no time to warn him of his danger, they might seize him and turn him back, without any real infringement of his liberty; for liberty consists in doing what one desires, and he does not desire to fall into the river. Nevertheless, when there is not a certainty, but only a danger of mischief, no one but the person himself can judge of the sufficiency of the motive which may prompt him to incur the risk: in this case, therefore (unless he is a child, or delirious, or in some state of excitement or absorption incompatible with the full use of the reflecting faculty), he ought, I conceive, to be only warned of the danger; not forcibly prevented from exposing himself to it. . . .

The right inherent in society to ward off crimes against itself by antecedent precautions, suggests the obvious limitations to the maxim, that purely self-regarding misconduct cannot properly be meddled with in the way of prevention or punishment. Drunkenness, for example, in ordinary cases, is not a fit subject for legislative interference; but I should deem it perfectly legitimate that a person who had once been convicted of any act of violence to others under the influence of drink, should be placed under a special legal restriction, personal to himself; that if he were afterwards found drunk, he should be liable to a penalty, and that if when in that state he committed another offense, the punishment to which he would be liable for that other offense should be increased in severity. The making himself drunk, in a person whom drunkenness excites to do harm to others, is a crime against others. So, again, idleness, except in a person receiving support from the public, or except when it constitutes a breach of contract, cannot without tyranny be made a subject of legal punishment; but if, either from idleness or from any other avoidable cause, a man fails to perform his legal duties to others, as for instance to support his children, it is no tyranny to force him to fulfill that obligation, by compulsory labour, if no other means are available. . . .

I have already observed that, owing to the absence of any recognized general principles, liberty is often granted where it should be withheld, as well as withheld where it should be granted; and one of the cases in which, in the modern European world the sentiment of liberty is the strongest, is a case where, in my view, it is altogether misplaced. A person should be free to do as he likes in his own concerns; but he ought not to be free to do as he likes in acting for another, under the pretext that the affairs of the other are his own affairs. The State, while it respects the liberty of each in what specially regards himself, is bound to maintain a vigilant control over his exercise of any power which it allows him to possess over others. This obligation is almost entirely disregarded in the case of the family relations, a case, in its direct influence on human happiness, more important than all others taken together. The almost despotic power of husbands over wives need not be enlarged upon here, because nothing more is needed for the complete removal of the veil, than that wives should have the same rights, and should receive the protection of law in the same manner, as all other persons; and because, on this subject, the defenders of established injustice do not avail themselves of the plea of liberty, but stand forth openly as the champions of power. It is in the case of children, that misapplied notions of liberty are a real obstacle to the fulfillment by the State of its duties. One would almost think that a man's children were supposed to be literally, and not metaphorically, a part of himself, so jealous is opinion of the smallest interference of law with his absolute and exclusive control over them; more jealous than of almost any interference with his own freedom of action; so much less do the generality of mankind value liberty than power. Consider, for example, the case of education. Is it not almost a self-evident axiom, that the State should require and compel the education, up to a certain standard, of every human being who is born its citizen? Yet who is there that is not afraid to recognize and assert this truth? Hardly any one indeed will deny that it is one of the most sacred duties of the parents (or, as law and usage now stand, the father), after summoning a human being into the world, to give to that being an education fitting him to perform his part well in life towards others and towards himself. But while this is unanimously declared to be the father's duty, scarcely anybody, in this country, will bear to hear of obliging him to perform it. Instead of his being required to make any exertion or sacrifice for securing education to the child, it is left to his choice to accept it or not when it is provided *gratis!* It still remains unrecognized that to bring a child into existence without a fair prospect of being able, not only to provide food for its body, but instruction and training for its mind, is a moral crime, both against the unfortunate offspring and against society; and that if the parent does not fulfill this obligation, the State ought to see it fulfilled, at the charge, as far as possible, of the parent. . . .

It is not a matter of education only, that misplaced notions of liberty prevent moral obligations on the part of parents from being recognized, and legal obligations from being imposed, where there are the strongest grounds for the former always, and in many cases for the latter also. The fact itself, of causing the existence of a human being, is one of the most responsible actions in the range of human life. To undertake this responsibility—to bestow a life which may be either a curse or a blessing—unless the being on whom it is to be bestowed will have at least the ordinary chances of a desirable existence, is a crime against that being. And in a country either over-peopled, or threatened with being so, to produce children, beyond a very small number, with the effect of reducing the regard of labour by their competition, is a serious offense against all who live by the remuneration of their labour. The laws which, in many countries on the Continent, forbid marriage unless the parties can show that they have the means of supporting a family, do not exceed the legitimate powers of the State: and whether such laws be expedient or not (a question mainly dependent on local circumstances and feelings), they are not objectionable as violations of liberty. Such laws are interferences of the State to prohibit a mischievous act—an act injurious to others, which ought to be a subject of reprobation, and social stigma, even when it is not deemed expedient to superadd legal punishment. Yet the current ideas of liberty, which bend so easily to real infringements of the freedom of the individual in things which concern only himself, would repel the attempt to put any restraint upon his inclinations when the consequence of their indulgence is a life or lives of wretchedness and depravity to the offspring, with manifold evils to those sufficiently within reach to be in any way affected by their actions. When we compare the strange respect of mankind for liberty, with their strange want of respect for it, we might imagine that a man had an indispensable right to do harm to others, and no right at all to please himself without giving pain to anyone.

I have reserved for the last place a large class of questions respecting the limits of government interference, which, though closely connected with the subject of this Essay, do not, in strictness, belong to it. These are cases in which the reasons against interference do not turn upon the principle of liberty; the question is not about restraining the actions of individuals, but about helping them; it is asked whether the government should do, or cause to be done, something for their benefit, instead of leaving it to be done by themselves, individually or in voluntary combination.

The objections to government interference, when it is not such as to involve infringement of liberty, may be of three kinds.

The first is, when the thing to be done is likely to be better done by individuals than by the government. Speaking generally, there is no one so fit to conduct any business, or to determine how or by whom it shall be conducted, as those who are personally interested in it. This principle condemns the interferences, once so common, of the legislature, or the officers of government, with the ordinary processes of industry. But this part of the subject has been sufficiently enlarged upon by political economists, and is not particularly related to the principles of this Essay.

The second objection is more nearly allied to our subject. In many cases, though individuals may not do the particular thing so well, on the average, as the officers of government, it is nevertheless desirable that it should be done by them rather than by the government, as a means to their own mental education—a mode of strengthening their active faculties, exercising their judgment, and giving them a familiar knowledge of the subjects with which they are thus left to deal. This is a principal, though not the sole, recommendation of jury trial (in cases not political); of free and popular local and municipal institutions; of the conduct of industrial and philanthropic enterprises by voluntary associations. These are not questions of liberty, and are connected with that subject only by remote tendencies; but they are questions of development. It belongs to a different occasion from the present to dwell on these things as parts of national education; as being, in truth, the peculiar training of a citizen, the practical part of the political education of a free people, taking them out of the narrow circle of personal and family selfishness, and accustoming them to the comprehension of joint interests, the management of joint concerns—habituating them to act from public or semi-public motives, and guide their conduct by aims which unite instead of isolating them from one another. Without these habits and powers, a free constitution can neither be worked nor preserved; as is exemplified by the too-often transitory nature of political freedom in countries where it does not rest upon a sufficient basis of local liberties. The management of purely local business by the localities, and of the great enterprises of industry by the union of those who voluntarily supply the pecuniary means, is further recommended by all the advantages which have been set forth in this Essay as belonging to individuality of development, and diversity of modes of action. Government operations tend to be everywhere alike. With individuals and voluntary associations, on the contrary, there are varied experiments, and endless diversity of experience. What the State can usefully do is make itself a central depository, and active circulator and diffuser, of the experience resulting from many trials. Its business is to enable each experimentalist to benefit by the experiments of others, instead of tolerating no experiments but its own.

The third and most cogent reason for restricting the interferences of government, is the great evil of adding unnecessarily to its power. Every function superadded to those already exercised by the government causes its influence over hopes and fears to be more widely diffused, and converts, more and more, the active and ambitious part of the public into hangers-on of the government, or of some part which aims at becoming the government. If the roads, the railways, the banks, the insurance offices, the great joint-stock companies, the universities, and the public charities, were all of them branches of the government; if, in addition, the municipal corporations and local boards, with all that now devolves on them, became departments of the central administration; if the employees of all these different enterprises were appointed and paid by the government, and looked to the government for every rise in life; not all the freedom of the press and popular constitution of the legislature would make this or any other country free otherwise than in name. And the evil would be greater, the more efficiently and scientifically the administrative machinery was constructed—the more skillful the arrangements for obtaining the best qualified hands and heads with which to work it.

If every part of the business of society which required organized concert, or large and comprehensive views, were in the hands of the government, and if government offices were universally filled by the ablest men, all the enlarged culture and practiced intelligence in the country, except the purely speculative, would be concentrated in a numerous bureaucracy, to whom alone the rest of the community would look for all things: the multitude for direction and dictation in all they had to do; the able and aspiring for personal advancement. To be admitted into the ranks of this bureaucracy, and when admitted, to rise therein, would be the sole objects of ambition. Under this regime, not only is the outside public ill-qualified, for want of practical experience, to criticize or check the mode of operation of the bureaucracy, but even if the accidents of despotic or the natural working of popular institutions occasionally raise to the summit a ruler or rulers of reforming inclinations, no reform can be effected which is contrary to the interest of the bureaucracy. Such is the melancholy condition of the Russian empire, as shown in the accounts of those who have had sufficient opportunity of observation. The Czar himself is powerless against the bureaucratic body; he can send any one of them to Siberia, but he cannot govern without them, or against their will. On every decree of his they have a tacit veto, by merely refraining from carrying it into effect. In countries of more advanced civilization and of a more insurrectionary spirit, the public, accustomed to expect everything to be done for them by the State, or at least to do nothing for themselves without asking from the State not only leave to do it, but even how it is to be done, naturally hold the State responsible for all evil which befalls them, and when the evil exceeds their amount of patience, they rise against the government, and make what is called a revolution; whereupon somebody else, with or without legitimate authority from the nation, vaults into the seat, issues his orders to the bureaucracy, and everything goes on much as it did before; the bureaucracy being unchanged, and nobody else being capable of taking their place. . . .

Karl Marx and the Socialist Response to Capitalism

Kathleen Callanan Martin

As the Industrial Revolution and the ideas of liberalism spread out across Europe during the early nineteenth century, not everyone was happy about the changes that ensued. Landed aristocrats and members of the upper clergy, of course, were concerned about the possible loss of the privileges they enjoyed under the old order. For many working people, too, the tide of change was worrisome. Cities began to grow quickly and haphazardly as workers streamed in from the countryside looking for jobs; the inhabitants of their overcrowded, disease-ridden slums endured a truly miserable (and often short) existence. Conditions were no better at work, as people worked extremely long hours under dangerous conditions for very low pay and lost their jobs abruptly during downturns in trade. The abolition of guild privileges may have been good for the growth of the economy in the long run, but in the short run it was experienced as a disaster by craftsmen who lost their independence, status, and sometimes their comfortable standard of living as well.[1] And of course liberals, with their fervent belief in *laissez-faire* and minimal government, actively opposed laws intended to ameliorate any of these problems. To them it seemed obvious that a system of political liberty and a self-regulating economy would yield the most progress in the end. To many workers, who could not meet the property requirements for the vote and who desperately needed improvement in their living and working conditions, this seemed like an alliance of the propertied against the defenseless workers. They were attracted, therefore, to the growing body of ideas called socialism.

Socialism is not a single doctrine that is easy to define. Since its origin in the early nineteenth century, many people with very different ideas have called themselves socialists. The movement is based on the political ideas of the Enlightenment. For most socialists, the most important of these ideas were the equality of all men and the potential to solve human problems by the application of reason. They valued cooperation over individualism, but they did not deny the value of the individual; they argued that each individual must be given an opportunity to develop to the best of his potential — clearly not a likely outcome for a malnourished, illiterate child living in a pestilential slum. Surely, they argued, an increasingly enlightened and wealthy society can do better. Over time socialists have proposed a wide variety of means to this end, including government ownership, worker control, or collective regulation of some or all industries.[2]

Not surprisingly, in early nineteenth-century Europe the center of the socialist movement was the revolutionary city of Paris. But the ideas of socialism were widespread and tended to become increasingly popular in any given country as it began to industrialize. This popularity was given a substantial push in the year 1848, when Paris once again became the scene of a revolution, and a revolutionary wave seemed to be spreading across Europe.

A number of factors contributed to the wave of rebellions and revolutions that occurred in Europe in 1848, and the combination of them differed from one area to the next. Several consecutive years of bad harvests had raised the price of food considerably or, in some cases, caused severe famine. (The Irish Potato Famine is the most famous of these disasters; it caused the death by starvation of about a million Irish and sent even more across the seas to North America and Australia.) Combined with a business recession that swelled the ranks of the unemployed, this caused tremendous hardship to the poor. Many urban artisans were desperate to reverse the erosion of their status and income under the pressure of industrialization. Many middle-class professionals wanted political liberties of the kind enjoyed by their counterparts in Britain. In some areas, particularly in yet-to-be-unified Italy and Germany and in portions of the Habsburg Empire, nationalism also played a significant role in popular unrest. In various combinations, these issues fed the chain reaction of rebellion once the news of revolutionary Paris began to spread. Over the course of the year the **Revolutions of 1848** affected most of Europe: Paris, Vienna, Prague, Hungary, the Papal States, Palermo and Naples, Munich, Berlin, Frankfurt, and many other areas. Even relatively stable and liberal Britain experienced, not a revolution, but a significant increase in popular protest against working conditions and agitation for extension of the right to vote to more people. While most of these revolutionary movements were in the end put down, often with great violence followed by an increase in repression of dissident views, for a time it looked like a mighty and irresistible tide of change was sweeping across Europe. And it was in the excitement of this moment that socialists Karl Marx and Friedrich Engels published their best-known book, *The Communist Manifesto.*

Karl Marx: the Man and the Ideas

Karl Marx was born in the city of Trier in the Rhineland in 1818, shortly after the Napoleonic occupation had brought revolutionary new ideas to this prosperous area of Germany. His father, an enthusiastic liberal and a respected lawyer who raised his son on the classic works of the Enlightenment, had converted to Protestantism to avoid the legal inequalities imposed on Jews. Like many fathers, he wanted his son to follow in his footsteps, so Karl Marx studied law at the University of Berlin. It was there that he encountered the philosophy of Hegel, very much in vogue in German intellectual circles of the day, and changed his focus from law to philosophy. He received his Ph.D. in philosophy from the University of Jena in 1841. But by the time his dissertation was accepted Marx's growing concerns about the social issues of the day had become stronger than his interest in teaching philosophy. "The philosophers have only interpreted the world in various ways;" he wrote in his *Theses on Feuerbach*; "the point, however, is to change it."[3]

Thus began Marx's career as a crusading radical journalist and editor, during which the legal authorities of several countries suppressed his publications and ejected him from the country on short notice. Marx and his family were in turn expelled from Paris, Brussels, and Cologne. In each place he made the acquaintance of the local socialists and other radicals and familiarized himself with their ideas. And in each place the legal authorities took a very dim view of the newspaper or journal in which these views were expressed, deeming it a threat to the *status quo*. During these years Marx made quite a few enemies and several friends, the most important of whom was his closest friend, **Friedrich Engels** (1820–95).

Engels, too, was German, the son of a very prosperous cotton textile manufacturer. His pious father, a Protestant evangelical, was displeased by his son's attraction to frivolous pursuits like dueling, poetry, and radical politics at the university. The remedy for this was to be immersion in the family business; after a period of training Engels assumed management of the Manchester branch of his father's firm. This gave Engels a very comfortable income but did not cure him of his interest in radical causes. In fact he used his early years in Manchester as the basis for research on the living and working conditions of factory workers in this mushrooming city. His book *The Condition of the Working Class in England*, published in 1844, paints a disturbing picture of life in the city's teeming slums and smoky factories. Marx very much admired this book; it helped to seal a friendship based on shared interests and ideas about the state of Europe in the early industrial age. Intellectually, Marx was very much the greater of the two, as Engels freely acknowledged, but Engels provided Marx with useful feedback in the development of his ideas and a much-needed supplement to his income, especially after Marx settled in England in 1849. When, in the heady days of the Revolutions of 1848, a small radical group calling themselves the Communist League wanted to publish a pamphlet of revolutionary goals, they entrusted the task of composing this to Karl Marx and Friedrich Engels.

Probably because of the atmosphere of the time, *The Communist Manifesto* strikes a far more militant tone than most of Marx's later writings. Subsequent Communist revolutions in Russia and China have caused many people to pay most attention to the vision of "the specter of Communism" said to be haunting Europe in the *Manifesto*'s opening pages. But even more influential, in the long run, has been Marx's analysis of history and of capitalism, of which this is the earliest coherent statement. True to his Hegelian roots, Marx saw the flow of history as a series of pitched battles between diametrically opposed forces. For Hegel these forces were contending ideas. For Marx, a thorough **materialist**, the opposed forces are classes whose economic interests are in conflict. "The history of all hitherto existing society," the *Manifesto* proclaims, "is the history of class struggles."[4] In any given era there is an exploiting class, which owns the means of production, and an exploited class, which does not. The resulting class struggle is the engine of historical change. The struggle between the feudal aristocracy and the rising middle class, for example, brought about the French Revolution and the beginnings of the modern era. In turn, according to Marx, the contemporary struggle between the triumphant bourgeoisie and the industrial proletariat they have called into existence to work in their factories will in the end inevitably destroy the liberal capitalist order and usher in the era of communism, in which the means of production will be collectively owned and managed for the good of everyone. This will happen not because of the greed, malice, or heroism of individuals, but because that is simply the way history works. Capitalism will collapse not because of the actions of revolutionaries but because it has created an ever-growing class of proletarians whose interests cannot be reconciled to those of their employers. "What the bourgeoisie produces, above all, is its own grave-diggers. Its fall and the victory of the proletariat are equally inevitable."[5]

Karl Marx, Historical Sociologist

The importance of Marx's ideas is by no means confined to the later development of revolutionary groups calling themselves Communist. His approach to history and culture has had a considerable influence on the social sciences. It was Marx who prompted Europeans to consider how much impact our material surroundings, economic standing, and cultural framework have on us as individuals. In fact Marx clearly exhibited what American sociologist C. Wright Mills would later call "The Sociological Imagination," an ability to place individual lives within the context of wider social forces, to connect biography with history. "Men make their own history," Marx wrote, "but they do not make it just as they please; they do not make it under circumstances chosen by themselves, but under circumstances directly encountered, given and transmitted from the past. The history of all the dead generations weighs like a nightmare on the brain of the living."[6] Men may have free will, but they do not create the circumstances into which they are born. Nor can they create an infinite number of different cultures from the material reality in which they live. To Marx, an **economic determinist**, it seemed clear that the economic basis of any given society will govern the values, ideas, and social arrangements of that society. Members of hunter-gatherer bands cannot be individualists, nor can they live in vast cities. As the industrial revolution advanced, therefore, social change was inevitable. "The hand-mill gives you society with the feudal lord; the steam-mill, society with the industrial capitalist."[7] To be sure, not all modern historians are economic determinists, but since Marx few have denied that changes in a society's economic arrangements are likely to have a major impact on other aspects of the society.

The French historian Henri Lefebvre has suggested that Marx's greatest influence on sociology may have been his attention to **ideology**, "one of the most original and comprehensive concepts Marx introduced."[8] Marx argued that "The ruling ideas of each age have ever been the ideas of its ruling class."[9] These ideas justify the existing disposition of power and wealth in that society and therefore serve a purpose in maintaining the *status quo*. Ever since Marx social scientists of many political persuasions have looked carefully at the religious, moral, and political ideas of a given society with the understanding that not everyone shares them and that they may serve the purposes of some groups better than others. From this perspective, too, systems of social stratification are studied as they actually function and are maintained, rather than as ideal blueprints of how society ought to be. Medieval concepts of society, for example, emphasized the God-given nature of the social order and the unimportance of riches and power in this life. These ideas were not only in harmony with traditional Christian thought but also far more conducive to maintenance of the existing system than to change in the interests of equality or fairness.

Another legacy of Marx is a concern for the **alienation** of modern man in the increasingly large and impersonal social arrangements of the contemporary world. This is one emphasis that Marx retained from his days as a philosopher; he often wrote of man's estrangement from himself in the working world, where the worker retains no control over his work and someone else profits from it more than the worker himself and his family. Crammed together in huge, impersonal factories and enormous, impersonal cities, man finds himself in a world where it seems that no connection exists between one man and another except for the "cash nexus" of "naked self-interest."[10] Since Marx's time, this progressive impoverishment of the inner life and emotional relationships of man as modernization takes place has been a continuing concern of many social analysts, socialist, liberal, and conservative alike.

Karl Marx, Economist

From the time of his arrival in England in 1849 until his death in 1883, Marx spent much of his time on a deep study of how capitalism arose, how it works, and what its future might be. He conducted much of his research in the Reading Room of the British Museum, reading all of the works of the classical political economists like Smith and Ricardo, their predecessors, and their followers. He plowed through voluminous statistics on the development of various industries throughout Europe and the world, the construction of railroads and canals, and the competition for expanded colonial empires, filling notebook after notebook with his findings. The result was *Capital,* never finished in Marx's lifetime and eventually published in three volumes. It was hardly an immediate success; it took four years for the first thousand copies of Volume I to be sold.[11] It is enormously long, mind-numbingly detailed, and read by very few people. But it deserves more attention than it receives, especially since the fall of the Communist regimes of Russia and Eastern Europe, because Marx's track record in predicting the future development of capitalism has been disturbingly accurate.

Marx predicted that capitalism would experience a secular trend toward falling profits, as well as an ever-increasing scale of industry and resultant decrease in the number of firms. He predicted the increasing severity of the business cycle, leading to worldwide economic depressions and crises, each worse than the previous. (In 1883 this idea seemed rather absurd to many people; by 1930 it seemed frighteningly possible.) He predicted that governments would find it impossible to deal adequately with these crises because they had no reach outside their national boundaries and were too intimately connected with the dominant capitalist class to be objective in their approach. He predicted globalization, the erosion of local and even national culture over time, and the dominance of multinational corporations against which no individual government can stand. In all of these instances, his foresight has been impressive.

Finally, Marx predicted, despite the enormous wealth created by capitalism (and celebrated in the *Communist Manifesto*), eventually the entire system would come crashing down, a victim of its own success. At the time of his death Marx did not expect to see this happen soon, but he was no less convinced than he had been in 1848 that eventually we will find "The conditions of bourgeois society are too narrow to comprise the wealth created by them."[12] The enormous social forces of production would have to be controlled not by the few, as private property, but by the many, collectively. However much this prospect heartened Karl Marx, this is not a future to which most citizens of the developed world in the post-Communist era would look forward with pleasure. And yet his record as a prophet of capitalism indicates that Marx was a man who understood capitalism very, very well. If we are to understand it well enough to have some control over our own destiny in a capitalist world, prudence would dictate that we not ignore his insights.

Notes

1. In the medieval period, organizations of master craftsmen had arisen to set standards for training, recognition of master status, and quality of workmanship of the finished goods. These organizations were called guilds; only their members could engage in the craft they regulated.

2. For a sense of just how wide a variety of ideas have been proposed under the banner of socialism, see Michael Newman, *Socialism: A Very Short Introduction* (Oxford: Oxford University Press, 2005).

3. Karl Marx, *Theses on Feuerbach*, in *Selected Works of Karl Marx and Friedrich Engels* (New York: International Publishers, 1972), 30.

4. Karl Marx and Friedrich Engels, *The Communist Manifesto*, in *Selected Works of Karl Marx and Friedrich Engels*, 35.

5. *The Communist Manifesto*, 46.

6. Karl Marx, *The Eighteenth Brumaire of Louis Bonaparte*, in *Selected Works*, 97.

7. Karl Marx, *The Poverty of Philosophy*, cited in David McLellan, *Karl Marx: His Life and Thought* (New York: Harper & Row, 1973), 164.

8. Henri Lefebvre, *The Sociology of Marx* (New York: Pantheon Books, 1968), 59. This is the first American edition, translated from the French by Norbert Guterman.

9. *The Communist Manifesto*, in *Selected Works*, 54.

10. *The Communist Manifesto*, in *Selected Works*, 38.

11. McLellan, 353.

12. *The Communist Manifesto*, in *Selected Works*, 41.

The Return of Karl Marx

John Cassidy

A hundred and fifty years ago, he sat in the British Museum analyzing the problems of capitalism and the virtues of Communism. He was wrong about Communism. Was he right about capitalism?

Early this summer, I enjoyed a weekend at the Long Island vacation home of a college friend—a highly intelligent and levelheaded Englishman whose career has taken him (by way of the upper echelons of the British Civil Service and a financial firm in the City of London) to a big Wall Street investment bank. There he has spent the last few years organizing stock issues and helping his firm milk the strongest market in living memory. Between dips in his pool, we discussed the economy and speculated about how long the current financial boom would last.

To my surprise, he brought up Karl Marx. "The longer I spend on Wall Street, the more convinced I am that Marx was right," he said.

I assumed he was joking.

"There is a Nobel Prize waiting for the economist who resurrects Marx and puts it all together in a coherent model," he continued, quite seriously. "I am absolutely convinced that Marx's approach is the best way to look at capitalism."

I didn't hide my astonishment. We had both studied economics during the early eighties at Oxford, where most of our teachers agreed with Keynes that Marx's economic theories were "complicated hocus-pocus" and Communism was "an insult to our intelligence." The prevailing attitude among bright students of our generation was that Marx's arguments were fit only for polytechnic lecturers and aspiring Labour Party politicians (many of whom are now right-wing Blairites). In the years since, his reputation has fallen lower still: Moscow's Institute of Marxism-Leninism is gone; the Chinese Red Army has retooled itself into a manufacturing business; even Fidel Castro is looking for outside investors. Nonetheless, I decided that if my host, with all his experience of global finance, reckoned Marx had something worthwhile to say, perhaps it was time to take a look.

Gathering the material proved easy. Hardly anybody reads Marx these days, so secondhand bookstores are overflowing with moldy translations of "The Communist Manifesto" and "Das Kapital." Some of his earlier works are harder to come by, but I picked up a hefty volume of selected writings edited by the British scholar David McLellan, and it contained everything from a letter Marx wrote home from the University of Berlin in 1837 to correspondence with his fellow-socialists when he was an old man living on Haverstock Hill, in London. I took the books with me on my August vacation and nibbled at them on the beach—plums like "Theories of Surplus Value," "The German Ideology," and "The Eighteenth Brumaire of Louis Bonaparte."

More than fifty years ago, Edmund Wilson noted that much of Marx's prose "hypnotizes the reader with its paradoxes and eventually puts him to sleep." The passing decades have not made the going any easier. Marx was ludicrously prolix (even Engels complained that his chapters were too long) and often willfully obscure. His favorite mode of argument was, as he put it, "coquetting with modes of expression peculiar to Hegel," and many of his expositions are practically bereft of meaning. (Try deciphering at bedtime this sentence from "Surplus Value": "The determinate social character of the means of production in capitalist production—expressing a particular production relation—has so grown together with, and in the mode of thought of bourgeois society is so inseparable from, the material existence of these means of production as means of production, that the same determinateness—categorical determinateness—is assumed even where the relation is in direct contradiction to it.") Not that Marx couldn't write. When he felt like it, he could compose simple declarative sentences that were, in Wilson's words, "dense with the packed power of high explosives." Parts of the "Manifesto" and "The Eighteenth Brumaire" are brilliantly written, and Marx's journalistic dispatches for Charles Dana's New York *Tribune* were eminently readable. Most of the time, though, Marx wrote as if parsimony and clarity were traps laid by the bourgeoisie for unsuspecting authors.

In spite of this, I gradually began to grasp what my friend had been talking about. In many ways, Marx's legacy has been obscured by the failure of Communism, which wasn't his primary interest. In fact, he had little to say about how a socialist society should operate, and what he did write, about the withering away of the state and so on, wasn't very helpful—something Lenin and his comrades quickly discovered after seizing power. Marx was a student of capitalism, and that is how he should be judged. Many of the contradictions that he saw in Victorian capitalism and that were subsequently addressed by reformist governments have begun reappearing in new guises, like mutant viruses. When he wasn't driving the reader to distraction, he wrote riveting passages about globalization, inequality, political corruption, monopolization, technical progress, the decline of high culture, and the enervating nature of modern existence—issues that economists are now confronting anew, sometimes without realizing that they are walking in Marx's footsteps.

The Moor, as Marx's children called him, because of his fearsome facial features, was born in the Rhineland city of Trier, which was then part of Prussia, in 1818. His father, a prosperous Jewish lawyer who was a convert to Christianity, urged his son to study, and Marx didn't need much encouragement. In 1841, he got his doctorate from the University of Jena—his thesis dealt with the natural philosophies of Democritus and Epicurus—but his radical views prevented him from getting a university post, and for the rest of his life he drifted between journalism and left-wing politics. During the eighteen-forties, he lived in Bonn, Paris, and Brussels. In the revolutionary year of

1848, he moved back to Paris, then to Cologne, and, finally (after being thrown out of Prussia), to London, where he remained until his death, in 1883.

Like many thinkers, Marx did his most novel cogitating in his twenties and thirties, then spend decades expanding ideas that he had developed as a young man. His basic insight, which he introduce in "The German Ideology" (1846), was reintroduced in recent times by James Carville: "It's the economy, stupid." Marx's own term for his theory was "the materialist conception of history," and it is now so widely accepted that analysts of all political views use it, like Carville, without any attribution. When conservatives argue that the welfare state is doomed because it stifles private enterprise, or that the Soviet Union collapsed because it couldn't match the efficiency of Western capitalism, they are adopting Marx's argument that economics is the driving force in human development. Indeed, as Sir John Hicks, a Nobel Prize-winning British economist, noted in 1969, when it comes to theories of history Karl Marx still has the field pretty much to himself. It is, Hicks wrote, "extraordinary that one hundred years after *Das Kapital* . . . so little else should have emerged."

Marx wasn't a crude reductionist, but he did believe that the way in which society organized production ultimately shaped people's attitudes and beliefs. Capitalism, for example, made human beings subjugate themselves to base avarice. "Money is the universal, self-constituted value of all things. It has therefore robbed the whole world, human as well as natural, of its own values," he wrote when he was twenty-five. "Money is the alienated essence of man's work and being. This alien essence dominates him, and he adores it." The language may be a bit strong, but has anything changed? The magazine racks are packed with titles like *Money, Smart Money, Worth*, and *Fortune;* it is difficult to turn on a television without hearing financial advice; and successful investors like Warren Buffett and George Soros are regularly lionized by the media.

The money-driven debasement of popular culture, epitomized by most of Hollywood's output, was also foreshadowed by Marx. In the "Grundrisse" (1857), he argued that the quality of the art a society produces is a reflection of the material conditions present at the time. Homer and Virgil reflected a naïve mythological view of nature, which wasn't sustainable in an age of machinery, railways, and electric telegraphs. "Where does Vulcan come in as against Roberts & Co.? Jupiter as against the lightning conductor? Hermes as against the Crédit Mobilier?" Marx asked. "What becomes of the Goddess Fama side by side with Printing House Square?" When these words were written, Dickens and Thackeray were writing for monthly magazines, most educated people had studied Latin, and capitalism hadn't yet demonstrated its ability to produce "The Jenny Jones Show."

"The Communist Manifesto," of which Marx was the co-author with Friedrich Engels, a fellow-Rhinelander, whose father owned an interest in a factory in Manchester, almost didn't get written. Engels wrote a first draft in late 1847, but Marx, who was busy, sat down to complete it only after receiving a desperate plea from his colleagues in the Communist League. Perhaps because of this deadline pressure, his language was much nattier than usual, and the final version, which appeared in February, 1848, contained some of his sharpest phrases: "A spectre is haunting Europe—the spectre of Communism," "The history of all hitherto existing society is the history of class struggles," "What the bourgeoisie produces, above all, is its own grave-diggers."

The book's misguided prophecies about capitalism's imminent demise have obscured a far more durable intellectual achievement: Marx's explanation in the "Manifesto" of how capitalism works. Unlike many of his followers, he never underestimated the power of the free market. "The bourgeoisie, during its rule of scarcely one hundred years, has created more massive and more colossal productive forces than have all preceding generations together," he wrote. "It has accomplished wonders far surpassing Egyptian pyramids, Roman aqueducts, and Gothic cathedrals; it has conducted expeditions that put in the shade all former Exoduses of nations and crusades." Moreover, this unprecedented productive spurt, otherwise known as the industrial revolution, was not confined to any one country, since the ever-present need for new markets "chases the bourgeoisie over the whole surface of the globe." Wherever the bourgeoisie go, Marx said, they undermine traditional ways of doing things. "All old-established national industries have been destroyed or are daily being destroyed," he wrote. "They are dislodged by new industries, whose introduction becomes a life-and-death question for all civilized nations." It wasn't just local businesses that suffered. Entire cultures were swept aside by the relentless forces of modernization and international integration. "The intellectual creations of individual nations become common property," he noted. "National one-sidedness and narrow-mindedness become more and more impossible, and from the numerous national and local literatures, there arises a world literature."

"Globalization" is the buzzword of the late twentieth century, on the lips of everybody from Jiang Zemin to Tony Blair, but Marx predicted most of its ramifications a hundred and fifty years ago. Capitalism is now well on its way to transforming the world into a single market, with the nations of Europe, Asia, and the Americas evolving into three rival trading blocs within that market. John Grisham's novels are translated into dozens of languages, teenagers in Australia wear Chicago Bulls caps, and almost everybody in business speaks English, the global language of money. Occasionally, some embattled group—French farmers, British miners, American autoworkers—puts up a fight for traditional interests, but its efforts always prove fruitless. Nothing can stop the permanent revolution that capitalism represents. "Uninterrupted disturbance of all social conditions, everlasting uncertainty and agitation distinguish the bourgeois epoch from all earlier ones," Marx wrote. "All that is solid melts into air, all that is holy is profaned, and man is at last compelled to face with sober senses his real conditions of life and his relations with his kind."

Globalization is set to become the biggest political issue of the next century. Richard Gephardt is already running for President on a "fair trade" platform, and populist, xenophobic parties are emerging in Russia, France, and many other countries. According to a recent World Bank study, Russia, China, India, Indonesia, and Brazil will all become major industrial powers within the next twenty-five years, and this will only increase the competitive pressures on other advanced nations. Even economists, who traditionally have been globalization's biggest defenders (on the ground that it creates more winners than losers), are now having second thoughts about its impact. Contemporary critics tend to use drier language than Marx did, but their message is similar. "The international integration of markets for goods, services, and capital is pressuring societies to alter their traditional practices, and, in return, broad segments of these societies are putting up a fight," Dani Rodrik, a Harvard economist, wrote in a path-breaking book, published earlier this year, entitled "Has Globalization Gone Too Far?" Rodrik pointed out that child labor, corporate tax avoidance, and shuttered American factories are all features of globalization. He didn't mention Marx directly—citations of his work are not good for the career prospects of an Ivy League economist—but he concluded that failure to meet the global challenge could lead to "social disintegration."

While Marx was exiled in London, he had plenty of time to read. Each day, he trudged to the British Museum and stayed there from ten until seven, studying obscure government reports and classical economists, such as Adam Smith and David Ricardo. The museum's famous Reading Room was an escape from the domestic squalor in which he daily left his wife, Jenny; his three children; and their maid (who in 1851 gave birth to his illegitimate child). Until 1856, when Jenny inherited some money, they all lived in two cramped rooms, and they were usually broke. At one point, a bailiff arrived to collect five pounds, but Marx didn't have it, so the debt collector seized "beds, linen, clothes, everything, even my poor baby's cradle," Jenny wrote to a friend. Marx, arrogant and crotchety even at the best of times, suffered from boils and piles, which occasionally prevented him from sitting in the British Museum ("I hope that the bourgeoisie, as long as they live, will have cause to remember my carbuncles," he wrote to Engels), but he never stopped working. Between 1848 and 1867, he published a number of economic works, culminating in "Das Kapital," which was, he said, an attempt to reveal "the economic law of motion of modern society."

In one way, Marx's efforts were a failure. His mathematical model of the economy, which depended on the idea that labor is the source of all value, was riven with internal inconsistencies and is rarely studied these days. Many of the constructs used by modern economists—such as supply-and-demand curves, production functions, and game theory—hadn't been conceived in the eighteen-sixties. A new textbook, "Principles of Economics," by N. Gregory Mankiw, a Harvard professor, mentions Marx just once in eight hundred pages, and that reference is pejorative.

Mankiw, quoting the turn-of-the-century economist Alfred Marshall, says that economics is "a study of mankind in the ordinary business of life," which answers questions like "Why are apartments so hard to find in New York City?" and "Why do airlines charge less for a round-trip ticket if the traveller stays over a Saturday night?" and "Why is Jim Carrey paid so much to star in movies?" Marx didn't dismiss such questions—although his labor theory of value was ill equipped to address them—but he considered them secondary to the real task of economics, which was to explain how society evolved over time.

One important lesson Marx taught is that capitalism tends toward monopoly—an observation that was far from obvious in his day—giving rise to a need for strong regulation. This problem subsequently seemed to have been taken care of by the reforms of Teddy Roosevelt and F. D. R., but the last decade has witnessed an unprecedented wave of mergers in sectors as diverse as entertainment, medicine, defense, and financial services. At the same time, budget cuts and conservative court rulings have undermined the effectiveness of government regulatory agencies, such as the Federal Trade Commission. Unless these trends are reversed, the inevitable result will be more mergers, higher prices, and fewer choices for consumers.

Marx's primary achievement as an economist was placing the entrepreneur and the profit motive front and center in the study of economic development. To the layman who reads the business pages, this may seem obvious, but it isn't obvious to professional economists. In neo-classical economics—the sort taught by Mankiw—consumers are the main focus of attention, while firms are merely "black boxes" that transform raw material and labor into commodities that people want to buy. In the world envisioned by this theory, the economy grows at a pace determined by the expansion of the labor force and the rate of technical progress, which appears like manna from Heaven and is not governed by market forces.

Marx's view of economic growth was darker and more complex. In his model, capitalists were a beleaguered species, constantly under pressure from competitors trying to enter their markets and steal their profits. Given such pressure, firms had to cut costs by investing in labor-saving machinery, forcing their employees to work harder, and developing new products. This process, which Marx called "accumulation," was the main reason that capitalism was so much more productive than previous social systems. In feudal times, the nobles consumed the economic "surplus" created by the peasants, but in the industrial society capitalists were forced to invest the surplus created by their employees or risk being swept aside by their rivals. "Accumulate! Accumulate! Accumulate! That is Moses and the Prophets," Marx declared.

This vision of economic growth was largely forgotten by the economics profession after Marx's death, but it was resurrected in the nineteen-forties by Joseph Schumpeter, a former Austrian finance minister turned Harvard academic. He labelled it "creative destruction." In recent years, Schumpeter's work has been formalized by a group of eminent and mathematically inclined theorists, including Paul Romer, of Stanford, and Philippe Aghion, of the University of London. Economists working in this field, which calls itself endogenous-growth theory, usually fail to credit Marx as their intellectual forefather (to do so would invite ridicule), but their models are undoubtedly Marxist in spirit, since their main aim is to demonstrate how technical progress emerges from the competitive process, and not from Heaven, as in the neoclassical model.

Marx's version of free enterprise also chimes with the views of many contemporary businessmen, who would rather be flogged than labelled Marxists. In the nineteen-eighties, for instance, Jack (Neutron Jack) Welch, Jr., the flinty but highly respected chairman of General Electric, transformed the company, closing down dozens of plants and firing tens of thousands of employees. The reasons he did so would have been familiar to any reader of Marx. "The events we see rushing toward us make the rough, tumultuous eighties look like a decade at the beach," Welch said at a shareholders' meeting in 1989. "Ahead of us are Darwinian shakeouts in every major marketplace, with no consolation prizes for the losing companies and nations."

In 1881, Jenny Marx died. Marx never got over the loss—"The Moor is dead, too," he said to Engels—and two years later he followed his wife to the grave. At his funeral, Engels eulogized him in a way that Marx would have liked, declaring, "Just as Darwin discovered the law of evolution in organic nature, so Marx discovered the law of evolution in human history." This wasn't quite true, but it wasn't altogether false. Capitalism certainly wasn't succeeded by Communism, but, just as certainly, it didn't survive in the Dickensian form that Marx had witnessed. During the century following his death, governments in industrialized countries introduced numerous reforms designed to improve the living standard of working people: labor laws, minimum-wage legislation, welfare benefits, public housing, public-health systems, inheritance levies, progressive income taxes, and so on. These ameliorative measures would have been labelled "socialism" in Marx's day; indeed, he prescribed many of them in the "Manifesto," and it is difficult to see how capitalism could have survived without them.

It is only in the past two decades that a systematic assault on social democracy has been carried out in the name of "economic efficiency." This right-wing backlash has produced a sharp upsurge in inequality, just as Marx would have predicted. Between 1980 and 1996, the share of total household income going to the richest five percent of the families in the country increased from 15.3 percent to 20.3 percent, while the share of the income going to the poorest sixty per cent of families fell from 34.2 percent to 30 percent. These changes represent an unprecedented redistribution of resources from poor to rich—each shift of one per cent represents about thirty-eight billion dollars.

Marx believed that the fundamental divide in any society is between the people who own the machinery and the factories used to make commodities (the "bourgeoisie") and the people whose only marketable asset is their capacity for work (the "proletarians"). This split is too rigid—it doesn't account for self-employed people, public-sector employees, and workers who own shares in their employer's firm—but there is no doubt that the biggest winners, by far, during the past two decades have been the people who control the means of production: chief executives and shareholders. In 1978, a typical chief executive at a big company earned about sixty times what a typical worker earned; in 1995, he took home about a hundred and seventy times as much. Shareholders have also done fabulously, and this has accentuated the increase in inequality. According to Edward Wolff, a professor of economics at New York University, half of all financial assets in the country are owned by the richest one percent of the population, and more than three-quarters of them are owned by the richest ten percent. A Federal Reserve Board survey shows that six in ten American families still own no stocks whatever, either directly or via 401(k) pension plans. And most families who do own stocks have total holdings worth less than two thousand dollars.

These figures suggest that one of Marx's most controversial ideas, the "theory of immiseration," may be making a comeback. He didn't believe, as some critics suggest, that wages could never rise under capitalism, but he did say that profits would increase faster than wages, so that workers would become poorer relative to capitalists over time, and this is what has happened during the last two decades. Inflation-adjusted average hourly wages are still below their 1973 levels, but profits have soared. In 1979, sixteen percent of all the money produced by the corporate sector went to profits and interest; today the figure is twenty-one percent.

A key question for the future, the answer to which will determine the fate of the soaring stock market and much else, is whether capital can hold on to its recent gains. The United Parcel Service strike and the raising of the minimum wage both suggest that workers are starting to recover some losses, but their bargaining power is limited, because many firms can easily relocate to countries where labor is cheaper. Marx, for one, had no doubt which side held the upper hand. "The worshipful capitalists will never want for fresh exploitable flesh and blood, and will let the dead bury their dead," he noted in "Wage-Labour and Capital."

Highgate Cemetery is just a short stroll from the bijou urban village of the same name in north London. To get there, you stroll past a row of designer stores and a bunch of English schoolchildren in blue-and-gray uniforms, turn left down a narrow lane, pass some tennis courts, and turn left again at a set of tall black gates. There to meet you is an elderly English lady named Kathleen, who is clad in a tweed skirt, a woolly sweater, and sensible shoes. With her strangled vowels, she might have just stepped out of an Agatha Christie novel. One afternoon last month, I took the bus from central London to Highgate and walked down to the cemetery to see her.

"Do many people come to visit Marx these days?" I asked as I handed over the admission fee of two pounds (one for entry, the other for a map of the graveyard).

"Oh, yes, some do, but I can't say why," Kathleen replied. "We've got a lot more interesting people here, you know. George Eliot, Sir Ralph Richardson. Are you sure you don't want to see them?"

I said I was sure, and Kathleen reluctantly directed me down a path to the cemetery's northwest corner, where I found a large marble tombstone topped with an imposing statue of Marx's head and the inscription "Workers of all lands unite." There were fresh flowers next to the grave, but only three people: two bearded students from Turkey and a young woman from South Korea who said she was a socialist. All were in London studying English.

"Marx is very big in Turkey, although Communism is illegal," one of the Turks told me. He added that he had been imprisoned briefly in Ankara for his socialist activities. He and his friend were tickled to be smoking Camels in front of Marx's grave.

I asked the visitors whether they had read any of Marx's works—"Das Kapital," in particular.

The young South Korean socialist said she hadn't.

"I tried it, but it is very big," the Turk who had been arrested volunteered.

"I started it, but I didn't understand it," his friend said.

We talked for about twenty minutes, and then I made my way back to Kathleen and asked her if Highgate was still a working cemetery. (It is. Rod Stewart's parents are buried there.) On the bus for central London, I wondered again why Marx is so little read these days.

Maybe it is because the economy is doing well, but even in good times he has lessons to teach us, such as the fact that raising workers' living standards depends on maintaining a low rate of unemployment—something that many orthodox economists denied until recently. Marx believed that wages were held down by the presence of a "reserve army" of unemployed workers who attempt to underbid the employed. Reduce the ranks of this army, he said, and wages would rise—just as they have started to do in the last year. Since the middle of 1996, the unemployment rate has averaged about five per cent, its lowest level in twenty-four years, and inflation-adjusted median hourly wages have risen by 1.4 per cent, their first appreciable rise in almost a decade.

Perhaps the most enduring element of Marx's work is his discussion of where power lies in a capitalist society. This is a subject that economists, with their fixation on consumer choice, have neglected for decades, but recently a few of them have returned to Marx's idea that the circumstances in which people are forced to make choices are often just as important as the choices. (Take the case of a robbery victim who is given the "choice" of handing over his money or being stabbed.) At Harvard, for example, Oliver Hart has developed a new theory of how firms operate which depends on the power struggle among shareholders, managers, and workers. Other economists are looking critically at the exercise of political power. Elhanan Helpman, another Harvard professor, and Gene Grossman, of Princeton, have constructed a formal model illustrating the way that the government is encouraged to introduce damaging trade policies by pressure from rival business lobbyists.

Marx, of course, delighted in declaring that politicians merely carry water for their corporate paymasters. "The executive of the modern State is but a committee for managing the common affairs of the bourgeoisie," he wrote in the "Manifesto," and he later singled out American politicians, saying they had been "subordinated" to "bourgeois production" ever since the days of George Washington. The sight of a President granting shady businessmen access to the White House in return for campaign contributions would have shocked him not at all. Despite his errors, he was a man for whom our economic system held few surprises. His books will be worth reading as long as capitalism endures.

Marx's view of free enterprise is now being echoed by many businessmen who would rather be flogged than labelled Marxists.

Nationalism and Nations

John W. Mackey

Along with industrialization, a central feature of the nineteenth century was the spread of ideologies. Especially in the Western parts of Europe, more concentrated urban populations, which were becoming increasingly literate, were increasingly drawn to systems of ideas that they believed promoted their interests and would help to bring about the sorts of progress that Enlightenment thinking encouraged. In addition to Classical Liberalism and early ideas of socialism, one of the most powerful of these ideologies was what we call **nationalism**. Though it came in several varieties and displayed a tendency to change over time, by the end of the nineteenth century, nationalism had emerged as perhaps the most powerful ideology yet to appear in Western society. As such, it was intimately connected to the process of modernization.

The Power and Authority of the Modern Nation State

The modern **nation state** is one of the most significant and powerful of all human institutions. The nation state organizes the political lives of a given people in a particular land area over which it has sovereign jurisdiction. It creates laws that regulate behavior and judicial systems and punishments to deal with the violators of laws. The modern state also provides for a wide variety of human needs through the creation of bureaucracies and government agencies. While some states offer a high degree of personal liberty to their citizens, others are repressive or even totalitarian in nature; the latter are often met with anger, dissent, and resistance from their citizenry.

Although nation states vary widely in the ways they govern, all successful states are able to function because they can wield power. Among the types of power identified by sociologist Max Weber is the power of **physical force**. Nation states can use physical force to impose their will, and to that end they organize police and military services. Weber also argued that another type of power might be called **latent force**, or the threat of physical force. Nation states utilize latent force as well; for example, citizens of a particular nation may be dissuaded from violating a law for fear of facing the physical force of the police. The state may benefit, then, from both the use of physical force and its looming possibility.

But Weber believed that governing by physical force alone is not optimal or even efficient for a well-run state. Thus, modern nation states govern on the basis of their **authority**. Authority is power that is presumed to be legitimate by those who are subject to it. Many modern states have created constitutional systems and institutions that provide the justification for the exercise of power, a type of authority Weber called **rational-legal authority**. Thus, in an effective modern nation state, citizens participate constructively in their societies not merely because they fear the force of the state, but because they feel part of a legitimate system that is based on reasonably fair and rational principles.

Both the nation state and its corresponding ideology, known as **nationalism**, are generally considered to have been products of the European nineteenth century. As the effects of the Enlightenment and the Industrial Revolution spread through the continent, nation states and nationalism assumed various forms. But whatever the different environments that affected them, Europeans began to identify strongly with the concept of "the nation."

The Early Nineteenth Century: Liberal and Romantic Nationalism

As the century began, **liberal nationalism** was on the rise as a political force, and **Romantic nationalism** sparked the imaginations of many newly patriotic Europeans, who began to identify strongly with a nation. Romantic nationalists usually defined the nation terms of a shared history, as well as common language and customs. Historians credit the French Revolution with giving birth to both types of early nationalism. Revolutionary leaders such as the Jacobins emphasized the ideal of loyalty to the nation, and they defined the nation not as a class or ruling power, but as the French people themselves. According to the republican ideals of the Revolution, individuals were no longer to consider themselves loyal to a particular monarch or family, nor to a region or locality; the people of France were to be *citizens* of a republic, not *subjects* of a monarch. As Rousseau had argued, citizenship obligated individuals to actively participate in their own governance, while absolutist rule based on blind obedience was equivalent to slavery.[1] The nationalism of the French Revolution was based on Enlightenment values, active citizenship, representative institutions, and devotion to the concept of the people as the nation.

The Napoleonic Wars facilitated the spread of the nationalist spirit of the French Revolution. As Napoleon's armies marched through Europe in the early years of the nineteenth century, they brought their nationalist enthusiasms with them, encouraging the subjects of absolutist states to liberate themselves. Their message found a receptive audience, especially among peoples who saw themselves as a distinctive national or ethnic group under the control of a foreign power or within a multi-ethnic empire. Thus, enthusiasm for what is sometimes called **liberal nationalism** was unleashed across Europe. Liberal nationalists believed that the modern, constitutional nation state was the ideal institution for the expression of the will of the nation and the safeguarding of individual liberty. They regarded absolutism as tyrannical and obsolete.

The old, conservative order in Europe resisted this spreading ideology, viewing it as a threat to stability, tradition, and the entrenched European power system. But despite the conservative backlash in that followed Napoleon's final defeat in 1815, liberal nationalism continued to gain momentum that could not be reversed. Critics found the old, conservative order increasingly incapable of meeting the needs and desires of modernizing societies, and enthusiasm for representative institutions grew accordingly. Minority populations in multi-ethnic empires in particular began to demand national self-determination, new institutions, and political independence.

Among the earliest victories for nineteenth-century nationalism took place in Greece, which had long been under the control of the Turkish Ottoman Empire. In 1821 Greek nationalist leaders asserted the right to nationhood, and by 1830 they had gained the support of several major European states. Armed resistance forced the Ottoman Empire to recognize the independence of a new Greek nation state. Throughout Europe, the Greek War of Independence was hailed as a victory of the unstoppable force of liberty against despotism, further energizing the movement.

In the following decades, other nationalist movements in Europe met both significant successes and abject failures. In 1848, an uprising in France provoked a chain reaction of rebellions in numerous other European nations (see Chapter 13). Though most of these failed, it was clear that nationalism had become a widespread popular force, as nationalist groups, often tied to youth movements, continued to demand national self-determination for their people. For example, the multi-ethnic Austrian Habsburg Empire was shaken by revolts of nationalist Germans, Hungarians, Poles, Czechs, Romanians, and Serbs, among others. Other nationalist revolutionary movements occurred in Ireland, the German states, and the Italian peninsula.

This liberal form of nationalism was dominant among nationalist political movements in the first half of the nineteenth century. But there existed other forms of nationalist sentiment in Europe, including what is often called **Romantic nationalism**. While liberal nationalism was based on rational republican values, Romantics stressed the uniqueness of a particular people and their history. They suggested that each people had a national essence, or a series of traits and qualities they believed to be inherent. Such an essence was not a rational phenomenon, but rather something more like a spiritual quality. German Romantics called this essence the *Volksgeist* or "spirit of the people." Romantic nationalism tended to emphasize the ancient or even timeless nature of the nation and its traditions, and of the historical unity of the nation. Historical evidence shows, however, that such beliefs were frequently quite exaggerated, and many national "traditions" (like forms of "national dress") are in fact quite modern inventions.[2]

In stressing the inherent uniqueness of people rather than universal human principles, Romantic nationalism commonly highlighted the differences between nations and peoples. Informed by Romantic nationalism, the seemingly benign love of country and culture often evolved into **chauvinism**—"my nation is great" tended to become "my nation is superior to yours." Bigotry and stereotyping often accompanied Romantic nationalism, inciting violence and conflict between states or between members of different national or ethnic groups within a state.

In the first half of the nineteenth century, nationalism, in both liberal and Romantic expressions, inspired activists and revolutionaries from Greece to Ireland, and from Poland to Italy. And while these forms of nationalism differed, they could also operate in conjunction. In the latter half of the nineteenth century, however, nationalism in Europe changed in character. As the nationalism of this period helped form new European nation states, it also came to be more closely associated with power politics, conservatism, and racism. Among the major events that accompanied the growth of nineteenth-century nationalism were the unification of Italy and the birth of the modern German nation state.

The Late Nineteenth Century: Unification and Power Politics

Despite the efforts of liberal nationalists in the revolutions of 1848, at mid-century the Italian peninsula had remained a collection of separate states, many under the control of other European powers. Liberal and Romantic Italian nationalists yearned for a unified state that would reflect their vision of the common culture and history of the Italian people. But it would take a series of bold political moves and military calculations to bring about a unified Italy.

While a number of factors contributed to the eventual success of Italian unification, the process was led by the military efforts and power politics exercised after mid-century by Count Camillo di **Cavour**, the prime minister of the Kingdom of Piedmont-Sardinia. His calculated alliances with great powers like France and Prussia enabled successful military campaigns against Austria and the forces of the Papacy, with inspiring leadership provided by Giuseppe **Garibaldi**, a veteran of the failed nationalist uprising of 1848. Largely due to the vision and efforts of these two individuals, a new state emerged in 1861 as the Kingdom of Italy, a constitutional monarchy under the leadership of the king of Piedmont-Sardinia. The final pieces of the puzzle were added during the next decade with the addition of Venice and the city of Rome. While republican liberal nationalists had provided some of the early sparks, the creation of modern Italy only succeeded through the use of military force and bold diplomatic maneuvering.

The other major political development during this period was the creation of a unified German state, which was composed of the varied collection of former principalities that had emerged from the Napoleonic Wars. The process of German unification is a good example of how nationalism became a force of the political "right" in the second half of the nineteenth century. While Germany lacked political unity prior to 1871, there did exist a popular concept of "Germany" as a place where the German-speaking people lived. German nationalists relied on this ethnic consciousness in their efforts to consolidate a single political entity.

The key figure in the unification of Germany was the aristocratic Prussian chancellor **Otto von Bismarck**. The two large ethnically German states of Austria and Prussia were both potential leaders of any movement towards German unification. When Bismarck defeated Austria in the Austro-Prussian War of 1866, he created a Prussian-led confederation of Northern German states that became the precursor of a unified Germany. Then, by provoking another war, this time with France (the Franco-Prussian war of 1870-71), Bismarck induced most of the remaining German territories to join his coalition, consolidating his leadership over the larger part of the German-speaking world.

This new Germany hardly resembled the fulfillment of republican liberal nationalist dreams. It was literally a German Empire, complete with the first "German

Emperor," Wilhelm I, while the Imperial Chancellor Bismarck controlled of the levers of political power. In Bismarck's hands, the German state was powerful and conservative, retaining the traditional institutions of monarchy and aristocracy and attacking socialist movements and parties. The "Iron Chancellor" skillfully exploited German nationalist sentiments to promote the power of the state, while enacting reforms, including ambitious social welfare programs, that rallied popular enthusiasm among the masses. In Bismarck's Germany, nationalism became a phenomenon of the political right, as its conservative leaders appealed to national unity and loyalty to the state as alternatives to class loyalty and class conflict.

While the cases of Italy and Germany demonstrated how this phenomenon could unify states, nationalism could also be based on a separatist agenda. Irish and Hungarian nationalists in 1848, for example, wished to separate from a larger political entity (Britain and the Austrian Empire, respectively) and enjoy self-determination in independent nation states. They had limited success in each case; fully independent, separate Irish and Hungarian states would be a product of the twentieth century. Other situations were more complicated. In some parts of Eastern Europe, for example, distinct ethnic groups had shared the same territory for centuries, often with one group dominating another. In such places, nationalist appeals frequently resulted not in newly unified, culturally homogenous states, but in political and social instability. Nationalist appeals in such places as Romania and Serbia encouraged neighbors who had grudgingly learned to coexist to take up arms against each other to redress "historical wrongs." Such tensions contributed in a major way to the war that exploded in 1914.

Extreme Nationalism

During the same decades that brought about Italian and German unification, most forms of nationalism in Europe grew more zealous and militaristic. **Extreme nationalists** championed the superiority of their own people, while disparaging those of other nations. Their views were increasingly influenced by the development of **Social Darwinism** and so-called **scientific racism**. Social Darwinists took Darwinian ideas about evolution out of their intended contexts, and commonly argued that history can be seen as a struggle among nations or peoples who display varying levels of sophistication or evolution. They trumpeted a far different message than Enlightenment liberals; while the latter spoke of human equality, nineteenth century Social Darwinists emphasized what they believed to be significant evolutionary differences between races and nations.[3]

Similarly, scientific racism held that it was possible to use scientific methods to identify biological differences among racial groups, and it promoted the concept of a world racial hierarchy. In a number of long-since discredited "scientific" inquiries, scientific racists claimed to illustrate the superiority of the "white" race over African and Asian peoples. Such biological beliefs about the nature of human groups, combined with mistaken Darwinist notions, helped create a distinctively racial form of nationalism as the nineteenth century wore on. **Racial nationalism** contended that human history is a clash between nations and/or races in which the only the "fittest" peoples would survive. Racial and extreme nationalists celebrated war and conflict, arguing that the defeat of inferior peoples on the field of battle would cleanse the world of the weak and allow the strong to prosper. Thus, nationalists urged the masses to willingly sacrifice their lives for the greatness of their nation. The brutally violent racial imagery and glorification of war employed by such virulent strains of nationalism influenced twentieth-century movements like Nazism.

Extreme nationalism also became infused with **anti-Semitism** in the late nineteenth century. Prejudice, discrimination, and even waves of violence against Jews were not new in Europe at this time. But anti-Semitism, when linked with extreme forms of racial nationalism, began to take on a new character.4 Extreme nationalists began to describe Jews as racially distinct and inferior to supposedly "authentic" Europeans. Unlike the anti-Semites of the Middle Ages, racial nationalists argued that Jews could not be "cured" or assimilated by converting to Christianity. They were presumed to be a foreign and inferior race of people whose presence contaminated the purity of the "national race." This particular form of racism found formal voice in anti-Semitic political movements and parties in Austria and Germany in the 1880s and 1890s, but was not limited to those nations.

Nationalism and Identity

The concept of the nation state is essential in our modern political lives and the contemporary system of international relations. It emerged from the ideology of nationalism that first appeared in the wake of the French Revolution and Napoleonic Wars. The liberal nationalists of the early nineteenth century tended to argue that the modern state was the ideal institution to safeguard personal liberty and Enlightenment values. Concurrently, early Romantic nationalists created works of art and literature, and started movements that grew from their belief in the inherent, distinctive, and ancient qualities of their people.

As the nineteenth century progressed, nationalism became more closely associated with the political right. As the German Chancellor Bismarck illustrated, conservative forces could harness or manipulate nationalist feelings to quell class conflict and strengthen loyalty to the state. In more extreme forms of nationalism, often connected to Social Darwinist, anti-Semitic, or racist ideas, the world was portrayed as a brutal clash of nations and/or races, in which only the strongest peoples would and should survive.

As a social phenomenon, the appeal of nationalism, even extreme nationalism, is understandable. Members of European societies that had been shaken by economic change and political stability faced severe crises of identity. The forces of urbanization, industrialization, secularism, rationalism, and skepticism had transformed social stratification systems, demolished traditional ways of life, and created complex, confusing new sets of social norms. Even while prosperity increased for the majority of people, the social fabric was disintegrating, in ways that worried observers like Emile Durkheim, Ferdinand Tönnies, and Max Weber. As individuals longed for something that might give meaning to their lives within the rapidly developing *gesellschaft*, nationalist ideologies seemed to fill the void. Nationalism would become one of history's most powerful forces.

One of the most important impacts of nationalism was that it helped to create a climate of competition and rivalry among the nation states of the western world. Such competition would have far-ranging effects and consequences. The nation-state system created the arms races, territorial disputes, alliance systems, and conditions for conflict that led to the great catastrophe of World War I. More immediately, the competitive rivalries among western states that grew out of nationalism also played out across the globe, as a rapid drive to create vast overseas colonial holdings that we call the Age of Empire.

Notes

1. Rousseau, SC, Book 1, Part 4

2. For a thorough study of the creation of nationalist traditions, see Eric J. Hobsbawm and Terence Ranger, eds., *The Invention of Tradition* (Cambridge, 1992).

3. For an in-depth explanation of the faulty science and biological determinism that fueled Social Darwinism and scientific racism, see Stephen Jay Gould, *The Mismeasure of Man* (New York, 1981).

4. See Donald L. Niewyk, *The Holocaust: Problems and Perspectives of Interpretation* (Boston, 2003) and George L. Mosse, *Masses and Man: Nationalist and Fascist Perceptions of Reality* (New York, 1980).

References and Suggested Readings:

Anderson, Benedict. *Imagined Communities: Reflections on the Origin and Spread of Nationalism*. London: Verso, 1983.

Breuilly, John. *Nationalism and the State*. Chicago: University of Chicago Press, 1994.

Gould, Stephen Jay. *The Mismeasure of Man*. New York: Norton, 1981.

Hobsbawm, Eric J. and Terence Ranger, eds. *The Invention of Tradition*. Cambridge and New York: Cambridge University Press, 1992.

Hobsbawm, Eric J. *Nations and Nationalism since 1780: programme, myth, reality*. Cambridge and New York: Cambridge University Press, 1992.

Kohn, Hans. *The Idea of Nationalism: a study in its origins and background*. New York: Macmillan, 1961.

Mosse, George L. *Masses and Man: Nationalist and Fascist Perceptions of Reality*. New York: Howard Fertig, 1980.

Niewyk, Donald L., ed. *The Holocaust: Problems and Perspectives of Interpretation*. Boston: Houghton Mifflin, 2003.

Rousseau, Jean-Jacques. *The Social Contract*.

Smith, Anthony D. *National Identity*. London: Penguin, 1991.

The New Nationalism and Racism

Heinrich von Treitschke

It is not suggested that the following selection was connected directly with Darwinism. The new bellicose nationalism and racism were, however, contemporary with, and flourished in, the Darwinian world. Nor should it be inferred that they were peculiar to Germans. Nevertheless, Heinrich von Treitschke (1834–96), historian and university professor, was one of the chief exponents of the new nationalism. A liberal in his youth, he devoted his mature years to extolling the mission of Prussia to unify Germany and of Bismarck's united Germany to lead Europe and the world. His magnum opus was his History of Germany in the Nineteenth Century *(first volume 1879). The following selections are from his lectures on politics and the state, delivered at Berlin in the 1880s and 1890s.*

The State is the people, legally united as an independent entity. By the word "people" we understand briefly a number of families permanently living side by side. This definition implies that the State is primordial and necessary, that it is as enduring as history, and no less essential to mankind than speech. History, however, begins for us with the art of writing; earlier than this men's conscious recollection of the past cannot be reckoned with. Therefore everything which lies beyond this limit is rightly judged to be prehistoric. We, on the other hand, must deal here with man as an historical being, and we can only say that creative political genius is inherent in him, and that the State, like him, subsists from the beginning. The attempt to present it as something artificial, following upon a natural condition, has fallen completely into discredit. We lack all historical knowledge of a nation without a constitution. Wherever Europeans have penetrated they have found some form of State organization, rude though it may have been. This recognition of the primordial character of the State is very widespread at the present day, but was in fact discovered in the eighteenth century. Eichhorn, Niebuhr, and Savigny were the first to show that the State is the constituted people. It was indeed a familiar fact to the Ancients in their great and simple Age. For them the State was a divinely appointed order, the origins of which were not subject to inquiry.

* * *

If, then, political capacity is innate in man, and is to be further developed, it is quite inaccurate to call the State a necessary evil. We have to deal with it as a lofty necessity of Nature. Even as the possibility of building up a civilization is dependent upon the limitation of our powers combined with the gift of reason, so also the State depends upon our inability to live alone. This Aristotle has already demonstrated. The State, says he, arose in order to make life possible; it endured to make good life possible.

* * *

Ultramontanes and Jacobins both start with the assumption that the legislation of a modern State is the work of sinful man. They thus display their total lack of reverence for the objectively revealed Will of God, as unfolded in the life of the State.

* * *

. . . if we simply look upon the State as intended to secure life and property to the individual, how comes it that the individual will also sacrifice life and property to the State? It is a false conclusion that wars are waged for the sake of material advantage. Modern wars are not fought for the sake of booty. Here the high moral ideal of national honour is a factor handed down from one generation to another, enshrining something positively sacred, and compelling the individual to sacrifice himself to it. This ideal is above all price and cannot be reduced to pounds, shillings, and pence. Kant says, "Where a price can be paid, an equivalent can be substituted. It is that which is above price and which consequently admits of no equivalent, that possesses real value." Genuine patriotism is the consciousness of co-operating with the body-politic, of being rooted in ancestral achievements and of transmitting them to descendants. Fichte has finely said, "Individual man sees in his country the realisation of his earthly immortality."

This involves that the State has a personality, primarily in the juridical, and secondly in the politico-moral sense.

* * *

Treat the State as a person, and the necessary and rational multiplicity of States follows. Just as in individual life the ego implies the existence of the non-ego, so it does in the State. The State is power, precisely in order to assert itself as against other equally independent powers. War and the administration of justice are the chief tasks of even the most barbaric States. But these tasks are only conceivable where a plurality of States are found existing side by side. Thus the idea of one universal empire is odious—the ideal of a State co-extensive with humanity is no ideal at all. In a single State the whole range of culture could never be fully spanned; no single people could unite the virtues of aristocracy and democracy. All nations, like all individuals, have their limitations, but it is exactly in the abundance of these limited qualities that the genius of humanity is exhibited. The rays of the Divine light are manifested, broken by countless facets among the separate peoples, each one exhibiting another picture and another idea of the whole. Every people has a right to believe that certain attributes of the Divine reason are exhibited in it to their fullest perfection. . . .

The features of history are virile, unsuited to sentimental or feminine natures. Brave peoples alone have an existence, an evolution or a future; the weak and cowardly perish, and perish justly. The grandeur of history lies in the perpetual conflict of nations, and it is simply foolish to desire the suppression of their rivalry. Mankind has ever found it to be so. The Kingdoms of the Diadochi and the hellenized nations of the East were the natural reaction from the world-empire of Alexander. The extreme one-sidedness of the idea of nationality which has been formed during our century by countries big and small is nothing but the natural revulsion against the world-empire of Napoleon. The unhappy attempt to transform the multiplicity of European life into the arid uniformity of universal sovereignty has produced the exclusive sway of nationality as the dominant political idea. Cosmopolitanism has receded too far.

These examples show clearly that there is no prospect of a settlement of international contradictions. The civilization of nations as well as of individuals tends to specialization. The subtleties of personal character assert themselves proportionately to increase of culture, and with its growth even the differences between nations become more sharply defined. In spite of the increased facilities of communications between different countries, no blending of their peculiarities has taken place; on the contrary, the more delicate distinctions of national character are far more marked today than in the Middle Ages. . . .

Further, if we examine our definition of the State as "the people legally united as an independent entity," we find that it can be more briefly put thus: "The State is the public force for Offence and Defence." It is, above all, Power which makes its will to prevail, it is not the totality of the people as Hegel assumes in his deification of it. The nation is not entirely comprised in the State, but the State protects and embraces the people's life, regulating its external aspects on every side. It does not ask primarily for opinion, but demands obedience, and its laws must be obeyed, whether willingly or no. . . .

The State is not an Academy of Arts. If it neglects its strength in order to promote the idealistic aspirations of man, it repudiates its own nature and perishes. This is in truth for the State equivalent to the sin against the Holy Ghost, for it is indeed a mortal error in the State to subordinate itself for sentimental reasons to a foreign Power, as we Germans have often done to England.

We have described the State as an independent force. This pregnant theory of independence implies firstly so absolute a moral supremacy that the State cannot legitimately tolerate any power above its own, and secondly a temporal freedom entailing a variety of material resources adequate to its protection against hostile influences. Legal sovereignty, the State's complete independence of any other earthly power, is so rooted in its nature that it may be said to be its very standard and criterion. . . .

The notion of sovereignty must not be rigid, but flexible and relative, like all political conceptions. Every State, in treaty making, will limit its power in certain directions for its own sake. States which conclude treaties with each other thereby curtail their absolute authority to some extent. But the rule still stands, for every treaty is a voluntary curb upon the power of each, and all international agreements are prefaced by the clause "Rebus sic stantibus." No State can pledge its future to another. It knows no arbiter, and draws up all its treaties with this implied reservation. This is supported by the axiom that so long as international law exists all treaties lose their force at the very moment when war is declared between the contracting parties; moreover, every sovereign State has the undoubted right to declare war at its pleasure, and is consequently entitled to repudiate its treaties. Upon this constantly recurring alteration of treaties the progress of history depends; every State must take care that its treaties do not survive their effective value, lest another Power should denounce them by a declaration of war; for antiquated treaties must necessarily be denounced and replaced by others more consonant with circumstances.

It is clear that the international agreements which limit the power of a State are not absolute, but voluntary self-restrictions. Hence, it follows that the establishment of a permanent international Arbitration Court is incompatible with the nature of the State, which could at all events only accept the decision of such a tribunal in cases of second- or third-rate importance. When a nation's existence is at stake there is no outside Power whose impartiality can be trusted.

* * *

If we apply the test of "autarchy" we perceive that, as Europe is now constituted, the larger States are constantly gaining influence in proportion as our international system assumes a more and more aristocratic complexion. The time is not yet very distant when the adhesion or withdrawal of such States as Piedmont and Savoy could actually decide the fate of a coalition. Today such a thing would be impossible. Since the Seven Years' War the domination of the five great Powers has been necessarily evolved. The big European questions are decided within this circle. Italy is on the verge of being admitted into it, but neither Belgium, Sweden, nor Switzerland have a voice unless their interests are directly concerned.

The entire development of European polity tends unmistakeably to drive the second-rate Powers into the background. . . .

On close examination then, it becomes clear that if the State is power, only that State which has power realizes its own idea, and this accounts for the undeniably ridiculous element which we discern in the existence of a small State. Weakness is not itself ridiculous, except when masquerading as strength.

* * *

When we begin to consider the aim of the State we are immediately confronted with the old vexed question which has needlessly fretted both the learned and the ignorant, namely—Should we look upon it as a means towards the private ends for which its citizens strive, or are those citizens means towards the great national ends of the State? The severely political outlook of the ancient world favoured the second alternative; the first is maintained by the modern social conception of the State, and the eighteenth century believed itself to have discovered in it the theory that the State should be treated only as an instrument to promote the aims of its citizens.

But, as Falstaff would say, this is "a question not to be asked," for ever since it has been considered at all, it has been universally agreed that the rights and duties of the State and its members are reciprocal. There can be no two opinions on that point. But parties which are bound together by mutual obligations and rights cannot stand to each other in the relations of means to an end, for means only exist to serve an end, and there can be no reciprocity between them. The Christian point of view has destroyed the ancient conception of the State, and the Christian would be false to himself if he did not reserve that immortal and intransitory something, which we call conscience, as his own private and peculiar possession.

In one of his greatest books, *The Foundations of the Metaphysics of Ethics,* Kant logically develops the principle that no human being may be used merely as an instrument, thereby recognizing the divinely appointed dignity of man. Conversely, to regard the State as nothing but a means for the citizens' ends is to place the subjective aspect too high. The greatness of the State lies precisely in its power of uniting the past with the present and the future; and consequently no individual has the right to regard the State as the servant of his own aims but is bound by moral duty and physical necessity to subordinate himself to it, while the State lies under the obligation to concern itself with the life of its citizens by extending to them its help and protection.

* * *

The next essential function of the State is the conduct of war. The long oblivion into which this principle had fallen is a proof of how effeminate the science of government had become in civilian hands. In our century this sentimentality was dissipated by Clausewitz, but a one-sided materialism arose in its place, after the fashion of the Manchester school, seeing in man a biped creature, whose destiny lies in buying cheap and selling dear. It is obvious that this idea is not compatible with war, and it is only since the last war that a sounder theory arose of the State and its military power.

Without war no State could be. All those we know of arose through war, and the protection of their members by armed force remains their primary and essential task. War, therefore, will endure to the end of history, as long as there is multiplicity of States. The laws of human thought and of human nature forbid any alternative, neither is one to be wished for. The blind worshipper of an eternal peace falls into the error of isolating the State, or dreams of one which is universal, which we have already seen to be at variance with reason.

Even as it is impossible to conceive of a tribunal above the State, which we have recognized as sovereign in its very essence, so it is likewise impossible to banish the idea of war from the world. It is a favourite fashion of our time to instance England as particularly ready for peace. But England is perpetually at war; there is hardly an instant in her recent history in which she has not been obliged to be fighting somewhere. The great strides which civilization makes against barbarism and unreason are only made actual by the sword. Between civilized nations also war is the form of litigation by which States make their claims valid. The arguments brought forward in these terrible law suits of the nations compel as no argument in civil suits can ever do. Often as we have tried by theory to convince the small States that Prussia alone can be the leader in Germany, we had to produce the final proof upon the battlefields of Bohemia and the Main.

Moreover war is a uniting as well as a dividing element among nations; it does not draw them together in enmity only, for through its means they learn to know and to respect each other's peculiar qualities. . . .

The grandeur of war lies in the utter annihilation of puny man in the great conception of the State, and it brings out the full magnificence of the sacrifice of fellow-countrymen for one another. In war the chaff is winnowed from the wheat. Those who have lived through 1870 cannot fail to understand Niebuhr's description of his feelings in 1813, when he speaks of how no one who has entered into the joy of being bound by a common tie to all his compatriots, gentle and simple alike, can ever forget how he was uplifted by the love, the friendliness, and the strength of that mutual sentiment.

It is war which fosters the political idealism which the materialist rejects. What a disaster for civilization it would be if mankind blotted its heroes from memory. The heroes of a nation are the figures which rejoice and inspire the spirit of its youth, and the writers whose words ring like trumpet blasts become the idols of our boyhood and our early manhood. He who feels no answering thrill is unworthy to bear arms for his country.

The Age of Empire

John W. Mackey

We can see the Crusades in the Middle Ages and the creation of overseas trading networks in the Early Modern Period as precursors to the more modern phenomenon that we call **imperialism**. During the second half of the nineteenth century, powerful western nation states embarked an energetic program of seizing and formalizing possession over much of the world, in what has often been called the **Age of Empire**.[1] One critical difference from the earlier era of colonization was that the Industrial Revolution had given Europeans the technological and military advantages that allowed them to conquer and colonize non-western lands, often quickly, easily, and brutally. This made the nineteenth and early twentieth century process both qualitatively and quantitatively different from anything that had come before.

Motives for Empire

Like earlier efforts at overseas expansion, there were various motives and goals behind the Age of Empire. Among the most obvious were economic. In previous centuries Europeans had sought to create colonies as potential sources of natural resources, slave labor, foodstuffs, or "exotic" products not available at home. As European economies had developed during the mercantilist age, their colonial endeavors relied upon increasingly higher levels of capital investment to achieve economies of scale, and by the time of the Industrial Revolution, this had created new, even more compelling economic needs. Not only could colonial territories provide raw materials and labor for factories, but they could also serve as captive markets for industrial goods produced in the colonizing country. European imperialists sought markets for their textiles in India and for opium in China; they mined diamonds and gold in Africa; and everywhere colonizing powers sought profit and competitive economic advantage over other colonial powers. As a result, indigenous economies were often weakened or even destroyed, and western-dominated investment-driven market systems took their place.

Proponents of imperialism, relying on the Classical Liberal arguments of David Ricardo and others, argued that it benefited colonizer and colonized alike by maximizing efficiency through comparative advantage. Though state involvement and monopolies were common features of this process, imperialism was often defended as the extension of "legitimate trade" across the globe. Others, however, attacked it as capitalistic exploitation, such as the Russian Communist revolutionary V.I. Lenin, who saw imperialism as the logical, and somewhat inevitable, expansion of capitalist profiteering beyond the industrialized world. He famously called it the "Latest Stage of Capitalism," arguing that as exploitation led to excess capital at home, capitalist economies would be driven to invest abroad in their quest for continued profits.

As critical as economic imperatives were, European cultural factors also supported imperialism. Westerners in the nineteenth century believed their centuries of progress had made their cultures, political institutions, and economies highly advanced in comparison to those of other societies. They often associated western civilization with civilization itself, and, influenced by Social Darwinist arguments, they viewed African and Asian peoples as primitive, or in some cases even savage or barbaric. Therefore, colonizers often spoke of their duty to carry out a **civilizing mission** in their empires. This attitude suggests that not only the colonizer, but also the colonized had something of great benefit to gain from the growth of empires. The belief in the duty of so-called advanced western nations to engage in a civilizing mission became known as "the white man's burden," a phrase taken from the title of a poem about America's involvement in the Philippines by British poet Rudyard Kipling. The civilizing mission rested on the notion that non-white people were incapable of advancement and self-government, and needed help from supposedly civilized westerners. A major component of this "civilizing mission," as in the earlier era, was the desire to spread Christianity.[2] A wave of missionary activity often followed conquest and the establishment of European rule, to help bring salvation to people whom they regarded as "heathens" and potential converts. Many Europeans held a deeply patronizing but optimistic view that the "unfortunate natives" could change and advance if exposed to the civilizing influence of Christianity and western culture. Building schools and hospitals as well as churches, missionaries considered it their duty to bring not only the Gospel but western advancement and western culture to the "backward" areas of the world.

But as the nineteenth century progressed, and Social Darwinism and scientific racism became more widespread, westerners became even more hardened in their attitudes and became less optimistic that Africans and Asians could be "improved." Yet as the twentieth century dawned and empires expanded, strategic considerations assumed more prominence. As European nations actively competed for overseas possessions, diplomatic tensions rose, heightening concern for the defensibility of the global trade routes that were the critical arteries of empire. Britain, France, Germany, and the United States, among others, sought places to establish military garrisons, fueling stations, and supply depots to protect and support both commercial and military traffic. Locations such as the Suez Canal, Singapore, and South Africa assumed enormous importance in the functioning of imperial systems, and for both politicians and military planners, securing their possessions from jealous imperial rivals became an essential priority.

The Global Reach of the New Imperialism

Between about 1870 and 1914, a great wave of colonization and growth of empires rapidly changed the world. Nineteenth-century nationalism fueled great rivalries among the powerful nation states of Europe, while Germany and the United States began to take their places as competitive world industrial powers. Each great power sought the prestige of a vast empire, as well as the presumed economic benefits this would bring.

Before the nineteenth century, European contact with Africa had been mostly confined to coastal areas. During the course of the century, however, western explorers, missionaries, and merchants began penetrating the interior of the continent, revealing great quantities of resources that might be exploited. As nationalistic fervor began to drive colonial competition ever more intensely, what became known the **"Scramble for Africa"** commenced during the 1880s. To minimize future conflicts among themselves in the "Dark Continent," European representatives at the Berlin Conference of 1884-5 literally divided up the continent with a map and a ruler, then set ground rules governing future colonial trade, settlement, and administration. By the eve of World War I, the nations of Britain, France, Belgium, Germany, Italy, Spain, and Portugal controlled nearly all of Africa; only Ethiopia, which had resisted Italian imperialist advances, and Liberia, a state founded for freed American slaves, remained independent. Many of the arbitrary and impractical colonial lines drawn at Berlin, which had largely ignored the traditional economies and settlement patterns of the local peoples, became the borders of the modern independent African nations that emerged after World War Two.

By the late nineteenth century, Europeans had already possessed colonial footholds in Asia for centuries. But the Age of Empire expanded and intensified their control. Britain held the largest and most prestigious imperial prize in its control of the "subcontinent" of India, accomplished through the state-supported efforts of the British East India Company, the largest privately funded company of the age. Britain also claimed significant colonies in Southeast Asia. The French had established a presence in Indochina (present-day Vietnam, Laos, and Cambodia), the Dutch held lucrative colonies in the East Indies (present-day Indonesia), and the expanding Russian empire had extended its tentacles into Manchuria and central Asia. By the end of the century, the United States took control of the Pacific islands of Hawaii, the Philippines, and Guam in a wave of colonialism in the era of the Spanish-American War. Meanwhile, numerous powers had forced major trade concessions from the declining Chinese Qing dynasty, helping to bring about its demise in the early twentieth century. In Asia, only Japan was largely successful in resisting foreign incursion. Modernizing on the Western model during the nineteenth century, Japan too became an imperial power, annexing Korea and Taiwan by 1910.

Though often of an informal nature, Western imperialism also touched other less-developed parts of the world, including Latin America and the Middle East. While European powers often recognized the independence of states, they were also able to enter into trade or diplomatic agreements that made sovereign nations economically, politically, and/or militarily dependent on one of the "Great Powers." For example, during most of the nineteenth century, British financial and trading firms came to dominate Brazilian exports of coffee, sugar, and cotton, making Brazil, in the minds of some, a *de facto* British colony. Other territories, including some that officially remained parts of the declining Ottoman Empire, became the focus of European competition for control of the resources they offered, such as petroleum, by the turn of the twentieth century. While European imperial powers did establish the occasional formal colony in these regions, for the most part western dominance was less direct, though sometimes no less thorough. As empires competed with each other for far-flung resources, an increasing proportion of the world's population became entangled in the expanding global economy.

Imperial Administration

The creation of empire was based on the ability to impose authority, and empire-builders devised new institutions to carry out the tasks of governance and administration. Depending on the circumstances, they employed a variety of strategies to govern their overseas possessions. Under the system of **direct rule**, imperial officials assumed formal, unambiguous control over the colony. In this arrangement, the new rulers might hire the services of low-level native administrators, but the real power was in the hands of foreigners who acted as direct representatives of the crown or parliament back home. An example of direct rule was the enormous, diverse territory of French West Africa, where the French Governor General in Dakar carried out the will of the government in Paris. Supported as necessary by French military forces largely composed of African troops, the Governor General enforced justice and oversaw the operations of both large French trading companies and evangelization efforts.

Other imperial territories were governed by a system of **indirect rule**, where the colonizers ruled through arrangements with local princes, aristocrats, or other indigenous elites. While ultimate authority usually rested in the hands of the colonizing power, indigenous leaders were responsible for many elements of local administration and often kept much of their traditional social systems intact. An example of indirect rule would be Britain's relationship with Malay leaders, known as sultans, whose rule was strengthened by British advisors, investment, and military support. While local elites did most of the day-to-day work of governance, both the British and the sultans profited from exports of minerals and agricultural products. The advantage of the system of indirect rule was that it enabled colonial powers to both gain and maintain control without exhausting their own manpower and resources.

Settler colonies were a different sort of colony, a type that had certain similarities to the colonies established by Spain in Central and South America during the sixteenth and seventeenth centuries. In such places settler populations from the colonizing country had a hand in creating institutions of self-government, and they often displaced indigenous populations through forced resettlement or even genocide. However, a significant difference from the Spanish model was that, during the Age of Empire, the rise of "modern" racial ideologies usually meant stricter segregation of settlers and natives. Canada, Rhodesia, Australia, and New Zealand—all British colonial holdings—are examples of settler colonies.

Somewhat ironically, imperialism ultimately generated the forces that would bring it down. Colonial regimes and the inequality they brought created anger and resentment among indigenous peoples. As a result, colonial dominance encouraged previously separate peoples to unify against foreign rule, eventually creating **nationalist movements** seeking independence. For example, resentment of British colonial rule caused Indians, many of whom had little in common except a desire to be free of colonial domination, to unify in the Indian National Congress (INC) in 1885. The INC demanded and received a voice in the colonial administration, and later emerged as a leading voice for Indian independence. Similar nationalist movements developed throughout the colonized world, and in the twentieth century, they helped dismantle empires and create entirely new nation states.

The Impact of the New Imperialism

The economic impacts of imperialism varied with the resources, demography, climate, and location of the colony. Since the dominant colonial powers orchestrated economic activity for their own benefit, without regard to the needs and traditions of indigenous peoples, the economic effects of imperialism were often brutally harsh and disruptive. Colonial economic imperatives often interfered with or destroyed traditional patterns of trade, agriculture, herding, and commodity production. In some areas, colonial powers imposed **single-crop agriculture**, seizing land to create plantations for the growing of export crops. In other areas, mining operations caused waves of migration, as indigenous people often traveled great distances to take cash-based employment so that they could pay the colonial taxes imposed upon them by foreign powers.

The New Imperialism served to reorder the global economy and social system. As a result of the vast extent of western colonization and the dominant position of European interests and those of white settlers, colonialism imposed what might be called an international system of stratification. And because positions of power, authority, wealth, and opportunity were reserved for white populations and European nations, imperialism contributed to pervasive attitudes of racial superiority. Both the inequalities and the attitudes promoted by imperialism still linger in the twenty-first century.

The intense and prolonged cultural contacts of imperialism resulted in a significant degree of social change. On the whole, because colonizing powers held the upper hand in colonial relationships, the impact of western cultures on non-western cultures was greater than the reverse, since western cultures, beliefs, and social systems held higher prestige within the colonial order. Of course, it did work in both directions; new products, new types of employment, greater contact with non-western people, and increased immigration into the west all contributed to significant social change. By the twentieth century, **cultural diffusion** could be found in the homes of both colonizer and colonized.[3] Englishmen enjoyed tea and tobacco from the empire while sitting in London, whereas Indians in Delhi often spoke English while wearing shirts made in Britain.

But the colonized often saw their cultures and societies transformed in a more thorough way than did the colonizers, as the sustained and profound forces of imperialism often led to **acculturation**. The influence of missionaries, western-style education systems, and the dominance of the economic and political culture of the colonizer often transformed indigenous societies and cultures almost beyond recognition. As a consequence, non-western people living in European colonies frequently wore western clothes, spoke European languages, attended Christian churches, and worked in colonial offices or western-owned businesses. Indeed, colonial penetration has been directly or indirectly responsible for the extinction of hundreds, and perhaps even thousands, of languages across the world, as well as the suppression of numerous native religions, and countless local customs and traditions.[4] By the time that many societies were able to assert their independence, the imperial legacy had already profoundly and irreversibly distorted traditional ways of life.

The age of imperialism grew out of great-power rivalries and competition, economic motives, and a western desire to carry out what they saw as a civilizing mission. In a short span of about forty years, the European powers and the United States colonized nearly all of Africa, as well as a significant portion of Asia and the Pacific islands. Colonialism reordered the world economy, with the western powers as the beneficiaries of African and Asian labor, resources, and markets at the expense of traditional indigenous economies. In effect, colonialism created a global form of stratification in which whites held the dominant position. Colonialism also brought profound changes to non-western cultural systems and political structures. As it did so, the Age of Empire also created great tensions that would have an enormous effect on the twentieth century, by contributing to the rivalries that would bring about World War I, and by creating new forms of nationalism that would challenge the colonial system itself.

Notes

1. In his trilogy of books chronicling the "long" nineteenth century (1789-1914), influential historian Eric J. Hobsbawm divides the century into "The Age of Revolution" from 1789 to 1848, "The Age of Capital" from 1848 to 1875, and "The Age of Empire" from 1875 to 1914.

2. See Andrew Porter, *Religion Versus Empire?: British Protestant Missionaries and Overseas Expansion, 1700-1914* (Manchester, 2004).

3. For more on the impact of imperialism on the cultures of the colonized, see Frederick Cooper and Ann Laura Stoler, eds., *Tensions of Empire: Colonial Cultures in a Bourgeois World* (Berkeley, 1997).

4. Daniel Nettle and Suzanne Romaine, *The Extinction of the World's Languages* (Oxford, 2002).

References and Suggested Readings:

Cain, P.J., and A.G. Hopkins, *British Imperialism: innovation and expansion, 1688-1914*. London and New York: Longman, 1993.

Cannadine, David. *Ornamentalism*. Oxford: Oxford University Press, 2001.

Cohn, Bernard S. *Colonialism and Its Forms of Knowledge*. Princeton, NJ: Princeton University Press, 1996.

Cooper, Frederick, and Ann Laura Stoler, eds. *Tensions of Empire: Colonial Cultures in a Bourgeois World*. Berkeley: University of California Press, 1997.

Hall, Catherine, and Sonya O. Rose, eds. *At Home with the Empire: Metropolitan Culture and the Imperial World*. Cambridge and New York: Cambridge University Press, 2007.

Hochschild, Adam. *King Leopold's Ghost: a story of greed, terror, and heroism in colonial Africa.* Boston: Houghton Mifflin, 1998.

Hobsbawm, Eric J. *The Age of Empire, 1875-1914.* New York: Pantheon Books, 1987.

Marshall, P.J., ed. *The Cambridge Illustrated History of the British Empire, Vol. III: The Nineteenth Century.* Cambridge: Cambridge University Press, 1996.

Nettle, Daniel, and Suzanne Romaine. *The Extinction of the World's Languages.* Oxford: Oxford University Press, 2002.

Porter, Andrew. *Religion Versus Empire?: British Protestant Missionaries and Overseas Expansion, 1700-1914.* Manchester and New York: Manchester University Press, 2004.

Said, Edward W. *Culture and Imperialism.* New York: Vintage, 1993.

Imperialism, the Latest Stage of Capitalism

V.I. Lenin

These are excerpts from a lengthy polemical pamphlet that Lenin wrote in 1916. For ideological reasons, the work was later renamed Imperialism, the Highest Stage of Capitalism, *the title by which it is commonly known today.*

The export of *goods* was characteristic of the old capitalism, under the complete control of free competition. For the new capitalism, controlled by monopoly, the export of *capital* has become characteristic . . .

Of course if capitalism could develop agriculture, which today has everywhere fallen terribly far behind industry, if it could raise the standard of living of the bulk of the population, who everywhere remain, despite dizzying technological progress, half-starved and impoverished—then there could be no talk of a capital surplus. And this is the argument usually advanced by *petit-bourgeois* critics of capitalism.[1] But then capitalism would not be capitalism, for both unevenness of development and semi-starvation living standards are fundamental, inevitable conditions and prerequisites of this mode of production. As long as capitalism remains capitalism, a surplus of capital will be deployed not to raise the general standard of living in a given country—since this would lower the profits of the capitalists—but to raise profits by exporting capital abroad to the backward countries. In these backward countries profits are usually high, because there is little capital, the price of land is comparatively low, wages are low, and raw materials are cheap. It is *possible* to export capital because a number of backward countries have already been drawn into the world capitalist economic system, major railway lines have been built or are under construction, the elementary conditions for industrial development have been secured, and so on. It is *necessary* to export capital because in several countries capitalism has become "over-ripe," and capital has no field for profitable investment, given the underdevelopment of agriculture and the poverty of the masses . . .

The export of capital influences the development of capitalism, greatly accelerating it in the countries to which it is directed. If therefore, to some extent, this export can lead to stagnation in the development of the exporting countries, this can happen only at the price of permitting an intensification of the further development of capitalism throughout the world . . .

[T]he defining characteristic of the period we are examining is the final partitioning of the world, final not in the sense that it cannot be *repartitioned*—repartition is possible, even inevitable—but in the sense that the colonial policy of the capitalist countries has *completed* the seizure of the unoccupied land on our planet. The world, for the first time, is completely partitioned, so henceforth there can be *only* repartition, that is, transfer from one "proprietor" to another, rather than from an ownerless to an "owned" state.

Thus we are living in a distinctive era of global colonial policy, which is very closely connected to the "latest stage in the development of capitalism"—finance capital . . .

It is not only the already-discovered sources of raw materials that are of interest to finance capital, but also potential sources, for technology is developing with incredible speed in our era, and land that is useless today can perhaps be made useful tomorrow if new methods are found (to this end a major bank can mount a special expedition of engineers, agronomists, etc.) and if a large expenditure of capital is made. The same principle applies to prospecting for mineral wealth, new methods of processing and utilizing raw materials, and so on. Hence the inevitable aspiration of finance capital to increase its territory. Just as the trusts capitalize their holdings at two or three times their value, taking into account "potential" profits in the future (and not just in the present) and subsequent results of monopoly, in general finance capital strives to capture as much land as it can, wherever and however it can, taking into account possible sources of raw materials, afraid of falling behind in the mad scramble for the last morsels of the unpartitioned world, or for the repartition of morsels already divided up.

. . . . . .

We must now try to summarize what we know, to gather together what has been said above about imperialism. Imperialism arose as a development of the fundamental characteristics of capitalism in general. But capitalism became capitalist imperialism only at a particular, very high stage of its development, when some of the fundamental characteristics of capitalism began to turn into their opposites, when the characteristics of the era of transition from capitalism to a higher socio-economic structure had taken form and revealed themselves. Economically, the most important thing was a change from capitalist free competition to capitalist monopoly.

Free competition is the essential characteristic of capitalism, and of commodity production in general; monopoly is the exact opposite of free competition, but the latter has transformed itself into monopoly before our very eyes, creating large-scale industry and forcing out the small, replacing the large with the even larger, pushing the concentration of industry and capital to the point where out of it has arisen and is arising monopoly:—cartels, syndicates, trusts—merging with the capital of the ten or so banks that control billions. At the same time the monopolies, which have arisen out of free competition, do not eliminate it but exist above and beside it, thus engendering a series of particularly acute and abrupt contradictions, clashes, and conflicts. Monopoly is the transition from capitalism to a higher system.

If we had to give the shortest possible definition of imperialism, we would therefore have to say that imperialism is the monopolistic phase of capitalism. This definition would capture the most important point for, on the one hand, the finance capital of a few enormous monopolistic banks has merged with the capital of the monopolist cartels of industrialists; and on the other hand, the partition of the world is a transition from a colonial policy that has freely extended to all territories as yet unseized by a capitalist power, to a colonial policy of monopolist possession of all the world's land, carried through to the end.

But excessively short definitions, useful as they are to sum up the most important points, are nonetheless insufficient, because we need to deduce from them the particularly essential features of the phenomenon that we must define. Therefore, without forgetting the conventional and relative significance of definitions—which can never encompass completely all the multitudinous features of a phenomenon in its full development—we must provide a definition of imperialism that includes the following five fundamental features: (1) the concentration of production and capital has reached such a high stage that it has produced monopolies which play a decisive role in economic life; (2) the merging of bank capital with industrial capital, creating on the basis of this "finance capital" a financial oligarchy; (3) the export of capital, as opposed to the export of goods, acquires a particularly important significance; (4) the formation of international monopolistic alliances of capitalists, dividing up the world among themselves; and (5) the completion of the territorial division of the globe by the major capitalist powers. Imperialism is capitalism at that stage of development when the dominance of monopoly and financial capital has been established, the export of capital has acquired outstanding importance, the division of the world by international trusts has begun, and the partition of all the earth's territories by the major capitalist countries has been completed.

. . . . . .

As we have seen, the deepest economic foundation of imperialism is monopoly. This is capitalist monopoly, *i.e.* monopoly that has arisen out of capitalism and exists in the general environment of capitalism—commodity production and competition—in permanent and irresolvable contradiction to this environment. Nevertheless, like all monopoly it inevitably creates a tendency toward stagnation and decay. Because monopoly prices are fixed, if only temporarily, to some extent incentives for technological—and consequently for all other—progress disappear. Furthermore, there arises the *economic* possibility that technological progress will be deliberately retarded. For example, in America a man named Owens invented a bottle-making machine that revolutionized the manufacture of bottles. The German cartel of bottle manufacturers bought the Owens patents and set them aside rather than use them. Of course, under capitalism monopoly can never totally and permanently eliminate competition in the global market . . . And of course the possibility of lowering production costs and raising profits by means of technological improvements is an impetus toward change. But the *tendency* toward stagnation and decay that is characteristic of monopoly will continue to operate, and in certain branches of industry, in certain countries, in certain periods of time, it will prevail.

Monopolist possession of particularly vast, rich, or conveniently located colonies will work in the same way.

Further, imperialism is an enormous accumulation of money capital in a handful of countries, reaching, as we have seen, the level of 100–150 million francs in securities. Hence the extraordinary growth of a class or, more accurately, a stratum of *rentiers, i.e.* people who live by "clipping coupons"—people entirely disconnected from participation in any kind of enterprise—people whose profession is idleness. The export of capital, one of the most essential foundations of imperialism, further intensifies this complete isolation of the *rentier* stratum from production and marks as parasitic the entire country that lives by exploiting the labor of several overseas countries and colonies.

. . . . . .

On the one hand the enormous amount of finance capital concentrated in a few hands, creating an extraordinarily extensive and dense network of relationships and connections that subordinates not only all of the medium-sized and small but even the very small capitalists and proprietors; on the other hand, the intensifying struggle against groups of financiers in the other nation-states for the partition of the world and domination over other lands—together these have brought about the unanimous conversion of the propertied classes to the imperialist cause. "Universal" enthusiasm about the prospects for imperialism, rabid defense of it, portraying it as attractively as possible—these are the signs of the times. Imperialist ideology even cozies up to the working class. There is no Chinese wall separating it from the other classes.[2] The leaders of today's so-called "Social Democratic" party in Germany[3] have truly earned the designation "social imperialist," *i.e.* socialists in word but imperialists in deed, while in 1902 Hobson had already noted the existence of "Fabian imperialists" in England, members of the opportunistic Fabian Society.[4]

. . . . . .

We have seen how the economic essence of imperialism is monopoly capitalism. This is what defines its place in history, for monopoly that develops in the context of free competition, to be exact *out of* free competition, is the transition from capitalism to a higher socio-economic structure. We must note in particular four principal aspects of monopoly, or principal manifestations of monopoly capitalism, that characterize the era we are examining.

First, monopoly arose out of the concentration of production at a very high stage of its development. This means monopolist associations of capitalists, cartels, syndicates, and trusts. We have seen what an enormous role they play in contemporary economic life. By the beginning of the 20th century they had achieved total supremacy in the advanced countries. Although the first steps toward forming cartels had been taken earlier by countries with high protective tariffs (Germany, America),

Great Britain, with her system of free trade, only slightly later displayed the same basic reality: the birth of monopoly out of the concentration of production.

Second, monopolies have accelerated the seizure of the most important sources of raw materials, especially for the basic and most highly cartelized industries of capitalist society: coal-mining and iron-making. Monopolistic control of the most important sources of raw materials has greatly increased the power of giant capital and intensified the antagonism between cartelized and non-cartelized industry.

Third, monopoly was an outgrowth of the banks. They have transformed themselves from modest intermediary enterprises into monopolists of finance capital. Some three to five enormous banks in each of the leading capitalist countries have accomplished the "intimate union" of industrial and finance capital; they have concentrated in their hands control of countless millions, constituting the greater part of the capital and monetary income of the entire nation. A financial oligarchy that imposes a dense network of relationships of dependency on absolutely all of the economic and political institutions of contemporary bourgeois society—this is the most striking manifestation of this monopoly.

Fourth, monopoly is an outgrowth of colonial policy. To the many "old" motives of colonial policy, finance capital has added a struggle for sources of raw materials, for the export of capital, for "spheres of influence"—*i.e.* zones for advantageous deals, concessions, monopolistic profits, *etc.*—in the end for economic territory in general. For example, when European colonial holdings comprised only 10% of Africa, as was the case in 1876, colonial policy could develop by non-monopolistic means—"free seizure" of territory, so to speak. But when, by 1900, 90% of Africa had been seized, when the whole world had been partitioned, inevitably the era of monopoly possession of colonies and, consequently, of particularly intense competition for the division and re-division of the world, began.

The extent to which monopoly capitalism has intensified all the contradictions of capitalism is well known. It will suffice to point out the high cost of living and the yoke of the cartels. This intensification of contradictions is the most powerful motive force of the transitional historical period that began with the conclusive victory of international finance capital.

Monopolies, oligarchies, a struggle for supremacy rather than for freedom, exploitation of an ever larger number of small or weak countries by a handful of wealthy or powerful nations[5]—all of this has engendered the distinguishing characteristics of imperialism which compel us to define it as parasitic or decaying capitalism. More and more conspicuously the creation of the "rentier state," the money-lender state, whose bourgeoisie increasingly lives off the export of capital and "clipping coupons," emerges as one of the tendencies of imperialism. It would be a mistake to think that this tendency toward decay precludes rapid growth of capitalism. On the contrary, in the era of imperialism certain branches of industry, certain strata of the bourgeoisie, and certain countries display, to a greater or lesser extent, now one, now another of these tendencies. Overall, capitalism is growing immeasurably faster than before. However, not only is this growth becoming more and more uneven in general, but the unevenness is particularly evident in the decay of the countries strongest in capital (Britain) . . .

In its turn, this extraordinarily fast-growing finance capital, precisely because it has grown so quickly, doesn't mind moving along to a "quieter" possession of colonies subject to seizure—and not by peaceful means alone—from richer countries. For the last few decades, economic development has proceeded even faster in the United States than in Germany; it is precisely *because* of this that the parasitic characteristics of the new American capitalism are so clearly evident. On the other hand, if you were to compare the republican American bourgeoisie with the monarchist bourgeoisie of Japan or Germany, you would see that enormous political differences weaken considerably in the era of imperialism—not because they are not important in general, but because in all of these instances we are talking about a bourgeoisie with the characteristic features of parasitism.

Receipt of high monopolistic profits by the capitalists in one of the many branches of industry, in one of the many countries, *etc.*, gives them the economic means to buy off certain strata of the workers—and for a while at least a significant minority of them—bringing them over to the side of a given industry or a given nation against all others. And the intensifying antagonism among the imperialist nations for the partition of the world strengthens this effort. This is the basis for the bond between imperialism and opportunism[6] that was evident earliest and most clearly in Britain, due to the fact that certain features of imperialist development were evident there much earlier than in other countries . . . In fact the extraordinary rapidity and loathsomeness of the development of opportunism do not guarantee its enduring success; the rapid growth of a malignant boil on a healthy organism can only hasten the boil's bursting, freeing the organism from it. Most dangerous of all in this respect are people who do not want to understand that the struggle against imperialism is an empty and dishonest phrase unless it is inseparably joined with the struggle against opportunism . . .

Notes

1. The phrase "*petit-bourgeois*" functions as a term of general-purpose abuse in the writings of early twentieth-century Communists. Strictly speaking it means "from the lower ranks of the bourgeoisie," but as commonly used it is not necessarily an accurate description of the class origins of the person or persons being denounced. Here as elsewhere, it can best be understood as meaning "people who think they are on the Left because they criticize capitalism, but who are actually capitalist dupes because they don't read enough Marx and/or don't interpret him the same way I do."

2. Lenin is referring, metaphorically, to the Great Wall of China.

3. The Social Democratic Party (SPD) was Germany's largest mass political party. Backed by the labor unions, it was a socialist party, but Lenin considered the SPD insufficiently Marxist and insufficiently critical of German imperialism.

4. The Fabian Society was a small but influential group of British social-ists led by Sidney and Beatrice Webb. For a variety of reasons too com-plicated to explain here, they actively supported continued expansion of the British Empire.

5. When Lenin says "small or weak," he is probably thinking not only of small Third World territories but also of China, which though vast and populous was also subject to commercial exploitation by the imperial powers because of its military weakness. When he says "wealthy or powerful," he is undoubtedly thinking not only of wealthy capitalist nations like Britain and France but also of his own country, Russia, which had just begun to industrialize and had little capital, but which had amassed considerable territory on its borders through military force.

6. Lenin considered support for imperialism by the leaders of a socialist party unprincipled. He uses the word "opportunism" here because he assumes that these leaders must be driven by unworthy motives: they are trying to curry favor with their national elites and/or trying to attract votes from their jingoistic countrymen. The possibility that they might be sincere, if perhaps mistaken, he does not consider.

Translated from the Russian and annotated by Kathleen Callanan Martin

The White Man's Burden

Rudyard Kipling

This famous poem, written by Britain's imperial poet, was a response to the American take over of the Phillipines after the Spanish-American War.

Take up the White Man's burden—
Send forth the best ye breed—
Go bind your sons to exile
To serve your captives' need;
To wait in heavy harness,
On fluttered folk and wild—
Your new-caught, sullen peoples,
Half-devil and half-child.

Take up the White Man's burden—
In patience to abide,
To veil the threat of terror
And check the show of pride;
By open speech and simple,
An hundred times made plain
To seek another's profit,
And work another's gain.

Take up the White Man's burden—
The savage wars of peace—
Fill full the mouth of Famine
And bid the sickness cease;
And when your goal is nearest
The end for others sought,
Watch sloth and heathen Folly
Bring all your hopes to nought.

Take up the White Man's burden—
No tawdry rule of kings,
But toil of serf and sweeper—
The tale of common things.
The ports ye shall not enter,
The roads ye shall not tread,
Go mark them with your living,
And mark them with your dead.

Take up the White Man's burden—
And reap his old reward:
The blame of those ye better,
The hate of those ye guard—
The cry of hosts ye humour
(Ah, slowly!) toward the light:—
"Why brought he us from bondage,
Our loved Egyptian night?"

Take up the White Man's burden—
Ye dare not stoop to less—
Nor call too loud on Freedom
To cloke your weariness;
By all ye cry or whisper,
By all ye leave or do,
The silent, sullen peoples
Shall weigh your gods and you.

Take up the White Man's burden—
Have done with childish days—
The lightly proferred laurel,
The easy, ungrudged praise.
Comes now, to search your manhood
Through all the thankless years
Cold, edged with dear-bought wisdom,
The judgment of your peers!

The Great War

Benjamin E. Varat

On June 28, 1914, in the Bosnian city Sarajevo, Gavrilo Princip, a 19-year old Serb nationalist, shot and killed Archduke Franz Ferdinand, heir to the Austro-Hungarian throne. His assassination set off a chain of events that led to the outbreak of a war in Europe that eventually resulted in the most costly conflict the world had yet experienced. Nearly forty million people, many of them civilians, would be killed, wounded, or missing by the time World War I ended.

What began as a European war ultimately spanned the globe. Men died fighting in Africa, the Middle East, South America, and Asia while Indians, Australians, South Africans, Canadians, Chinese and Senegalese soldiers perished in the trenches of Belgium and France. Millions of troops from the United States played the decisive role in ending the war. The sheer breadth and scope of World War I presents a conundrum to those who study it: how did the assassination of an Austro-Hungarian archduke result in the most destructive war the world had yet seen?

Franz Ferdinand's death is only a small part of the answer to why the Great Powers chose the battlefield over diplomacy. Alliance systems, nationalistic ideologies, the decay of multi-ethnic empires, an arms race, and incompetent leadership all played some part in precipitating war. Add to this mix the destabilizing effects of industrialization and mass social change, and a picture emerges of the Great Powers standing on a precipice, needing only a small push, to send them to their doom below.

Origins of the War

Untangling the origins of World War I begins in the Balkans, the region of Southeastern Europe that today includes parts or all of the following countries: Turkey, Greece, Bulgaria, Romania, Albania, Macedonia, Serbia, Kosovo, Croatia, Montenegro, Slovenia and Bosnia-Herzegovina.[1] A hodge-podge of national and religious divisions, the Balkans prior to World War I were marked by a rising sea of nationalist fervor that led to occasional wars and threatened to tear apart the two empires in the region, the Ottoman and Austro-Hungarian. The two Balkan Wars of 1912 and 1913 had largely dismantled the European portion of the Ottoman Empire, increasing the size of several nation-states like Serbia, Bulgaria, and Romania, but ultimately the conflicts left even the victors unsatisfied. Practically every nation sought further territory, which political leaders justified by appeals to nationalism and reference to historical myths that told of some long ago moment when all the people of this nation had lived together in a single state.

The Austro-Hungarian Empire was diverse political entity whose varied subjects owed allegiance to the Habsburg family, a dynasty that had controlled much of Central and Eastern Europe as Holy Roman Emperors since before the era of Martin Luther. In 1914, Emperor Franz Josef had already been in power for more than sixty-five years and was a deeply conservative man who hated the changes wrought by liberalism, industrialization, and especially ethnic nationalism. He and his advisors, increasingly insecure about their Great Power status, recognized the mortal threat this last ideology posed to the Austro-Hungarian empire and did everything in their power to suppress it. Of particular concern were the ethnic Serbs, millions of whom lived under Franz Josef's authority, but who clearly preferred to join their brethren in the Kingdom of Serbia just to the east and south. Even before the turn of the century, illegal Serb nationalist organizations had operated within the empire, stirring up popular resentment and assassinating Austrian officials, sometimes with the active support of Serbia's government. Gavrilo Princip was a member of one such organization, known as the **Black Hand**.

This explosive situation raised tensions with Russia, whose tsar saw himself as the protector of all ethnic Slavs, who included Serbs as well as Russians. However odd it may seem that the Russian tsar, who ruled a highly insecure, unstable multi-ethnic empire, should support ethnic nationalism, the fact remained that his support for Serbia placed Russia and Austria-Hungary on a collision course. By 1914, most observers saw war between them as inevitable. If this war occurred, it threatened to bring in the rest of the "Great Powers": Germany, France, and Great Britain.

Culture and treaties bound Germany and Austria-Hungary closely together. These states, both ruled by ethnic Germans, had an alliance dating back to the early 1880s. The treaties establishing this relationship, which became known as the **Triple Alliance** when Italy joined it, stated that any attack on one member was considered an attack on all of them. In other words, if the Russians initiated hostilities with Austria-Hungary, Germany and Italy were obligated to declare war on Russia.

But it was even more complicated than that, since Russia too had alliances. A close one existed with France that dated back to the 1890s. Humiliated by the loss of Alsace-Lorraine to Prussia in 1870, the French were determined to regain the region, but German unification the following year had left France comparatively weaker than its new neighbor. This made an alliance with Russia, resentful of German policies in the Balkans and desperate to modernize, a logical step. Thus was born the Franco-Russian alliance. French money flowed into Russia to build railroads and help industrialize and empire that was still quite backwards. France had successfully rearranged the European chessboard; hereafter, Germany faced the possibility of a two-front war.

The last of the "Great Powers," Great Britain, was an obvious alliance partner for neither France or Russia, and certainly not both. During most of the nineteenth century, Britain had tried to avoid continental entanglements, preferring to focus on its vast empire, which often led to conflicts with France and Russia, though seldom with

Germany. But everything changed for Britain in 1897 when German naval advisors to Kaiser Wilhelm II convinced him that Germany needed a large navy to have its own "place in the sun." Aspiring to be a global power, Germany started building a large deepwater navy that would command Britain's respect and vastly increase German prestige. Apparently none of the Germans considered that the British might see the building of a modern German fleet—whose apparent purpose was to challenge British naval supremacy—as a threat.

The British Parliament responded to the German naval expansion by approving huge new naval expenditures of its own. Meanwhile, British political leaders, worried by rising German power, accepted an alliance with France in 1904 that overturned nearly a thousand years of Anglo-French conflict. This was followed three years later by a series of agreements that created the alliance known as the **Triple Entente**, which divided the Great Powers of Europe into two antagonistic coalitions.

As discussed in earlier chapters, racial theories and nationalist fervor added further layers of tension. Social Darwinism gained wide popular appeal, especially in Germany, among people who completely misunderstood Darwin's theories of evolution and natural selection. Social Darwinists claimed that humans were naturally divided by distinct racial and physical characteristics into nations. War, they believed, was the natural state for nations, since it destroyed the weaker nations while only the fittest survived. Conflict also supposedly cleansed the nation of its weakest elements, those people somehow unfit to be part of the nation, whom the German historian Heinrich von Treitschke called "puny man."[2] The fact that no large-scale European wars had taken place since 1815 meant that such rhetoric was absorbed by citizens who had scarce knowledge of the nature of warfare, and even less sense of what it might be like when fought with industrial weaponry.

If war was the natural state for the nation, then the nation had to strengthened at all costs. Towards this goal, youth groups devoted to the active life cropped up in the early years of the twentieth century. The *Wandervogel* in Germany and Boy Scouts in Britain were but two examples of new organizations focused on liberating young people, mostly boys, from the confines of their sedate bourgeois lives and giving them a vigorous regimen of group exercise and outdoor activities. Leaders of such organizations explicitly connected their efforts with building national unity in the face of shadowy foreign and domestic threats.

No one doubted that such threats existed, and war scares were common in the years before World War I. Balkan instability, alliance systems, aggressive ideologies, and the ongoing rapid social change caused by modernization left many in Europe so unsettled that war—by then an abstract concept tied somehow to heroism and national honor—seemed positively desirable. All these factors provided kindling for a European conflagration. Gavrilo Princip's bullets provided the spark that set it alight.

Mobilization: July, 1914

The assassination of heir-apparent Franz Ferdinand in late June gave Austria-Hungary its excuse to finally act against the Kingdom of Serbia. Worried about Russian intervention, Austrian officials asked German leaders if they would support military action against Serbia. They responded affirmatively, promising to back

Austria even if Russia entered the conflict. This "blank check" was a key development in the run to war for two reasons. First, it allowed Austria to act freely against Serbia without worrying about Russia's response. Second, the "blank check" in essence gave Austria control over whether or not Germany went to war, because an Austrian declaration of war on Serbia committed Germany to fight.

In hindsight, German leaders faced a difficult set of circumstances in 1914. By then, they feared that the European balance-of-power had shifted against them. Their efforts to build a navy that could rival Britain's not only had failed—the British navy was still twice as large—but also left German finances severely strained. Meanwhile, Germany's potential enemies were only getting stronger. Russia was industrializing and each new year brought more railroads and a stronger military, while France, too, was increasing the size of its army. With Austria- Hungary, Germany's only real ally, destabilized by rising nationalist movements, 1914 appeared to many German officials as the last chance for victory before the balance of power shifted too far in the other direction. Diplomacy alone could not protect them, and Germany had shown little diplomatic skill in recent decades anyway. Thus the "blank check" was a means to bring war without having to assume responsibility for starting it. The German strategy ensured that once war came, it would involve all of Europe.[3]

The German war plan, known as the **Schlieffen Plan**, had been developed as a response to the Franco-Russian alliance of the early 1890s.[4] Count Alfred von Schlieffen, the head of the German General Staff, had feared the possibility of a two-front war, and believed that to avoid this, Germany needed to defeat one of its enemies before the other was ready to fight. In the early 1900s Schlieffen had assumed that the backward Russians would take about six weeks to mobilize their forces, and that this would allow Germany to focus all its efforts on taking Paris and destroying the French army before dealing with the Russian threat to the east. Therefore, the plan required the Germans to attack France the instant war broke out.

Since any delay in defeating France would leave Germany vulnerable to a Russian advance, Schlieffen wanted German forces to avoid the French defenses on the border with German-controlled Alsace-Lorraine. Instead, he planned to send the German army through neutral Belgium, which shared an unfortified border with France. This, he believed, would surprise the French, throw them off-balance and ultimately lead to a quick surrender. While the breach of Belgian neutrality might bring Great Britain into the war, this did not seem to worry Schlieffen because Britain lacked a sizeable army and its superior naval power would not matter much in what, he assumed, would be a six week campaign. Moreover, once Germany defeated France, German troops would vacate Belgium, removing the British rationale for war. According to his plan, success on the Western Front would ensure success on the Eastern Front; undistracted by a two-front war, the better-trained and better-equipped German forces would grind down the Russians even if the latter had more troops. The Schlieffen Plan was a gamble, but one the German leadership accepted, believing that no better alternative existed.

Austria-Hungary, with the German "blank check" safely deposited, presented an ultimatum to Serbia on July 23, the terms of which were designed to be rejected. Serbia, given forty-eight hours to respond, surprisingly accepted most of the terms and asked for negotiations on the remaining ones. When Austria replied that the ultimatum was absolute, mobilization began for both countries on July 28, leading Russia to mobilize two days later. The German high command—that France might choose to do nothing until Germany was fully engaged fighting Russia and only then declare war—then prepared a double ultimatum of impossible demands. They insisted that Russia must cease its mobilization and France must both publicly announce its neutrality and hand over its border fortresses to Germany. Both countries had twelve hours to comply. Neither did.

Military wheels moved faster than political ones did; industrial societies could ready and deploy troops in hours, instead of weeks. Because their military leaders perceived speed of mobilization as so central to victory, all four of the Continental powers were getting their troops onto trains even before most of the war declarations even took place. Germany and France both began to mobilize their armies on July 31, while German soldiers actually entered France on August 2, one day before the two countries officially went to war.

Regardless of when the actual declarations of war occurred, news of impending war provoked spontaneous celebrations in Paris, Berlin, St. Petersburg and Vienna. So many years of tension and fear made war seem almost a relief. On a far different note, British Foreign Secretary Sir Edward Grey remarked to a friend that "the lamps are going out all over Europe. We shall not see them lit again in our time."[5] World War I had begun.

The Guns of August, 1914

Forty-eight hours after mobilization began, German soldiers entered France and also took over the Luxembourg railroads. On August 4, exactly on schedule, the German army attacked Belgium. As Schlieffen had expected, Britain declared war on Germany, bringing the last Great Power into the conflict.

Winston Churchill, First Lord of the Admiralty, immediately ordered the British navy to blockade German ports, cutting Germany's supply lines with the outside world. Beyond this Britain could offer little immediate assistance to Belgium or France. Much of its existing army was stationed in Britain's overseas colonies, and it would take weeks to deploy them in Europe. In the meantime, the British government had to increase the size of their army. The call for volunteers found fertile ground in England; by 1916, nearly 2.5 million men had volunteered for what became known as the British Expeditionary Force (BEF).

While the British were organizing their war effort, in mid-August, the French army went barreling into Alsace-Lorraine to meet well-fortified German troops, leaving much of the Franco-Belgian border undermanned. When the German army swept deeper into Belgium, taking Brussels, French commanders frantically redeployed troops to meet the threat in the west. The massive casualties that resulted from these early clashes foreshadowed the war to come on the Western Front.

At the start, everything seemed to be going Germany's way, but two significant developments changed the trajectory of the war. First, on August 23, as German troops in Belgium approached the border with France, they ran into an unexpected storm of bullets around the city of Mons. Unknown to the German leadership, the first part of the BEF had arrived in France. Despite being significantly outnumbered, the British troops delayed the German advance for two days, time vitally needed for French commanders to move the French army. The second factor was that Russia was mobilizing faster than the Schlieffen Plan expected. Just as the BEF was making itself known in southern Belgium, the German leadership received word of Russian divisions attacking Austrian and under-manned German forces across a broad front in Eastern Europe.

The German high command panicked upon hearing of the Russian initiatives and immediately began moving men from the Western to the Eastern Front. This decision eventually proved the undoing of the Schlieffen Plan. Although the Germans quickly stabilized the east by defeating the Russian army at the Battle of Tannenberg in late August, the removal of hundreds of thousands of troops from the west left the German army too weak to carry out their strategy of defeating France quickly.

Even so, until the first of week of September, German forces kept up their momentum and pushed the French and British backwards across northern France. Frontline German units advanced to within thirty-five miles of Paris, close enough for their long-range artillery to hit the city. But this moment was to prove the high water mark for the German offensive. After this, further German advances became nearly impossible because of the troop diversions to Eastern Europe, the arrival of the British, ever longer supply lines, and troop exhaustion.

On September 5, 150,000 French and 70,000 British soldiers launched a major counterattack, in what became known as the **First Battle of the Marne**. It was a desperate struggle. When German units began breaking through the French line on the third day of fighting, threatening to capture Paris and put a quick end to the war, French reinforcements arrived from the capital in taxi cabs and rushed up to fill the gap, in one of the most famous moments of World War One. Buoyed by the additional troops and the bravery of the taxi drivers, French forces launched a surprise nighttime attack on September 8 that broke the German line, forcing them to retreat.

The "miracle of the Marne" saved Paris, but Entente troops were too cautious in pursuing the Germans, allowing them to stop their retreat after forty miles. Both sides began digging the network of trenches that characterized the **Western Front** and became the symbol of World War I. By the end of 1914, trenches extended almost four hundred miles, from a sliver of British-controlled Belgium on the Channel, across northern France, and down to Switzerland. Despite literally millions of casualties, this line of battle changed little until 1918.[6]

Expectations on all sides had been for a quick war, where everyone would be home by Christmas at the latest, but the failure of the Schlieffen Plan led to a type of war few expected and no one desired. World War I would destroy a generation of young men and shatter the Enlightenment belief that humans were logical, rational creatures destined to perfect the world.

The Horror Begins: Trench Warfare

War had changed, but few generals noticed it. In the minds of the military planners, war was a test of national will in which armies were supposed to go on the offensive, attacking the enemy until he disintegrated or surrendered; fighting spirit mattered above all else. But they had it all wrong. Science and engineering, the core of the

Industrial Revolution, now provided armies with heavy artillery, machine guns, poison gas, hand grenades, and flame throwers. Artillery and machine guns, the iconic weapons of World War I, favored defenders, not attackers. Human flesh could not withstand shell and bullet.

In Erich Maria Remarque's classic World War I novel, *All Quiet on the Western Front*, the main character, Paul Baümer, says that the spade was the soldier's most important possession.[7] Soldiers quickly discovered that narrow trenches, up to twelve feet deep, protected troops best. They reinforced their trench walls with metal plates and lay sand bags across the top, front and back, to block shrapnel and give protection when standing on the fire step to shoot at the enemy. Steel doors and zig-zag corners connected trenches so that they could easily be isolated and retaken if overrun by the enemy. Conditions inside the trench were appalling. Soldiers shared it with lice, rats, stagnant water, and dead comrades. Artillery shells roared overhead without end, punctuated occasionally by an enemy attack. Sleep was almost impossible.

Yet the trench was the safest place on the field of battle. While a trench held many horrors, the order to attack was even more terrifying. But attacks rarely achieved surprise, since they were usually announced by massive artillery bombardments. Generals, especially British and French, ordered hours and often days of advance shelling in the unshakeable but quite mistaken belief that doing so destroyed the enemy's trenches and the defenders within them. Intense shelling certainly rattled the enemy's nerves and a direct hit could destroy a trench, but the real effect of these long bombardments was to give the enemy time to reinforce the area to be attacked.

Once the artillery ceased and the attack whistles blew, soldiers leaped out of the trenches, desperate to get across the "no man's land" that lay between the opposing lines of trenches as quickly as possible. The landscape, however, prevented quick movement. Artillery shells cratered no man's land, making running difficult, although the craters provided shelter from artillery. Barbed wire and unseen landmines added further obstacles to attackers running directly into streams of machine-gun bullets. Those attackers who managed to successfully navigate no man's land threw hand grenades into the nearest enemy trench, hoping to kill its defenders before jumping into it. Yet taking a trench often proved pointless, since the enemy usually just fell back to the next line of trenches before striking back at the exhausted invaders. A successful counter-attack often mirrored the original attack, on the other side of no-man's land, with similarly inconclusive results.

As the war progressed, both sides on the Western Front came up with new weapons to end the stalemate. The Germans first used poison gas in April 1915 during an attack on British troops. A grey-green cloud passed over no-man's land and descended on the British who had no idea what it was until their lungs began collapsing. Panic ensued in the British lines and a massive gap opened as they fled. German troops, however, hesitated to approach the gassed areas themselves and pursued slowly. One ingenious British soldier, who recognized the gas as chlorine, took out a handkerchief, urinated on it, and pressed it to his mouth and nose, breathing normally. A chemical in the urine made the chlorine inactive; thus was born the first gas mask.

Gas attacks became a "normal" battlefield horror, one immortalized by Wilfred Owen, the famous World War I poet who died on the Western Front in 1918. His haunting poem, "Dulce et Decorum Est" describes a gas attack and the terrible death of a soldier unable to get his mask on in time.[8]

> "Gas! Gas! Quick, boys!
> —An ecstasy of fumbling,
> Fitting the clumsy helmets just in time;
> But someone still was yelling out and stumbling,
> And flound'ring like a man in fire or lime...
> Dim, through the misty panes and thick green light,
> As under a green sea, I saw him drowning."

Airplanes also played important roles on the World War I battlefields. Initially used for scouting, they soon carried machine guns and gravity-propelled bombs. Fighter planes fought battles in the sky while bomber planes added one more worry to the men trying to survive in the trenches. It was the airplane that first brought civilians into direct contact with the war, when each side began bombing industrial centers in an effort to undermine the enemy's war effort. The British, long protected by the their navy and the English Channel, found the bombing especially traumatic.

But neither poison gas nor planes brought movement back to the battlefield. It was a British invention, the tank, that finally overcame the barriers of crater, mine, barbed wire, and machine gun. Initially, British military officials did not understand the potential of this new industrial weapon and only the intervention of the First Lord of the Admiralty, Winston Churchill, pushed the project forward. By replacing conventional wheels with so-called caterpillar tracks, the tank could navigate almost any obstacle and, if sufficiently armored, ignore machine gun fire. The first tank action took place during the 1916 Battle of the Somme, but with limited numbers and still largely untested, they had little effect on the fighting. Only in the last months of the war, after dramatic improvements in armor and firepower, did the tank finally change battlefield dynamics. It would take another world war to fully reveal the tank's significance.[9]

Only the Dead Go Home

Another new weapon became the central feature of German naval strategy. Because of the strangling British blockade of its ports, the Germans turned to the submarine. With their navy bottled up and the blockade creating shortages of almost everything for civilians and soldiers, German submarines, known as "**U-boats**," began to attack Entente shipping in order to force the British navy to withdraw the blockade in favor of protecting merchant ships.

At first, German U-boats only sank merchant ships after giving the crew time to evacuate. This gentlemanly conception of warfare gave way in early 1915 to unrestricted submarine warfare, in which enemy ships were sunk with no prior warning. Considered illegal according to international law (as was the British blockade), the new German policy dramatically increased British shipping losses. This strategy, however, risked an international incident with the United States. American trade with Britain had increased tremendously since the war began, which meant merchant ships, either owned by U.S. firms or at least carrying Americans on them, constantly passed through the German designated war zone around the British Isles. Civilian cruise ships also continued to operate between the United States and Britain. The undiscerning nature of unrestricted submarine warfare made it practically inevitable that a German submarine would sink a ship that had a large number of Americans aboard.

This happened on May 7, 1915 when a German U-boat fired a single torpedo into the *Lusitania*, a British passenger liner en route from New York City to England. The ship sank within minutes, killing 1,198 people, including 128 Americans. Outrage emanated from all over the world, most prominently from American President Woodrow Wilson, who threatened war if Germany continued their submarine campaign. Despite German protests that the *Lusitania* carried war material, the threat of American involvement cowed the German government into revising its submarine policy. For the next eighteen months, German submarines operated under far more restrictions, somewhat reducing tensions with the U.S., but also ensuring that the British blockade remained in place.[10]

Meanwhile, World War I continued relentlessly through 1915 and 1916, quashing hopes of a quick war, while drawing in new countries anxious for the supposed spoils that victory might bring. The Ottomans had entered the war in December 1914 as an ally of Germany and Austria-Hungary, in the hope of recapturing lost territory and glory from a defeated Russia. Italy, which had refused to honor its Triple Alliance commitment at the outbreak of the war, turned coat and joined the Entente in April 1915 with promises of territorial gains in Southeastern Europe. Although neither addition significantly affected the outcome of the conflict, they did bring millions more soldiers and civilians into the inferno.

As the war in the trenches took its toll on the soldiers, another battle of sorts went on behind the lines, on the homefront. Survival in World War I, to say nothing of victory, required not just the strategies of generals or the strength of soldiers, but also the perseverance of those far behind the lines. While millions of men fought in the trenches, millions of women took their place in the factories and fields, trying to provide for soldiers and civilians alike. The war effort in each country required the involvement of all of a nation's citizens. Economic production, the ability of political leaders to keep their people unified, and the endurance of entire populations would go a long way toward determining the winners and losers of World War I.

Societal cohesion first began breaking down in Austria-Hungary and Russia. The incompetence of the Austrian high command forced the Germans to take increasing control of the Austro-Hungarian army, undermining its morale. Furthermore, due to the Allied blockade, Austria-Hungary suffered from major food shortages, leading to strikes and bread riots by the middle of 1916. A further blow, in November of the same year. was the death of Emperor Franz-Josef, whose presence alone had held together Austria-Hungary as a multi-national empire well into the age of nationalism. Continued military reverses created even more desperation, and the empire began to crack open along national lines. Army desertions rose, nationalist parties emerged, and street violence spread across the country. As 1916 waned, the question of victory or defeat in World War I appeared increasingly irrelevant to Austria-Hungary, since neither outcome seemed likely to prevent its collapse.

By this time, Russia too faced collapse. Each battlefield failure further demoralized the Russian army and weakened morale at home. Poor planning, a still underdeveloped transportation system, and the Ottoman closure of the Turkish Straits in late 1914 caused increasingly severe food shortages. Food riots and street violence erupted by 1916, and Russia, like Austria-Hungary, lacked political leadership capable of handling the crisis. Tsar Nicholas II, while a man of some intelligence, possessed minimal leadership skills, often relying on his unbalanced wife and her spiritual advisor, the infamous Rasputin, for advice on running the war. By late 1916, with army desertion rates reaching catastrophic levels and growing industrial strikes creating economic chaos, both the Russian war effort and Russia itself seemed on the verge of disintegration.

Russia's collapse would, of course, be good news for Germany, which desperately needed Russia's agricultural resources to feed a blockade-starved population. In addition, a German victory on the Eastern Front would potentially free millions of troops for duty on the Western Front, which might tip the balance in the West, bringing a German victory that left it dominating the entire continent. Such hopes, however, would be not realized in 1916, as Russia held on in the east and trench warfare continued to take its terrible toll on the soldiers in the west.

More Than Man Can Bear: Verdun and the Somme, 1916

The year 1916 would be remembered for two battles, **Verdun** and the **Somme** River, which nearly destroyed the armies involved and left long-lived scars on the landscape and people of Western Europe. The Battle of Verdun, a German effort to capture French fortresses two hundred miles east of Paris, resulted in nearly 800,000 casualties, almost all German and French. Artillery did most of the damage to body and soul as literally tens of millions of German and French shells rained down on soldiers. Periodic infantry offensives, none of which resulted in anything beyond human destruction, punctuated the ubiquitous shelling. In December, after ten months of fighting, the frontline was essentially unchanged. Only winter and the obscene casualty rate ended the battle.[11]

German and French troops pulled double-duty in 1916, for the Battle of the Somme overlapped Verdun. What began as a British offensive in July developed into one of the bloodiest battles ever fought. More than a million soldiers—British, French, and German—were killed and wounded before winter mercifully ended the slaughter. On the first day alone, the British suffered nearly 60,000 casualties, most of which resulted from a pointless charge across no man's land. Without needing to aim, German machine gunners fired into the tightly massed British infantry, exacting such a terrible toll that many refused to keep firing at retreating soldiers. When the battle ended in November, the British had gained less than a square foot of territory for every casualty.

There is no way to explain how traumatic the Somme was for the British, but one statistic offers some illumination. In 1917, about twenty-three million British, half the population, watched the silent film footage of the battle. This record number of viewers stood until 1977, when *Star Wars* surpassed it, and by then, Britain's population was sixty million.[12]

America Enters the War and Europe Begins to Disintegrate

By the end of 1916, German officials had come to believe that time was not on their side, and they decided to resume unrestricted submarine warfare in the desperate hope that Allied shipping losses would end the war before the United States effectively entered it. However, their renewed attacks, along with German diplomatic intrigues in Mexico, ignited American public opinion against Germany. Although Wilson had won re-election in 1916 at least partly on his promise that he would not send American boys to fight in Europe, he had little choice but to declare war on Germany on April 6. Events halfway around the world eased his decision. In March the Russian Tsar Nicholas II had abdicated, and although the Provisional Government that followed him was unstable (it lasted only until the fall of 1917), it was nominally democratic, and thus a far more palatable ally for Wilson and the United States. Meanwhile, the implementation of a convoy system vastly increased the safety of ships carrying supplies and men arriving in Europe from the United States.

This hardly assured victory for the Allies. The Provisional Government in Russia collapsed, and by autumn, Lenin and the Bolsheviks, a small but rapidly growing Marxist party, seized power and ended Russian involvement in the war.[13] As Russia fell apart, the countries fighting on the Western Front began another year of bloody, pointless battles until finally French soldiers mutinied, refusing to continue making suicidal attacks. By early June half the army had stopped taking orders, while sympathy strikes broke out among workers across France, further endangering the war effort until the appointment of a new French commander-in-chief ended the mutiny.

One Last Gamble: The Ludendorff Offensive, Spring 1918

During the winter of 1917-1918 Austria-Hungary slowly disintegrated, as did the Ottoman Empire, with the latter facing British-inspired rebellions in its Middle East possessions. But in March, 1918, the Bolsheviks sued for peace, and Russia was out of the war for good. With this, despite the collapse of its allies, Germany saw a momentary opportunity for victory. Once fighting ended in the east, their commanders immediately transferred hundreds of thousands of troops to the Western Front and began organizing what they hoped was a final victorious offensive. Their plan called for three million German troops to attack in northern France, to open a gap between British and French troops. The German army would then swivel towards the northwest, wipe out the British army, before sweeping back east to take Paris and conquer France. **The Ludendorff Offensive** would end the war and leave Germany the master of Europe. At least that was the plan.

The offensive began in March 1918, and for three months enjoyed success. German troops managed to cross the Marne River and threaten Paris for the first time since 1914. But that was as far as they got. Their advance cost them more than three hundred thousand casualties, while the same number of American troops arrived in France. The American Expeditionary Force, now more than a million men strong, played a main role in repelling the German threat. By late summer, an Allied counter-offensive soon retook all the territory Germany had captured the previous spring.[14] The German generals had gambled and lost.

The war would soon be lost as well. In the east, Austria-Hungary could no longer field an army, the Ottoman Empire had largely ceased to exist, and the Russian Civil War disrupted German control of the territory they had won in Eastern Europe. Germany itself began to fall apart; a naval rebellion and massive communist-directed protests made a revolution seem imminent. The Allies, with six million men and nearly unlimited supplies, approached the German border in late October. Nothing remained for Germany to do but surrender.

Rather than take responsibility for the defeat, Kaiser Wilhelm abdicated and fled to the Netherlands. On November 8 representatives from what remained of the German government met with the French to accept their terms. Although Kaiser Wilhelm and his generals had caused and lost the war, these officials, the core of the future Weimar Republic, would ultimately take the blame.

The war ended on November 11, 1918 at 11:00 A.M. Ten million soldiers lay dead. Another twenty million had been wounded and nearly eight million were missing, while almost seven million civilians had also died. The nations of Europe, whether victorious or defeated, lay in shambles. Before the end of the year, Woodrow Wilson had embarked across the Atlantic with his grand vision of peace forever. Citizens of the shattered societies of Europe desperately wanted to believe that the New World could teach the Old World how to live in harmony. It was a forlorn hope.

Notes

1. James Joll and Gordon Martel, *The Origins of the First World War*, Third Edition (London: Pearson-Longman, 2007). Joll's book, recently revised by Martel, is an eminently readable, sophisticated analysis of why the war began.

2. Heinrich von Treitschke, "The New Nationalism and Racism," in John McGrath (ed.), *Readings in Social Theory and Modernization*, Vol. II, Spring 2010 (New York: Learning Solutions, 2010), 207.

3. Fritz Fischer, *Germany's War Aims in the First World War* (New York: W. W. Norton & Company, Inc., 1967). When first published, Fischer's book evoked a storm of controversy for his claim that Germany was largely to blame for causing the war. Subsequent scholarship has pretty much confirmed, with some modification, this so-called Fischer Thesis. For a summary of this scholarship see Joll and Martel's text referenced above: Joll and Martel, *The Origins of the First World War*, 1-9.

4. John Keegan, *The First World War* (New York: Alfred A. Knopf, 1999), 28-36.

5. G.J. Meyer, *A World Undone: The Story of the Great War, 1914-1918* (New York: Bantam Dell, 2007), 149

6. Keegan, *The First World War*, 112-203; Captain B. H. Liddell Hart, *The Real War, 1914-1918* (Boston: Little, Brown and Company, 1930), 82-102.

7. Erich Maria Remarque, *All Quiet on the Western Front*, trans. A. W. Wheen (New York: Ballantine Books, 1929), 55-56, 104.

8. www.oucs.ox.ac.uk/ww1lit/collections/item/3303?CISOBOX=1&REC=5

9. Meyer, *A World Undone*, 260-264; Remarque, *All Quiet*, 105-118; Liddell Hart, *The Real War*, 248-255.

10. Meyer, *A World Undone*, 289-291.

11. Alistair Horne, *The Price of Glory: Verdun 1916* (London: Penguin Books, 1962).

12. www.national-army-museum.ac.uk/exhibitions/theSomme/

13. Michael Kort, *The Soviet Colossus: History and Aftermath,* Seventh Edition (New York: M. E. Sharpe, 2010); George F. Kennan, *Soviet Foreign Policy, 1917-1941* (Malabar, Florida: Robert E. Krieger Publishing Company, 1960).

14. Keegan, *The First World War*, 372-414.

Suggested Readings:

Horne, Alistair. *The Price of Glory: Verdun 1916.* London: Penguin Books, 1962.

Joll, James, and Gordon Martel. *The Origins of the First World War*, Third Edition London: Pearson-Longman, 2007.

Keegan, John. *The First World War*. New York: Alfred A. Knopf, 1999.

Kort, Michael. *The Soviet Colossus: History and Aftermath*, Seventh Edition. New York: M. E. Sharpe, 2010.

Meyer, G.J. *A World Undone: The Story of the Great War, 1914-1918*. New York: Bantam Dell, 2007.

Remarque, Erich Maria. *All Quiet on the Western Front*, trans. A. W. Wheen. New York: Ballantine Books, 1929.

Europe Between Wars

Jay P. Corrin

World War I turned out to be a watershed in European history. It produced a series of political, social, and economic crises that transformed the landscape of western culture. Ten million military deaths robbed nations of their future leaders. Germany and France lost some 16 percent of their male populations; to put this in context, a comparable proportion of America's current population would be 15 million adult males — and even in WWII, America's costliest conflict, the number of American dead was less than half a million. If this devastation wasn't enough, in 1918 the Spanish influenza epidemic began to sweep through a cold, hungry and weakened world, killing twice as many as had been taken in World War I.

In addition to the human cost, this conflict ravaged Europe's economy. The Germans lost 22 percent of their national treasure, while the Italians lost 26 percent of their wealth and France 30 percent. The British had expended more capital on the war than they had invested in all previous industrial and financial undertakings; by the end of 1918 Great Britain had ceased to be the world's banker and was instead, much like France, deeply in debt to the United States. The locus of world financial and industrial power shifted abruptly from Europe to America, a nation that was ill-prepared to assume the role of world leader.

The economic and social demands of waging a total war also had the effect of profoundly transforming capitalism. The liberal foundation of traditional capitalism was the idea that government should not engage in business activities and that the market mechanisms of supply and demand should regulate transactions. But even before 1914, increasing international competition had compelled governments to become more involved in their national economies by establishing tariffs to protect fledgling domestic industries and seeking new markets and raw materials by state-supported imperialist ventures. Once the war broke out, the belligerents needed to organize their economies more systematically, with an objective of "rationalizing" production to advance the nation's economic and military needs. Thus, state economic control only increased, as free competition was deemed too inefficient to respond to national emergencies. After the conflict ended, it was difficult for European nations to dismantle the bureaucratic institutions and mentalities that had managed their wartime economic systems, especially with the emergence of economic crises after 1919. The wartime shift to "planned" or "command" economies became permanent.

The economic challenge of reconstruction after the war was compounded by the imperative of dealing with huge national debts, which could only be ameliorated by higher taxes for years to come. All of its citizens were now faced with the prospect of declining economic and social development. Most significantly, no longer would Europe be the world's center of manufacturing, banking and overall economic power.

Peace Making

While the economic wreckage was unprecedented, the political situation was equally problematic. Given the wartime propaganda that demonized the enemy, it was very difficult if not impossible for the belligerents to draw up a satisfactory peace settlement. Fixed ideas, deep-seated angers, hatreds and fears became obstacles to rational and judicious political judgment.

As the victorious powers gathered in Paris in the bleak winter of 1919 to draw up peace treaties, much of Europe was mired in chaos and suffering. Russia was in the hands of **Bolsheviks**, violent communist revolutionaries who had declared their intention to spread unrest throughout the world in order to destroy bourgeois democracy and capitalism. The German and Austro-Hungarian empires had collapsed, creating political vacuums that several revolutionary regimes struggled to fill.

The world placed much hope in the visionary determination of American President **Woodrow Wilson**, who arrived in Paris to great fanfare in January 1919 with a message that promised freedom and peace. Indeed, Wilson was convinced that his ideas on the subject would eliminate the need for future wars altogether. The mechanisms for achieving this noble goal were contained in his famous "**Fourteen Points**," which, among other provisions, called for an end to secret treaties and secret diplomacy, which had been prime causal factors of World War I. He also called for freedom of the seas, ending barriers to international trade, armament reduction, colonial readjustments, the self-determination of nationalities, the promotion of democracy and, most important, an international organization to prevent conflict among states.

Unfortunately, Wilson ran into resistance in getting the victorious powers to accept his Fourteen Points. From the start, the Paris conference was crippled by conflicting goals and attitudes. The German delegates at the conference had hoped for moderation from British and French diplomats, in order to rebuild their nation along the lines of popular democracy, an experiment in government that had never been tried before in that country. But they were disappointed by the demands of their former enemies, whose political leaders were driven by the festering anger of their citizens, who insisted on German blood.

Wilson ultimately won support for what came to be called the **League of Nations**, a permanent international body in which states could discuss their interests and settle disputes without resorting to war. Yet this was among his few triumphs in Paris. The war in the west had been mostly fought on French soil, and her diplomats demanded that Germany should compensate France for war damages and expenses, so that they could rebuild their own economies and repay the huge war debts they owed the United States; Britain, at least initially, made similar claims, and both nations were apprehensive about the threat a revived Germany might pose. Under pressure from French diplomats the **Versailles Peace Treaty** contained the infamous Article 231, which was called by the Germans the "**war guilt clause.**" The article suggested that Germany had to accept full responsibility both for starting the war and making good on the losses and damage it had caused.

This was clearly unfair and inflamed German public opinion. Arguably, the British and French had been as responsible as Germany for stumbling into the war, but of course the spoils always go to the victors.[1] Almost immediately, the notion of "war guilt" provided an opening for extremist groups in Germany who aimed to overthrow the Versailles Peace Treaty, and even moderate Germans considered Article 321 a stain on their sense of national self-respect. Not only was the new German Republic burdened with the task of repaying unrealistic reparations, but the peace treaty also forbade the government from rebuilding an effective army and navy. Furthermore, it deprived Germany of all her former overseas colonies, which were now called "mandates" rather than the politically incorrect "colonies," and were turned over to the victors. The Versailles Treaty was so severe that even the allies felt conflicted, and as time went on, they became increasingly unwilling to enforce its terms.

Although German diplomats resisted the harsher terms of the Versailles Treaty, they gave way after the allies threatened to renew hostilities. The German statesmen who eventually signed the peace treaty would forevermore be damned for accepting such humiliation. This made it even more difficult for these politicians to create a workable liberal democracy. German agitators who demanded a full repudiation of the treaty found a ready audience among people who had previously known only monarchical authority and state paternalism. And the new government, known as the **Weimar Republic** (named after the city in which the democratic constitution was drafted—the capital remained in Berlin), received little support from the victorious powers that had forced the treaty upon them, since within a few years it became clear that the allies had become more concerned about protecting the Continent from Soviet Bolshevism than they were about Germany. France and Britain came to see the efficacy of using Germany as a shield against revolutionary communism, and generally closed their eyes to the Weimar government's endeavors to circumvent the treaty's strictures on rearmament.

Thus, the Versailles Peace Treaty proved to be a disaster. The perceived unfairness of German reparations and the stigma of war guilt sowed the seeds of social, economic and political unrest. The warnings of English economist **John Maynard Keynes** proved prophetic. He had warned that if Germany were not reintegrated into the European system, if its industrial potential went unrecognized, there could be no European-wide economic recovery, The ensuing economic difficulties would not be accepted mildly by those who suffered the most, said Keynes, and these rumblings could well spawn revolutionary upheaval. This was lost on the minds of the peacemakers who were bent on keeping Germany down, and the world would pay dearly for this oversight in the years to come.

New Geo-Political Challenges

Although Wilson succeeded in convincing the reluctant European powers to accept the League of Nations, he failed to get U.S. congressional approval, and the American government did not ratify the Versailles Treaty, although a separate peace agreement was signed between the U.S. and Germany sometime later. Unfortunately, this meant that Washington would not participate in executing the terms of what became the **Peace of Paris**, leaving a financially weakened Britain and France with the Herculean task of carrying out and enforcing its terms.[2] For the next few decades, as far as European statecraft was concerned, the U.S. once again retreated into splendid isolation, mistakenly assuming that its people could remain shielded from foreign power politics by the breadth of its oceans.

In addition to dealing with Germany, Europe's statesmen had a number of other challenges. The map of Europe also had to be redrawn, both to weaken Germany and to fill the open spaces caused by the collapse of the Russian, Austro-Hungarian and Ottoman Empires. This was complicated by the emergence, in Russia, of a communist regime bent on universal subversion. The ethnic-linguistic self-determination advocated by Wilson, along with a need to discourage communism, became the guiding principles in the creation of new nations, most of which were destined to be politically unstable and economically backward.

The regional conflicts these new nations engendered tore the continent apart up through the 1990s. After 1919 Austria and Hungary were vastly reduced in size, and several territories once part of their empire became independent states. Serbia merged with Croatia and Montenegro to become **Yugoslavia**, while the new state of **Czechoslovakia** arose from the combination of Czech, Slovakian, and Ruthenian homelands. None of these ethnic and religious mixings proved very stable. German irredentist claims during the 1930s contributed directly to the Second World War; more recently, in the 1990s, Yugoslavia disintegrated amid wars of "ethnic cleansing." As the historian E. J. Hobsbawm observed, the old chickens of Versailles once again came home to roost.[3]

The British and French were hardly better off. Their leaders were greatly disappointed when President Wilson made it clear that the U.S. expected them to rely on their own resources to recover from the war. The victors were deeply in debt to Washington, and the Americans, as good capitalists, expected to be repaid. In the spring of 1919 the U.S. Secretary of the Treasury announced that all American government loans to its wartime allies would be terminated. The Europeans had expected either a cancellation of their American debts so as to allow their own economies to recover, or at least Washington's support for a recovery plan, along the lines of what later became the Marshall Plan that helped Europe recover from World War II. But the Americans believed in the free market, and any future European loans and credits would have to come not from American taxpayers but from private capitalists on Wall Street. The American return to what amounted to economic nationalism convinced the French to press even harder for reparation payments from Germany, so as to stimulate their own economic recovery and repay debts to the U.S.

Cultural Despair

The Great War also brought about a transformation of Western culture. The beginning of the twentieth century had seemed to represent a full flowering of bourgeois liberal civilization. There were of course muted tones of pessimism and a handful of critics of middle-class mentalities (Friedrich Nietzsche, for example), but for the most part the century had opened with continuing faith in the progress made possible by democracy, liberal capitalism and the contributions of science. Living standards had been improving everywhere on the Continent and political pluralism seemed to be carrying the day. Indeed, even large-scale war seemed a thing of the past. But the unprecedented destruction of World War I and the consequent economic and political crises it produced led to radical changes in outlook and growing pessimism about the future. The cultural mind-set of the post-war era was symbolized by a plethora of literary and artistic trends. As early as 1918, for example, the German philosopher of history Oswald Spengler published a widely-read book entitled *The Decline of the West*. Its central theme was that Western civilization was in an advanced stage of dementia and would soon die. Even the titles T. S. Eliot gave to two of his best-known poems captured the sense of impending doom, *The Waste Land* (1922) and *The Hollow Men* (1925). The latter concluded with the following lines:

> This is the way the world ends
> Not with a bang but a whimper

"The Lost Generation" was a term used to describe many of the writers of the inter-war years, several of whom became literary vagabonds, seemingly in search for a way of life that could give more meaning to a world in turmoil. Almost all the major literary figures of the era—D. H. Lawrence, Andre Gide, Ernest Hemingway, James Joyce, Rupert Graves, T. S. Eliot—were marked wanderers who chose to live and write in other people's countries.

Since the secular religions of liberalism, democracy and capitalism appeared to have failed, a number of intellectuals pursued "strange new gods" by embracing communism (Jean-Paul Sartre and Arthur Koestler) or its totalitarian counterpart, **fascism** (Ezra Pound and Wyndham Lewis). Still others returned to Christianity, as it appeared that the secular god of liberalism, with its belief in progress, had proven false. Many of these intellectuals (Eliot, Jacques Maritain, Karl Barth) found in original sin and Christian humility an antidote to the shallow morality of the pre-war liberals and socialists who believed in rationality and the perfectibility of man.

In art we find **Dadaism**, a nonsense word for a movement based on the conviction that everything was nonsensical. Here is a sample of how Dada expressed the incongruity of bourgeois life and the absurdity of the age in poetry:

> The aeroplane weaves through telegraph wires and the fountain sings the same song.
> At the rendezvous of the coachmen the aperitif is orange but the locomotive mechanics have blue eyes.
> The lady has lost her smile in the woods.[4]

Dada soon gave way to **Surrealism**, a form of artistic expression that reflected Freud's sense of the irrational, the subconscious and the bizarre; its best-known practitioners were the painters Salvador Dali, Marc Chagall, Paul Klee and Pablo Picasso. The balance and harmony of traditional classical music, which had expressed the rationality and order of a gentler and more humane world, were now replaced by new experiments in atonality. Arnold Schonberg, for instance, abandoned traditional scales for what was called the twelve-tone scale, music that sounded purely cacophonous to the uninitiated. Igor Stravinsky's world premier of *Sacre du Printemps* (Rites of Spring) in 1913 sounded so outlandish to his audience that it provoked a full-scale riot. The police were called in and Stravinsky saved himself from a furious crowd by jumping through a window backstage. Yet Stravinsky's music was clearly anticipating the confusions and uncertainties of a new era. An advocate of this futuristic musical style wrote:

> The art of combining musical sounds reached its peak at the end of the nineteenth century. In the music of the future the sounds of our mechanical civilization—its machinery and crowded cities—will be subtly combined into an art of noises.

Popular culture, on the other hand, reflected less despair and foreboding than it did escapism. When the world economic downturn set in by the 1930s, "the people" found solace from their angst in record-breaking airplane flights of Charles Lindbergh, the thrilling crime escapades of Bonnie and Clyde, and movie stars such as the dancing wonders of Fred Astaire and Ginger Rogers. This was when Walt Disney began creating an alternative reality in animal magic and dreamy escapist kingdoms inhabited by the likes of Mickey Mouse, On one level, all this represented the expansion of democratic culture to the common people. While elitists like T. S. Eliot found such attractions insipid, and popular culture itself cheapening, now the "little people" were on the rise, as mass newspapers and magazines with minimum intellectual content began to pander to rather mundane thrills and tastes. While these developments may have represented the expansion of popular democracy, some wondered if it was wise to feed the base impulses of the masses.

New Economic Challenges

Another major feature of Europe during the interwar years was the growing size and responsibilities of the political state. Since the functioning of its many bureaucracies required increases in taxes, it became obligatory for governments to expand the franchise and satisfy mass demands. Budgets began to expand so as to provide for security and public services. Big government and big industry merged together, and as manufacturing expanded so did its need for capital. Increasingly, cartels and oligopolistic organizations capable of amassing huge pools of capital came to dominate the market; these business enterprises in turn developed close affiliation with their respective governments. "The day of combination is here to stay," observed John D. Rockefeller: "Individualism is gone never to return." What this also meant, especially in Europe, where state social welfare was more advanced, was that when economic conditions deteriorated the people held their governments responsible.

Europe's combatants had financed the cost of fighting the war through loans, all of which had to be repaid when the conflict ended, and their desperate monetary policies contributed to postwar inflation. For example, in France and Italy between 1913 and 1926, prices of most goods rose 250 percent or more. In France, much of the post-war reconstruction was supposed to be financed by loans, which were to be repaid from German reparations, and this led to a nine-fold increase in public debt by 1926. This was especially devastating for those on fixed incomes, such as wage earners, creditors, and pensioners. Small businesses suffered as well, since they had to replenish their stock at higher costs. At the same time, governments had to increase taxes to pay for this mounting public debt. Adding to these problems was the fact that civilians who had purchased war bonds from their governments now were repaid with depreciated currency.

Britain, and France to a lesser extent, saw recovery through the restoration of international trade. Yet such recovery required the participation of Germany as a prosperous trading partner, and this was compromised by the collection of war reparations. Unfortunately economic recovery proved to be a slow and painful process. During the war the combatants had experienced difficulty in meeting their economic needs through their own productive capacities. After hostilities ended, the lesson taken from this was to strive for economic self-sufficiency. A spirit of economic nationalism swept the Continent, as domestic markets were closed to foreign products. The U.S. compounded the problem by imposing high tariffs that restricted the market for European goods. Such protectionist policies only served to retard the restoration of international trade.

The situation was far worse in the defeated countries, where currencies had largely collapsed. In Austria prices rose 4,000 times their pre-war level; in Hungary prices multiplied 23,000 times; in Poland 2,500,000 times. Germany's inflation was even worse. Their hyperinflation was due largely to France and Belgium's decision in 1923 to invade the Ruhr, Germany's industrial heartland, because its government had fallen delinquent on war reparations, in this case by failing to deliver a thousand telephone poles. Without an army to resist the invasion, the Weimar politicians commanded workers to resist by undertaking a general strike, and in order to compensate the workers the government simply printed money. This resulted in probably the highest level of inflation in world history, as prices rose by a multiple of a thousand billion. Money essentially became worthless, and many used it for fuel, since it was cheaper than purchasing wood or coal. This catastrophic situation was only relieved by American intervention, when short-term loans from U.S. banks under the **Dawes Plan** stabilized the Deutschmark.

Thanks to American intervention Germany for the next few years enjoyed not only social stability but even modest economic growth. Unfortunately, this "Indian summer" of quietude was abruptly shaken by the onslaught of a world-wide economic depression. The catastrophe was the consequence of a multitude of factors, including structural weaknesses in the U.S. economy and careless speculation, which led to the crash of the American stock market and the insolvency of domestic banks and financial institutions. Wall Street responded by calling in loan payments from the German banks. The ensuing economic crash in Germany, a country already struggling to adjust to the requisites of democratic politics, was far more severe than anything that hit the American heartland. John Maynard Keynes's earlier prognostications of what could happen to men and women in the despair of economic loss proved tragically prophetic. As savings, jobs and hopes for the future vanished peddlers of extremist political views found ready audiences for their messages of hate.

References and Suggested Readings:

Aldcroft, Derek H. *From Versailles to Wall Street*, 1919-1929. Berkeley, CA: University of California Press.

Aldcroft, Derek H. *The European Economy, 1914-2000*. London: Routledge, 2001.

Ambrosius, Gerold, *A Social and Economic History of Twentieth-Century Europe*. Cambridge, MA, 1989.

Bessel, Richard, Germany *After the First World War*. Oxford, UK: Oxford University Press, 1993.

Galbraith, John Kenneth. *The Great Crash, 1929*. Boston, 1961.

Hobsbawm, E.J., *The Age of Extremes: A History of the World, 1914-1991*. New York: Random House, 1994.

Kindleberger, *The World in Depression, 1929-1939*. Berkeley, CA: University of California Press, 1986.

Silverman, Dan P. *Reconstructing Europe After the Great War*. Cambridge, MA: Harvard University Press,1982.

Notes

1. There was no specific language regarding a "war guilt clause" in Article 231, but the stricture was interpreted rather loosely as blaming the Kaiser and the German military for starting the conflict. The article was inserted in the treaty by an American delegate to the Reparations Commission in order to protect Germany against allied demands to pay all the costs of the war, Article 321 in fact declared Germany *morally* responsible for the war and its consequences but legally liable only for narrowly defined damages specified in the treaty. (See William Keylor, *The Twentieth-Century World: A International History* [New York, 1984] p. 85). The myth of the "war guilt clause" was employed with great effect by German governments up through the 1920s as a political tool to fan resentments against what it considered the injustices of the Versailles Treaty, Hitler used this myth with consummate success in overturning strictures on German rearmament.

2. It should be pointed out that the Versailles Peace Treaty was simply a part of what was the Peace of Paris, This treaty only applied to Germany. Various other treaties were drawn up as part of the Peace of Paris and were named after several parks and royal chateaux in that city, These included the Treaty of Saint Germain with Austria; Trianon with Hungary; Sevres with Turkey and Neuilly with Bulgaria.

3. E. J. Hobsbawm, *The Age of Extremes: A History of the World, 1914-1991* (New York, 1994), p. 31.

4. Roland N. Stromberg, *An Intellectual History of Modern Europe* (New York, Appleton-Century-Crofts, 1966), p. 380.

On the Democratic Welfare State

Franklin D. Roosevelt

Franklin D. Roosevelt was born in 1882 at Hyde Park, N.Y. He was educated at Groton, Harvard, and the Columbia Law School. He served as Assistant Secretary of the Navy, 1913–1920. In 1921 he suffered a severe attack of infantile paralysis, but in subsequent years he recovered the partial use of his legs. He was governor of New York, 1929–1933, and President of the United States from 1933 until his death on April 12, 1945.

His second inaugural address on January 20, 1937, surveyed the achievements of his first term and the problems requiring further action. It is presented as an expression of the New Deal philosophy of democracy.

This address has been reprinted in various volumes, including The Public Papers and Addresses of Franklin D. Roosevelt, 1937 Volume, *New York, The Macmillan Company, 1941.*

When four years ago we met to inaugurate a President, the Republic, single-minded in anxiety, stood in spirit here. We dedicated ourselves to the fulfillment of a vision—to speed the time when there would be for all the people that security and peace essential to the pursuit of happiness. We of the Republic pledged ourselves to drive from the temple of our ancient faith those who had profaned it; to end by action, tireless and unafraid, the stagnation and despair of that day. We did those first things first.

Our covenant with ourselves did not stop there. Instinctively we recognized a deeper need—the need to find through government the instrument of our united purpose to solve for the individual the ever-rising problems of a complex civilization. Repeated attempts at their solution without the aid of government had left us baffled and bewildered. For, without that aid, we had been unable to create those moral controls over the services of science which are necessary to make science a useful servant instead of a ruthless master of mankind. To do this we knew that we must find practical controls over blind economic forces and blindly selfish men.

We of the Republic sensed the truth that democratic government has innate capacity to protect its people against disasters once considered inevitable, to solve problems once considered unsolvable. We would not admit that we could not find a way to master economic epidemics just as, after centuries of fatalistic suffering, we had found a way to master epidemics of disease. We refused to leave the problems of our common welfare to be solved by the winds of chance and the hurricanes of disaster.

In this we Americans were discovering no wholly new truth; we were writing a new chapter in our book of self-government.

This year marks the one hundred and fiftieth anniversary of the Constitutional Convention which made us a nation. At that Convention our forefathers found the way out of the chaos which followed the Revolutionary War; they created a strong government with powers of united action sufficient then and now to solve problems utterly beyond individual or local solution. A century and a half ago they established the Federal Government in order to promote the general welfare and secure the blessings of liberty to the American people.

Today we invoke those same powers of government to achieve the same objectives.

Four years of new experience have not belied our historic instinct. They hold out the clear hope that government within communities, government within the separate States, and government of the United States can do the things the times require, without yielding its democracy. Our tasks in the last four years did not force democracy to take a holiday.

Nearly all of us recognize that as intricacies of human relationships increase, so power to govern them also must increase—power to stop evil; power to do good. The essential democracy of our Nation and the safety of our people depend not upon the absence of power, but upon lodging it with those whom the people can change or continue at stated intervals through an honest and free system of elections. The Constitution of 1787 did not make our democracy impotent.

In fact, in these last four years, we have made the exercise of all power more democratic; for we have begun to bring private autocratic powers into their proper subordination to the public's government. The legend that they were invincible— above and beyond the processes of a democracy—has been shattered. They have been challenged and beaten.

Our progress out of the depression is obvious. But that is not all that you and I mean by the new order of things. Our pledge was not merely to do a patchwork job with second-hand materials. By using the new materials of social justice we have undertaken to erect on the old foundations a more enduring structure for the better use of future generations.

In that purpose we have been helped by achievements of mind and spirit. Old truths have been relearned; untruths have been unlearned. We have always known that heedless self-interest was bad morals; we know now that it is bad economics. Out of the collapse of a prosperity whose builders boasted their practicality has come the conviction that in the long run economic morality pays. We are beginning to wipe out the line that divides the practical from the ideal; and in so doing we are fashioning an instrument of unimagined power for the establishment of a morally better world.

This new understanding undermines the old admiration of worldly success as such. We are beginning to abandon our tolerance of the abuse of power by those who betray for profit the elementary decencies of life.

In this process evil things formerly accepted will not be so easily condoned. Hardheadedness will not so easily excuse hard-heartedness. We are moving toward an era of good feeling. But we realize that there can be no era of good feeling save among men of goodwill.

For these reasons I am justified in believing that the greatest change we have witnessed has been the change in the moral climate of America.

Among men of goodwill, science and democracy together offer an ever-richer life and ever-larger satisfaction to the individual. With this change in our moral climate and our rediscovered ability to improve our economic order, we have set our feet upon the road of enduring progress.

Shall we pause now and turn our back upon the road that lies ahead? Shall we call this the promised land? Or, shall we continue on our way? For "each age is a dream that is dying, or one that is coming to birth."

Many voices are heard as we face a great decision. Comfort says, "Tarry a while." Opportunism says, "This is a good spot." Timidity asks, "How difficult is the road ahead?"

True, we have come far from the days of stagnation and despair. Vitality has been preserved. Courage and confidence have been restored. Mental and moral horizons have been extended.

But our present gains were won under the pressure of more than ordinary circumstance. Advance became imperative under the goad of fear and suffering. The times were on the side of progress.

To hold to progress today, however, is more difficult. Dulled conscience, irresponsibility, and ruthless self-interest already reappear. Such symptoms of prosperity may become portents of disaster! Prosperity already tests the persistence of our progressive purpose.

Let us ask again: Have we reached the goal of our vision of that fourth day of March, 1933? Have we found our happy valley?

I see a great nation, upon a great continent, blessed with a great wealth of natural resources. Its hundred and thirty million people are at peace among themselves; they are making their country a good neighbor among the nations. I see a United States which can demonstrate that, under democratic methods of government, national wealth can be translated into a spreading volume of human comforts hitherto unknown, and the lowest standard of living can be raised far above the level of mere subsistence.

But here is the challenge to our democracy: In this nation I see tens of millions of its citizens—a substantial part of its whole population—who at this very moment are denied the greater part of what the very lowest standards of today call the necessities of life.

I see millions of families trying to live on incomes so meager that the pall of family disaster hangs over them day by day.

I see millions whose daily lives in city and on farm continue under conditions labeled indecent by a so-called polite society half a century ago.

I see millions denied education, recreation, and the opportunity to better their lot and the lot of their children.

I see millions lacking the means to buy the products of farm and factory and by their poverty denying work and productiveness to many other millions.

I see one-third of a nation ill-housed, ill-clad, ill-nourished.

It is not in despair that I paint you that picture. I paint it for you in hope—because the Nation, seeing and understanding the injustice in it, proposes to paint it out. We are determined to make every American citizen the subject of his country's interest and concern; and we will never regard any faithful, law-abiding group within our borders as superfluous. The test of our progress is not whether we add more to the abundance of those who have much; it is whether we provide enough for those who have too little.

If I know aught of the spirit and purpose of our Nation, we will not listen to Comfort, Opportunism, and Timidity. We will carry on.

Overwhelmingly, we of the Republic are men and women of good will; men and women who have more than warm hearts of dedication; men and women who have cool heads and willing hands of practical purpose as well. They will insist that every agency of popular government use effective instruments to carry out their will.

Government is competent when all who compose it work as trustees for the whole people. It can make constant progress when it keeps abreast of all the facts. It can obtain justified support and legitimate criticism when the people receive true information of all that government does.

If I know aught of the will of the people, they will demand that these conditions of effective government shall be created and maintained. They will demand a Nation uncorrupted by cancers of injustice and, therefore, strong among the nations in its example of the will to peace.

Today we reconsecrate our country to long-cherished ideals in a suddenly changed civilization. In every land there are always at work forces that drive men apart and forces that draw men together. In our personal ambitions we are individualists. But in our seeking for economic and political progress as a nation, we all go up, or else we all go down, as one people.

To maintain a democracy of effort requires a vast amount of patience in dealing with different methods, a vast amount of humility. But out of the confusion of many voices rises an understanding of dominant public need. Then political leadership can voice common ideals, and aid in their realization.

In taking again the oath of office as President of the United States, I assume the solemn obligation of leading the American people forward along the road over which they have chosen to advance.

While this duty rests upon me I shall do my utmost to speak their purpose and to do their will, seeking Divine guidance to help us each and every one to give light to them that sit in darkness and to guide our feet into the way of peace.

For comparisons between democracy and other ideals, see Joseph A. Leighton, *Social Philosophies in Conflict: Fascism and Nazism, Communism, Liberal Democracy*, New York, Appleton-Century-Crofts, Inc., 1937; C. E. Merriam. *The New Democracy and the New Despotism*, New York, Whittlesey House, 1939; Kurt London. *Backgrounds of Conflict*, New York, The Macmillan Company, 1945.

Down and Out in the Great Depression: Letters from the Forgotten Man

Edited by Robert S. McElvaine

[February, 1936]

Mr. and Mrs. Roosevelt.
Wash. D.C.
Dear Mr. President:

I'm a boy of 12 years. I want to tell you about my family My father hasn't worked for 5 months He went plenty times to relief, he filled out application. They won't give us anything. I don't know why. Please you do something. We haven't paid 4 months rent, Everyday the landlord rings the door bell, we don't open the door for him. We are afraid that will be put out, been put out before, and don't want to happen again. We haven't paid the gas bill, and the electric bill, haven't paid grocery bill for 3 months. My brother goes to Lane Tech. High School. he's eighteen years old, hasn't gone to school for 2 weeks because he got no carfare. I have a sister she's twenty years, she can't find work. My father he staying home. All the time he's crying because he can't find work. I told him why are you crying daddy, and daddy said why shouldn't I cry when there is nothing in the house. I feel sorry for him. That night I couldn't sleep. The next morning I wrote this letter to you. in my room. Were American citizens and were born in Chicago, Ill. and I don't know why they don't help us Please answer right away because we need it. will starve Thank you.

God bless you.

[Anonymous]
Chicago, Ill.

[Canton, Georgia
July 22, 1935]

[President Franklin D. Roosevelt:]

dear Sur as you are the president of our State it looks like you could do Something to help out the poor white people the negroes can get work where the poor white man canot and his family are one Starvation The negroes are in post offices getting $1000 dollars a month and white families Suffering and it is not write just look at it your Self if it was your family in Canton Ga there is a negro working in the post office and white men cant get a job to feed his family and a white woman up holding for just Such as that and negroes being worked ever where instead of white men it dont look like that is rite and is not rite and lay off white men where there is a large family and keep men with big farms and just a man and wife and both at work unless there are something done the poor people will pursh to death will you please help the poor people out this relief work is not helping the poor out just make $300 a week them that uses the pick and Shovel and the ofice men and woman gets the rest there is to many in office for the poor working man to get any pay. rote by a woman that has a large family and is on Sufference

[Anonymous]

Troy, N.Y.
Jan. 2, 1935.

Dear Mrs. Roosevelt,

About a month ago I wrote you asking if you would buy some baby clothes for me with the understanding that I was to repay you as soon as my husband got enough work. Several weeks later I received a reply to apply to a Welfare Association so I might receive the aid I needed. Do you remember?

Please Mrs. Roosevelt, I do not want charity, only a chance from someone who will trust me until we can get enough money to repay the amount spent for the things I need. As a proof that I really am sincere, I am sending you two of my dearest possessions to keep as security, a ring my husband gave me before we were married, and a ring my mother used to wear. Perhaps the actual value of them is not high, but they are worth a lot to me. If you will consider buying the baby clothes, please keep them (rings) until I send you the money you spent. It is very hard to face bearing a baby we cannot afford to have, and the fact that it is due to arrive soon, and still there is no money for the hospital or clothing, does not make it any easier. I Have decided to stay home, keeping my 7 year old daughter from school to help with the smaller children when my husband has work. The oldest little girl is sick now, and has never been strong, so I would not depend on her. The 7 year old one is a good willing little worker and somehow we must manage—but without charity.

If you still feel you cannot trust me, it is allright and I can only say I donot blame you, but if you decide my word is worth anything with so small a security, here is a list of what I will need-but I will need it very soon.

2 shirts, silk and wool. size 2

3 pr. stockings, silk and wool, 4 1/2 or 4

3 straight flannel bands
2 slips—outing flannel
2 muslim dresses
1 sweater
1 wool bonnet
2 pr. wool booties
2 doz. diapers 30 × 30—or 27 × 27
1 large blanket (baby) about 45″ or 50″
3 outing flannel nightgowns

If you will get these for me I would rather no one knew about it. I promise to repay the cost of the layette as soon as possible. We will all be very grateful to you, and I will be more than happy.

Sincerely yours,
Mrs. H. E. C.

Seattle, Wash.
Dec. 12—1934

Federal Emergency Relief
Administration
1734 New York Ave N. W.
Washington D.C.
Gentlemen:

When the Home Owners Loan Corporation first opened in Seattle, I made an application for a loan, the mortgage was for $2,000.00 on a 6 room house and nearly an acre of land, during the last two years conditions have been so adverse with me that I have been unable to make any payments on the interest neither have I been able to pay the taxes, the mortgages at first agreed to take the Government bonds, but when certain repairs were included, the total amount the Government would loan was not enough to pay the mortgagee all his money in fact it would show a loss of nearly $400.00 after all *acrued interest* together with all taxes and repairs, so the mortgagee refused to take the bonds, and consequently my loan was rejected although I was one of the first to apply. I took it up with the repair department, to let me do the painting and repair the roof myself and in that way give the extra money to the mortgagee but just when it seemed I was about to get my loan through the Government stopped all loans, and since the mortgagee has been hot on my trail demanding me to give him a *deed* or he will foreclose at once.

Gentlemen, this is *all* I have in the *world* my home and family. I have four boys and a little girl all in school this is an Ideal place to raise my family to be good american citizens, we have enough good ground to raise lots of garden stuff and this goes a long way toward keeping the table, we are now forced on relief and it seems that everything comes at once, if they are allowed to take away my little home I don't know what I'll do, I understand the Government is planning to supply homes for those who have none, it would be 100 times better in my particular case if the Government would make it possible for me to keep my own little home.

I always have been able to give my family a decent living until economic conditions got so bad I was unable to make it go any longer.

I am inclosing the last letter I received from the mortgagee.

I sincerely believe if the Government will help me save my place, it wont be long be long before I will again be on my feet, I think, the *worry* and wear and tear for fear that the mortgagee would try and foreclose on me has kind of gotten me down a little, I have not been well for two or three weeks, but I'm sure if I can secure help from the Government at this time of my distress, it wont be long till I will again be on my feet.

I sincerely *hope* and *pray* you will come to my aid and help me save my home for my family, if I should loose it I don't know what I'll do as I have *no other place to go*, if I can save it, I will be able to raise my family to be *good useful citizens*.

My place is worth about $3500.00 but to me it is my *home*. where I have a lovely happy family, good loving wife, who is thrifty, energetic, and who makes a home what it should be, we teach our children to love God, go to Sunday school and train them to live to be *proper Americans* who love their country, and if needs be give their lives for it.

I believe God will see us through some way but it has been the hardest thing I have had to go through, this maybe His way so I'm writing to you *asking and praying* that you will do something to save our little home.

I am sure the President, if he only knew, would order that something be done, God Bless him. he is doing all he can to relieve the suffering and I am sure his name will go down in history among the other *great men* of our country.

Respectfully Yours

A. G. [male]

Seattle

Wash

The Rise of Fascism

Jay P. Corrin

Political and social unrest had haunted Europe long before the onset of the Great Depression. A good example of this can be seen in the post-war situation in Italy. Italy had fought on the side of the victors. Her contributions had been negligible yet losses severe, owing in large part to grossly incompetent field commanders. Compounding the misery was the nation's anger at being insufficiently rewarded at the peace conference with adequate spoils of war in terms of territorial gains. The Italian economy, weak even before 1914, had quickly slipped into a serious economic depression at the war's conclusion. The heavy war debt, high levels of taxation, rampant inflation, surging unemployment and food shortages brought Italy to the precipice of revolution. Workers went on strike and attacked factories, the unemployed rioted in the streets, and peasants seized large estates and destroyed property. Meanwhile, Italy's parliamentary politicians bickered and dithered while the nation moved closer to anarchy. Into this miasma of disorder stepped **Benito Mussolini**.

Mussolini (1883-1945) was the son of a fiercely anti-clerical blacksmith, and his early education had been disrupted by dismissal from a Catholic seminary for putting a knife in one of his classmates. After this, Mussolini became somewhat of a vagabond, skipping from one country to another to avoid military service. During these peregrinations he managed to pick up a smattering of socialist ideas and paid his keep by serving as a trade union organizer and left-wing radical journalist. Mussolini's political and cultural ideas were deeply influenced by George Sorel's *Reflections on Violence* and the writings of Friedrich Nietzsche. After numerous tirades against Italy's conquest of Ethiopia—socialists at the time were pacifist and anti-imperialist—Mussolini was arrested. After release from jail in 1912 he became editor of Milan's *Avanti* ("Forward"), the leading socialist newspaper in Italy. Yet with the outbreak of World War I he suddenly shifted his political orientation: Mussolini became an outspoken supporter of Italy's intervention in the conflict, which his socialist comrades vehemently opposed. At this point Mussolini took on the role of an ultra-nationalist and joined the army, where he rose to the rank of corporal. A political opportunist, a thug and a braggart, Mussolini was also clever, dynamic, and ambitious, and perfected his skills as a demagogic orator.

After the war, Mussolini had hoped to recover standing with his socialist comrades in order to advance his political career, namely to become master of Italy. But when his former associates rebuffed him, he decided to move to the other end of the political spectrum by organizing an anti-socialist movement. He called this group the *Fascio di combattimento*, and his first recruits to what became the Fascist Party were ex-soldiers and unemployed youth. Because of the country's growing fear of Soviet-inspired communism, Mussolini soon attracted financial support from wealthy industrialists and landowners who found the thuggery of Fascist *squadristi* useful for breaking up strikes and bashing the heads of unruly peasants. Mussolini dressed his followers in black shirts, gave them discipline through military training and promised to bring order to the mess that was Italy. The Fascists became especially popular with those who feared disorder and a communist takeover, including some of the most powerful interests in Italy: the captains of industry, bankers, the urban middle classes, wealthy landowners and the Roman Catholic Church. By 1921 Mussolini's party had 300,000 members and through the use of violence and intimidation won some 35 seats in elections to the Chamber of Deputies. The Fascists dreamed of Italy once again becoming a world power, claiming that the historical accomplishments of their Roman ancestors could supply the inspiration to make this reality.

In the autumn of 1922, Mussolini's "**Blackshirts**" began to overthrow local governments in Milan and Bologna. This was accompanied by generous doses of street violence against those the Fascists accused of threatening the national order, such as communists, alleged communists, socialists, Christian socialists and even ordinary people whose version of reality differed from that of Mussolini. Besides using rubber truncheons and chains, the Blackshirts' instrument of choice was castor oil, since when taken in large quantities it produced violent spasms of vomiting and diarrhea.

The culmination of these activities occurred in late October when the Fascists undertook their famous **March on Rome** (Mussolini conveniently stayed safely at home) aimed at taking over the nation's government. Although the liberal-democratic coalition cabinet in Rome tried to secure itself by declaring martial law, the king refused to approve it, and when the cabinet resigned, the weak and distraught King Victor Emmanuel III appointed Mussolini his prime minister. Although he was given only temporary emergency power to restore order and initiate reforms, Mussolini forced through parliament a new law that permitted a quick national election. In yet another campaign of terror, replete with lethal doses of physical violence and castor oil, the Fascists claimed a majority of votes in a rigged election. By April 1924 their domination of Italy was complete.

But what was the Fascist program for reform? What ideology was to guide the Fascist political vision? Never had Mussolini articulated a positive set of ideas for reconstructing the country. He only claimed that Italy needed a spiritual revolution facilitated by a Nietzschean "will to power" to generate action against enemies of the state. In practice Mussolini presented himself as Fascism personified: a chauvinist demagogue working up the crowds, a virile dictator shouting marching orders to disciplined soldiers (Mussolini liked to pose bare-chested for the cameras) and to youthful supporters in black-colored shirts who would beat up the weak and cowardly. The goal was to reconstruct the Roman Empire through force, with Mussolini as the new Caesar. How could this be done? Through war alone, said Mussolini, since it "brings up the highest tension, all human energy and puts the stamp of nobility upon the people who have the courage to meet it." The message was clear: beware all those men with no chests!

In order to legitimize his use of power Mussolini turned to the philosopher Giovanni Gentile to provide him with an ideology of Fascism. Gentile wrote up the definition, which was widely published as Mussolini's own philosophy. What emerged was an eclectic and jumbled mix of ideas from a variety of sources, including Hegel, Nietzsche, Sorel, Treitschke and a number of other idealist writers who celebrated anti-rational impulses. Fascism glorified the use of force and war as the noblest of human activities, and it denounced liberalism, capitalism, democracy, socialism and communism. Most significantly Fascism deified the state as the supreme embodiment of the human spirit. In the words of the English writer G. K. Chesterton, "Fascism was nationalism gone mad."

In 1925 Mussolini undertook an agreement with Italian industrialists and bankers that gave them privileges in return for supporting the Fascist Party. This partnership, which Mussolini called "**corporativism**," was presented as the vehicle for ending class conflict. In reality the arrangement simply assured the dominance of capitalism and the control of labor and professional groups. The so-called corporativist economic structure was to eliminate the free market and, through planning and management, reallocate resources for maximal efficiency. In practice corporativism was nothing more than a rhetorical mask to hide the creation of a command economy under the control of big business. Trade unions were abolished, except those controlled by Fascists. State propaganda went into high gear. Images of Mussolini were posted throughout the country; radio and films depicted him as "Il Duce," or "the leader." Although Mussolini was himself an atheist, he saw the necessity of cultivating the support of the Catholic Church. In February 1929 Mussolini settled all political problems with the Church with an agreement that gave the Pope sovereign control over the territory around St. Peter's Basilica and the Vatican. The Lateran Treaty recognized the role of the Church in education and guaranteed the Italian marriage laws. The Church, in return, was to recognize the Fascist regime and absent itself from politics.

The Case of Germany

Varieties of fascism had considerable appeal throughout Europe. Mussolini's brand was the first of its kind and had considerable influence giving birth to imitators. The greatest triumph of the creed emerged in Germany. **Adolf Hitler** was inspired by his Italian counterpart, but he carried Mussolini's musings to a level of reality that literally altered the course of world history.

Adolf Hitler was certainly Mussolini's best pupil. He was born in Austria (1898) and did not become a German citizen until 1932. Son of an Austrian customs official with high social aspirations, Hitler lost his father at the age of fourteen and two years later his mother. The latter's passing was a severe blow, since Hitler was unusually attached to his overindulgent mother, whose death from breast cancer he blamed on her Jewish doctor. At the age of sixteen he dropped out of school and soon thereafter drifted around the cosmopolitan city of Vienna after being denied admittance to a local academy as an art student. These years were marked by poverty as Hitler refused any jobs of menial labor and survived sometimes in squalor by selling inferior-quality postcards and watercolors of his own making.

Vienna was the capital of the multi-ethnic Hapsburg Empire and was frequented by wealthy noblemen of eastern Europe driving through the streets in fashionable carriages, laborers of mixed nationalities attached to international Marxism, and successful Jews who had become assimilated to the German culture of the Empire and occupied distinguished positions in business, banking, medicine, law, education and journalism. Hitler hated them all, somehow convinced that their very existence was the cause of his own failures. He was also exceedingly race conscious. Considering himself to be of pure German blood, he looked down with disdain upon those he considered racial hybrids. Hitler's categories of hatreds were legion, including of course Jews (he was pathologically anti-Semitic), aristocrats, capitalists, socialists (especially Marxists), foreigners, people of "mixed breeds" and all those with physical disabilities (in his mind a potential source of gene pollution). Hitler's intense aversion to the cosmopolitanism of Vienna led him in 1913 to the German city of Munich, capital of Bavaria, where presumably he would find people of superior racial stock absent the stain of "mongrelization."

Life in more amenable surroundings still remained difficult and fraught with personal failure for this insolent drifter until August of 1914. Like so many other young people in Europe who felt isolated and alienated from what was considered the drab routine of peace, Hitler found that the onslaught of world war provided an exciting opportunity for the kind of action that could give life new meaning. Suddenly what was a lonely and impersonal existence was transformed by the passions of patriotism and conflict that roused in some individual soldiers a fresh sense of belonging in their search for something greater than the self. For many this "rain of fire and steel" lifted the individual out of isolation and merged him into a greater whole. Upon hearing about the outbreak of hostilities Hitler fell to his knees and thanked God for allowing him to live in such propitious times.

By all accounts Hitler was a worthy soldier but, like Mussolini, failed to rise any higher than the rank of corporal. As was the case with many other soldiers, when peace returned Hitler felt an emotional and moral let-down, longing for the close companionship produced by trench combat that raised life to exalted levels of meaning. After discharge he returned to the city of Munich, which at this juncture was a caldron of political unrest. In 1919 a Bavarian Socialist Republic, with Munich as its capital, was declared with the active support of Moscow. The federal government eventually crushed this experiment in communism, but its legacy produced a deep aversion to all forms of socialism, liberalism and democratic ideas. Bavaria itself swarmed with violent secret societies and paramilitary organizations led by frustrated former military officers who found the post-war peace settlement forced on Germany intolerable.

This was an environment that enabled Hitler to finally discover his true talent, which was not artistic but a unique ability to move crowds with demagogic speeches. He was given a job with the army's political instruction program to combat socialist and democratic propaganda among demobilized soldiers, with the aim of keeping alive their patriotic and military spirits. At the army's urging Hitler joined a small organization called the German Worker's Party. He soon took over as leader and changed the name to the **National Socialist Workers' Party**, whose members became known as **Nazis**, a name derived from the German pronunciation of the first two syllables of the word National.

Germany after the war was socially and politically fractious owing to persistent economic problems and the unpopularity of its government, the fledgling democratic **Weimar Republic**. This was Germany's first experiment in participatory politics, which would have been a difficult undertaking even in the best of times given the country's tradition of monarchical paternalism. The post-war governing constitution was drawn up in the city of Weimar, which had been selected for this important event in part because it had been the home of two of Germany's most esteemed philosophers, Goethe and Schiller. The city also was one of the centers of 18th-century European cosmopolitanism and represented different values from the militaristic and authoritarian legacy of Berlin.

The Weimar Republic was in trouble from its birth after being saddled with accepting the harsh and unpopular Versailles peace settlement. Many Germans associated the government with humiliation and defeat, due in large part to the myth of a "**stab in the back**," the idea that the war was lost not on the battlefield but through a political sellout by those who dominated the new Republic. Right-wing groups spread rumors that communists and Jews associated with the Weimar leadership clique purposely had weakened the nation with its betrayal of the German military by prematurely signing an armistice. This negative image was compounded by the harsh peace terms: lost territory and people, restrictions on the military and unfair reparations.

Attempts by the Weimar Republic to establish legitimacy and maintain social peace were undermined by repeated economic, political and diplomatic crises in the 1920s. The country was plagued by a number of military threats from extremists on both the political right and left throughout the decade. Two of the Republic's most promising leaders were assassinated, and a major source of social unrest was post-war inflation. However, once the inflation was reined in by American loans through the Dawes Plan of 1923, there was a substantial economic recovery and Germany experienced economic growth. Industrial output expanded, workers secured good wages and the government expanded social welfare services. All this came crashing to the ground with the onslaught of global depression triggered by the American stock market debacle. U.S. banks called in their international loans and the German economy collapsed.

It was the Depression that opened the door to the Nazis, who had previously remained small and ineffectual. Hitler earlier had managed to make a name for himself in 1923 when he was involved in the so-called "Beer Hall Putsch" against the Bavarian state government in Munich. This attempted coup failed, and Hitler was put on trial where he availed himself of the opportunity to air his extremist political views. Although he was given a five-year prison sentence, Hitler was pardoned after only a year, a reflection of the government's ambivalence about challenges to democracy. It was during this prison term that Hitler wrote *Mein Kampf* ("My Struggle"), a rambling, bilious screed against communists, liberals and Jews and also a disjointed, confusing attempt to articulate a political philosophy. This turgid literary farrago became the bible of the Nazi Party. Today's audience would find it largely unreadable.

Once the Depression set in, the Nazi Party, which initially attracted unemployed soldiers and criminals, or as one historian put it "the gutter elite," stepped out of the shadows and attracted broader popular support. Hitler inveighed against the Treaty of Versailles, denouncing Weimar democracy for fomenting class struggle, division and weakness. He called for a "real democracy" of the German Volk, a pure master race who would be united as a vital force behind the leadership of a strong leader, the Nazi *Fuhrer*. Hitler also railed against unfair taxes, unearned incomes, the power of great trusts, land speculators, and above all the Jews, whom he accused of running both capitalism and international communism. Nazi doctrine, claimed Hitler, speaks for the German "little men."

The party performed well in the 1930 general election; its representation in the Reichstag national assembly increased from twelve to more than one hundred. For the next two and half years, divisions within the Reichstag between social democrats, conservatives, liberals, Nazis and communists paralyzed the government. The streets turned to mayhem as Hitler's paramilitary thugs or storm troopers known as the Brown Shirts battled communists. A new election in July 1932 produced a substantial increase in Nazi Reichstag seats. Finally, after numerous failed efforts to put together a stable government, the aged and near senile President Paul von Hindenburg appointed Hitler chancellor on January 30, 1933.

In this position of power Hitler called for another election in March, while unleashing the Brown Shirts to beat up the opposition in the guise of preserving public order from communist subversion. Some five days before the scheduled March 5th election, the Reichstag (Germany's legislative assembly) was set ablaze. Although it is likely that the Nazis themselves started the fire, Hitler blamed the communists for the crime and used his emergency powers as chancellor to outlaw the Communist Party. The Nazis still failed to capture the majority of Reichstag seats, but Hitler managed to win the support of several key conservatives from other parties, who thought they could control him once in power, and forced through the so-called **Enabling Act**, which gave him emergency dictatorial power for a period of four years. The dictatorship quickly became permanent. Hitler now put in place the domestic infrastructures that would rid the nation of its internal enemies, reorganized both the economic and social order, and launched a massive military buildup that created full employment and provided the requisite muscle for creating what he called the "**Third Reich**," an empire that would last for a thousand years.

Where did the Nazis find their audience? Initially they appealed to the demoralized and disenchanted, especially demobilized lesser army officers. Among Hitler's leading followers were Hermann Goering, a WWI air fighter ace and drug addict who became second in command. Rudolph Hess, a humorless and rather stupid man, assumed command of Nazi political action. Ernst Rohm, a sexual pervert, was the leader of the S.A. (*Sturmabteilung*) or Brown Shirts. Other key Nazis included Julius Streicher, a pornographer and rapist who always appeared in public with a whip; Paul Joseph Goebbels, a club footed and acid-tongued chief propagandist, who was one of the few Nazis with a high education; and Heinrich Himmler, a former chicken farmer and failed fertilizer salesman given leadership of the SS (*Schutzstaffel*). All these men were supposed to represent the purity of the "Aryan race," a mythical people that appeared in the writings of Nietzsche and were believed to move the wheels of history. Hitler, on the other hand, had no illusions about the character of the men who became his leaders and followers. Such elements, he admitted, were unusable in time of peace:

> ...but in turbulent periods it is quite different...fundamentally, they were just overgrown children...they were simply creatures, all of a piece...from the beginning I knew that one could make a party only with elements like that...I especially looked for people of disheveled appearance. A bourgeois in a stiff collar would have bitched up everything."[1]

As the economy deteriorated, frustrated university graduates who could not find employment were drawn to Hitler's message. The Nazis also won the support of dis- affected workers by promising good wages; medium and small-scale entrepreneurs who were offered protection from chain stores and trade union wage demands; mem- bers of the middle and lower middling classes whose savings had been wiped out in the Depression; farmers who were promised subsidies for their crops; and eventually Germany's leading industrialists, who saw a strong Nazi state an important buffer against communism and the prospect of profits under Hitler's proposed rearmament campaign. In short, the Nazis succeeded in winning support from the broadest cross- section of German society who feared the uncertainties of market capitalism as well as the revolutionary agenda of communism.

Could it be said that a "horde of barbarians" had set up their tents in Germany? Some two months after Hitler was named chancellor, the novelist Thomas Mann wrote of a new type of revolution, one "without underlying ideas, against ideas, against everything nobler, better, decent, against freedom, truth and justice." Mann noted that the "common scum" had taken control of the state "accompanied by vast rejoicing on the part of the masses."[2]

What followed this revolution, however, would not improve the lot of the German masses. As a central feature of their dictatorship the Nazis classified Jews as "un-German" and eventually deprived them not only of their property but also civil rights and citizenship. This foreshadowed the state-organized **Holocaust** leading to the elimination of some six million European Jews. All political parties except the Nazis were outlawed, a secret political police called the **Gestapo** (*Geheime Staatspolizei*) suppressed all ideas and behaviors contrary to the Fuhrer's and arrested or killed all who were considered threats to the state. Churches, both Protestant and Catholic, were brought under control of the regime and schools and institutions of higher learning indoctrinated the next generation of Nazi citizens. All facets of the media were coordinated to propound Nazi racial doctrines. Full employment was assured through extensive public works projects (the *autobahn*, the world's first superhighway was one result) and, most importantly, a vast rearmament program was put in place to build the massive military apparatus Hitler needed to achieve the Reich of a thousand years. Now, with his political competitors vanquished, and the German masses roaring their approval in Goebbels's giant, torchlight demonstra- tions, Hitler could proudly proclaim "Today Germany, tomorrow the world."

Understanding the Varieties of Fascism

Fascism and its most virulent German variety were spawned by the collapse of the bourgeois cultural order triggered by the Great War. There are several possible explanations for the fascist phenomenon. On one level we can see it as a response to the inherent problems of modernity, a concrete historical illustration of what can occur when social change — either bad or good — takes place so quickly that individuals are no longer able to make meaningful connections between their sense of self and the institutions that previously had provided linkages to a broader social matrix. This resulted in what the French sociologist Emile Durkheim called "anomie," a feeling of rootlessness caused by the collapse of normative values. The process appears to have occurred in many countries after the trauma of world war and the subsequent economic crisis culminating in the Great Depression.

Those countries where the move to modernization had been difficult, where the values of a liberal democratic order had not had the sufficient time to establish historical roots, were prime candidates for a fascist experience. Fascist-style movements found their greatest audiences in Spain, Portugal, Italy, Germany and various eastern European countries. None of these states had a large middle class to serve as a buffer between the higher and lower social orders, and they also lacked the bourgeois cultural confidence needed to stanch fascist-type appeals. Nor had these countries reached any popular consensus on political values and institutional structures. It is significant that the U.S., Canada, Great Britain and the other Commonwealth countries as well as nearly all the nations of Western Europe were spared the triumphs of this scourge.

Certainly one of fascism's singular appeals was to rescue the isolated, atomized individual alienated by the rapidity of social change brought by what Ferdinand Tönnies called *gesellschaft* ("modern corporation") and to reintegrate him once again into a traditional *gemeinschaft* ("community"). Anxiety about the collapse of communal solidarity had intensified in Europe as early as the late nineteenth century when industrial conflict, urbanization, and rising immigration rattled the traditional sense of community. Jarring transformations brought about by these accelerating changes had captured the attention of European sociologists such as Georg Simmel, Emile Durkheim, Tönnies and others, who noted in their work the disruptions of traditional social relationships brought about by what today we recognize as the advancement of modernization. This collective sense of social dislocation had been exacerbated by World War I. In the midst of the consequent social, psychological and economic chaos many were prepared—much as the 17th-century philosopher Thomas Hobbes had predicted—to sacrifice individual freedom for the security that comes from the immersion of self into a larger authoritarian social collectivity. This was one answer to Durkheim's anomie, the purposeless drift of people without social ties. It has been said that the Nazis offered a "false *gemeinschaft*" as an antidote to the insecurities of modernity, a totalitarian dynamic in which the "I" becomes the "We."

Yet can we simply associate fascism as the rejection of modernity? Mussolini, for example, was a great admirer of the Italian "**Futurists**," a cult that celebrated the attributes of modernity in the symbol of its movement: a racing automobile signalizing the liberating virtues of action in a rapid leap into the future. The "Futurist Manifesto" dismissed the cultural legacies of the past preserved in museums and libraries, while praising the revitalizing values of speed and violence. One of the founders of the Futurist movement, the artist Filippo Tommaso Marinetti, was a fan of Mussolini's emphasis on action and violence and a Fascist himself. Hitler, for his part, may have borrowed Tönnies' term for the "People's Community" (*Volksgemeinschaft*) he hoped to create (Tönnies was a supporter of the Nazis), but on another level he sought an alternative modernity, a technically advanced and militarily powerful society in which "modernity's strains and divisions would be smothered" by the party's totalitarian powers of integration and control.[3]In this respect technology would be used to manage the stresses of modernization but in the context of a traditional yet authoritarian *Volks* community. Even the Nazi's barbarous war against the Jews was based on modern so-called "eugenic science," a willingness to weed out the weak and racially impure that rejected moral values in the quest of an aesthetic of the perfect human specimen, notwithstanding the contradictions of Aryan physical and mental superiority represented by Himmler, Goebbels and other members of Hitler's "gutter elite."

Some historians have asserted that the Nazi version of fascism can best be understood as the natural culmination of German history, which from the days of Luther revealed a tendency to seek protection from the vagaries of modernity by submitting to the powerful, either like the secular princes who protected Protestants from Rome at the time of Luther's apostasy, or to submit completely to an all-powerful God, which Luther preferred to the popes. Subsequent German history was shaped by its people's submission to strong political and religious authorities, who never gave democracy a chance to deepen its roots either in German politics or in the popular psyche. Germany had been forged into a modern state by the "Iron Chancellor" Prince Otto von Bismarck and his Prussian Junkers, a military aristocracy who scorned liberals and devoted their lives to serve as military leaders for an authoritarian and paternalistic monarchy. This was supposedly a military tradition that Hitler and the Nazis manipulated to establish their empire.

The problem with this explanation, however, is that Hitler and his National Socialists got most of their support from Bavaria, the Catholic part of Germany that always resisted the lead of the northern Prussians Protestants who represented the military elites. Moreover, the German army officer class was suspicious of Hitler from the beginning and only after much struggle submitted to Nazi leadership. Even the claim that Nazi anti-Semitism was a unique product of Germany's hatred of Jews must be challenged by the fact that other countries in eastern Europe traditionally were even more anti-Semitic than the Germans, and many willingly collaborated in assisting the Nazis in their so-called "final solution."

An equally incomplete explanation for fascism comes from Marxist historians. They have emphasized the centrality of economic factors and class struggle as forces for bringing successes to Mussolini and Hitler. In their view the varieties of fascism represented the last desperate stage of the bourgeois elite's struggle to maintain their wealth and privileges against the claims of working- class revolution. They suggest that in a moment of great crises wealthy industrialists, bankers and landowners threw their support to Mussolini or Hitler to prevent the collapse of capitalism. Both dictators certainly initiated short-term policies and programs that benefited these groups and thereby staved off a communist takeover. Yet it is clear in the long run that both dictators used the elites to advance their own megalomaniacal agendas. Indeed, from the outset Mussolini and Hitler generated popular support by attacking bourgeois capitalist values. In the long run neither dictator was beholden to bourgeois economic or cultural interests, and they systematically eliminated market mechanisms in favor of a command economy that was geared not for capitalist profits but for military success. Finally, their respective irrational foreign policy decisions only served to destroy the wealth and class values of such elites.

In the final analysis we might well argue that fascism was a product of modernization. But we can perhaps best understand the complexities of the fascist historical moment not as a *reaction against* modernization but rather as a *consequence* of modernization. Fascism's relationship to modernity was complex and ambivalent, but it does reveal to us how certain forms of political movements and ideologies can engineer anti-modernizing sentiments into channels that maximize the powers of party and state. It should also be kept in mind that Italian Fascism and National Socialism in Germany required not merely the complicity of ordinary people but also the acquiescence or assistance of traditional elites. These men had a distaste for the crudities of fascist militants, but they believed that allowing the vulgarians into the governing arena would serve to tame the beasts. They were wrong.

References and Suggested Readings:

Arendt, Hannah. *The Origins of Totalitarianism*. New York: World Publishing Co., 1964.

Bullock, Alan. *Hitler: A Study in Tyranny*. New York: Harper & Row, 1962.

Cassels, Alan. *Fascist Italy*. New York: Thomas Crowell, 1968.

Fest, Joachim. *Hitler*. New York: Harcourt, Brace, Jovanovich, 1974.

Gay, Peter. *Weimar Culture: The Outsider as Insider*. New York: Harper & Row, 1968.

Kirkpatrick, Ivone. *Mussolini: A Study in Power*. New York: Hawthorn Books, 1964.

Nolte, Ernst. *Three Faces of Fascism*. New York: New American Library, 1969.

Orlow, Dietrich. *A History of Modern Germany: 1871 to the Present*. Englewood Cliffs, NJ: Prentice Hall, 1987.

Payne, Stanley. *A History of Fascism: 1914-1945*. Madison, WS: 1995.

Paxton, Robert. *The Anatomy of Fascism*. New York: Random House, 2004.

Smith, Denis Mack. *Mussolini*. New York: Knopf, 1982.

Turner, Henry, ed. *Reappraisals of Fascism*. New York: 1975.

Notes

1. Excerpts from *Hitler's Table Talk*, p.107, as cited in Alan Bullock, *Hitler: A Study in Tyranny*, revised edition (New York, NY, 1962), p. 83.

2. Quoted in Robert O. Paxton, *The Anatomy of Fascism* (New York, 2004), p. 7.

3. *Ibid.*, p. 13. This is the view of Jeffrey Herb, *Reactionary Modernism: Technology, Culture and Politics in Weimar and the Third Reich*, Cambridge, MA, 1984, and Henry A. Turner, Jr., *Reappraisals of Fascism*, New York, NY, 1975.

The Anatomy of Fascism

Robert O. Paxton

Fascism was the major political innovation of the twentieth century, and the source of much of its pain. The other major currents of modern Western political culture—conservatism, liberalism, socialism—all reached mature form between the late eighteenth century and the mid-nineteenth century. Fascism, however, was still unimagined as late as the 1890s. Friedrich Engels, writing a preface in 1895 for his new edition of Karl Marx's *The Class Struggles in France*, clearly believed that wider suffrage would inexorably deliver more votes to the Left. Both time and numbers, Engels was certain, were on the socialists' side. "If it [the growing socialist vote] continues in this fashion, by the end of this [nineteenth] century we [socialists] shall conquer the major part of the middle strata of society, petty bourgeois and peasants, and grow into the decisive power in the land." Conservatives, Engels wrote, had noticed that legality was working against them. By contrast, "we [socialists], under this legality, get firm muscles and rosy cheeks and look like life eternal. There is nothing for them [the conservatives] to do but break through this legality themselves."[1] While Engels thus expected that the Left's enemies would launch a preemptive attack, he could not imagine in 1895 that this might win mass approval. Dictatorship against the Left amidst popular enthusiasm—that was the unexpected combination that fascism would manage to put together one short generation later.

. . . what fascists *did* tells us at least as much as what they *said*. What they said cannot be ignored, of course, for it helps explain their appeal. Even at its most radical, however, fascists' anticapitalist rhetoric was selective. While they denounced speculative international finance (along with all other forms of internationalism, cosmopolitanism, or globalization—capitalist as well as socialist), they respected the property of national producers, who were to form the social base of the reinvigorated nation.[40] When they denounced the bourgeoisie, it was for being too flabby and individualistic to make a nation strong, not for robbing workers of the value they added. What they criticized in capitalism was not its exploitation but its materialism, its indifference to the nation, its inability to stir souls.[41] More deeply, fascists rejected the notion that economic forces are the prime movers of history. For fascists, the dysfunctional capitalism of the interwar period did not need fundamental reordering; its ills could be cured simply by applying sufficient political will to the creation of full employment and productivity.[42] Once in power, fascist regimes confiscated property only from political opponents, foreigners, or Jews. None altered the social hierarchy, except to catapult a few adventurers into high places. At most, they replaced market forces with state economic management, but, in the trough of the Great Depression, most businessmen initially approved of that. If fascism was "revolutionary," it was so in a special sense, far removed from the word's meaning as usually understood from 1789 to 1917, as a profound overturning of the social order and the redistribution of social, political, and economic power.

Yet fascism in power did carry out some changes profound enough to be called "revolutionary," if we are willing to give that word a different meaning. At its fullest development, fascism redrew the frontiers between private and public, sharply diminishing what had once been untouchably private. It changed the practice of citizenship from the enjoyment of constitutional rights and duties to participation in mass ceremonies of affirmation and conformity. It reconfigured relations between the individual and the collectivity, so that an individual had no rights outside community interest. It expanded the powers of the executive—party and state—in a bid for total control. Finally, it unleashed aggressive emotions hitherto known in Europe only during war or social revolution. These transformations often set fascists into conflict with conservatives rooted in families, churches, social rank, and property. We will see below[43] when we examine more fully the complex relationship of complicity, accommodation, and occasional opposition that linked capitalists with fascists in power, that one cannot consider fascism simply a more muscular form of conservatism, even if it maintained the existing regime of property and social hierarchy.

It becomes hard to locate fascism on the familiar Right-Left political map. Did the fascist leaders themselves know, at the beginning? When Mussolini called his friends together at the Piazza San Sepolcro in March 1919, it was not entirely clear whether he was trying to compete with his former colleagues in the Italian Socialist Party on the Left or to attack them frontally from the Right. Where on the Italian political spectrum would what he still sometimes called "national syndicalism" find its place?[44] Indeed, fascism always retained that ambiguity.

Fascists were clear about one thing, however: they were not in the middle. Fascist contempt for the soft, complacent, compromising center was absolute (though fascist parties actively seeking power would need to make common cause with centrist elites, against their common enemies on the Left). Their scorn for liberal parliamentarianism and for slack bourgeois individualism, and the radical tone of their remedies for national weakness and disunity, always jarred with their readiness to conclude practical alliances with national conservatives against the internationalist Left. The ultimate fascist response to the Right-Left political map was to claim that they had made it obsolete by being "neither Right nor Left," transcending such outdated divisions and uniting the nation.

Another contradiction between fascist rhetoric and fascist practice concerns modernization: the shift from rural to urban, from handwork to industry, the division of labor, secular societies, and technological rationalization. Fascists often cursed faceless cities and materialist secularism, and exalted an agrarian utopia free from the rootlessness, conflict, and immorality of urban life.[45] Yet fascist leaders adored their fast cars[46] and planes,[47] and spread their message by dazzlingly up-to-date techniques of propaganda and stagecraft. Once in power, they forced the industrial pace in order to rearm. Thus it becomes difficult to posit the essence of fascism solely in either anti-modernist reaction[48] or in modernizing dictatorship.[49]

Creating Fascist Movements

Postwar Germany offered particularly fertile soil to popular-based antisocialist movements of national revival. Germans had been shaken to their roots by defeat in 1918. The emotional impact was all the more severe because German leaders had been trumpeting victory until a few weeks before. So unbelievable a calamity was easily blamed on traitors. The plummet in German fortunes from the bold Great Power of 1914 to the stunned, hungry loser of 1918 shattered national pride and self-confidence. Wilhelm Spannaus later described his feelings upon returning to his hometown in 1921 after years of teaching in a German school in South America:

> It was shortly after the Spartakus uprising in the Rhineland: practically every windowpane was broken on the train in which I reentered Germany, and the inflation was reaching fantastic proportions. I had left Germany at the height of the power and glory of the Wilhelmine Reich. I came back to find the Fatherland in shambles, under a Socialist republic.[6]

Spannaus became the first respectable citizen of his town to join the Nazi Party, and, as an intellectual leader (he owned the local bookstore), he carried many other citizens with him.

Footloose veterans, their units melting away, unable to find work or even food, were available for extremism of either Left or Right. Some turned to Bolshevik Russia for their inspiration, as in the short-lived Munich Soviet Republic of spring 1919. Others clung to the nationalism already spread by the wartime propaganda movement, the Fatherland Front. Some of these nationalist veterans joined mercenary units (Freikorps) formed under the command of regular army officers to fight what they regarded as Germany's internal enemies. In January 1919 they murdered the socialist leaders Rosa Luxemburg and Karl Liebknecht in revolutionary Berlin. The following spring they crushed socialist regimes in Munich and elsewhere. Other Freikorps units continued battling Soviet and Polish armies along the still-undemarcated Baltic frontier well after the armistice of November 1918.[7]

Corporal Adolf Hitler,[8] back on active duty with Army Group Command IV in Munich after recovering from the hysterical blindness he suffered upon learning of German defeat, was sent by Army Intelligence in September 1919 to investigate one of the many nationalist movements that were sprouting in the postwar disorder. The German Workers' Party (DAP) had been created at the end of the war by a patriotic locksmith, Anton Drexler. Finding a handful of artisans and journalists who dreamed of winning workers to the nationalist cause but had no idea of how to go about it, Hitler joined them and received party card No. 555. He soon became one of the movement's most effective speakers and a member of its directing committee.

In early 1920 Hitler was put in charge of the DAP's propaganda. With the help of sympathetic army officers such as Captain Ernst Röhm and some wealthy Munich backers,[9] Hitler greatly expanded the party's audience. Before nearly two thousand people in a big Munich beer cellar, the Hofbräuhaus, on February 24, 1920, Hitler gave the movement a new name—the Nationalsozialistische Deutsche Arbeiterpartei (NSDAP, or "Nazi" Party, for short)—and presented a program of twenty-five points mixing nationalism, anti-Semitism, and attacks on department stores and international capital. The following April 1, he left the army to devote himself full-time to the NSDAP. He was increasingly recognized as its leader, its *Führer*.[10]

As the immediate postwar turmoil eased, such activist nationalist sects faced less hospitable conditions in Europe. Governments gradually established a toehold on legitimacy. Borders were set. Bolshevism was contained within its Russian birthplace. Some semblance of peacetime normalcy returned to most parts of Europe. Even so, the Italian Fascists, the Hungarian officers, and the Austrian and German National Socialists persisted. Similar movements arose in France[11] and elsewhere. They clearly expressed something more enduring than a momentary nationalist spasm accompanying the final paroxysm of the war.

The Immediate Background

A political space[12] for mass-based nationalist activism, mobilized against both socialism and liberalism, had been only dimly visible in 1914. It became a yawning gap during World War I. That conflict did not so much create fascism as open up wide cultural, social, and political opportunities for it. Culturally, the war discredited optimistic and progressive views of the future, and cast doubt upon liberal assumptions about natural human harmony. Socially, it spawned armies of restless veterans (and their younger brothers)[13] looking for ways to express their anger and disillusion without heed for old-fashioned law or morality. Politically, it generated economic and social strains that exceeded the capacity of existing institutions—whether liberal or conservative—to resolve.

The experience of World War I was the most decisive immediate precondition for fascism. The successful campaign to bring Italy into the war in May 1915 (the "radiant May" of Fascist mythology) first brought together the founding elements of Italian Fascism. "The right to the political succession belongs to us," proclaimed Mussolini at the founding meeting of the Fasci di Combattimento in March 1919, "because we were the ones who pushed the country into war and led it to victory."[14]

The Great War was also, it must be added, at the root of much else that was violent and angry in the postwar world, from Bolshevism to expressionist painting. Indeed, for some authors, the Great War by itself suffices to explain both Fascism and Bolshevism.[15] Four years of industrialized slaughter had left little of Europe's legacy unaltered and nothing of its future certain.

Before 1914, no living European could have imagined such brutality in what was then considered the most civilized part of the globe. Wars had become rare, localized, and short in Europe in the nineteenth century, fought out by professional armies that impinged little on civilian society. Europe had been spared the likes of the American Civil War or the War of the Triple Alliance (Brazil, Argentina, and Uruguay) against Paraguay, which reduced the Paraguayan population by half between 1864 and 1870. When, in August 1914, a petty Balkan conflict erupted out of control into a total war among the European Great Powers, and when those powers managed to sustain the slaughter of an entire generation of young men over four years, it seemed to many Europeans that their civilization itself, with its promise of peace and progress, had failed.

The Great War had also lasted far longer than most people had imagined possible for urbanized industrial countries. Most Europeans had assumed that highly differentiated populations packed into cities, dependent upon massive exchanges of consumer goods, would be simply incapable of enduring years of massive destruction. Only primitive societies, they thought, could support long wars. Contrary to expectations, Europeans discovered, beginning in 1914, how to mobilize industrial productivity and human wills for long years of sacrifice. As trench warfare approached the limits of human endurance, so war governments approached the limits of regimentation of life and thought.[16]

All the belligerent governments had experimented with the manipulation of public opinion. Germany's attempt to motivate the entire civilian population in the Fatherland Front was one of the most coercive examples, but all of them worked to shape their citizens' knowledge and opinions. The economies and societies of all the belligerent countries, too, had been deeply transformed. European peoples had endured their first prolonged experience of universal national service, rationing of food, energy, and clothing, and full-scale economic management. Despite these unprecedented efforts, however, none of the belligerents had achieved its goals. Instead of a short war with clear results, this long and labor-intensive carnage had ended in mutual exhaustion and disillusion.

The war posed such a redoubtable challenge that even the best-integrated and best-governed countries barely managed to meet its strains. Badly integrated and governed countries failed altogether to meet them. Britain and France allocated materiel, assigned people to duties, distributed sacrifice, and manipulated the news just successfully enough to retain the allegiance of most of their citizens. The recently unified German empire and Italian monarchy did less well. The Habsburg empire broke apart into its constituent nationalities. Tsarist Russia collapsed into chaos. Those dislocated countries where a landless peasantry was still numerous and where a disfranchised middle class still lacked basic liberties polarized to the Left (as in Russia). Those with a large but threatened middle class, including family farmers, polarized against the Left and looked for new solutions.[17]

At the end of the war, Europeans were torn between an old world that could not be revived and a new world about which they disagreed bitterly. As war economies were dismantled too quickly, wartime inflation spun out of control, making a mockery of the bourgeois virtues of thrift and savings. A population that had come to expect public solutions to economic problems was thrown into uncertainty.

Mobilizing Passions

. . . fascism became fully developed only after its practitioners had quietly closed their eyes to some of their early principles, in the effort to enter the coalitions necessary for power. Once in power, as we will see, fascists played down, marginalized, or even discarded some of the intellectual currents that had helped open the way.

To focus only on the educated carriers of intellect and culture in the search for fascist roots, furthermore, is to miss the most important register: subterranean passions and emotions. A nebula of attitudes was taking shape, and no one thinker ever put together a total philosophical system to support fascism. Even scholars who specialize in the quest for fascism's intellectual and cultural origins, such as George Mosse, declare that the establishment of a "mood" is more important than "the search for some individual precursors."[59] In that sense too, fascism is more plausibly linked to a set of "mobilizing passions" that shape fascist action than to a consistent and fully articulated philosophy. At bottom is a passionate nationalism. Allied to it is a conspiratorial and Manichean view of history as a battle between the good and evil camps, between the pure and the corrupt, in which one's own community or nation has been the victim. In this Darwinian narrative, the chosen people have been weakened by political parties, social classes, unassimilable minorities, spoiled rentiers, and rationalist thinkers who lack the necessary sense of community. These "mobilizing passions," mostly taken for granted and not always overtly argued as intellectual propositions, form the emotional lava that set fascism's foundations:

- a sense of overwhelming crisis beyond the reach of any traditional solutions;
- the primacy of the group, toward which one has duties superior to every right, whether individual or universal, and the subordination of the individual to it;
- the belief that one's group is a victim, a sentiment that justifies any action, without legal or moral limits, against its enemies, both internal and external;[60]
- dread of the group's decline under the corrosive effects of individualistic liberalism, class conflict, and alien influences;
- the need for closer integration of a purer community, by consent if possible, or by exclusionary violence if necessary;
- the need for authority by natural leaders (always male), culminating in a national chief who alone is capable of incarnating the group's destiny;
- the superiority of the leader's instincts over abstract and universal reason;
- the beauty of violence and the efficacy of will, when they are devoted to the group's success;
- the right of the chosen people to dominate others without restraint from any kind of human or divine law, right being decided by the sole criterion of the group's prowess within a Darwinian struggle.

The "mobilizing passions" of fascism are hard to treat historically, for many of them are as old as Cain. It seems incontestable, however, that the fevers of increased nationalism before World War I and the passions aroused by that war sharpened them. Fascism was an affair of the gut more than of the brain, and a study of the roots of fascism that treats only the thinkers and the writers misses the most powerful impulses of all.

Long-Term Preconditions

Longer-term shifts in fundamental political, social, and economic structures also helped prepare the way for fascism. As I pointed out at the beginning, fascism was a latecomer among political movements.[61] It was simply inconceivable before a number of basic preconditions had been put in place.

One necessary precondition was mass politics. As a mass movement directed against the Left, fascism could not really exist before the citizenry had become involved in politics. . . .

Unlike conservatives and cautious liberals, fascists never wanted to keep the masses out of politics. They wanted to enlist, discipline, and energize them. In any event, by the end of World War I, there was no possible turning back to a narrow suffrage. Young men almost everywhere had been summoned to die for their countries, and one could hardly deny the full rights of citizenship to any of them. Women, too, whose economic and social roles the war had expanded enormously, received the vote in many northern European countries (though not yet in France, Italy, Spain, or Switzerland). While fascists sought to restore patriarchy in the family and the workplace, they preferred to mobilize sympathetic women rather than disfranchise them, at least until they could abolish voting altogether.[65] . . .

After 1917, of course, the Left was no longer gathering itself and waiting for its moment, as it had been doing before 1914. It was threatening to march across the world at the head of a seemingly irresistible Bolshevik Revolution. The fright given the entire middle and upper classes by Lenin's victory in Russia, and the anticipated success of his followers in more industrialized Germany, is crucial for understanding the panicky search during 1918–22 for some new kind of response to Bolshevism.

The fire-bells set off by Bolshevism transformed into emergencies the difficulties already faced by liberal values and institutions in the aftermath of World War I.[67] All three key liberal institutions—parliament, market, school—dealt poorly with these emergencies. Elected representatives struggled to find the necessary minimum of common ground to make difficult policy choices. Assumptions about the adequacy of a self-regulating market, even if believable in the long run, seemed laughably inadequate in the face of immediate national and international economic dislocations. Free schooling no longer seemed sufficient by itself to integrate communities shaken by the cacophony of opposing interests, cultural pluralism, and artistic experiment.

Recruitment

We have repeatedly encountered embittered war veterans in our account of the founding of the first fascist movements. Fascism would have remained a mere pressure group for veterans and their younger brothers, however, if it had not drawn in many other kinds of recruits.[89]

Above all, the early fascists were young. Many of the new generation were convinced that the white-bearded men responsible for the war, who still clung to their places, understood nothing of their concerns, whether they had experienced the front or not. Young people who had never voted before responded enthusiastically to fascism's brand of antipolitical politics.[90]

Several features distinguished the most successful fascisms from previous parties. Unlike the middle-class parties led by "notables" who condescended to contact their publics only at election time, the fascist parties swept their members up into an intense fraternity of emotion and effort.[91] Unlike the class parties—socialist or bourgeois—fascist parties managed to realize their claim to bring together citizens from all social classes. These were attractive features for many.[92]

Early fascist parties did not recruit from all classes in the same proportions, however. It was soon noticed that fascist parties were largely middle class, to the point where fascism was perceived as the very embodiment of lower-middle-class resentments.[93] But, after all, all political parties are largely middle class. On closer inspection, fascism turned out to appeal to upper-class members and voters as well.[94]

Early fascism also won more working-class followers than used to be thought, though these were always proportionally fewer than their share in the population.[95] The relative scarcity of working-class fascists was not due to some proletarian immunity to appeals of nationalism and ethnic cleansing. It is better explained by "immunization" and "confessionalism":[96] those already deeply engaged, from generation to generation, in the rich subculture of socialism, with its clubs, newspapers, unions, and rallies, were simply not available for another loyalty.

Workers were more available for fascism if they stood outside the community of socialists. It helped if they had a tradition of direct action, and of hostility to parliamentary socialism: in Italy, blackleg marble workers in traditionally anarchist Carrara,[97] for example, or the Genoese seamen organized by Captain Giuseppe Giulietti, who followed first D'Annunzio and then Mussolini. The unemployed, too, had been separated from organized socialism (which, under the harsh and divisive conditions of economic depression, appeared to value employed workers more than the unemployed). The unemployed were more likely to join the communists than the fascists, however, unless they were first-time voters or from the middle class.[98] A similar rootedness in the parish community probably explains the smaller proportion of Catholics than Protestants among the Nazi electorate.

Special local conditions could draw proletarians to fascism. A third of the members of the British Union of Fascists in rundown East London were unskilled or semi-skilled workers, recruited through resentment at recent Jewish immigrants, disillusion with the feckless Labour Party, or anger at communist and Jewish assaults upon BUF parades.[99] The Hungarian Arrow Cross won a third of the votes in heavily industrial central Budapest (Csepel Island), and had success in some rural mining areas, in the absence of a plausible Left alternative for an antigovernment protest vote.[100]

Whether fascism recruited more by an appeal to reason than to the emotions is hotly debated.[101] The evident power of emotions within fascism has tempted many to believe that fascism recruited the emotionally disturbed or the sexually deviant. It needs to be reemphasized that Hitler himself, while driven by hatreds and abnormal obsessions, was capable of pragmatic decision-making and rational choices, especially before 1942. To conclude that Nazism or other forms of fascism are forms of mental disturbance is doubly dangerous: it offers an alibi to the multitude of "normal" fascists, and it ill prepares us to recognize the utter normality of authentic fascism. Most fascist leaders and militants were quite ordinary people thrust into positions of extraordinary power and responsibility by processes that are perfectly comprehensible in rational terms. Putting fascism on the couch can lead us astray. Suspicions about Hitler's own perverse sexuality rest on no firm evidence,[102] though he was notoriously no conventional family man. Both homosexuals (such as Ernst Röhm and Edmund Heines of the SA) and violent homophobes (Himmler, for example) were prominent in the masculine fraternity that was Nazism. But there is no evidence that the proportion of homosexuals was higher among Nazis than in the general population. The issue has not risen for Italian Fascism.

The fascist leaders were outsiders of a new type. New people had forced their way into national leadership before. There had long been hard-bitten soldiers who fought better than aristocratic officers and became indispensable to kings. A later form of political recruitment came from young men of modest background who made good when electoral politics broadened in the late nineteenth century. One thinks of the aforementioned French politician Léon Gambetta, the grocer's son, or the beer wholesaler's son Gustav Stresemann, who became the preeminent statesman of Weimar Germany. A third kind of successful outsider in modern times has been clever mechanics in new industries (consider those entrepreneurial bicycle makers Henry Ford, William Morris, and the Wrights).

But many of the fascist leaders were marginal in a new way. They did not resemble the interlopers of earlier eras: the soldiers of fortune, the first upwardly mobile parliamentary politicians, or the clever mechanics. Some were bohemians, lumpen-intellectuals, dilettantes, experts in nothing except the manipulation of crowds and the fanning of resentments: Hitler, the failed art student; Mussolini, a schoolteacher by trade but mostly a restless revolutionary, expelled for subversion from Switzerland and the Trentino; Joseph Goebbels, the jobless college graduate with literary ambitions; Hermann Goering, the drifting World War I fighter ace; Heinrich Himmler, the agronomy student who failed at selling fertilizer and raising chickens.

Yet the early fascist cadres were far too diverse in social origins and education to fit the common label of marginal outsiders.[103] Alongside street-brawlers with criminal records like Amerigo Dumini[104] or Martin Bormann one could find a professor of philosophy like Giovanni Gentile[105] or even, briefly, a musician like Arturo Toscanini.[106] What united them was, after all, values rather than a social profile: scorn for tired bourgeois politics, opposition to the Left, fervent nationalism, a tolerance for violence when needed.

What Is Fascism?

The moment has come to give fascism a usable short handle, even though we know that it encompasses its subject no better than a snapshot encompasses a person.

Fascism may be defined as a form of political behavior marked by obsessive preoccupation with community decline, humiliation, or victim-hood and by compensatory cults of unity, energy, and purity, in which a mass-based party of committed nationalist militants, working in uneasy but effective collaboration with traditional elites, abandons democratic liberties and pursues with redemptive violence and without ethical or legal restraints goals of internal cleansing and external expansion.

Fascism according to this definition, as well as behavior in keeping with these feelings, is still visible today. . . .

"Giving up free institutions," especially the freedoms of unpopular groups, is recurrently attractive to citizens of Western democracies, including some Americans. We know from tracing its path that fascism does not require a spectacular "march" on some capital to take root; seemingly anodyne decisions to tolerate lawless treatment of national "enemies" is enough. . . .

Its further progress is not inevitable, however. Further fascist advances toward power depend in part upon the severity of a crisis, but also very largely upon human choices, especially the choices of those holding economic, social, and political power. Determining the appropriate responses to fascist gains is not easy, since its cycle is not likely to repeat itself blindly. We stand a much better chance of responding wisely, however, if we understand how fascism succeeded in the past.

"The Anatomy of Fascism" by Robert O. Paxton © 2004 by Robert Paxton, Vintage Books, 1400033918.

The Doctrine of Fascism

Benito Mussolini

Benito Mussolini—former schoolteacher, journalist, and WWI veteran—was the main figure in the Italian political movement known as "Fascism," a term he coined. Mussolini and the Fascists seized power during the 1920s, which they held until Italy was liberated by Allied forces during World War Two.

When, in the now distant March of 1919, I summoned a meeting at Milan . . . of the surviving members of the interventionist Party who had themselves been in action, and who had followed me since the creation of the Fascist Revolutionary Party (of 1915), I had no specific doctrinal attitude in mind. I had a living experience of one doctrine only—that of Socialism, from 1903–4 to the winter of 1914—that is to say, about a decade; and from Socialism itself, even though I have taken part in the movement first as a member of the rank and file and later as a leader, yet I had no experience of its doctrine of action. A unanimous, universally accepted theory of Socialism did not exist after 1905. . . . In the great stream of Fascism are to be found ideas which began with Sorel, Peguy, with Lagardelle in the "Mouvement Socialiste," and with the Italian trade union movement which throughout the period of 1904–14 was sounding a new note in Italian Socialist circles. . . .

After the war, in 1919, Socialism was already dead as a doctrine; it existed only as hatred. The *Popolo d'Italia* was then given the subtitle of "The newspaper of ex-servicemen and producers," and the word "producers" was already the expression of a mental attitude. Fascism was not the nursling of a doctrine worked out beforehand with detailed elaboration; it was born of the need for action and it was itself from the beginning practical rather than theoretical; it was not merely another political party but, even in the first two years, in opposition to all political parties as such. . . . If one were to re-read . . . the report of the meeting in which the *Fasci Italiani di combattimento* were constituted, one would there find no ordered expression of doctrine, but a series of aphorisms, anticipations, and aspirations which, when refined by time from the original ore, were destined after some years to develop into an ordered series of doctrinal concepts, forming the Fascists' political doctrine—different from all others either of the past or the present day.

"If the bourgeoisie," I said then, "think that they will find lightning-rods in us, they are the more deceived; we must start work at once. . . . We want to accustom the working class to real and effectual leadership, and also to convince them that it is no easy thing to direct an industry or a commercial enterprise successfully. . . . We shall combat every retrograde idea, technical or spiritual. . . . When the succession to the seat of government is open, we must not be unwilling to fight for it. We must make haste; when the present regime breaks down, we must be ready at once to take its place. It is we who have the right to the succession, because it was we who forced the country into the War, and led her to victory. The present method of political representation cannot suffice, we must have a representation direct from the individuals concerned. It may be objected against this program that it is a return to the conception of the corporation, but that is no matter. . . . Therefore, I desire that this assembly shall accept the claims of national trades-unionism from the economic point of view. . . ."

Now is it not a singular thing that even on this first day in the Piazza San Sepolcro that word "corporation" arose, which later, in the course of the Revolution, came to express one of the creations of social legislation at the very foundation of the regime?

The years which preceded the March to Rome were years of great difficulty, during which the necessity for action did not permit of research or any complete elaboration of doctrine. The battle had to be fought in the towns and villages. There was much discussion, but—what was more important and more sacred—men died. They knew how to die. Doctrine, beautifully defined and carefully elucidated, with headlines and paragraphs, might be lacking; but there was to take its place something more decisive—Faith. . . . But, since there was inevitably some lack of system, the adversaries of Fascism have disingenuously denied that it had any capacity to produce a doctrine of its own, though that doctrine was growing and taking shape under their very eyes, even though tumultuously; first, as happens to all ideas in their beginnings, in the aspect of a violent and dogmatic negation, and then in the aspect of positive construction which has found its realization in the laws and institutions of the regime as enacted successively in the years 1926, 1927, and 1928. . . .

Above all, Fascism, the more it considers and observes the future and the development of humanity quite apart from political considerations of the moment, believes neither in the possibility nor the utility of perpetual peace. It thus repudiates the doctrine of Pacifism—born of a renunciation of the struggle and an act of cowardice in the face of sacrifice. War alone brings up to its highest tension all human energy and puts the stamp of nobility upon the peoples who have the courage to meet it. All other trials are substitutes, which never really put men into the position where they have to make the great decision—the alternative of life or death. Thus a doctrine which is founded upon this harmful postulate of peace is hostile to Fascism. And thus hostile to the spirit of Fascism . . . are all the international leagues and societies, which, as history will show, can be scattered to the winds when once strong national feeling is aroused by any motive—sentimental, ideal, or practical. This anti-pacifist spirit is carried by Fascism even into the life of the individual; the proud motto of the Squadrista, "*Me ne frego*" (I do not hear), written on the bandage of the wound, is an act of philosophy not only stoic, the summary of a doctrine not only political—it is the education to combat, the acceptance of the risks which combat implies, and a new way of life for Italy. Thus the Fascist accepts life and loves it, knowing nothing of and despising suicide; he rather conceives of life as duty and struggle and conquest, life which should be high and full, lived for oneself, but above all for others—those who are at hand and those who are far distant, contemporaries, and those who will come after. . . ."

Such a conception of life makes Fascism the complete opposite of that doctrine, the base of the so-called scientific and Marxian Socialism, the materialist conception of history; according to which the history of human civilization can be explained simply through the conflict of interests among the various social groups and by the change and development in the means and instruments of production. That the changes in the economic field . . . have their importance no one can deny; but that these factors are sufficient to explain the history of humanity excluding all others is an absurd delusion. Fascism, now and always, believes in holiness and heroism; that is to say, in actions influenced by no economic motive, direct or indirect. And if the economic conception of history be denied . . . it follows that the existence of an unchangeable and unchanging class war is also denied. And above all Fascism denies that class war can be the preponderant force in the transformation of society. These two fundamental concepts of Socialism being thus refuted, nothing is left of it but the sentimental aspiration—as old as humanity itself—towards a social convention in which the sorrows and sufferings of the humblest shall be alleviated. But here again Fascism repudiates the conception of economic happiness. . . . Fascism denies the materialist conception of happiness as a possibility, and abandons it to its inventors, the economists of the first half of the nineteenth century: that is to say, Fascism denies the validity of the equation, well-being=happiness, which would reduce men to the level of animals, caring for one thing only—to be fat and well-fed—and would thus degrade humanity to a purely physical existence.

After Socialism, Fascism combats the whole complex system of democratic ideology; and repudiates it, whether in its theoretical premises or in its practical application. Fascism denies that the majority, by the simple fact that it is a majority, can direct human society; it denies that numbers alone can govern by means of a periodical consultation, and it affirms the immutable, beneficial, and fruitful inequality of mankind, which can never be permanently leveled through the mere operation of a mechanical process such as universal suffrage. The democratic regime may be defined as from time to time giving the people the illusion of sovereignty, while the real effective sovereignty lies in the hands of other concealed and irresponsible forces. Democracy is a regime nominally without a king, but it is ruled by many kings—more absolute, tyrannical, and ruinous than one sole king, even though a tyrant. This explains why Fascism, having first in 1922 (for reasons of expediency) assumed an attitude tending towards republicanism, renounced this point of view before the March to Rome; being convinced that the question of political form is not today of prime importance. . . .

A party which entirely governs a nation is a fact entirely new to history, there are no possible references or parallels. Fascism uses in its construction whatever elements in the Liberal, Social, or Democratic doctrines still have a living value; it maintains what may be called the certainties which we owe to history, but it rejects all the rest—that is to say, the conception that there can be any doctrine of unquestioned efficacy for all times and all peoples. . . . Political doctrines pass, but humanity remains; and it may rather be expected that this will be a century of Fascism. For if the nineteenth century was the century of individualism (Liberalism always signifying individualism) it may be expected that this will be the century of collectivism, and hence the century of the State. . . .

Every doctrine tends to direct human activity towards a determined objective; but the action of men also reacts upon the doctrine, transforms it, adapts it to new needs, or supersedes it with something else. A doctrine then must be no mere exercise in words, but a living act; and thus the value of Fascism lies in the fact that it is veined with pragmatism, but at the same time has a will to exist and a will to power, a firm front in face of the reality of "violence."

The foundation of Fascism is the conception of the State. Fascism conceives of the State as an absolute, in comparison with which all individuals or groups are relative, only to be conceived of in their relation to the State. . . .

The Fascist State has drawn into itself even the economic activities of the nation, and through the corporative social and educational institutions created by it, its influence reaches every aspect of the national life and includes, framed in their respective organizations, all the political, economic and spiritual forces of the nation. A State which reposes upon the support of millions of individuals who recognize its authority, are continually conscious of its power and are ready at once to serve it, is not the old tyrannical State of the medieval lord nor has it anything in common with the absolute governments either before or after 1789. The individual in the Fascist State is not annulled but rather multiplied, just in the same way that a soldier in a regiment is not diminished but rather increased by the number of his comrades. The Fascist State organizes the nation, but leaves a sufficient margin of liberty to the individual; that latter is deprived of all useless and possibly harmful freedom, but retains what is essential. . . .

The Fascist State is an embodied will to power and government; the Roman tradition is here an ideal of force in action. According to Fascism, government is not so much a thing to be expressed in territorial or military terms as in terms of morality and the spirit. It must be thought of as an empire—that is to say, a nation which directly or indirectly rules other nations, without the need for conquering a single square yard of territory. For Fascism, the growth of empire, that is to say the expansion of the nation, is an essential manifestation of vitality, and its opposite a sign of decadence. Peoples which are rising, or rising again after a period of decadence, are always imperialist; any renunciation is a sign of decay and of death.

Fascism is the doctrine best adapted to represent the tendencies and the aspirations of a people, like the people of Italy, who are rising again after many centuries of abasement and foreign servitude. But empire demands discipline, the co-ordination of all forces and a deeply felt sense of duty and sacrifice; this fact explains many aspects of the practical working of the regime, the character of many forces in the State, and the necessarily severe measures which must be taken against those who would oppose this spontaneous and inevitable movement of Italy in the twentieth century, and would oppose it by recalling the outworn ideology of the nineteenth century . . . for never before has the nation stood more in need of authority, of direction, and of order. If every age has its own characteristic doctrine, there are a thousand signs which point to Fascism as the characteristic doctrine of our time. For if a doctrine must be a living thing, this is proved by the fact that Fascism has created a living faith; and that this faith is very powerful in the minds of men, is demonstrated by those who have suffered and died for it.

Total War: World War II

Michael G. Kort

The coming to power of **Adolf Hitler** and the **Nazi Party** in Germany was the crucial link in a chain of events that ultimately led to World War II. To be sure, during the 1930s there were undemocratic regimes both in Asia and Europe whose aggressive designs threatened international peace. In East Asia, even before Hitler came to power and began destabilizing Europe, Japan had seized the huge Chinese territory of Manchuria and turned it into a puppet state. In southern Europe, Fascist Italy under Benito Mussolini moved to expand its colonial possessions in Africa and to act on its territorial ambitions elsewhere in the Mediterranean region. Yet only Germany among the world's growing assortment of fascistic and authoritarian countries had the military and economic potential to challenge the international order established after World War I. Hitler's rise to power in 1933 added a key catalyst to that mix: the will and ruthlessness to undertake aggression.

Between 1933 and 1939 the world's most powerful democracies, still traumatized by the carnage of World War I and desperate to remain at peace, ignored or tried to wish away Hitler's growing threat. These sentiments were dominant not only in Europe, which had suffered the most during World War I, but also in the United States, where **isolationist** public opinion deeply opposed to American entanglement in European crises and possibly another war. The deep mistrust Europe's democratic leaders held for the Soviet Union, a totalitarian regime officially committed to promoting Communist revolutions worldwide, further stymied efforts to stand up to Nazi Germany. The result was the most total and destructive war in human history.

Hitler's World View

Hitler initially masked the threat Nazi Germany posed to other countries by claiming that his major foreign policy goal was to undo what he claimed were injustices imposed on Germany by the **Treaty of Versailles**. Although during the 1920s the World War I peace settlement had been substantially revised in Germany's favor, some of those claims were not considered entirely illegitimate abroad. This certainly was true in Great Britain, where by the 1930s some prominent politicians were arguing that the post-World War I peace settlement had treated Germany too harshly;

some even believed that certain remaining restrictions on Germany, such as limits on its armaments and the demilitarization of its western region called the Rhineland, were no longer sustainable or worth defending. This unwillingness to stem the growth of German power was reinforced by the notion that a strong Germany would prevent Soviet expansion; it would serve as a "bulwark against Bolshevism," as the saying went at the time.

But in fact Hitler had far more radical and far-reaching goals than righting any alleged wrongs of the post–World War I settlement. He based his objectives on Nazi racial ideology, which asserted that the German people were inherently superior to everyone else and destined to rule as the world's "master race." According to Nazi doctrine, Germans were hemmed in by their current borders and needed additional room to live—*Lebensraum* in German—in order to prosper and, indeed, to survive. This view mandated Germany's territorial expansion, into areas both populated by ethnic German minorities as well as those populated by other peoples, such as the Slavs of Poland and the Soviet Union, whose "inferiority" justified their expulsion or enslavement. To achieve a stronger Germany, Hitler planned a series of conquests, initially against Germany's immediate neighbors, later against the Soviet Union, and finally against the United States. As historian Gerhard L. Weinberg has noted, Hitler planned "to bring about a total demographic and racial reordering of the globe." [1]

The worst fate by far of any people awaited Europe's Jews, and indeed Jews anywhere in the world who fell into Nazi hands. An extraordinarily fanatical and violent **anti-Semitism** was at the core of Hitler's world view. To him, Jews were even worse than the subhuman Slavs or any other group. In Hitler's twisted, hate-filled mind, Jews were evil incarnate, and as such were the main and mortal enemy of the Aryan Germans. Hitler was convinced that Germany would never be safe as long as the Jewish people had any influence in the world, and as early as 1920 he openly called for their complete extermination. Unlike with Slavs or even the despised Gypsies, there was no room for any Jews at all in the new order that Hitler promised to bring about. This in turn explains why Hitler launched his "war against the Jews," as historian Lucy Dawidowicz has aptly called it, immediately upon coming to power, and well before he plunged Europe into World War II. [2] That assault began with a campaign to drive all Jews from Germany: it expanded quickly from harassment, boycotts, street violence, and far-reaching discrimination to depriving Jews of German citizenship and seizing their businesses and property. Once war came—having announced in January 1939 during a speech to the German parliament that war would bring "the annihilation of the Jewish race in Europe"—Hitler turned this assault against the Jews into a systematic campaign to round up and murder every Jewish man, woman, and child living in the expanding area under Nazi control. [3]

Appeasement and the Road to War

The road from the Nazi rise to power in Germany to the outbreak of World War II was paved by a policy known as **appeasement**: a series of concessions by Europe's democratic powers that, in the hope of avoiding another major war, allowed Hitler to do and take what he wanted. In 1933 Hitler pulled Germany out of the **League of Nations**. Emboldened by British and French indecision, he then announced a program of rearmament, including the building of an air force, in direct violation of the Treaty of Versailles. Once again Britain and France failed to react. In 1935, when Italy invaded and conquered the African country of Ethiopia, neither country, nor the League of Nations, offered anything but verbal criticism, a weak reaction that did nothing but anger Mussolini and push him closer to Hitler. Their continued failure to act further encouraged Hitler, who in 1936 again violated the Treaty of Versailles by placing military forces in the Rhineland.

That same year a civil war broke out in Spain, when fascist forces led by General Francisco Franco rebelled against the recently elected republican government, which was led by a leftist coalition. While Britain and France, where public opinion was deeply divided on the issue, declined to intervene in Spain, Germany and Italy provided substantial aid to Franco. The Soviet Union gave limited aid to the republican side, but Soviet intervention did as much harm as good because of Stalin's efforts to strengthen local Communists. The result, after almost three years of fighting, was a fascist victory and a serious defeat for democracy—not only in Spain but in Europe as a whole.

By then, British and French appeasement had enabled Hitler to assert control over two other European countries, Austria and Czechoslovakia. The Nazis were popular in German-speaking Austria, where Hitler had been born and raised and which had close cultural and historical ties to Germany. The Austrians were divided on whether they wanted to become part of Germany, but Hitler did not allow them to decide the matter for themselves. In early 1938, after threatening invasion, and having again intimidated Britain and France, he occupied Austria and annexed it to Germany.

The most notorious act of British and French appeasement involved Czechoslovakia, by the late 1930s central Europe's only remaining democracy. Established after the dismantling of the Austro-Hungarian Empire in 1918, Czechoslovakia was home to a number of distinct ethnic groups, including a significant German population along its borders with Germany and Austria in a territory known as the Sudetenland. The Sudetenland's mountainous topography made it vital to Czechoslovakia's ability to defend itself from potential German aggression. After seizing Austria, Hitler demanded that Czechoslovakia cede this area to Germany. However, Czechoslovakia had mutual defense agreements with France and the Soviet Union, as well as a modern army well positioned to defend its territory, and its leaders were willing to stand up to the Hitler if they had international support.

That support was not forthcoming. Neither Britain, which had just begun a rearmament program, nor France was prepared for war. Instead, British prime minister **Neville Chamberlain** tried to appease Hitler to avoid hostilities. In September he and French leader Edouard Daladier met with Hitler and Mussolini in the southern German city of Munich, without the presence of statesmen from either the Soviet Union or Czechoslovakia itself. Chamberlain and Daladier caved in to Hitler, agreeing that Germany should have the Sudetenland. Deserted by Europe's strongest democracies, Czechoslovakia had to accept the **Munich Agreement**. When Chamberlain returned to London, he announced to cheering crowds that he had secured "peace in our time." Another British politician, **Winston Churchill**, saw it differently. Having noted that Britain and France had faced a choice between war and dishonor, Churchill grimly and presciently observed, "They chose dishonor; they will have war."[4]

At Munich Hitler had promised to respect the sovereignty of what remained of Czechoslovakia, while Britain and France in turn guaranteed that country's truncated boundaries. In early 1939, those assurances crumbled into dust as Germany seized the western section of the country and set up a puppet state on what remained. Next Hitler made a series of demands that threatened the territorial integrity of Poland. These demands finally convinced Europe's leading appeasers that Hitler's objectives were far more extensive than they had believed and that he could not be bought off by further concessions. Britain and France both announced that they would go to war to protect Poland from Germany.

As war clouds gathered during the spring and summer of 1939, Britain and France attempted to surround Germany, as they had done during World War I, by negotiating an alliance with the Soviet Union. That effort was undermined from the start by mutual suspicions between democratic and capitalist London and Paris on the one hand and totalitarian and communist Moscow on the other. Stalin, meanwhile, had his own plans. He desperately wanted to buy time for the Soviet Union to prepare for war; in addition he believed that conflict between the democracies and Nazi Germany would weaken both sides and facilitate future communist expansion into central and western Europe. So while the Soviet Union negotiated with Britain and France, it simultaneously secretly negotiated with Germany. Ideology aside, Hitler and Stalin, totalitarian dictators both, were more comfortable dealing with each other than with democratic leaders. Statesmen in London and Paris, however, never seriously considered the possibility that Nazi Germany and the Soviet Union, sworn ideological archenemies, could work together, which may explain why the British and French negotiated with the Soviets with a marked lack of urgency.

Thus, the Western democracies were stunned when in late August of 1939 Berlin and Moscow announced they had signed a nonaggression treaty. The **Nazi-Soviet Pact** included a secret protocol in which the two sides divided Poland and other spoils elsewhere in Eastern Europe. Hitler could now do as he pleased, free from the potential military nightmare of simultaneously having to fight Britain and France in the west and Soviet Russia in the east. In fact, for the next two years the Soviet Union in effect functioned as a German ally, supplying Hitler with a wide range of supplies vital to the Nazi war machine.

Fewer than ten days after the signing of the Nazi-Soviet nonaggression pact, and less than a generation since the end of last great conflict that had brought such ruin to the continent, Europe was again at war.

Blitzkrieg, the Battle of Britain, Barbarossa, and Pearl Harbor, 1939-1941

World War II began when Nazi Germany invaded Poland on September 1, 1939. Britain and France declared war on Germany two days later. In assaulting Poland, Germany unveiled its concept of **Blitzkrieg**, or lightening war, in which rapidly moving ground forces, supported by advanced mobile weaponry, could overrun, surround, and annihilate slower moving opponents. Both tanks and aircraft, the key weapons in *Blitzkrieg*, had been used in World War I, and all of the major powers had developed far more advanced models during the interwar period. But the way the Germans used them in their slashing war of rapid movement was new and devastating. Poland was defeated within a month and disappeared from the map of Europe: its western half in German hands; its eastern half, in accordance with the Nazi-Soviet pact, occupied by Soviet troops and under Moscow's control.

The winter of 1939-1940 is known as the "Phony War," as there was little serious fighting after the seizure of Poland. Britain and France awaited Germany's next move, the former protected by the English Channel and the latter hunkered down behind a series of supposedly impregnable fortifications along its German border known as the Maginot Line. Meanwhile, the Soviet Union invaded neighboring Finland to seize strategic border territory. Although ultimately victorious, Stalin's army performed poorly, leaving Britain and France skeptical about Soviet military preparedness and prowess. The Soviets also forcefully annexed Lithuania, Latvia, and Estonia, three small countries on the shore of the Baltic Sea that in 1918 had taken advantage of the collapse of the Russian Empire to establish their independence. The Germans resumed offensive operations in the spring of 1940, occupying Denmark and Norway against limited opposition.

Blitzkrieg returned with suddenness and a vengeance in May, when German armored forces used speed, surprise, and overwhelming firepower to outflank French and British units in Holland, Belgium and then France. The French army crumbled, while the British retreated to the French port of Dunkirk on the English Channel coast. In ten desperate days, as the Germans pounded at Dunkirk's defensive perimeter, the British conducted a desperate evacuation of their remaining soldiers and a smaller number of French troops. Though the "Miracle of Dunkirk" significantly boosted Britain's morale and ability to continue the war, it could not negate the stunning victory the Germans had achieved. France surrendered a few weeks later, allowing Germany to occupy the northern part of the country, including Paris, while a puppet regime under World War I hero Marshall Henri Petain was set up in the southern French town of Vichy. The record of collaboration with the Germans over the next four years, both by the Vichy regime and authorities in occupied France, forms one of the darkest pages in France's history.

The defeat of France left Britain standing alone. However, Winston Churchill, the critic of the Munich Agreement, had become Prime Minister, and the British rallied behind his fierce determination never to surrender, dashing Hitler's hopes that Britain would make peace. That meant Germany would have to invade Britain, but to cross the English Channel the Germans needed control of the air. The stage was set for the **Battle of Britain**, the first genuine air war in history and, as such, the beginning of a new era in warfare. This time it was the British who made the best use of modern weapons, specifically newly developed single-wing fighter aircraft, most notably the Spitfire, and radar, a system of using radio waves to detect incoming aircraft from afar. The battle began in August with attacks on British air force bases; later the Germans bombed London and other cities in an effort to break British civilian morale. But German aircraft losses were so severe that in by mid-September Hitler cancelled his invasion plans, by which time British bombers were hitting German bases along the French and Belgian coasts. The bombing of British cities, and thus the Battle of Britain itself, continued into the spring of 1941.

By then Britain was being bolstered by American aid. Because of isolationist sentiment, the United States was still officially neutral in the war. This remained the case even though President Franklin Roosevelt was convinced that Britain could not defeat Germany and that Nazi Germany represented a mortal threat to the United States. Although his options were limited, Roosevelt did what he could to prepare Americans for the struggle ahead. As early as 1938 he began a massive rearmament program, and in 1940 the first American peacetime military draft increased the size of the army to one million men. Roosevelt also used what authority he had to funnel aid to Britain, culminating in the 1941 Lend-Lease program under which the United States provided military supplies and equipment to Britain without demanding payment.

Meanwhile, on June 22, 1941, the course and nature of World War II changed in a flash when Hitler broke his non-aggression pact with Stalin and attacked the Soviet Union. In launching **Operation Barbarossa**, Germany sent more than three million troops, 2,500 tanks, and 2,700 aircraft against the Soviet Union. The Soviet Union's military force was even larger than Germany's, but its officer corps had been ravaged by Stalin's purges of the 1930s, and its units facing the Germans were unprepared for war because Stalin refused to listen to intelligence reports of an imminent German attack. The Soviets suffered appalling initial losses, but their country's vast expanses and reserves enabled them to absorb these defeats without collapsing. As summer turned to fall and then into an early and bitterly cold Russian winter, the German advance stalled. German troops reached the outskirts of both Leningrad and Moscow, but failed to take either city. What followed during the next four years on the so-called eastern front was a titanic fight to the death, unequaled in scale and savagery in the history of warfare, between the world's two great totalitarian powers.[5]

As the German advance ground to a halt on the frozen Russian plains, events in the tropical Pacific Ocean changed World War II in yet another fundamental way. In 1937 Japan had launched an all-out invasion of China. The goal was to reduce China to the status of a dependency as part of an overall strategy of making Japan the dominant power in East Asia. By September 1940, Japan had garnered support for its ambitions through a pact with Germany and Italy that created an alliance known as the **Axis**. By then, the United States was applying economic pressure on Japan to force Tokyo to withdraw from China, which culminated in mid-1941 with an oil embargo. The military officers who controlled the Japanese government correctly recognized the United States as the main obstacle to their plans, and they knew they could not win a long war against the United States because of America's enormous industrial power. They therefore decided to try to destroy the U.S. Pacific fleet, based at **Pearl Harbor** in Hawaii, in the hope that a crippling defeat in the Pacific and concerns about Germany would induce Washington to accept Japan's East Asian ambitions.

The attack on Pearl Harbor, carried out on December 7, 1941, achieved complete surprise and did great damage to the U.S. fleet. However, the key U.S. warships—its aircraft carriers—were at sea at the time and escaped destruction. On December 8, the United States declared war on Japan. Three days later, fulfilling Germany's treaty obligations to Japan, Hitler declared war on the United States. The last of the world's major powers was now fully committed to World War Two, a colossal struggle that would be fought on more than half a dozen major fronts, on four continents and on three of the world's oceans.[6]

The Grand Alliance, 1942-1944

The events of December 1941 gave birth to a partnership between the United States, Great Britain, and the Soviet Union that Churchill dubbed the **Grand Alliance**. In fact, it was strange rather than grand, a tenuous union between two capitalist democracies on the one hand and a totalitarian communist regime on the other, held together only by the threat posed by Nazi Germany. In addition, the United States and Britain were at war with both Germany and Japan while the Soviet Union was at war only with Germany, having signed a non-aggression pact with Japan in 1941. However, from the start Roosevelt and Churchill agreed that most resources would be devoted to defeating Germany, whose industrial and technological strength made it by far a greater menace than Japan. By signing a document drafted by the United States called the "Declaration of the United Nations," several dozen lesser powers in effect became junior members of the Grand Alliance.

The Grand Alliance looked formidable on paper, especially in light of America's unmatched industrial power. But in late 1941, despite having begun rearmament, the United States was unprepared for all-out war and both Britain and the Soviet Union had been severely weakened by their initial defeats. As a result, during the spring of 1942 German forces were able to push deeper into the Soviet Union in several areas, including in the south where they approached the Soviet oil fields south of the Caucasus Mountains near the Caspian Sea. In North Africa, a German army advanced eastward toward the Suez Canal, a key lifeline for the British. Another vital but tenuous British lifeline, formed by supply ships crossing the Atlantic from the United States, was under deadly attack from German submarines. In Asia and the Pacific, the Japanese overran the Philippines; seized Burma, Malaya, and Singapore; occupied Indochina; and swept southward through the Netherlands East Indies and the Solomon Islands, putting themselves in position to threaten Australia. By mid-1942 there was a very real danger that the Axis powers would win the war.

Then the tide of battle began to turn, with the first major allied victories coming in the Pacific. In May 1942 American and Japanese naval forces clashed northeast of Australia in the **Battle of the Coral Sea**. The battle was notable for two reasons. Although militarily a draw, it ended the Japanese advance toward Australia. Of equal significance, Coral Sea ushered in a new era in naval warfare: the age of the aircraft carrier. For the first time in history the opposing warships never saw each other; all the fighting was done by airplanes flying from aircraft carriers. In June came the far more decisive **Battle of Midway**, where four Japanese aircraft carriers dueled with three American carriers near tiny Midway Island, the site of a U.S. military base. Critically, the Americans had broken the Japanese naval codes and therefore learned of Tokyo's plan to attack Midway. They were ready when the Japanese arrived. In a short, fierce battle on June 4, American carrier-based dive bombers sank all four Japanese carriers, while only one American carrier was lost. The Americans had struck a crippling blow: although the Japanese navy remained a formidable force, the losses it suffered at Midway ended its ability to take the offensive against growing U.S. forces in the Pacific.

Another major Allied victory, this time on the hot desert sands of North Africa, followed in October when the British defeated the Germans less than 100 miles west of the Suez Canal at the **Battle of El Alamein**. Most important of all, on the frozen Russian steppe, the Soviet Red Army crushed the Germans in the **Battle of Stalingrad**, fought over control of a strategically important city on the Volga River. After German forces reached the city in August 1942, the Soviet defenders turned the battle into a debilitating house-to-house, room-to-room war of attrition before launching a counterattack in November that encircled and trapped the invaders. The frigid Russian winter also closed in on the Germans with temperatures as low as minus 30 degrees. When the end came in February 1943, about 90,000 German soldiers surrendered, all that remained from a force that had once numbered more than 330,000. For the first time in the war, a German army had not only been defeated but entirely destroyed. It was a crucial turning point: after Stalingrad, with rare exceptions—most notably the greatest tank clash in history in July 1943 at the **Battle of Kursk**—German forces on the eastern front were in retreat.

From the day the United States entered the war, the military objective essential to ultimate victory was to invade France. This would enable American, British, and other allied troops to attack Germany from the west, thereby creating a "**second front**" in addition to the eastern front where German and Soviet forces were engaged. However, it proved impossible to mount such a complex and risky assault during 1942 and 1943. After defeating the German and Italian forces in North Africa, the Allies landed in Italy in 1943. But Allied troops advanced slowly up the mountainous Italian peninsula —they did not take Rome until June 1944—while Germany itself was protected from attack via Italy by the Alps.

Until the Allies landed in France in June 1944, the only way to strike directly at Germany from the west was by air. The weapon used was the newly developed long-range bomber, an aircraft based on cutting-edge technology and powered by four engines, that was refined further as more advanced models appeared during the war. The idea behind what was called **strategic bombing** was to cripple Germany's (and Japan's) ability to make war by destroying its industrial infrastructure. The problem with implementing this idea in practice was that the technology did not yet exist to enable bombers—flying at high altitude and under attack from anti-aircraft fire and enemy fighters—to hit specific industrial targets such as factories, a tactic known as "precision" bombing. Early Allied bombing missions often missed their targets by miles, suffering heavy losses in the process. As a result, both the American and British air forces in practice had to adopt what was called "area" bombing, that is, attacking entire cities, which meant, inevitably, civilian casualties. Some observers, both then and now, have been critical of that policy, especially as it was carried out in 1945 during the last months of the war. However, as military historian Robin Neillands has stressed, the "alternative was not to attack at all but to leave the enemy's homeland an intact arsenal of aggression."[7] As it turned out, strategic bombing forced the Germans to devote considerable quantities of weapons and troops to air defense. These otherwise could have been deployed against Allied soldiers on the battlefield, which in turn would have increased Allied casualties and lengthened the war. Such difficult choices were an unavoidable consequence of total war, where the destruction of civilian and industrial areas became inseparable from the destruction of the enemy's military forces.

In the end, the ability to wage total war rested on the industrial strength and capacity of the combatants, and it was not long before all of the major powers had organized their economies for the war effort. It is here that the industrial power of the United States, which far exceeded that of any other country, was decisive. The United States had the world's largest and most modern industrial plant when the war began, and the gap separating it from the others grew as the war continued. During the course of the conflict the United States produced more than 300,000 aircraft of all kinds, including newly developed fighter planes and high-tech, long range bombers that pulverized German and Japanese cities. Its shipyards produced 88,000 landing craft, 215 submarines, 147 aircraft carriers—including massive, fast-moving vessels that could carry up to 90 aircraft—and almost a thousand other warships. The United States also produced thousands of tanks, artillery, rifles, and other equipment for its armed forces and those of its allies. American Lend-Lease supplies, extended to the Soviet Union in the summer of 1941, included thousands of trucks, jeeps, field telephones, locomotives, railway cars, and aircraft, to say nothing of millions of boots and belts; these were crucial to the Red Army's mobility and ability to sustain its offensives from 1942 to 1945. The Soviet Union made enormous sacrifices, produced vast quantities of its own weapons, and ultimately fought and defeated two-thirds of the German army, but without Lend-Lease, as Stalin himself admitted to his closest aides, the Soviets would have been forced out of the war.

The Holocaust

During World War II, Japan's military forces committed mass murder and other war crimes throughout China and elsewhere in Asia. Its army engaged in terror killing and rape, deployed biological and chemical weapons against Chinese troops and civilians, and treated captives and prisoners of war with great brutality. Japanese scientists and doctors at the notorious **Unit 731** biological warfare facility in Manchuria did hideous experiments on prisoners, fully as dreadful as what the Nazis did in their concentration and death camps. Japanese authorities throughout Asia carried out policies that caused widespread starvation. All of this, and more, was done under direction from Tokyo.[8]

Nazi Germany treated conquered peoples, especially in Poland and the Soviet Union, with horrible cruelty and committed mass murder on a staggering scale. For example, immediately after occupying its share of Poland, the Germans murdered thousands of Polish intellectuals, clergy, and other members of the elite in order to deprive the country of its leadership. More than three million Soviet prisoners of war, almost 60 percent of those taken captive, died from maltreatment at German hands. But the Germans reached further to yet another realm of evil. Driven by the fanatically virulent Nazi version of anti-Semitism, Germany during World War II attempted to wipe out the entire Jewish people, for no other reason other than because they were Jews. All Jewish men, women, and children, no matter where they lived and how much effort it required to round them up, were targeted for extermination. The entire military and civilian institutional infrastructure of the German state was enlisted in the effort, and industrial scale methods using the most modern technology available were developed to facilitate the killing process. This effort continued throughout the war, notwithstanding that it used scarce resources and personnel that could have helped the increasingly desperate war effort against the Allies. Even against the horrific background of what Germany did to conquered people across the length and breadth of Europe, Hitler's war against the Jews stands out as something qualitatively distinct. It was and remains a genocidal crime unique in human history.[9]

Only about 600,000 Jews lived in Germany in 1933, and many of them had emigrated by 1939. Then the invasion of Poland brought more than 2 million Polish Jews under Nazi control. The Nazis uprooted these Jews from their homes and forced them into ghettos, most of which were in Polish cities that already had large Jewish populations. The most famous of these ghettos, in effect huge prisons surrounded by high walls and fences, was in Warsaw, Poland's capital. Conditions in these severely overcrowded ghettos were terrible and quickly grew worse as deportees arrived from other parts of Poland and elsewhere in Europe. There was not enough food, fuel, or other necessities of life. The few Jews who had jobs worked as slave laborers for the Nazi war machine. People began to die immediately, especially the elderly, infirm, and young children, with the death toll quickly reaching the hundreds of thousands.

The process of outright extermination of Jews began with the invasion of the Soviet Union in June 1941. Specially recruited and trained units called *Einsatzgruppen* spearheaded the killing in the Soviet Union, relying primarily on machine guns to massacre their victims. The *Einsatzgruppen* were assisted by other German military and police units and often by local collaborators. During 1941 alone the Nazis murdered 500,000 Jews on Soviet soil. By the end of the war the *Einsatzgruppen* and other mobile killing units operating in the Soviet Union had murdered at least 1.5 million Jews.

At some point during late 1940 or early 1941 Hitler made the decision to systematically murder all the Jews, although his actual order has never been found and almost certainly was given verbally. On July 31, 1941, **Hermann Goering**, Hitler's closest aide, ordered the **SS**, the elite Nazi organization that controlled Germany's secret police (the Gestapo) and its system of concentration camps, to submit "an overall plan of the preliminary organizational, practical, and financial measures for the execution of the intended **final solution** (*Endlosing*) of the Jewish question."[10] Construction of death camps began that summer, and in on January 20, 1942, the **SS** convened a meeting known as the **Wannsee Conference** for representatives from key institutions of the Nazi German state to coordinate the extermination of European Jewry.

It was in the death camps—Chelmno, Treblinka, Sobibor, Majdanek, Belzec, and **Auschwitz**, the largest, a factory of death capable of killing 12,000 people in a single day—that modern science and technology were enlisted in the service of genocide.

The victims arrived by train packed so densely in cattle cars that many had died en route. They came from the ghettos of Poland and, often having been rounded up with the aid of modern IBM punch-card technology, from all over Europe. Most were immediately murdered in specially designed gas chambers disguised as showers using a recently developed vermicide called Zyklon-B. Their bodies were then reduced to ashes in massive crematoria, again specially designed. Aside from being faster than the machine guns of the *Einsatzgruppen*, this industrial system of murder had the important advantage of not being face-to-face, a situation that had caused severe morale and psychological problems among *Einsatzgruppen* personnel. By 1945, the Nazis had murdered a total of six million Jews, two-thirds of the entire Jewish pre-war population of Europe.

One of the most disturbing questions about the Holocaust is why the United States and Britain, despite having detailed information about what was happening no later than 1942, did virtually nothing to stop the slaughter. There certainly were possibilities such as allowing additional Jewish refugees entry into their countries or other areas they controlled, and/or bombing the rail lines to Auschwitz. Part of the answer is the widespread persistence of anti-Semitism, including in high places where policy was made, the most notable examples being the British Foreign Office and the U.S. State Department. Ultimately, however, as historian Robert S. Wistrich has noted, saving Jews from the Nazis was "marginal" to Roosevelt and Churchill, the leaders in the position to do the most, when balanced against the "larger global and military and diplomatic strategy" involved in winning the war itself.[11]

Left on their own and confronted by overwhelming German power and often by indifference and hostility from non-German populations among whom they lived, the Jews of Europe resisted as best they could. Many of those who managed to avoid capture fought in resistance movements from the cities of France to the forests of the Soviet Union. The first armed urban uprising against the Nazis by anyone in occupied Europe was carried out by poorly armed Jews in the **Warsaw Ghetto** in April 1943. They held out against the mighty German army for three weeks. There also were revolts in other ghettos and in several of the death camps, including Auschwitz, although none of these actions could stop the German death machine.

Once the death camps were in operation, the Holocaust was carried out with cold bureaucratic and industrial efficiency. It employed the resources and expertise of the most important branches of the modern, totalitarian German state. In that regard the Holocaust was a function of modernity, as it could not have been implemented without modern technology and institutional organization. At the same time, the motives were strictly primitive. The political leaders who set in motion the ultra-modern Nazi death machine and the bureaucrats who ran it were driven by a pre-modern bigotry— anti-Semitism—with deep roots in European civilization that stretch back to ancient times. Absent that inherited centuries-old hatred, updated to be sure with racial pseudoscience during the nineteenth century and given unprecedented virulence by Hitler and other Nazis in the twentieth, there would not have been a Holocaust. Made technically possible by modernity, its ultimate cause was an old and deeply entrenched cultural demon that modern Western humanistic and liberal values dating from the Renaissance and Enlightenment could not overcome. In short, the Holocaust was modern only in its implementation; its roots lay in pre-modern inhumanity.

Endgame and Reckoning: June 1944-August 1945

On June 6, 1944, ever since known as **D-Day**, a huge armada crossed the English Channel and American, British, and other Allied forces and landed on five beaches along the **Normandy** coast of France. As with so many World War II operations that set new standards, the Normandy invasion was the largest and most complex amphibious military operation in history. Overcoming strong German resistance, Allied troops slowly pushed inland, and the vise on Nazi Germany began to close. By the spring of 1944, Soviet forces, bolstered by huge quantities of Lend-Lease equipment and supplies, were advancing rapidly westward, and in some places on southern portions of the eastern front had driven beyond the Soviet Union's 1939 borders. The Allies suffered some setbacks, most seriously in the **Battle of the Bulge**, which from mid-December 1944 to late January 1945 became the largest and costliest battle in the history of the U.S. Army. But while painful, these setbacks were temporary. By the end of January 1945, American, British, and other Allied forces had reached, and in some places even inched across, Germany's western border, while in the east the Soviet Red Army had expelled the Germans from most of central Europe and had even overrun part of eastern Germany.

Hitler's last hope to turn the tide of battle rested on a group of new ultra-modern weapons. They included the ME-262, the world's first operational jet fighter, and the jet-powered V-l, a pilotless aircraft packed with explosives was used to bomb London and other targets. Most futuristic of all was the V-2 rocket, a supersonic weapon years ahead of its time. These and other weapons were impressive demonstrations of German technological skills and, frighteningly, how far ahead of the Allies the Germans were in certain areas. Fortunately, they reached combat much too late to change the course of the war. Their main impact at the time was to cause a race between the United States and the Soviet Union to get their hands on the advanced German technology and the scientists and engineers who had produced it. As weapons that would affect the balance of power between nations, they belonged to the postwar era.

Meanwhile, by early 1945 the time had arrived to plan for the postwar peace. This effort took place during February 1945 at a conference between Roosevelt, Churchill, and Stalin at Yalta, a resort along the Soviet Union's Black Sea coast. Important agreements were reached at Yalta regarding the occupation of Germany. However, the Soviet Union's clear intent to set up a Communist-controlled puppet regime in Poland and concerns about how Moscow would deal with the other countries occupied by the Red Army caused serious divisions between Roosevelt and Churchill on the one hand and Stalin on the other. The fear in Washington and London was that the Soviet Union, having helped prevent Germany from dominating Europe, was now poised to do the very same thing. In retrospect, it is evident that rather than establishing the basis for a genuine postwar peace, the **Yalta Conference** set the stage for the **Cold War**. The subsequent **Potsdam Conference**, which took place from mid-July to early August, after Germany had surrendered, only deepened the divisions between the two sides, especially as the Soviet Union tightened its grip on Poland and other countries in eastern Europe.

Their disagreements about what would happen after the war notwithstanding, between February and April the Allies carried the war into German territory. On April 25, American and Soviet units met near the center of the country at the Elbe River. By then Soviet forces had reached Berlin, where Hitler committed suicide on April 30 as the Stalin's troops completed their conquest of the city after a bloody house-to-house struggle that cost hundreds of thousands of casualties. On May 8, Germany finally surrendered, ending the war in Europe.

Attention now shifted to the Pacific and Japan. By the spring of 1945, the United States had driven Japan back from its conquests in the Pacific, although Japanese forces were still entrenched in China, Indochina, and the Netherlands East Indies, among other places. Since late 1944, once the United States had taken and built airfields on the Marianas Islands, its huge new B-29 bombers—streamlined, high-tech wonders with technological features found on no other aircraft—had been pounding Japan. Yet despite terrible damage to its cities and casualties to its civilians, Japan showed no signs of surrendering.

Meanwhile, as the fighting approached Japan island-by-island, American casualties mounted. Japanese garrisons one after another refused to surrender and fought to the last man. In the battle for **Iwo Jima**, a five-week struggle during February-March 1945 that had been expected to take four days, the United States suffered almost 27,000 casualties, including more than 6,800 dead, to take an island eight miles square. The Japanese garrison of 22,000 fought until it was virtually wiped out; only a few hundred soldiers, most of them wounded, survived. The pattern was the same on **Okinawa** in April, where Japanese suicide kamikaze pilots crashing their planes into warships offshore turned that battle into the costliest in the history of the U.S. Navy.

The next battle on the agenda was the invasion of the Japanese home islands. No one knew what the final cost of defeating Japan would be, but estimates of 500,000 or more total American casualties were not unusual. With access to information from broken Japanese military and diplomatic codes, American leaders knew that Japan's government, controlled by military hardliners, was unwilling to surrender on terms satisfactory to the United States and its allies. Allied policy was to demand unconditional surrender, a condition already imposed on Nazi Germany. Unconditional surrender was considered vital because the Allies were determined to occupy Germany and Japan, punish war criminals, and impose reforms that would prevent those countries from causing another war. The Japanese wanted to negotiate an end to the war that would let them retain their authoritarian and militaristic form of government and part of their empire. Meanwhile, as the decrypted enemy cables told Washington, Japan was preparing its defenses for the initial American invasion at the precise points where U.S. forces were slated to land. By the summer of 1945, those defenses already were much stronger than U.S. military intelligence had predicted just a few months earlier.

It is against this background that the use of the atomic bomb against Japan must be understood.[12] The urgent, top-secret project to develop an atomic bomb, known as the **Manhattan Project**, had been initiated in 1942 because of fears that Germany was trying to build such a bomb. Those fears were based on dramatic progress in atomic physics during the 1930s, in particular the success by German scientists in creating atomic fission. Between 1942 and 1945 Manhattan Project scientists further pioneered a whole range of scientific and engineering areas; almost everything involved in the project was technologically path breaking. On July 16, 1945, at a remote desert site in New Mexico, the designers of the bomb successfully tested a device they called the "gadget," which exploded with the incredible force of 18,000 tons of TNT. World War II had brought the world into the atomic age.

The atomic bomb had been developed for use against Germany, but the war in Europe had ended before Manhattan Project scientists and engineers had completed their work. By the time an atomic bomb was ready, only Japan was still fighting, and even though its cities and industrial infrastructure had already been devastated by aerial bombing, its government steadfastly refused to surrender. Harry S. Truman, who had become president upon Roosevelt's death in April 1945, led a war-weary country, and like his predecessor saw the bomb as a potentially necessary means with which to end the war. On July 26, the United States, Great Britain, and China issued the **Potsdam Declaration**, demanding that Japan surrender or face "prompt and utter destruction," though it offered some concessions not offered to the Germans.[13] However, despite the urging of its foreign minister to at least consider it, the Japanese government rejected the Potsdam Declaration outright. This made the employment of atomic bombs inevitable.

In this historical context, the sole purpose of these bombs is clear: they were used to force Japan to surrender and thereby end the war as soon as possible. On August 6, a B-29 dropped an atomic bomb on Hiroshima, virtually destroying the city in a matter of seconds. When no response came from Tokyo after three days, Nagasaki was bombed, with similar results. Meanwhile, on August 8 the Soviet Union honored the pledge it made at Yalta by declaring war on Japan. Despite all of this, with key ministers determined to fight to the bitter end, Japan's government remained deadlocked about whether to surrender. This caused **Emperor Hirohito** to take the unprecedented step of personally ordering the government to sue for peace. Japan offered to surrender on August 10, although on terms unacceptable to the Allies. After several days of negotiations, Japan accepted Allied terms based on the Potsdam Declaration and surrendered on August 14. The formal ceremony ending World War II took place on September 2, 1945.

Costs and Results

World War II led to the destruction of German Nazism and Japanese militarist authoritarianism, but at a staggering cost. The war's death toll, military and civilian, probably approached 60 million, including the six million Jews murdered in the Holocaust. An estimated 27 million people died in the Soviet Union alone, although some of those losses must be attributed to the callous and wasteful way Stalin's regime fought the war. From the Atlantic deep eastward far into the Soviet Union much of Europe was a wasteland, its cities strewn with rubble and millions of refugees on the move. In Asia, vast swaths of destruction stretched across China, the Philippines, and Japan itself. Of all the world's industrial powers, only the United States, despite having suffered 400,000 dead between 1941 and 1945, emerged from the war largely undamaged and with the resources to begin a new era of prosperity.

The war ended the era of European dominance in international affairs. The United States, Britain, the Soviet Union, and France occupied defeated Germany, which no longer existed as an independent nation. Britain and France, albeit on the winning side, were exhausted, so much so that their colonial empires, along with those of other European states, soon would begin to crumble. Even more disturbing, the threat posed to Europe by one totalitarian power, Nazi Germany, had been defeated only to be replaced by the threat posed by another, the Soviet Union. The expansion of Soviet power into central Europe and the strength of local Communist forces in countries such as France and Italy raised the specter of Soviet domination of the continent. The only apparent counter to that threat was a non-European power, the United States. With Japan defeated and under American occupation, the United States also was the only counter to the expansion of Soviet influence in the Far East.

With the decline of Europe, the United States and the Soviet Union emerged as the world's dominant powers. As they built up their nuclear arsenals in the first post-war decade—the Soviet Union, having successfully spied on the Manhattan Project, exploded its first atomic bomb in 1949—they would be dubbed superpowers. Their global rivalry, in effect a struggle between democratic capitalism and totalitarian communism, would be known as the Cold War. The United States and the Soviet Union managed to avoid a catastrophic nuclear war with each other. But for more than four decades they and the rest of the world lived through a difficult time, a tense nuclear standoff punctuated by a series of crises and non-nuclear conflicts in which the superpowers sparred with each other indirectly. That "hard and bitter peace," as John F. Kennedy called it, was yet another painful legacy of World War II.[14]

Notes

1. Gerhard L. Weinberg, *Visions of Victory: The Hopes of Eight World War II Leaders* (New York: Cambridge University Press, 2005), p. 18. Weinberg is also the author of the monumental *A World at Arms: A Global History of World War II* (1994), the standard history of that war. A second edition of that book was published in 2005.

2. See Lucy S. Dawidowicz, *The War Against the Jews*, 1933-1945 (New York: Holt, Rinehart, and Winston), 1975.

3. Quoted in Leni Yahil, *The Holocaust: The Fate of European Jewry* (New York: Oxford University Press, 1987), p. 115

4. Quoted in Roland N. Stromberg, *Europe in the Twentieth Century*, fourth edition (Upper Saddle River: Prentice Hall, 1997), p. 236.

5. See, for example, Richard Overy, *Russia's War: A History of the Soviet War Effort, 1941-1945* (1997) and David M. Glantz and Jonathan House, *When Titans Clashed: How the Red Army Stopped Hitler* (1995).

6. The standard work on the Pacific War remains Ronald H. Spector, *The Eagle Against the Sun: The American War With Japan* (1985). A recent outstanding work that covers the last year of that war, from grand strategy to the experiences of ordinary soldiers, sailors, and airmen who actually fought it, is Max Hastings, *Retribution: The Battle for Japan*, 1944-45 (2008).

7. Robin Neillands, *The Bomber War: The Allied Offensive Against Germany* (Woodstock and New York: Overlook Press, 2001), p. 389. See also Max Hastings, *Armageddon: The Battle for Germany, 1944-1945* (2005), pp. 289-337, especially pp. 306-309. Hastings writes that until 1945 "there seems little difficulty in justifying the bomber offensive militarily and morally, as a matter of both desirability and necessity." Hastings is less certain with regard to 1945, but also observes: "We should recognize...that it is far easier to pass such judgments amid the relative tranquility of the twenty-first century that it seemed in 1945, when Hitler's nations was still doing its utmost to kill American and British people, together with millions of Nazi captives, by every means within its power."

8. See Werner Gruhl, *Imperial Japan's World War Two, 1931-1945* (2007) for a overview of how Japan fought the war.

9. Lucy Dawidowicz makes the following key point about the Holocaust: "The deaths of the 6 million European Jews were not a byproduct of the war. The Jews did not die as a consequence of the indiscriminate reach of bombs or gunfire or of the unselective fallout of deadly weapons. Nor were they the victims of the cruel and brutal expedience that actuated the Nazis to kill the Soviet prisoners of war and the Polish elite. Those murders were intended as a means to practical ends: they were meant to protect and to consolidate the position of the Germans as the undisputed masters over Europe. The murder of the Jews and the destruction of Jewish communal existence were, in contrast, *ends in themselves*, [italics added] ultimate goals to which the National Socialist state had dedicated itself." See Lucy S. Dawidowicz, *The Holocaust and the Historians* (Cambridge: Harvard University Press, 1981), p. 13.

10. Quoted in Yahil, *The Holocaust*, p. 255.

11. Robert S. Wistrich, *Hitler and the Holocaust* (New York: Modern Library, 2001), p. 196. This is the best short overview of the Holocaust and some of the key debates surrounding it.

12. The definitive work on the atomic bombing of Japan is Richard B. Frank, *Downfall: The End of the Japanese Imperial Empire* (1999). See also Robert James Maddox, *Weapons for Victory* (1995), Edward J. Drea, *MacArthur's Ultra: Codebreaking and the War Against Japan, 1942-1945* (1992), D.M. Giangreco, *Hell to Pay: Operation DOWNFALL and the Invasion of Japan, 1945-1947* (2009), and Michael Kort, *The Columbia Guide to Hiroshima and the Bomb* (2007). These works, and others, demonstrate that there is no basis for the charge made by some historians and commentators that the dropping of the bomb was motivated even in part by an intent to intimidate the Soviet Union with regard to postwar matters.

13. "The Potsdam Declaration," July 26, 1945. In Michael Kort, *The Columbia Guide to Hiroshima and the Bomb* (New York: Columbia: University Press, 2007), pp. 226-227.

14. "Inauguration Speech of President John F. Kennedy, January 20, 1961. Available online. http://www.jfklibrary.org/Historical+Resources/Archives/Reference+Desk/Speeches/JFK/003POF03Inaugural01201961.htm (Accessed May 29, 2009)

References and Suggested Readings:

Davidowicz, Lucy S. *The Holocaust and the Historians*. Cambridge: Harvard University Press, 1981.

_____. *The War Against the Jews*, 1933-1945. New York: Holt, Rinehart, and Winston, 1975.

Dziewanowski, M.K. *War at Any Price: World War II in Europe*, second edition. Englewood Cliffs: Prentice Hall, 1991.

Drea, Edward J. *MacArthur's Ultra: Codebreaking and the War Against Japan, 1942-1945*. Lawrence: University Press of Kansas, 1992.

Fischer, Klaus P. *Nazi Germany: A New History*. New York: Continuum, 1995.

Frank, Richard B. *Downfall: The End of the Japanese Imperial Empire*. New York: Random House, 1999.

Giangreco, D.M. *Hell to Pay: Operation DOWNFALL and the Invasion of Japan, 1945-1947*. Annapolis: Naval Institute Press, 2009.

Glantz, David M. and Jonathan House, *When Titans Clashed: How the Red Army Stopped Hitler*. Lawrence: University Press of Kansas, 1995.

Gruhl, Werner. *Imperial Japan's World War Two, 1931-1945*. New Brunswick: Transaction Publishers, 2007.

Hastings, Max. *Armageddon: The Battle for Germany, 1944-1945*. New York: Vintage 2005.

_____. *Retribution: The Battle for Japan, 1944-45*. New York: Knopf, 2008.

Kort, Michael. *The Columbia Guide to Hiroshima and the Bomb*. New York: Columbia University Press, 2007.

Lipstadt, Deborah. *Denying the Holocaust: The Growing Assault on Truth and Memory*. New York: Plume, 1993.

Lyons, Michael J. *World War II: A Short History*, fourth edition. Upper Saddle River: Pearson, 2004.

Maddox, Robert James. *Weapons for Victory*. Columbia and London: University of Missouri Press, 1995.

Neillands, Robin. *The Bomber War: The Allied Offensive Against Germany*. Woodstock and New York: Overlook Press, 2001.

Overy, Richard. *Russia's War: A History of the Soviet War Effort, 1941-1945*. New York: Penguin, 1997.

Spector, Ronald H. *The Eagle Against the Sun: The American War With Japan*. New York: Free Press, 1985.

Stromberg, Roland N. *Europe in the Twentieth Century*, fourth edition. Upper Saddle River: Prentice Hall, 1997.

Weinberg, Gerhard L. *A World at Arms: A Global History of World War II*. Cambridge: Cambridge University Press, 1994.

_____. *Visions of Victory: The Hopes of Eight World War II Leaders*. New York: Cambridge University Press, 2005.

Wistrich, Robert S. *Hitler and the Holocaust*. New York: Modern Library, 2001.

Yahil, Leni. *The Holocaust: The Fate of European Jewry*. New York: Oxford University Press, 1987.

The Good War

Studs Terkel

A Chance Encounter

ROBERT RASMUS

I've lived about thirty-eight years after the war and about twenty years before. For me it's B.W. and A.W.—before the war and after the war. I suspect there are a lot of people like me. In business, there'll be times when I say. This really worries the heck out of me, but it's really minor compared to having to do a river crossing under fire. (Laughs.)

He is six feet four or five, graying. He is a business executive, working out of Chicago. Obviously he's kept himself in pretty good shape. His manner is gentle, easy, unruffled.

I get this strange feeling of living through a world drama. In September of '39 when the Germans invaded Poland, I was fourteen years old. I remember my mother saying, "Bob, you'll be in it." I was hoping she'd be right. At that age, you look forward to the glamour and have no idea of the horrors.

Sure enough, I was not only in the army but in the infantry. Step by logistic step, our division was in combat. You're finally down to one squad, out ahead of the whole thing. You're the point man. What am I doing out here—in this world-cataclysmic drama—out in front of the whole thing? (Laughs.)

You saw those things in the movies, you saw the newsreels. But you were of an age when your country wasn't even in the war. It seemed unreal. All of a sudden, there you were right in the thick of it and people were dying and you were scared out of your wits that you'd have your head blown off. (Laughs.)

I was acutely aware, being a rifleman, the odds were high that I would be killed. At one level, animal fear. I didn't like that at all. On the other hand, I had this great sense of adventure. My gosh, going across the ocean, seeing the armies, the excitement of it. I was there.

This wouldn't have been true of most, but I was a skinny, gaunt kind of mama's boy. I was going to gain my manhood then. I would forever be liberated from the sense of inferiority that I wasn't rugged. I would prove that I had the guts and the manhood to stand up to these things. There were all these things, from being a member of the Western world to Bobby Rasmus, the skinny nineteen-year-old who's gonna prove that he can measure up. (Laughs.)

I remember my mother during my thirty-day furlough. Continuous weeping. She said, "Bob, you've got to tell your captain you're too tall to be a rifleman." (Laughs.) The only way I could get her off that was to say, "I'll tell him, Ma." Of course, I didn't.

I was in training at Fort Benning, Georgia. If you got sick and fell back more than a week, you were removed from your battalion. I got the flu and was laid back for eight days. I was removed from my outfit where all my buddies were. I was heartbroken.

My original group went to the 106th Division and ended up being overwhelmed in the Battle of the Bulge. I remember letters I sent my buddies that came back: Missing in action. Killed in action. These were the eighteen-year-olds. It was only because I got the flu that I wasn't among them.

When I went in the army, I'd never been outside the states of Wisconsin, Indiana, and Michigan. So when I woke up the first morning on the troop train in Fulton, Kentucky, I thought I was in Timbuktu. Of course, I was absolutely bowled over by Europe, the castles, the cathedrals, the Alps. It was wonderment. I was preoccupied with staying alive and doing my job, but it seemed, out of the corner of my eye, I was constantly fascinated with the beauty of the German forests and medieval bell towers. At nineteen, you're seeing life with fresh eyes.

The first time I ever heard a New England accent was at Fort Benning. The southerner was an exotic creature to me. People from the farms. The New York street-smarts. You had an incredible mixture of every stratum of society. And you're of that age when your need for friendship is greatest. I still see a number of these people. There's sort of a special sense of kinship.

The reason you storm the beaches is not patriotism or bravery. It's that sense of not wanting to fail your buddies. Having to leave that group when I had the flu may have saved my life. Yet to me, that kid, it was a disaster.

Kurt Vonnegut, in *Slaughterhouse Five*, writes of the fire bombing of Dresden and the prisoner-of-war train in Germany. A lot of my buddies who were captured were on that train. I didn't know that until three days ago when a middle-aged guy with white hair like mine stopped me on the street and said, "Hey, aren't you Bob Rasmus?" I said, "Aren't you Red Prendergast?" He'd been in the original training group, gone to the 106th Division, taken to Germany, was on the troop train that got strafed. I knew him for about five months, thirty-nine years ago, and had never set eyes on him since. I was only in combat for six weeks, but I could remember every hour, every minute of the whole forty-two days.

In Boston Harbor, we actually saw the first visible sign of the war: an Australian cruiser tied up next to the troop ship. There was a huge, jagged hole in the bow. The shape of things to come. There was a lot of bravado, kidding.

Our impression of France, those of us who grew up in the thirties, was French maids, French poodles, a frivolous type of people. So it was striking to see these stolid peasants walking behind horse-drawn plows. The area we were in had not yet been hit by the war. I was struck by the sheer beauty of the countryside, the little villages, the churches. This sort of thing the impressionists did.

Going to the front, I can remember the cities in Belgium: Liège, Namur. We were going through towns and villages. We were hanging out of the cars of the trains and on the roofs. We had all this extra candy from our K rations and would just throw them out to the kids. There was a sense of victory in the air. They had already been liberated. They were elated.

All of a sudden, the tone changes. You get off the train on the border in that little corner of Holland and Germany. We're near Aachen, which had been absolutely leveled by Allied bombings. Rubble, nothing but rubble. Here was the ancient city of Aix-la-Chapelle, just a sea of rubble. We've had forty-eight hours enjoying being part of the victorious army. Now the party's over. You're within a few miles of the front. You're off the train into trucks. You hear gunfire in the distance.

Everybody sobered up very rapidly. We drove on for a few miles and there was a second city, Düren, totally wiped out. It was one of the most bombed-out cities in Germany. Now we're moving forward on foot.

They moved us into what they called a quiet front. Our division occupied a frontage on the Rhine, south of Cologne. We simply relieved another division that had been there, the Eighth. We moved into the same foxholes. You know it's getting close. It's still sort of exciting. Nobody's gotten killed yet. To me, it was interesting because of the architecture. From the distance I could see the Cologne cathedral, with the twin towers.

We stayed in bombed-out buildings. It was almost surreal. Here's a cross-section of a four-story, where every room is open to the atmosphere on one side and there's another room that is still intact. This was true all the way through Europe.

The very first night, our squad was in comfortable quarters. Our one side was completely open, but on the other side were beds and kitchens and what-not. It was almost theatrical. Since the Germans were the enemy and evil, we never had any sense of guilt that we were in somebody's apartment. Any abuse of the apartment, like throwing dishes out the window, was what they deserved. Whatever was there in the way of food and drink, we would make use of.

One of the things we had was this old music box. It could play whole melodies. We had two disks. One was "Silent Night" and the other was "We Gather Together to Ask the Lord's Blessing." I had a typical Lutheran churchgoing background. Here am I hearing a Christmas carol and a hymn that I'd sung many times in church.

I was sort of schizophrenic all through this period. I was a participant, scared out of my wits. But I was also acutely aware of how really theatrical and surreal it was.

Three days later we pulled out, crossed the Rhine, and cut off a German pocket. As we were moving out of this area of sheared-off buildings, there were courtyards with fruit trees in blossom. And there were our heavy mortars blasting away across the river. I had been seeing shadowy figures moving around. Were they infiltrators or just a bush that I was imagining? And there in sight was the Cologne cathedral amidst all this wreckage.

We've seen a little of the war now. We've seen planes dropping bombs over on the other side. We've sent out patrols, have captured prisoners. But we really hadn't been in it ourselves. It was still fun and dramatics. When the truck took us from Cologne south through Bonn, for me it was, Hey, Beethoven's birthplace! But when we crossed a pontoon bridge and I saw a balloon of fire, I knew the real combat was going to begin. I had the feeling now that we were gonna be under direct fire, some of us were gonna be killed. But I was also enormously affected by the beauty of the countryside. We were in rolling hills and great forests. It stretched out for mile after mile. I could almost hear this Wagnerian music. I was pulled in two directions: Gee, I don't wanna get killed. And, Boy, this is gorgeous country.

Our uniforms were still clean. We were still young kids who hadn't seen anything. You could see these veteran troops. Their uniforms were dirty, they were bearded, there was a look in their eyes that said they'd been through a lot. A sort of expression on their faces—You're gonna find out now. A mixture of pity and contempt for the green-horns.

We started seeing our first dead, Germans. You drew the obvious inference: if Germans were dead, the Americans were getting killed farther up the line. Night fell, we were up within a couple of miles of where the action would begin. We were passing through our artillery emplacements. Incessant firing. It was reassuring to see how much artillery we had, but disturbing to see all these German dead. I had never seen a dead body before, except in a funeral home.

We were told that the next morning we would be on the attack. I remember the miserable cold. By this time, I had taken up cigarette smoking, wondering what my mother would think when I came back. (Laughs.) I felt sickish, I was cold, I was scared. And I couldn't even get one last cigarette.

We were awakened before dawn. I honestly don't know whether I dreamed it or whether it really happened. I've asked buddies I've seen since the war: Can you remember these ambulances and army surgeons getting their gear out? I have such an absolute recollection of it, but nobody else remembers it. It had a dreamlike quality: just seeing surgeons ready to work. Here we were still healthy, still an hour or two away from actual combat. It added to the inevitability that really bad, bad things were going to happen.

Our platoon of thirty men was to take a small town. At the time, I was a bazooka man. I'll never forget that sense of unreality as we were moving through the woods to this village, which we could just see a few hundred yards away. There were sheep grazing in the fields. By now there's gunfire: machine guns, rifle fire, mortar shells.

You'd lost your sense of direction. This was not a continuous front. These were piercing, probing actions. You'd take a town, then to the next river, then across the river and then the next one. This was the first. Now I can see actual mortar shells landing in this meadow. German 88s. They were hitting the tile roofs of these houses and barns. My initial reaction: they're not hurting anything. Oh, a few tiles, being knocked loose, but it's still a beautiful sunny day. The meadow is lovely. Here we are in a medieval village. This reaction lasted three seconds. These sheep started getting hit. You were seeing blood. Immediately you say, Soon it's gonna be us torn up like these animals. You sense all these stages you've gone through. And now (laughs), the curtain has gone up and you're really in it.

We captured that town without any casualties. I think the German troops had moved out. My confidence is coming back a little. Gee, we captured a town and didn't even see a German. Later that afternoon, we were moving up to take another town. We have a sense that things aren't going too well. We seem out of radio contact with the other rifle companies. I sense an apprehension by our officers.

All of a sudden, we spotted a group of German soldiers down by the slope of this hill, perhaps fifty. We were strung out, a couple of platoons. We would be on the ground, get up on command, and start firing right into this group of Germans. We did catch them by surprise. They responded quickly, firing back, machine guns and rifles. We had them well outnumbered, our company, about 240. We did the march-and-fire. It was a new maneuver we'd never done in training. We learned. I noticed that some of our guys were getting hit. It was all in a few minutes. We killed most of the Germans. A few might have gotten away, but we wiped them out. Our guys were getting killed, too. Irony again, the first one killed was our platoon sergeant.

You have to understand the culture of our company. Most of our privates were college types. They had been dumped en masse into these infantry divisions. The cadre of noncommissioned officers were old-timers. They were mostly uneducated country types, many of them from the South. There was a rather healthy mutual contempt between the noncoms and the privates. This sergeant was the most hated man. One of the nineteen-year-olds, during maneuvers, was at the point of tears in his hatred of this man who was so unreasonable and so miserable. He'd say, "If we ever get into combat, I'm gonna kill 'im. First thing I'll do." Who's the first one killed? This sergeant. I'm sure it was enemy fire. I would bet my life on it. I'm sure the guys who said they would kill him were horrified that their wish came true.

My best friend was leaning against a tree. We were waiting for further instructions. He had this sly grin on his face. I was so aghast. It didn't occur to me that one of our people had done it. I'm really sure we didn't. "I'm gonna kill 'im" is said a million times. Added to the horror of our first dead is that he's the one all of us hated so much.

I'm sure our company was typical. We had x percent of self-inflicted wounds. There's no question that a guy would blow his toe off to get out of combat. People would get lost. These combat situations are so confused that it's very easy to go in the other direction. Say you get lost, get sick, get hurt. By the time you get back to your outfit, a couple of days have gone by.

We remember examples of Caspar Milquetoast: ordinary people showing incredible heroism. But you have to accept the fact that in a cross section of people—in civilian life, too—you've got cowards and quitters. Our radio man shot up his radio: he thought we were going to be captured. Panic. I became a bazooka man because our bazooka man threw his weapon away and I picked it up. He ran off.

Our captain said, "Pick up the bodies. We don't leave our dead to the enemy." We're now cut off and have to join the rest of our battalion. We had to improvise stretchers. I took off my field jacket and turned the arms inside out. We poked rifles through the arms and fashioned a stretcher. We got the sergeant on ours and, jeez, half his head was blown off and the brains were coming out on my hands and on my uniform. Here's the mama's boy, Sunday school, and now I'm really in it.

I remember lying in that slit trench that night. It was a nightmare. I'd now seen what dead people look like, the color out of their face. I think each person in my squad went through this dream of mine. Daylight came and we moved out into another town. This is twenty four hours of experience.

Those who really went through combat, the Normandy landings, the heavy stuff, might laugh at this little action we'd been in, but for me . . . We were passing people who were taking over from us, another company. We had one day of this. Our uniforms were now dirty and bloody and our faces looked like we'd been in there for weeks. Now we had the feeling: You poor innocents.

We weren't able to bring those bodies back with us. The mortar fire became too much. The next morning, our squad was assigned to go back and recover the bodies. It was sunshine and quiet. We were passing the Germans we killed. Looking at the individual German dead, each took on a personality. These were no longer an abstraction. These were no longer the Germans of the brutish faces and the helmets we saw in the newsreels. They were exactly our age. These were boys like us.

I remember one, particularly. A redhead. To this day, I see the image of this young German soldier sitting against a tree. This group was probably resting, trying to make their escape. The whole thing might have been avoided had we been more experienced and called down in German for them to surrender. They probably would have been only too glad. Instead, out of fear, there was this needless slaughter. It has the flavor of murder, doesn't it?

What I remember of that day is not so much the sense of loss at our two dead but a realization of how you've been conditioned. At that stage, we didn't hate the Germans just for evil the country represented, their militarism, but right down to each individual German. Once the helmet is off, you're looking at a teen-ager, another kid. Obviously you have to go on. There are many, many more engagements.

A few days, later, we're in Lüdenscheid. It's near the Ruhr pocket. Two Allied armies had crossed the Rhine fifteen miles apart. It's a pincer movement, closing in a pocket of 350,000 Germans. Under Field Marshal Model, I believe. They just don't surrender overnight. They're gonna fight it out. Our job, all the way through Germany, was to move as fast as you could on trucks, on tanks, until you came up against resistance. Some towns fell without a battle. Others, quite a bit of resistance. You'd assume the worst.

You were constantly behind the lines and then moved up. You'd pass through your artillery and you knew you were getting closer. Pretty soon things would thin out. Just an hour earlier there were an awful lot of GIs around. As you got closer to action, it was only your platoon, and then it was your squad ahead of the other two. You were the point man for the squad.

I thought, This is incredible. We've got these great masses of troops, of quartermasters and truckers and tanks and support troops, and then all of a sudden it's so lonely. (Laughs.) You're out ahead of the whole thing.

In Lüdenscheid, we were in the hills looking down. It was dead silence in the town, except that you became aware of German ambulances with the big red crosses on the roofs. We didn't know whether it was a trick. There was something mysterious about that sight. The bells started tolling in the city. You didn't know what to make of it. Was this the opening of a major battle? Were they going away? There was very little resistance and we took the town.

Now I began to get an inkling of some other evil abroad. We were very much aware that the Germans had mobilized the Poles, the French, the captive countries, into workers on farms and in factories. As each town was captured, you were liberating Slavs, Poles, French, whatever. It was often highly emotional. The idea of those death camps still hadn't reached us at all. I marvel as I think back on it. When we took Lüdenscheid, our platoon stayed overnight in what was a combination beer hall, theater, festival-type thing, with a stage and a big dance floor. There in the middle of the floor was this mountain of clothing. I realize now that was probably the clothing they'd taken from the people that went to Dachau or another camp. It really didn't register with us what that might have been. You knew this wasn't just a Salvation Army collecting clothes. I remember it because that was the day Roosevelt died.

Every town had a certain number of slave laborers. It might range from handfuls to hundreds, depending on whether there was industry in that town. The final one we captured in the Ruhr was Letmathe. There was a large number of Italian laborers who worked in a factory. There were quite a few Russians. The military government hadn't yet moved in. I remember the Russians taking the horses and running them up and down the street to get their circulation up and then kill them for food. A Russian was going to kill the horse with a hatchet. I wasn't up to shooting the horse myself, but I let him use my pistol. We were aware of the starvation and the desperate measures they would take.

You had these spontaneous uprisings where the slave laborers and war prisoners the Germans had in these towns would just take over. It was very chaotic.

I remember where a Russian was in the process of strangling a German in the cellar of our building. This was a moment of truth for me. I was still nurturing the notion that every individual German was evil and the Russians were our allies. Somehow I got the picture that the Russian was carrying out vengeance. He claimed this German had killed his buddy. In that confused situation you couldn't tell whether it was true or whether it was a grudge carried out or what. It didn't take much deliberation to stop it. The Russian broke out in tears when I wouldn't let him kill the German. He just sobbed. Reflecting on it later, I had reason to believe his story was true. But I wasn't up to letting it happen.

We were aware that the Russians had taken enormous losses on the eastern front, that they really had broken the back of the German army. We would have been in for infinitely worse casualties and misery had it not been for them. We were well disposed toward them. I remember saying if we happen to link up with 'em, I wouldn't hesitate to kiss 'em.

I didn't hear any anti-Russian talk. I think we were realistic enough to know that if we were going to fight them, we would come out second best. We hadn't even heard of the atomic bomb yet. We'd just have to assume that it would be masses of armies, and their willingness to sacrifice millions of troops. We were aware that our leaders were sparing our lives. Even though somebody would have to do the dirty work in the infantry, our leaders would try to pummel the enemy with artillery and tanks and overpower them before sending the infantry in. If that was possible.

I've reflected on why people my age and with my experience don't have that spontaneous willingness to be part of the nuclear freeze. It's the sense that the Germans were willing to lose millions of men. And they did. Every German house we went to, there would be black-bordered pictures of sons and relatives. You could tell that most of them died on the eastern front. And the Russians lost twenty million.

Later, we were back in the States being retrained for the Japanese invasion. The first atom bomb was dropped. We ended halfway across the Pacific. How many of us would have been killed on the mainland if there were no bomb? Someone like me has this specter.

In the final campaign down through Bavaria, we were in Patton's army. Patton said we ought to keep going. To me, that was an unthinkable idea. The Russians would have slaughtered us, because of their willingness to give up so many lives. I don't think the rank of the GIs had any stomach for fighting the Russians. We were informed enough through press and newsreels to know about Stalingrad. I saw the actual evidence in those black-bordered pictures in every German household I visited. Black border, eastern front, nine out of ten.

I have more disapproval of communism today than ever. I think our government did try to stimulate a feeling about good Uncle Joe. The convoys to Murmansk. We had this mixed feeling: Gee, we're glad they did the lion's share, the overwhelming bulk of the dying, the breaking the back of the German armies. And individually, they can't be all that bad. In any case, we don't want to fight 'em. (Laughs.)

The thing that turned me against the Vietnam War was an issue of *Life* magazine in '68. It had a cover picture of the hundred men that died in Vietnam that week. I said, Enough. I don't want to stand here as a veteran of World War Two saying that we somehow took a stand that was admirable. We are bad as the rest if we don't think independently and make up our own minds. We were willing to go along as long as it seemed an easy victory. When it really got tough, we started re-examining.

World War Two was utterly different. It has affected me in many ways ever since. I think my judgment of people is more circumspect. I know it's made me less ready to fall into the trap of judging people by their style or appearance. In a short period of time, I had the most tremendous, experiences of all of life: of fear, of jubilance, of misery, of hope, of comradeship, and of the endless excitement, the theatrics of it. I honestly feel grateful for having been a witness to an event as monumental as anything in history and, in a very small way, a participant.

Rosie

PEGGY TERRY

She is a mountain woman who has lived in Chicago for the past twenty years. Paducah, Kentucky is her hometown. She visits it as often as her meager purse allows.

The first work I had after the Depression was at a shell-loading plant in Viola, Kentucky. It is between Paducah and Mayfield. They were large shells: anti-aircraft, incendiaries, and tracers. We painted red on the tips of the tracers. My mother, my sister, and myself worked there. Each of us worked a different shift because we had little ones at home. We made the fabulous sum of thirty-two dollars a week. (Laughs.) To us it was just an absolute miracle. Before that, we made nothing.

You won't believe how incredibly ignorant I was. I knew vaguely that a war had started, but I had no idea what it meant.

Didn't you have a radio?

Gosh, no. That was an absolute luxury. We were just moving around, working wherever we could find work. I was eighteen. My husband was nineteen. We were living day to day. When you are involved in stayin' alive, you don't think about big things like a war. It didn't occur to us that we were making these shells to kill people. It never entered my head.

There were no women foremen where we worked. We were just a bunch of hillbilly women laughin' and talkin'. It was like a social. Now we'd have money to buy shoes and a dress and pay rent and get some food on the table. We were just happy to have work.

I worked in building number 11. I pulled a lot of gadgets on a machine. The shell slid under and powder went into it. Another lever you pulled tamped it down. Then it moved on a conveyer belt to another building where the detonator was dropped in. You did this over and over.

Tetryl was one of the ingredients and it turned us orange. Just as orange as an orange. Our hair was streaked orange. Our hands, our face, our neck just turned orange, even our eyeballs. We never questioned. None of us ever asked, What is this? Is this harmful? We simply didn't think about it. That was just one of the conditions of the job. The only thing we worried about was other women thinking we had dyed our hair. Back then it was a disgrace if you dyed your hair. We worried what people would say.

We used to laugh about it on the bus. It eventually wore off. But I seem to remember some of the women had breathing problems. The shells were painted a dark gray. When the paint didn't come out smooth, we had to take rags wet with some kind of remover and wash that paint off. The fumes from these rags—it was like breathing cleaning fluid. It burned the nose and throat. Oh, it was difficult to breathe. I remember that.

Nothing ever blew up, but I remember the building where they dropped in the detonator. These detonators are little black things about the size of a thumb. This terrible thunderstorm came and all the lights went out. Somebody knocked a box of detonators off on the floor. Here we were in the pitch dark. Somebody was screaming, "Don't move, anybody!" They were afraid you'd step on the detonator. We were down on our hands and knees crawling out of that building in the storm. (Laughs.) We were in slow motion. If we'd stepped on one . . .

Mamma was what they call terminated—fired. Mamma's mother took sick and died and Mamma asked for time off and they told her no. Mamma said, "Well, I'm gonna be with my mamma. If I have to give up my job, I will just have to." So they terminated Mamma. That's when I started gettin' nasty. I didn't take as much baloney and pushing around as I had taken. I told 'em I was gonna quit, and they told me if I quit they would blacklist me wherever I would go. They had my fingerprints and all that. I guess it was just bluff, because I did get other work.

I think of how little we knew of human rights, union rights. We knew Daddy had been a hell-raiser in the mine workers' union, but at that point it hadn't rubbed off on any of us women. Coca-Cola and Dr. Pepper were allowed in every building, but not a drop of water.

You could only get a drink of water if you went to the cafeteria, which was about two city blocks away. Of course you couldn't leave your machine long enough to go get a drink. I drank Coke and Dr. Pepper and I hated 'em. I hate 'em today. We had to buy it, of course. We couldn't leave to go to the bathroom, 'cause it was way the heck over there.

We were awarded the navy E for excellence. We were just so proud of that E. It was like we were a big family, and we hugged and kissed each other. They had the navy band out there celebrating us. We were so proud of ourselves.

First time my mother ever worked at anything except in the fields—first real job Mamma ever had. It was a big break in everybody's life. Once, Mamma woke up in the middle of the night to go to the bathroom and she saw the bus going down. She said, "Oh my goodness, I've overslept." She jerked her clothes on, throwed her lunch in the bag, and was out on the corner, ready to go, when Boy Blue, our driver, said, "Honey, this is the wrong shift." Mamma wasn't supposed to be there until six in the morning. She never lived that down. She would have enjoyed telling you that.

My world was really very small. When we came from Oklahoma to Paducah, that was like a journey to the center of the earth. It was during the Depression and you did good having bus fare to get across town. The war just widened my world. Especially after I came up to Michigan.

My grandfather went up to Jackson, Michigan, after he retired from the railroad. He wrote back and told us we could make twice as much in the war plants in Jackson. We did. We made ninety dollars a week. We did some kind of testing for airplane radios.

Ohh, I met all those wonderful Polacks. They were the first people I'd ever known that were any different from me. A whole new world just opened up. I learned to drink beer like crazy with 'em. They were all very union-conscious. I learned a lot of things that I didn't even know existed.

We were very patriotic and we understood that the Nazis were someone who would have to be stopped. We didn't know about concentration camps. I don't think anybody I knew did. With the Japanese, that was a whole different thing. We were just ready to wipe them out. They sure as heck didn't look like us. They were yellow little creatures that smiled when they bombed our boys. I remember someone in Paducah got up this idea of burning everything they had that was Japanese. I had this little ceramic cat and I said, "I don't care, I am not burning it." They had this big bonfire and people came and brought what they had that was made in Japan. Threw it on the bonfire. I hid my cat. It's on the shelf in my bathroom right now. (Laughs.)

In all the movies we saw, the Germans were always tall and handsome. There'd be one meanie, a little short dumpy bad Nazi. But the main characters were good-lookin' and they looked like us. The Japanese were all evil. If you can go half your life and not recognize how you're being manipulated, that is sad and kinda scary.

I do remember a nice movie, *The White Cliffs of Dover*. We all sat there with tears pouring down our face. All my life, I hated England, 'cause all my family all my life had wanted England out of Ireland. During the war, all those ill feelings just seemed to go away. It took a war.

I believe the war was the beginning of my seeing things. You just can't stay uninvolved and not knowing when such a momentous thing is happening. It's just little things that start happening and you put one piece with another. Suddenly, a puzzle begins to take shape.

My husband was a paratrooper in the war, in the 101st Airborne Division. He made twenty-six drops in France, North Africa, and Germany. I look back at the war with sadness. I wasn't smart enough to think too deeply then. We had a lotta good times and we had money and we had food on the table and the rent was paid. Which had never happened to us before. But when I look back and think of him . . .

Until the war he never drank. He never even smoked. When he came back he was an absolute drunkard. And he used to have the most awful nightmares. He'd get up in the middle of the night and start screaming. I'd just sit for hours and hold him while he just shook. We'd go to the movies, and if they'd have films with a lot of shooting in it, he'd just start to shake and have to get up and leave. He started slapping me around and slapped the kids around. He became a brute.

Some fifteen years before, Peggy had recalled her experiences during the Great Depression. She and her young husband were on the road. "We were just kids. I was fifteen and he was sixteen. . . . It was a very nice time, because when you're poor and you stay in one spot, trouble just seems to catch up with you. But when you're moving from town to town, you don't stay there long enough for trouble to catch up with you."*

One of the things that bothered him most was his memory of this town he was in. He saw something move by a building and he shot. It was a woman. He never got over that. It seems so obvious to say—wars brutalize people. It brutalized him.

The war gave a lot of people jobs. It led them to expect more than they had before. People's expectations, financially, spiritually, were raised. There was such a beautiful dream. We were gonna reach the end of the rainbow. When the war ended, the rainbow vanished. Almost immediately we went into Korea. There was no peace, which we were promised.

I remember a woman saying on the bus that she hoped the war didn't end until she got her refrigerator paid for. An old man hit her over the head with an umbrella. He said, "How dare you!" (Laughs.)

Ohh, the beautiful celebrations when the war ended. They were selling cigarettes in Paducah. Up until that hour, you couldn'ta bought a pack of cigarettes for love or money. Kirchoff's Bakery was giving away free loaves of bread. Everybody was downtown in the pouring rain and we were dancing. We took off our shoes and put 'em in our purse. We were so happy.

The night my husband came home, we went out with a gang of friends and got drunk. All of us had a tattoo put on. I had a tattoo put up my leg where it wouldn't show. A heart with an arrow through it: Bill and Peggy. When I went to the hospital to

*Hard Times: An Oral History of the Great Depression (New York: Pantheon Books, 1970), p.48.

have my baby—I got pregnant almost as soon as he came home—I was ashamed of the tattoo. So I put two Band-Aids across it. So the nurse just pulls 'em off, looks at the tattoo, and she says, "Oh, that's exactly in the same spot I got mine." She pulled her uniform up and showed me her tattoo. (Laughs.)

I knew the bomb dropped on Hiroshima was a big terrible thing, but I didn't know it was the horror it was. It was on working people. It wasn't anywhere near the big shots of Japan who started the war in the first place. We didn't drop it on them. Hirohito and his white horse, it never touched him. It was dropped on women and children who had nothing to say about whether their country went to war or not.

I was happy my husband would get to come home and wouldn't be sent there from Germany. Every day when the paper came out, there'd be somebody I knew with their picture. An awful lot of kids I knew, went to school and church with, were killed.

No bombs were ever dropped on us. I can't help but believe the cold war started because we were untouched. Except for our boys that went out of the country and were killed, we came out of that war in good shape. People with more money than they'd had in years.

No, I don't think we'd have been satisfied to go back to what we had during the Depression. To be deprived of things we got used to. Materially, we're a thousand times better off. But the war turned me against religion. I was raised in the fundamentalist faith. I was taught that I was nothing. My feeling is if God created me, if God sent his only begotten son to give his life for me, then I am something. My mother died thinking she was nothing. I don't know how chaplains can call themselves men of God and prepare boys to go into battle. If the Bible says, Thou shalt not kill, it doesn't say, Except in time of war. They'll send a man to the electric chair who in a temper killed somebody. But they pin medals on our men. The more people they kill, the more medals they pin on 'em.

I was just so glad when it was over, because I wanted my husband home. I didn't understand any of the implications except that the killing was over and that's a pretty good thing to think about whether you're political or not. (Laughs.) The killing be over forever.

JEAN WOOD

She is a matronly-looking Londoner visiting New York, where her daughter has a job.

I was a dancer on the stage and just beginning to make my way. I was married and had one baby. My mother took care of her, so I was free and the world was my oyster. I was twenty-five. That war cut out my life till I was thirty-five.

Although the war ended after six years, we still had rationing and tightening our belts and, at one stage or another, no roof over our heads. My husband was in the Royal Artillery. He was wounded. He was never the same man again. He died from his war wounds, some years afterwards. I get a minute widow's pension.

I was due to have another baby when the blitz was at its height. That was 1940. We had a lull between 1939 and the summer of 1940. When the war broke out, I was dancing at a seaside resort. Ballet. I remember gazing out over the English Channel: how could people go to war on such a lovely day and kill each other? It was so unreal.

What was real was that everybody around me downed their tools and clambered to get to the recruiting office. Stores were left unattended, banks closed down. I'd left my little girl with my mother. I said to my husband, "For God's sake, let's get our little girl out of London." So we got her out. The government said, If you're out of London with a child, please stay put. You're more of a nuisance coming back to London.

I went back to seaside. They said there'd be a lull. They paid you to be evacuated. We were billeted in different people's homes. I had a terrible billet. The woman wouldn't even let me boil a kettle of hot water. She wouldn't let me iron my baby's clothes. She wouldn't let me keep the baby carriage in the house. She said, "Outside. It stays in the rain." I had to put the baby in a damp carriage.

The first day war was declared, the air-raid siren went off. People dived under the most ridiculous places, thinking the Luftwaffe was coming over. (Laughs.) They did feel silly when it was a false alarm. My God, is that what we're going to do? Fling ourselves down into the gutter and all that?

My husband said, "I'll go to the nearest big town and try to put the money down on a house. So at least you'll have your own roof and be safe." On the way, he volunteered to go into the army. He didn't have to go. He was thirty-four, and they weren't calling up that age yet. He said, "I may as well go in now and get it over with." I had to stay with this dreadful woman for a while. He went off and left me.

The war didn't start until the blitz. In October it started. First they bombed two schools in daylight. The kids were all laid out. We couldn't believe it. That was in Croydon.

The seaside was worse than London. When I'd been there, we'd had 109 dogfights overhead. I'd seen our Battle of Britain boys spiraling down. I'd also seen them do a victory roll when they shot a German airplane down. These boys went up day and night, in these Spitfires, almost stuck together with chewing gum. The mother of two of them lived quite near me. She lived in fear and trembling. We lived near the Spitfire airfield and we got terrible bombings. Here is where we were supposed to be safe.

One day I took my little girl shopping in the main little street. A German plane came down and started to machine-gun us. I ran into a store and put her and myself under the shop counter. I had my behind sticking out. (Laughs.) The machine gun was going bang! bang! bang! all up the road.

They had public underground shelters. They held maybe a couple of hundred. You could dodge in any time there was an air raid. There was no warning in these dogfights. You just looked up and saw planes coming down, machine-gunning. It was mostly bombers; our Spitfire boys were fighting back.

We also had our own air-raid shelter that the government issued. In the country, it was a steel table. You had it in your bedroom or living room. You all crawled underneath it. It was not very high, and if you were pretty big, it was awful to get under. (Laughs.) You'd stay under it for hours.

If you were in a big town, like London or Manchester, there was one in the garden. I don't know which was worse. The garden one was concrete or old tin and it was terribly damp. It used to be up to here with water. Such was the fortitude of the ordinary working class that they made little cozy living rooms in it. (Laughs.) They took their bird down there or their cat. The cat was always the last one: "Where's the cat?"

I had an aunt killed through coming up to make a cup of tea. The siren had just gone all clear. (Demonstrates pitch.) She came up the steps, said to her husband, "I'll make a nice hot cup of tea." They'd been there all night, listening to the crashing and bombing. She put the kettle on and with that, the bomb threw a direct hit on the house.

It was nothing to have the people who lived opposite's furniture blow through your window. We acquired all kinds of furniture we never owned. We ended up with a medley of furniture. Most people did. I had an old aunt of eighty who ended up like a film star's dressing table. How it shot into her garden, all that lovely furniture. (Laughs.)

You had air-raid wardens who were very good. These were men who weren't fit for service or worked in key jobs, and after they finished work, they'd be air-raid wardens. They would help you. They would drag the dead out. My husband once was coming home on leave through London. He was days late because he kept stopping at buildings, pulling out the dead. It was awful.

I had four daughters, all except one born during the war. When I went to have one of them, we didn't have ambulances. I had to go out into the blitz with all the fires raging, to try to get to a phone you could still use, call my doctor. He sent two men with a little truck, with a plank across it. I lay on it. There was no light and no signs, in case the Germans came. These two men were so hopeless, I almost gave birth in the truck. We fell down a big bomb crater and I almost tipped over. But you took it all in your stride. It looked as if you were going to live this way the rest of your life.

When I had my third baby, I stood in the room and said, "Please, God, if you're going to kill us with these bombs, let's all die together now, at night." One didn't know how many children to take under you, like a bird, put them under your wing. I thought if I had two here, and that one was over there, she might get killed and leave me with these two. You had to sort of lay on top of them, so that you'd all be killed together. Never thought I had it in me.

I never thought I could sit and read to children, say, about Cinderella, while you could hear the German planes coming. Sometimes a thousand a night came over, in waves. We had a saying, (says it staccato) I'm gonna getcha, I'm gonna getcha. That's how the planes sounded. You'd hear the bomb drop so many hundred yards that way. And you'd think, Oh, that missed us. You'd think, My God, the next one's going to be a direct hit. But you'd continue to read: "And the ugly sister said"—and you'd say, "Don't fidget, dear." And you'd think, My God, I can't stand it. But you bore up. And I wasn't the bravest of people, believe me.

You had hunches. About half past three you'd say, "I won't sleep over there tonight. I'll put them all over here 'cause I have a hunch that that part of the wall will come down." Or what few neighbors were left would say, "Why don't you bring all the kids over to me tonight and let's all sing and play cards. We won't bother with Jerry tonight." Now would it be safer that side of the road or this side? We'll go over there.

I did fire-watch. And that's frightening. You got up on the roof with a steel helmet on. You're supposed to have a protective jacket. The fire bombs were round balls. They'd come onto roofs and start fires. So the government gave you a bucket of sand and a shovel. Charming. (Laughs.) You stood there till the bomb fell. And you'd shovel it up quick and throw it into the bucket of sand. I didn't do that for long, because I fell pregnant again.

Most of the bombs were in working-class areas. I know there was a big thing about Buckingham Palace had a bomb, but they were all under a beautiful shelter. The working class caught it the worst because of the dock areas. And gasometers and electrical power stations. They aimed for those things. They thought if they demoralized the working class, they weren't going on with the war. For some reason, that never happened.

I had an aunt who was bombed out three times. My grandmother, who was eighty-odd, was bombed out and left clinging to the stairs, with her hair alight. The air-raid wardens got her out. She said, "I must go back for my hat." They took her in a truck with a lot of other elderly people to a safety zone.

I had to stay with my mother-in-law once. Sometimes the raids came before the siren went off, so you weren't down in the shelter. Land mines came down by parachute and laid whole streets low. It was like a bombed-out piece of land. This airplane was very low dropping the fire bombs, dropping them everywhere she was going. She did this terrific zigzag all across this field, hopping and leaping, hopping and leaping. Afterwards, people ran to get the parachute, 'cause with this parachute, we could make ourselves clothes. Clothes rationing was terribly strict. My husband got me a piece, and I made the children little dresses out of this nylon.

A lot of flowers grew on these bombed spaces, especially one in particular. It was a stalk with a lot of little red spots. It was like a weed, really. It was called London pride.

There was the blitz, when all London caught fire, except Saint Paul's Cathedral, thank God. That's why every time I go to Saint Paul's, I say, Oh, you're still there, thank God. Everything was in flames that night. It was like daylight, the flames.

I saw schoolchildren killed one Saturday morning. No warning. That's when the V-2s came. They were like big telegraph poles that shot through the air. No pilot, no nothing. They went into a building and laid low a whole street. On this morning, kids were shopping at Woolworth's. You couldn't buy much. You couldn't buy candy without your coupons. My mother's house was two blocks over and we heard this terrible crash. We all ran out to see. It was this Woolworth's and all these kiddies' bodies were brought out. They said they buried them. They don't know what arms and legs belong to people's arms and legs. They had cardboard coffins. We made so many, but we never made enough.

Then we had the V-1s. They were the planes that came over belching fire. It was amazing when the first one came down—in a working-class area, as usual. The fire went *chuchuchu, chuchuchu*. When the fire stopped, they circled and circled. You could almost pinpoint where it's going to land. We all ran to see it. When's the pilot going to get out? We were going to take him prisoner. But there was no pilot.

After that, there was another lull while they thought up the next monstrosity: the V-2s. You had no warning of those. At least with the V-1s you could hear a *bububu, bububu* with the fire. You could see the fire. If the war had gone on ten days longer, they might have had the atom bomb. All these things were getting up to that. The blitz began in 1940 when the French let us down at Dunkirk, and lasted until the Normandy landing.

We had bouncing bombs, too. They dropped a bomb here and it didn't stay there. It bounced over a building.

There was a great camaraderie, too. People were down there with their sleeping blankets and their bags of goodies or rations. I don't know of one case where anybody took advantage of you. Even going to the bathroom, they might try to hang a little curtain or something. It was "After you, luv." "That's all right, duck, you go." People developed terrifically high morals.

Being a dancer and a singer, I took over an empty house with my bunch of evacuees. These were very poor people. They hadn't even the little things in life. They didn't know which way to turn. Their husbands were in the war. God knows if they were dying or what. So I said, "Come on, girls, let's all get together to scrub the place out." We managed to get a rickety old piano through these rich ladies. I used to play songs and keep 'em all singin' in the afternoon while another two ladies made cups of tea and served little cookies. That cheered 'em up. We'd say, "Come on, let's have a singsong." And we turned the top floor into a playpen with Girl Scouts taking care of the babies to give these poor mothers a break. They, who had babies by day and night, with landladies who were horrible to 'em.

One time when I was evacuated, I was given a house that people had just fled. It was a lovely place. I could never have had one like it in my normal life. These very upper-class people said, "You look a nice type. We know you'll take care of it, so we'll give it to you as long as we're gone." It had a swing in the garden and everything. It was all done through an evacuee council. They commandeered any empty house. In wartime they can make laws overnight, so people who left their property had it confiscated for the duration.

It was getting near D-Day. Normandy, 1944.

They let me stay in their house an extra five years after the war, because I didn't have anyplace to come back to in London. They were a vicar and his wife, who'd lost a son in a Nazi prison camp. The old vicar had died, and this lady was going to New Zealand and live with her daughter. I paid a very minimum rent. It just paid her taxes.

At that time, you were lucky if you had a corner in somebody else's room. There were no houses for people to come back to. It was surviving as best you could. I know Americans have never had the experience of being bombed out. I don't ever wish it on them, either. But I do wish they wouldn't be so keen to get into wars, because one day it will come back on your territory and God help you. I was sorry for the Germans, too. They must have suffered. You have such silly ideas when you're young: Oh, if I could see Adolf Hitler, I'd shoot him myself tomorrow. Oh, Hitler's dead, isn't that marvelous? But that's not the end of your troubles.

When the war ended, we thought it was going to be a better world. I remember feeling so elated, I really do. I don't think I've ever had such good feelings since. I could see everybody being kind to each other 'cause we'd been through such dreadful things.

The housing was terrible. When the men came back from service and found their wives sleeping in these subway shelters and weeks went on, they took over the Savoy Hotel and became squatters. It was the best hotel in London at the time. The working people rallied around them. They went to these big hotels and the servicemen would let down buckets on ropes and we all put what bits of food we had in them. They occupied those hotels for ages. The authorities were petrified. They thought it was going to be Bolshevism or something. The squatting went on spasmodically for about six months. Then they put up prefabricated houses. They built them in one day. Every available construction worker was busy putting up these houses.

At that time, our family had no home. So my husband said he'd be a sandwich man. You know? Wear a placard in front and back with a sign and parade up and down: You have houses for the tourists, but none for your servicemen. I called a newspaper and told them this is what he planned to do. Within two days, we were offered a nice place to live.

The war took a disastrous chunk out of my life. I gave up thinking about my profession. I had a war-wounded husband and four children. I became a different personality. Before the war, I saw everything through rose-colored glasses and lived for music and my dancing. After the war, I began to study things. I had to help educate my children. I had to adjust to never ever having any money, 'cause we existed on my husband's war pension. I put behind me looking into store windows, 'cause you knew you never were going to be able to buy anything in the way of pretty clothes. Never coveting anything off anybody, because that would only make you old and hateful-looking.

It's taken a lot of maybes and pleasures from me, but I began to see people and events in a certain light. I'm always looking for the economic reason why people do this or why a government does this. It's not always nice to know. (Laughs.)

Maybe I'm pessimistic. Maybe we'll see a lovely new era come. I'm so worried now for my grandchildren. I feel so sorry for them. But then, maybe somebody should have felt sorry for me, growing up in World War Two. (Laughs.) Yet with all its horrors, it made people behave better toward each other than they thought they could.

Housewives during the war were far better cooks than they've been ever since. Can you believe that? We had so little to manage with, we became inventive. If one managed to get a little bit of rice and you had a piece of chop meat, you would mix the two together and make it spread further. If you managed any sultanas or raisins, you scotched all the bits of bread you had together with water and made a gorgeous pudding. If you managed to get some syrup and some brown sugar, if you were lucky, you could make toffee for the kids. So we did fantastic swaps.

I had a very nice lady and her husband, neighbors. She was having her son on leave and she didn't have any meat for him. But that particular day, the butcher let me have some rabbit. In wartime, we et horsemeat and whale steaks, so rabbit was a taste treat. I didn't want the rabbit, 'cause I'd rather give my small children an egg, if I could get eggs. So I took the rabbit round to her. She was so thrilled. On that particular day, her son was killed. We could have flung the rabbit anywhere, for all we cared. He was such a nice boy, a young officer, nineteen years old.

OLEG TSAKUMOV

It is a beautiful Sunday morning of June 22, 1941. The sky is clear, the day quiet. All Leningrad is in a holiday mood. It always is at this time of the year. The summer solstice has begun, when the sun does not set in Leningrad. Girls in their pretty dresses and young men in their white ice-cream pants have been walking all night long on these streets, their arms entwined, singing songs.

Suddenly, a voice on the streets' loudspeakers is saying, Vinomania! Vinomania! Attention! Attention! Hitler has attacked and his armies have crossed the Russian border around four o'clock that morning.

The siege of Leningrad was to begin on the seventh of September and go on unrelenting for nine hundred days. Nobody knows how many people in Leningrad died. It was surely a million. It may have been a million five. Almost half the people of the city died. Imagine New York or Chicago with half its people dead.

They were months of horror. The bones and remains of people at the end of the siege were stacked higher than buildings.

In the winter, there is no light. No heat. It is 20 below zero. A slice of bread a day—bread made of sawdust and glue. There's no water, no transportation. How did people survive under those conditions? I don't know.

When the radio was on, the metronome tick-ticked. It was like the city's heartbeat. Without it, there was no outward sign that this city was alive.

—Harrison Salisbury, reflections on a summer day in 1982. It was shortly after we visited the mass grave at Leningrad.

A poet, living in Leningrad.

I was six when the war began. That Sunday morning, my family took me to the Pushkin Museum. After that, everything was wiped out.

What I most remember is the snow, winter, cold, fog. It eats people. The houses were like dead houses. The smoke was alive, the people were dead. The smoke came from the damaged houses, the fire bombs. One hundred thousand were dropped on Leningrad.

When I was seven, I spoke on the radio. I read a poem, "To the Victory Day." It was long before the victory. It was important for the soldiers at the front to hear this childish voice on the radio, to know that the children of Leningrad were alive. This was no less important than the projectiles. Later, much later, I read my own poem about a very young, small, skinny, very hungry boy who was so small he could walk under the table. Myself, of course.

The most difficult days were when my mother could not get up from bed to go to work. She was too weak from hunger. I went to the kindergarten by myself. With my steps as a man, it is not a far distance. To a man, they are snow heaps. To me, this little boy, they were snow mountains.

In this silent city, there came these sudden bursts of sound. The explosions. I was very frightened, and it was such a long distance to school.

We ate what you give to horses. Oats. In the summer, we picked up grass, boiled it, and ate it. It was food on our minds all the time. Morning was the best time of the day, when you get up. You think something might turn up, you might get something to eat. All the days became one long day and night. Imagine nine hundred such days. It seemed forever.

Victory day? On the ninth of May, 1945, we went to a small opera theater. It was *Iolanthe*. Suddenly the performance stopped and the director came out and said that the Germans surrendered. Everybody in the theater went to the square. I saw hundreds of thousands of people dancing, embracing each other. Tossing the soldiers in the air. They were crying and kissing each other. I was nine years old.

The Cold War

Benjamin E. Varat

The Grand Alliance was a marriage of necessity, forced into existence by the threat of Adolf Hitler. The Soviet Union had shared an enemy and nothing else with Britain and the United States. The ideological conflict between them was so irreconcilable that even during the darkest days of the war, disagreements and mistrust existed between ostensible allies. While the combined efforts of these three nations defeated the threat of fascism, their victory left little optimism that the communist and capitalist worlds could work together after the war. In light of this, it is hardly surprising that a dominant feature of the following decades was the tense, ideologically driven struggle known as the **Cold War**, which affected politics, economic development, and social development around the globe.

Origins of the Cold War

We can trace the origin of this struggle to the fundamentally incompatible postwar priorities of the United States and Great Britain, on the one hand, and Soviet Union, on the other. While Churchill and Roosevelt considered German recovery necessary for a larger European recovery, Stalin wanted Germany permanently weakened so that it could never again threaten the Soviet Union. While the democratic powers anticipated postwar freedom for the countries of Eastern Europe, the Soviet leader had no intention of loosening his military control of the areas he was seizing from the Nazis, and planned to keep them as Soviet-dominated "buffer states" that would serve to protect the Soviet Union from Western aggression. Most fundamentally, the two systems of capitalism and communism contained ideologically opposed visions of what the postwar world should look like. The result was a divided Europe: a western half recovering from the war with the help of American investment and military power, and an eastern half controlled by the closed, dark world of the Soviet Union.

During the last stages of the war, Soviet, British, and American leaders had arrived at many general agreements concerning what would happen after the war ended. Yet few of these were specific, and most of the tough decisions were put off until later. When the Nazis finally surrendered in May, 1945, the Red Army held all of Eastern Europe between the Soviet Union and the middle of Germany, while Anglo-

American forces controlled most of Western Europe. The eastern part of Germany, including the capital of Berlin was under Soviet occupation, while the western parts, and half of Berlin were held by the Allies.

Neither side was eager to loosen their hold on these territories. The Potsdam Conference in July largely confirmed this division of Europe, including the formal partition of Germany, when new American President Harry Truman and Churchill grudgingly agreed to some of Stalin's demands. Needing to give a positive public spin on the conference, Anglo-American representatives played up Stalin's statements about free elections, while no one discussed the potential long-term significance of having two massive armies each occupying half of a devastated Europe. Thus, the foundations of the Cold War were established even before Japan surrendered.

Meanwhile, during the last phases of World War Two, as the Big Three discussed the shape of the postwar world, they resurrected the idea of international government that had failed during the interwar period with the demise of the largely ineffective League of Nations. A new international body, known as the **United Nations**, emerged almost immediately following the peace, and it was dedicated to resolving matters of international concern before they got out of control. The UN charter embraced the principles of cooperation in international law, international security, economic development, social progress, human rights, and the achievement of world peace.[1] Its General Assembly, where most debate took place, had representatives from all recognized sovereign states, while much of the organization's decision-making capability lay in a smaller Security Council. In the following decades, the United Nations occasionally deployed multi-national "peacekeeping" forces to troubled areas, though they often found themselves powerless to prevent violence and atrocities. Nevertheless, the United Nations offered a useful forum for airing differences, and provided a framework for international cooperation on issues of health, education, and economic development that has undoubtedly saved and enriched the lives of millions, especially children in the developing world.

In addition, new initiatives were taking place in the area of global economics. The **Bretton Woods Agreements** of 1943, worked out by economists representing dozens of different nations, set the stage for postwar economic stability and cooperation. They developed guidelines concerning international trade and currency valuations to facilitate trade and avoid the sorts of monetary chaos that had prolonged the Great Depression. Among other achievements, Bretton Woods established two new institutions, the **International Monetary Fund** (**IMF**) and the International Bank for Reconstruction and Development (**World Bank**). Both of these were created to give financial assistance, through credit and debt restructuring, to struggling economies in order to promote overall global economic development, which they hoped would promote peace and stability through the world.

These earnest initiatives towards international cooperation enjoyed uneven success in the postwar era. Perhaps their biggest problem was the fact that neither the United Nations nor any other international body had the power to infringe on the principle of national sovereignty. While the United Nations undoubtedly created valuable opportunities for cooperation, the political leaders of individual nations could not be expected to abandon the priority of national interest even in the face of widespread international disapproval. In the postwar world, one recurrent problem was that national interest was often tied up with the intractable ideological struggle between communism and capitalism.

Soviet-American relations slowly deteriorated through the remainder of 1945 and into 1946, as Stalin consolidated his hold on Eastern Europe through intimidation and violence. Occasionally he allowed elections and nullified the results when local communist parties received little support, while some promised elections never took place at all. In other places, such as in Iran, Greece, and Turkey, provocative Soviet actions increased diplomatic tension. Since both the Soviet Union and the United States were permanent members of the Security Council, and a single veto could derail any resolution, the Security Council often was powerless to affect struggles around the globe related to the Cold War. Mutual mistrust dominated the relationship between the former allies, and from that point on, virtually every move the other side made was regarded as suspicious.

Containment

Stalin shocked the world in early February 1946 when he addressed the Soviet people to tell them that another war was on the horizon: a massive conflict between the communists and capitalists that would be started by the United States and its allies. In March, Churchill gave the Western response, the strongly-worded **Iron Curtain Speech** in which he explicitly spoke of a Soviet-enforced division of Europe. Churchill's pronouncement brought the serious disagreements that were evolving into the Cold War into high relief. Though it was clear that there was a fundamental clash of interests, Stalin puzzled the leaders of the Western democracies. What were his goals? Did he intend to act aggressively, like a Hitler, or would he work more subtly, behind the scenes, to undermine the capitalist democracies? Most importantly, after listening to his February speech, did he want World War III?

Worried that defeating Hitler had simply opened the door to Stalin's conquest of Europe, Truman began to forge a concrete strategy, known as **containment**, to deal with the apparent communist threat. He based this policy upon the analysis provided by **George Kennan**, a long-time American diplomat and historian specializing in Russia. Kennan linked Stalin's apparent paranoia to the historical Russian concern with protection from invasion and argued that Stalin's aggressiveness in Eastern Europe and elsewhere was primarily another chapter in this Russian desire for security. Furthermore, he persuaded Truman that Stalin likely hoped to avoid direct conflict with capitalist countries, relying instead on internal subversion to extend communist power in the world.

Kennan believed that the Cold War would be fought through propaganda, the success or failure of dueling economic systems, an occasional limited conflict, and the strength of one's allies; he felt that a "hot war" was unlikely if the United States handled the conflict correctly. To do so, Kennan called on the United States to build alliances with countries along the periphery of the Soviet sphere, especially those of western and southern Europe. The means to accomplish this were American economic aid and political support , which could rebuild them while discouraging the growth of communism. Eventually, he hoped, other countries around the world would recognize the advantages of democracy and capitalism, while the comparative economic inefficiency and brutality of Soviet rule would become apparent and undermine Soviet influence. Kennan was confident that if the American people and their leaders remained calm in the face of communist provocation, the Soviet Union would be dumped into the "dustbin of history" and the Cold War brought to a peaceful, successful end.[2]

Truman accepted Kennan's containment concept, which remained the foundation of American Cold War policy until the conflict itself ended in 1989. As the world's only relatively intact capitalist industrial power, the United States had the means to provide enormous economic and political support to the war-devastated European countries west of the Iron Curtain. The most important American initiative in this direction was the 1947 **Marshall Plan**, which supplied billions of reconstruction dollars to the democratic governments of Western Europe. These commitments demonstrated that the United States would not return to isolationism, as it had so disastrously after World War I, but intended to protect and support Western Europe during its time of rebuilding.

The Marshall Plan proved a remarkable success, allowing the shattered economies of Western Europe to rebuild their manufacturing capacities and put their people back to work. By the time the program ended in 1952, most of Western Europe had begun an economic expansion that would last nearly thirty years. Not only did such aid stimulate global economic growth and development, but, as Kennan had foreseen, it also undermined support for communist parties in these resurgent European democracies, which dashed Stalin's hopes of expanding communist influence in Western Europe. The Marshall Plan represented a major triumph for American foreign policy by not only revitalizing the global economy, but also strengthening global democracy, which at the outset of World War II had seemed in danger of extinction.

The United States scored another public relations success in postwar Germany. While Marshall Plan money stimulated rapid rebuilding and recovery in the three western zones of the divided nation, Stalin pillaged and impoverished the Soviet-controlled eastern zone. In mid-1948 Stalin cut off Western land access to the German capital of Berlin, located within the eastern zone, in violation of the Yalta agreements. This created a major diplomatic confrontation known as the **Berlin Crisis**. With the borders cut off, the United States and its allies refused to abandon the free citizens in the western part of Berlin by flying in supplies in a dramatic operation known as the Berlin Airlift. This defiance forced Stalin to back down. The result was the formation of the democratic nation of West Germany, which quickly turned into a thriving democracy with a powerful industrial base. Meanwhile, Stalin created East Germany, a Soviet-dominated police state that offered its citizens neither freedom nor prosperity. Divided Germany, which included a divided Berlin, provided a stark example of the fundamental differences between postwar capitalist and communist societies.

Polarization

Kennan's emphasis on economic and political support for American allies soon proved too passive for American policymakers and public opinion, which became increasingly fearful of communist hordes tearing across the globe in an orgy of slaughter and destruction. Thus, containment began to rely increasingly upon military assistance, including at times the introduction of American troops into countries seemingly threatened by communist takeover. The first hints of this change came in April 1949 at the end of the Berlin crisis, with the creation of the **North Atlantic Treaty Organization** (**NATO**), a military alliance binding together the United States, Canada, and Western Europe. NATO served as the template for a series of additional American-led security alliances that eventually spanned the globe from Latin America to the Middle East to Asia. In response, the Soviets constructed their own alliance, the **Warsaw Pact**, which essentially placed the armies of Eastern Europe directly under Soviet Red Army control and left Europe divided between two powerful military coalitions. Developments elsewhere only heightened tensions. The Soviet Union successfully tested its own atomic device in 1949, while in the same year, the Mao Zedong-led communists triumphed in the Chinese Civil War to take over the world's most populous country. The next year, the **Korean War** erupted between the communist-supported north and the UN-supported south.

As the Cold War heated up overseas, both politicians and the public in the United States became preoccupied with the supposed threat posed by domestic communist activity. From 1950 to 1954, Senator Joseph McCarthy led a highly public and destructive "witch hunt" for communist spies and traitors within the American government. Although he never actually found a communist spy of any importance, McCarthy and his cronies created mass hysteria that severely limited American policy options and further polarized international relations. Thus, when North Korea, with Soviet encouragement, attacked American-backed South Korea in late June 1950, Truman did not want to appear "soft on communism," and thus felt compelled to commit hundreds of thousands of troops to the Korean peninsula and dramatically increase defense spending. The war in Korea dragged on for three years towards an inconclusive end, while American and allied forces faced not only North Korean troops, but over a million Chinese soldiers. Stalin's death in 1953 removed a volatile element from the tense international situation, but did little to lessen the mutual mistrust between the superpowers.

By the mid-1950s, containment had evolved into a rigid set of policies, based on the threat of military force instead of the promise of economic aid and political freedom. American leaders, preoccupied with stopping the spread of global communism, began to actively promote anticommunist governments throughout the world. Meanwhile, new Soviet leader Nikita Khrushchev put together a global Soviet-led network to battle what he called "capitalist imperialism," sending military advisors, weapons, and money to sympathetic political movements around the world. The post-World War II world provided many areas of fertile ground for this ideologically driven conflict between the two "superpowers" of the U.S. and the USSR, nowhere more so than in the many newly independent nations that were emerging from decades of colonial rule.

Decolonization and Proxy Wars

Before and during World War II, nationalist movements of various sorts had emerged in many colonial territories to demand freedom from their European masters. The postwar situation provided them with opportunities to try and make political self-determination a reality, as the exhausted nations of Europe generally lacked both the resources and the will to reassert their control. The Cold War competition between capitalism and communism powerfully shaped the process of **decolonization**, where former colonies became independent nations, that was a central feature of world history from the 1940s into the 1970s.[3]

Decolonization sometimes occurred relatively peacefully, as with the British withdrawal from India or the French from Morocco and Tunisia, and sometimes after a brutal war, as with the British in Malaysia and the French in Vietnam and Algeria. In almost all cases, though, the exit of the imperial nation left a power vacuum that various local groups tried to fill. These newly independent states were already burdened by challenges that had arisen out of the colonial legacy of exploitation, and were generally economically, politically, and socially unstable. This seemed to offer opportunities for Soviet and American leaders to expand their influence. They used many new states as pawns in the superpower competition, often providing massive assistance to competing groups that further destabilized nations and even entire regions. Efforts among these newly independent countries to avoid involvement in the Cold War went nowhere. These emerging states often suffered from such poor governance and economic underdevelopment that financial offerings from a superpower were usually irresistible, even though the citizens of such nations rarely benefited from them, since much of it went to military spending or corrupt politicians. Ultimately, the combination of Cold War ambitions and the instability of these newly independent states was a toxic mixture that played out in bloody **proxy wars** within and between developing nations.

Decolonization dramatically changed societies across the developing world. Self-rule meant that political control had passed from the imperial power into indigenous (native) hands. After decades of being exploited and living as second class citizens, the peoples of the underdeveloped world believed that now they would determine their own future, one full of peace and prosperity. A boundless optimism arose, born in the belief that the national unity forged through combating and then defeating imperialism would remain intact and rocket these new countries into the modern, industrial world.

With some exceptions, however, all of this optimism proved terribly misplaced. Rather than a rapid and gentle passage into the modern world, many of these new states experienced a destructive combination of neo-imperialism, political corruption, ethnic hatred, and the Cold War. All these factors worked against development and often stalled significant progress for years. Much of the social change of the Cold War period, therefore, was not due to the modernization process, but resulted from authoritarian governments, political violence, and civil wars, all of which forced people to adapt to a world far different from the old colonial structure. Colonialism in some sense had ended, but in its place arose a set of problems that would haunt much of the underdeveloped world even after the end of the Cold War.

One problem, which manifested especially in Africa, was the ongoing economic exploitation of the new nation by its old colonial master. Although the Europeans provided substantial money and technical assistance, much of it went into modernizing the process of extracting natural resources rather than redistributing land, mechanizing farming, or developing an industrial base. Europeans saw little advantage to changing the unequal economic relationships of colonialism, since they needed these resources for their own industry, as had been the case since the second industrial revolution in the late 1800s. The ex-colonies continued to act as suppliers of cheap natural resources for the industrialized countries, who then used these resources to produce the far more lucrative finished industrial products. Foreign aid often came as loans, from the former colonial powers, organizations such as the IMF and World Bank, or from other industrialized nations. Much of this money went to the military, badly planned development projects, or corrupt politicians, which frequently resulted in crippling debt that led to even more economic dependency. Underdeveloped countries employed diplomacy and embargo threats to force the Europeans into more equitable trade and aid relationships, but homegrown industrialization was still quite difficult to achieve.

In many places, a combination of poor governance, a lack of civil society, and ethnic strife undermined national unity, which left many of these new states unstable and plagued by internal and external conflict. Africa again suffered most from these problems, both because the borders of these new countries rarely conformed to neat ethnic divisions and also because of the rapidity of decolonization. Often, the imperial power left in a hurry, relinquishing governing responsibility to an ill-prepared leadership. Once in power, the new leaders proved unable to establish political institutions that could meet the basic needs of an ethnically diverse population. Struggles for power ensued, struggles that divided the country along ethnic, linguistic, and religious fault lines. Since few of these nations possessed legal and political outlets for protest, violence became the only means for settling grievances and redistributing power and wealth.

Thus, governments rose and fell with alarming regularity in many underdeveloped countries. Often the only institution capable of imposing order was the military, but it too proved to be a source of instability, frequently overthrowing popularly elected civilian governments. Military-dominated authoritarian regimes were usually more interested in stealing the development aid and the profits from the export of natural resources than in building modern, economically independent societies.

For the most part, the Cold War only hindered the modernization process for the underdeveloped world. From Asia to the Middle East to Africa to Latin America, the U.S.-Soviet clash intensified civil strife and prevented meaningful development. For example, U.S. interference in Latin America, which stemmed from both historical and Cold War contexts, often prioritized political and economic stability over true modernization and development. Many right-wing, authoritarian regimes that worked to keep the old social order intact received substantial American support, while Soviet leaders responded by funneling money and weapons to communist guerrilla groups. The resulting conflicts between well-armed combatants left civilians in the crossfire.

Occasionally a communist victory reversed the roles, but communist governments proved even less adept than their "right-wing" counterparts at providing for their populations. Countries as diverse as Cambodia, Angola, and Nicaragua tried to follow the Soviet or Chinese communist models of industrialization, ignoring how disastrous both had been. This frequently disrupted whatever economic development already existed and set back the industrialization process by decades. American-backed anti-communist groups in many of these countries added further chaos by destabilizing such governments and creating even more misery in people's lives. The Cold War, ultimately, reinforced the problems underdeveloped countries had inherited from neo-imperialism and a lack of civil institutions.

Glimmers of hope existed, notably in Asia and Latin America, where countries had a somewhat longer experience with self-rule and ethnic divisions were less intense, but substantial progress eluded much of the developing world during this period. At the end of the Cold war, many of these newly independent countries had advanced little since they had thrown off colonial control decades earlier.

Deterrence and Détente

By the 1960s, the Iron Curtain marked a stark divide between the communist and capitalist halves of Europe, and the Berlin Wall that physically separated the former German capital had become a potent symbol of the global ideological struggle. While "proxy wars" continued to rage outside of Europe, the two coalitions stared at each other in Europe across barbed wire. Despite the obvious mutual hostility and ideological incompatibility, one intriguing element of the Cold War was the fact that the Soviets and Americans never directly took up arms against each other. Despite Stalin's grim warning in 1946, World War Three never happened.

The unlikely "peace" of the Cold War came largely from an even more unlikely source: the nuclear bomb. Hiroshima and Nagasaki had illuminated the awesome and horrifying power of atomic weapons, and by the early 1950s, American and Soviet efforts had developed hydrogen bombs, nearly five hundred times more powerful than the atomic bombs of 1945. Although the nuclear arms race drained Soviet and American coffers and sometimes panicked their populations, superpower possession of nuclear weapons led, somewhat ironically, to a certain stability in the Cold War. This was largely due to the shocking simplicity of the nuclear equation: the destruction of Washington would ensure the destruction of Moscow, and vice-versa. No rational leader would contemplate such a tradeoff. In this way, peace was guaranteed by **deterrence**, the certainty that any use of nuclear weapons would lead to an annihilating counterstrike. "Victory" in a nuclear war would be impossible, or at least so costly as to be pointless. This situation of what became known as "mutually assured destruction" left both sides largely unwilling to take risks that might result in an all-out direct war.

The two superpowers did get perilously close to a nuclear holocaust in the **Cuban Missile Crisis** of October, 1962. Khrushchev precipitated the crisis by secretly putting nuclear weapons in communist Cuba as in attempt to even the Soviet-American nuclear balance, which at that time decisively favored the U.S. President Kennedy, upon learning of the missiles, publicly proclaimed that the United States would not allow them to remain in Cuba. For several tense days, the world held its collective breath in expectation of a nuclear exchange that might dwarf the damage caused by

World War Two. Finally, Khrushchev decided not to risk a nuclear holocaust, and agreed to remove the missiles. The Cold War remained cold.[4]

In two cases, Vietnam and Afghanistan, conflicts in developing nations compelled the United States and Soviet Union, respectively, to directly deploy substantial numbers of their own troops. In each case, this intervention resulted in a long war that was costly and unpopular, and disastrous for both the superpowers and the nations where the fighting took place.

By the time the U.S. sent troops into Vietnam in 1965, the Vietnamese already had experienced decades of French colonization. This had been followed by a brutal Japanese occupation during the Second World War and an extensive war of independence against France that lasted until 1954. In that year, superpower maneuvering split Vietnam into a communist North and American-backed South, ensuring a decade of civil war before American President Lyndon Johnson decided that containing communism required a massive military commitment to South Vietnam. Eight years of fighting accomplished little beyond further massive destruction.. Although American President Richard Nixon claimed victory for democracy when he began withdrawing American troops, North Vietnam conquered the south and reunified Vietnam under communist rule in 1975.

To the surprise of some, North Vietnam's victory meant little in the Cold War. Despite the "fall" of Vietnam, no Asian countries of any significance went communist thereafter. Kennan had been proved correct: while a communist victory in an undeveloped country ultimately did not matter, the full blown American intervention in a local conflict had traumatic results at home by promoting social and political instability.

Meanwhile, the Soviet Union used much of its yearly budget on closing the substantial "missile gap" that had led to Khrushchev's dangerous gamble in the Cuban Missile Crisis. By the late 1960s, the Soviet Union achieved approximate nuclear parity equality with the U.S., opening the door to superpower negotiations on how to stop this hugely expensive arms race. The mutual recognition that the arms race could not continue led to successes at the negotiating table that characterized the relaxation of tensions known as the **Détente** period of the Cold War. Although international crises, especially in the Middle East, reminded everyone that the superpowers were still enemies, for most of the 1970s, the Soviets and Americans sought to reduce tensions. And while the Cold War showed no signs of ending, better Soviet-American relations allowed the world to breathe a little easier.

Détente, however, proved temporary. The Soviets, who had apparently learned nothing from the U.S. misadventure in Southeast Asia, jumped into their own quagmire in December 1979 when they sent one hundred thousand Red Army troops into Afghanistan. This mountainous nation, which bordered several Central Asian Soviet Republics, had experienced many difficulties over the previous century, including interference by Britain and Russia before World War I and a series of civil wars thereafter. Despite a period of stability after World War II, a stagnant economy and ethnic divisions slowly undermined societal cohesion until a full-fledged civil war finally broke out in 1978, when a Soviet-backed Marxist party took power. The Soviet troops fought changing coalitions of guerrilla armies in a region where the difficult terrain nullified their advantage in military power. Much like the Americans in Vietnam, Soviet leaders continued to pursue the unattainable goal of military victory, fearing that defeat would seriously damage their international prestige and weaken communist rule at home. The Cold War flared anew, as covert American aid supported Afghan rebels, many of whom were Islamic fundamentalists who abhorred the official atheism of Communism.

The 1980 American presidential election further inflamed the situation by bringing into office a hardcore anti-communist, Ronald Reagan, who saw the world largely in black and white terms. American/Soviet relations hit their nadir in the early 1980s with massive American defense spending and military assistance given to every anti-communist group around the world, while Reagan's anti-Soviet rhetoric echoed the blunt accusations of the McCarthy era. The Soviet regime responded in kind; their military spending further strained a teetering Soviet economy that was already reeling from inefficiency and corruption.

Vietnam and Afghanistan highlighted a basic Cold War dilemma the superpowers faced, the dilemma articulated by Kennan at the dawn of the conflict: with no actual fighting between the two main combatants, the struggle had to play out in the hearts and minds of the world population. Prestige mattered more than numbers of tanks and propaganda was as powerful as nuclear weapons. As the Cold War stretched across the globe, the United States and the Soviet Union found themselves entangled in local problems and issues that mattered little to superpower security and had little to do with communism or capitalism.

Gorbachev and the End of the Cold War

Despite the massive economic and social problems faced by the USSR by 1985 **Mikhail Gorbachev**, who took power as General Secretary of the Soviet Union in 1985, perceived them as solvable. Gorbachev, at fifty fours old much younger and more vigorous than his predecessors, attacked them with energy. He spent his first four years in power trying to make the Soviet Union a more open, prosperous society through internal reforms, reducing Cold War tensions, and ending the occupation of Afghanistan. It was a noble, well-meant effort. It also ultimately destroyed the Soviet Union.

Gorbachev's reforms at home, most notably his willingness to allow a more open society, undermined communist power in Eastern Europe where most citizens loathed the USSR's domination of their countries. Gorbachev's decision to countenance criticism and change in the Soviet Union raised a fundamental question: if the Soviet people could question their government, why couldn't the Czechs or Hungarians or East Germans do the same?

Protests against communist rule began in Eastern Europe late in 1988. By early 1989, Gorbachev made it known to the communist leadership of Eastern Europe that he would not intervene in their internal affairs, in contrast to the iron hand frequently used by earlier Soviet leaders. Without the Red Army to back them, communists quickly lost control of the situation in Poland and Hungary, resulting in open borders and free elections in each state. East Germans, taking their cue from Poland and Hungary, began massive street protests that summer, which intensified in the fall. With communist control obviously crumbling, the East German leadership ended all travel restrictions between East and West Berlin. On November 9, East and West Berliners hesitantly approached the Berlin Wall that day and found the border crossings open. With sledgehammers, saws, and bare hands, they tore pieces from this symbol of the Cold War and a massive party began on top of the wall.

In subsequent months, the communist governments in Stalin's former "buffer states" recognized the futility of clamping down on public demands for political freedoms. One by one, they liberalized their governments and created multiparty states with elections. In every case except Romania, they accomplished this without significant violence. Meanwhile, Eastern Europe's overthrow of communism encouraged the various non-Russian peoples of the Soviet Union to demand states of their own, free from Moscow's control. The Union of Soviet Socialist Republics crumbled into a collection of separate states, and, by the end of 1991, it had ceased to exist.

Gorbachev's actions ensured that the Cold War ended peacefully. He deserves tremendous praise for this outcome, but ultimately he failed in his own task: to make the Soviet Union work better. His reforms at home became increasingly frantic and incoherent as both the extent of the problems and the Soviet people's hatred of the regime became clear. With the demise of the Soviet Union, the Cold War was over, ending a chapter in history that had created a great deal of misery, but undoubtedly could have created a great deal more.

By the early 1990s, many observers hoped that the end of this communist-capitalist ideological struggle might usher in a new era of global peace. However, such optimism was not entirely warranted. Sectarian violence, often connected to religious and ethnic ideologies, continued to emerge in various corners of the globe, including the Middle East, the former Yugoslavia, and Rwanda. Meanwhile, the pace of modernization continued to quicken, though at an uneven rate that contributed to international and domestic tensions. As the new millenium dawned, it was becoming clear that few societies could effectively escape involvement in global issues, and that the fates of the diverse populations around the world were becoming linked ever more tightly together.

Notes

1. "Charter of the United Nations," *United Nations Website*, http://www.un.org/en/documents/charter/intro.shtml. Accessed 9/10/10.

2. On decolonization as a process, see John Springhal *Decolonization Since 1945: The Collapse of European Overseas Empires* (London: Palgrave MacMillan, 2001).

3. The best source for understanding Kennan's ideas is John Lewis Gaddis, *Strategies of Containment: A Critical Appraisal of Postwar American National Security Policy* (New York: Oxford University Press, 1982), 25-53.

4. Aleksandr Fursenko and Timothy Naftali, *Khrushchev's Cold War: The Inside Story of an American Adversary* (New York: W. W. Norton & Company, 2006), 465-492.

References and Suggested Readings:

Fursenko, Aleksandr and Timothy Naftali. *Khrushchev's Cold War: The Inside Story of an American Adversary*. New York: W. W. Norton & Company, 2006.

Gaddis, John Lewis. *Strategies of Containment: A Critical Appraisal of Postwar American National Security Policy*. New York: Oxford University Press, 1982.

Springhal, John. *Decolonization Since 1945: The Collapse of European Overseas Empires*. Studies in Contemporary History. London: Palgrave MacMillan, 2001.

The End of History?

Francis Fukuyama

Francis Fukuyama is deputy director of the State Department's policy planning staff and former analyst at the RAND Corporation. This article is based on a lecture presented at the University of Chicago's John M. Olin Center for Inquiry Into the Theory and Practice of Democracy. The author would like to pay special thanks to the Olin Center and to Nathan Tarcov and Allan Bloom for their support in this and many earlier endeavors. The opinions expressed in this article do not reflect those of the RAND Corporation or of any agency of the U.S. government.

In watching the flow of events over the past decade or so, it is hard to avoid the feeling that something very fundamental has happened in world history. The past year has seen a flood of articles commemorating the end of the Cold War, and the fact that "peace" seems to be breaking out in many regions of the world. Most of these analyses lack any larger conceptual framework for distinguishing between what is essential and what is contingent or accidental in world history, and are predictably superficial. If Mr. Gorbachev were ousted from the Kremlin or a new Ayatollah proclaimed the millennium from a desolate Middle Eastern capital, these same commentators would scramble to announce the rebirth of a new era of conflict.

And yet, all of these people sense dimly that there is some larger process at work, a process that gives coherence and order to the daily headlines. The twentieth century saw the developed world descend into a paroxysm of ideological violence, as liberalism contended first with the remnants of absolutism, then bolshevism and fascism, and finally an updated Marxism that threatened to lead to the ultimate apocalypse of nuclear war. But the century that began full of self-confidence in the ultimate triumph of Western liberal democracy seems at its close to be returning full circle to where it started: not to an "end of ideology" or a convergence between capitalism and socialism, as earlier predicted, but to an unabashed victory of economic and political liberalism.

The triumph of the West, of the Western *idea*, is evident first of all in the total exhaustion of viable systematic alternatives to Western liberalism. In the past decade, there have been unmistakable changes in the intellectual climate of the world's two largest communist countries, and the beginnings of significant reform movements in both. But this phenomenon extends beyond high politics and it can be seen also in the ineluctable spread of consumerist Western culture in such diverse contexts as the peasants' markets and color television sets now omnipresent throughout China, the cooperative restaurants and clothing stores opened in the past year in Moscow, the Beethoven piped into Japanese department stores, and the rock music enjoyed alike in Prague, Rangoon, and Tehran.

What we may be witnessing is not just the end of the Cold War, or the passing of a particular period of postwar history, but the end of history as such: that is, the end point of mankind's ideological evolution and the universalization of Western liberal democracy as the final form of human government. This is not to say that there will no longer be events to fill the pages of *Foreign Affair's* yearly summaries of international relations, for the victory of liberalism has occurred primarily in the realm of ideas or consciousness and is as yet incomplete in the real or material world. But there are powerful reasons for believing that it is the ideal that will govern the material world *in the long run.* To understand how this is so, we must first consider some theoretical issues concerning the nature of historical change.

I

The notion of the end of history is not an original one. Its best known propagator was Karl Marx, who believed that the direction of historical development was a purposeful one determined by the interplay of material forces, and would come to an end only with the achievement of a communist utopia that would finally resolve all prior contradictions. But the concept of history as a dialectical process with a beginning, a middle, and an end was borrowed by Marx from his great German predecessor, Georg Wilhelm Friedrich Hegel.

For better or worse, much of Hegel's historicism has become part of our contemporary intellectual baggage. The notion that mankind has progressed through a series of primitive stages of consciousness on his path to the present, and that these stages corresponded to concrete forms of social organization, such as tribal, slave-owning, theocratic, and finally democratic-egalitarian societies, has become inseparable from the modern understanding of man. Hegel was the first philosopher to speak the language of modern social science, insofar as man for him was the product of his concrete historical and social environment and not, as earlier natural right theorists would have it, a collection of more or less fixed "natural" attributes. The mastery and transformation of man's natural environment through the application of science and technology was originally not a Marxist concept, but a Hegelian one. Unlike later historicists whose historical relativism degenerated into relativism *tout court,* however, Hegel believed that history culminated in an absolute moment—a moment in which a final, rational form of society and state became victorious.

It is Hegel's misfortune to be known now primarily as Marx's precursor, and it is our misfortune that few of us are familiar with Hegel's work from direct study, but only as it has been filtered through the distorting lens of Marxism. In France, however, there has been an effort to save Hegel from his Marxist interpreters and to resurrect him as the philosopher who most correctly speaks to our time. Among those modern French interpreters of Hegel, the greatest was certainly Alexandre Kojève, a brilliant Russian emigre who taught a highly influential series of seminars in Paris in the 1930s at the *Ecole Practique des Hautes Etudes.*[1] While largely unknown in the United States, Kojève had a major impact on the intellectual life of the continent. Among his students ranged such future luminaries as Jean-Paul Sartre on the Left and Raymond Aron on the Right; postwar existentialism borrowed many of its basic categories from Hegel via Kojève.

Kojève sought to resurrect the Hegel of the *Phenomenology of Mind*, the Hegel who proclaimed history to be at an end in 1806. For as early as this Hegel saw in Napoleon's defeat of the Prussian monarchy at the Battle of Jena the victory of the ideals of the French Revolution, and the imminent universalization of the state incorporating the principles of liberty and equality. Kojève, far from rejecting Hegel in light of the turbulent events of the next century and a half, insisted that the latter had been essentially correct.[2] The Battle of Jena marked the end of history because it was at that point that the *vanguard* of humanity (a term quite familiar to Marxists) actualized the principles of the French Revolution. While there was considerable work to be done after 1806—abolishing slavery and the slave trade, extending the franchise to workers, women, blacks, and other racial minorities, etc.—the basic *principles* of the liberal democratic state could not be improved upon. The two world wars in this century and their attendant revolutions and upheavals simply had the effect of extending those principles spatially, such that the various provinces of human civilization were brought up to the level of its most advanced outposts, and of forcing those societies in Europe and North America at the vanguard of civilization to implement their liberalism more fully.

The state that emerges at the end of history is liberal insofar as it recognizes and protects through a system of law man's universal right to freedom, and democratic insofar as it exists only with the consent of the governed. For Kojève, this so-called "universal homogenous state" found real-life embodiment in the countries of postwar Western Europe—precisely those flabby, prosperous, self-satisfied, inward-looking, weak-willed states whose grandest project was nothing more heroic than the creation of the Common Market.[3] But this was only to be expected. For human history and the conflict that characterized it was based on the existence of "contradictions": primitive man's quest for mutual recognition, the dialectic of the master and slave, the transformation and mastery of nature, the struggle for the universal recognition of rights, and the dichotomy between proletarian and capitalist. But in the universal homogenous state, all prior contradictions are resolved and all human needs are satisfied. There is no struggle or conflict over "large" issues, and consequently no need for generals or statesmen; what remains is primarily economic activity. And indeed, Kojève's life was consistent with his teaching. Believing that there was no more work for philosophers as well, since Hegel (correctly understood) had already achieved absolute knowledge, Kojève left teaching after the war and spent the remainder of his life working as a bureaucrat in the European Economic Community, until his death in 1968.

To his contemporaries at mid-century, Kojève's proclamation of the end of history must have seemed like the typical eccentric solipsism of a French intellectual, coming as it did on the heels of World War II and at the very height of the Cold War.

To comprehend how Kojève could have been so audacious as to assert that history has ended, we must first of all understand the meaning of Hegelian idealism.

II

For Hegel, the contradictions that drive history exist first of all in the realm of human consciousness, i.e. on the level of ideas[4]—not the trivial election year proposals of American politicians, but ideas in the sense of large unifying world views that might best be understood under the rubric of ideology. Ideology in this sense is not restricted to the secular and explicit political doctrines we usually associate with the term, but can include religion, culture, and the complex of moral values underlying any society as well.

Hegel's view of the relationship between the ideal and the real or material worlds was an extremely complicated one, beginning with the fact that for him the distinction between the two was only apparent.[5] He did not believe that the real world conformed or could be made to conform to ideological preconceptions of philosophy professors in any simple-minded way, or that the "material" world could not impinge on the ideal. Indeed, Hegel the professor was temporarily thrown out of work as a result of a very material event, the Battle of Jena. But while Hegel's writing and thinking could be stopped by a bullet from the material world, the hand on the trigger of the gun was motivated in turn by the ideas of liberty and equality that had driven the French Revolution.

For Hegel, all human behavior in the material world, and hence all human history, is rooted in a prior state of consciousness—an idea similar to the one expressed by John Maynard Keynes when he said that the views of men of affairs were usually derived from defunct economists and academic scribblers of earlier generations. This consciousness may not be explicit and self-aware, as are modern political doctrines, but may rather take the form of religion or simple cultural or moral habits. And yet this realm of consciousness *in the long run* necessarily becomes manifest in the material world, indeed creates the material world in its own image. Consciousness is cause and not effect, and can develop autonomously from the material world; hence the real subtext underlying the apparent jumble of current events is the history of ideology.

Hegel's idealism has fared poorly at the hands of later thinkers. Marx reversed the priority of the real and the ideal completely, relegating the entire realm of consciousness—religion, art, culture, philosophy itself—to a "superstructure" that was determined entirely by the prevailing material mode of production. Yet another unfortunate legacy of Marxism is our tendency to retreat into materialist or utilitarian explanations of political or historical phenomena, and our disinclination to believe in the autonomous power of ideas. A recent example of this is Paul Kennedy's hugely successful *The Rise and Fall of the Great Powers*, which ascribes the decline of great powers to simple economic overextension. Obviously, this is true on some level: an empire whose economy is barely above the level of subsistence cannot bankrupt its treasury indefinitely. But whether a highly productive modern industrial society chooses to spend 3 or 7 percent of its GNP on defense rather than consumption is entirely a matter of that society's political priorities, which are in turn determined in the realm of consciousness.

The materialist bias of modern thought is characteristic not only of people on the Left who may be sympathetic to Marxism, but of many passionate anti-Marxists as well. Indeed, there is on the Right what one might label the *Wall Street Journal* school of deterministic materialism that discounts the importance of ideology and culture and sees man as essentially a rational, profit-maximizing individual. It is precisely this kind of individual and his pursuit of material incentives that is posited as the basis for economic life as such in economic textbooks.[6] One small example will illustrate the problematic character of such materialist views.

Max Weber begins his famous book, *The Protestant Ethic and the Spirit of Capitalism*, by noting the different economic performance of Protestant and Catholic communities throughout Europe and America, summed up in the proverb that Protestants eat well while Catholics sleep well. Weber notes that according to any economic theory that posited man as a rational profit-maximizer, raising the piece-work rate should increase labor productivity. But in fact, in many traditional peasant communities, raising the piece-work rate actually had the opposite effect of *lowering* labor productivity: at the higher rate, a peasant accustomed to earning two and one-half marks per day found he could earn the same amount by working less, and did so because he valued leisure more than income. The choices of leisure over income, or of the militaristic life of the Spartan hoplite over the wealth of the Athenian trader, or even the ascetic life of the early capitalist entrepreneur over that of a traditional leisured aristocrat, cannot possibly be explained by the impersonal working of material forces, but come preeminently out of the sphere of consciousness—what we have labeled here broadly as ideology. And indeed, a central theme of Weber's work was to prove that contrary to Marx, the material mode of production, far from being the "base," was itself a "superstructure" with roots in religion and culture, and that to understand the emergence of modern capitalism and the profit motive one had to study their antecedents in the realm of the spirit.

As we look around the contemporary world, the poverty of materialist theories of economic development is all too apparent. The *Wall Street Journal* school of deterministic materialism habitually points to the stunning economic success of Asia in the past few decades as evidence of the viability of free market economics, with the implication that all societies would see similar development were they simply to allow their populations to pursue their material self-interest freely. Surely free markets and stable political systems are a necessary precondition to capitalist economic growth. But just as surely the cultural heritage of those Far Eastern societies, the ethic of work and saving and family, a religious heritage that does not, like Islam, place restrictions on certain forms of economic behavior, and other deeply ingrained moral qualities, are equally important in explaining their economic performance.[7] And yet the intellectual weight of materialism is such that not a single respectable contemporary theory of economic development addresses consciousness and culture seriously as the matrix within which economic behavior is formed.

Failure to understand that the roots of economic behavior lie in the realm of consciousness and culture leads to the common mistake of attributing material causes of phenomena that are essentially ideal in nature. For example, it is commonplace in the West to interpret the reform movements first in China and most recently in the Soviet Union as the victory of the material over the idea—that is, a recognition that ideological incentives could not replace material ones in stimulating a highly productive modern economy, and that if one wanted to prosper one had to appeal to baser forms of self-interest. But the deep defects of socialist economies were evident thirty or forty years ago to anyone who chose to look. Why was it that these countries moved away from central planning only in the 1980s? The answer must be found in the consciousness of the elites and leaders ruling them, who decided to opt for the "Protestant" life of wealth and risk over the "Catholic" path of poverty and security.[8] That change was in no way made inevitable by the material conditions in which either country found itself on the eve of the reform, but instead came about as the result of the victory of one idea over another.[9]

For Kojève, as for all good Hegelians, understanding the underlying processes of history requires understanding developments in the realm of consciousness or ideas, since consciousness will ultimately remake the material world in its own image. To say that history ended in 1806 meant that mankind's ideological evolution ended in the ideals of the French or American Revolutions: while particular regimes in the real world might not implement these ideals fully, their theoretical truth is absolute and could not be improved upon. Hence it did not matter to Kojève that the consciousness of the postwar generation of Europeans had not been universalized throughout the world; if ideological development had in fact ended, the homogenous state would eventually become victorious throughout the material world.

I have neither the space nor, frankly, the ability to defend in depth Hegel's radical idealist perspective. The issue is not whether Hegel's system was right, but whether his perspective might uncover the problematic nature of many materialist explanations we often take for granted. This is not to deny the role of material factors as such. To a literal-minded idealist, human society can be built around any arbitrary set of principles regardless of their relationship to the material world. And in fact men have proven themselves able to endure the most extreme material hardships in the name of ideas that exist in the realm of the spirit alone, be it the divinity of cows or the nature of the Holy Trinity.[10]

But while man's very perception of the material world is shaped by his historical consciousness of it, the material world can clearly affect in return the viability of a particular state of consciousness. In particular, the spectacular abundance of advanced liberal economies and the infinitely diverse consumer culture made possible by them seem to both foster and preserve liberalism in the political sphere. I want to avoid the materialist determinism that says that liberal economics inevitably produces liberal politics, because I believe that both economics and politics presuppose an autonomous prior state of consciousness that makes them possible. But that state of consciousness that permits the growth of liberalism seems to stabilize in the way one would expect at the end of history if it is underwritten by the abundance of a modern free market economy. We might summarize the content of the universal homogenous state as liberal democracy in the political sphere combined with easy access to VCRs and stereos in the economic.

III

Have we in fact reached the end of history? Are there, in other words, any fundamental "contradictions" in human life that cannot be resolved in the context of modern liberalism, that would be resolvable by an alternative political-economic structure? If we accept the idealist premises laid out above, we must seek an answer to this question in the realm of ideology and consciousness. Our task is not to answer exhaustively the challenges to liberalism promoted by every crackpot messiah around the world, but only those that are embodied in important social or political forces and movements, and which are therefore part of world history. For our purposes, it matters very little what strange thoughts occur to people in Albania or Burkina Faso, for we are interested in what one could in some sense call the common ideological heritage of mankind.

In the past century, there have been two major challenges to liberalism, those of fascism and of communism. The former[11] saw the political weakness, materialism, anomie, and lack of community of the West as fundamental contradictions in liberal societies that could only be resolved by a strong state that forged a new "people" on the basis of national exclusiveness. Fascism was destroyed as a living ideology by World War II. This was a defeat, of course, on a very material level, but it amounted to a defeat of the idea as well. What destroyed fascism as an idea was not universal moral revulsion against it, since plenty of people were willing to endorse the idea as long as it seemed the wave of the future, but its lack of success. After the war, it seemed to most people that German fascism as well as its other European and Asian variants were bound to self-destruct. There was no material reason why new fascist movements could not have sprung up again after the war in other locales, but for the fact that expansionist ultranationalism, with its promise of unending conflict leading to disastrous military defeat, had completely lost its appeal. The ruins of the Reich chancellory as well as the atomic bombs dropped on Hiroshima and Nagasaki killed this ideology on the level of consciousness as well as materially, and all of the proto-fascist movements spawned by the German and Japanese examples like the Peronist movement in Argentina or Subhas Chandra Bose's Indian National Army withered after the war.

The ideological challenge mounted by the other great alternative to liberalism, communism, was far more serious. Marx, speaking Hegel's language, asserted that liberal society contained a fundamental contradiction that could not be resolved within its context, that between capital and labor, and this contradiction has constituted the chief accusation against liberalism ever since. But surely, the class issue has actually been successfully resolved in the West. As Kojève (among others) noted, the egalitarianism of modern America represents the essential achievement of the classless society envisioned by Marx. This is not to say that there are not rich people and poor people in the United States, or that the gap between them has not grown in recent years. But the root causes of economic inequality do not have to do with the underlying legal and social structure of our society, which remains fundamentally egalitarian and moderately redistributionist, so much as with the cultural and social characteristics of the groups that make it up, which are in turn the historical legacy of premodern conditions. Thus black poverty in the United States is not the inherent product of liberalism, but is rather the "legacy of slavery and racism" which persisted long after the formal abolition of slavery.

As a result of the receding of the class issue, the appeal of communism in the developed Western world, it is safe to say, is lower today than any time since the end of the First World War. This can be measured in any number of ways: in the declining membership and electoral pull of the major European communist parties, and their overtly revisionist programs; in the corresponding electoral success of conservative parties from Britain and Germany to the United States and Japan, which are unabashedly pro-market and anti-statist; and in an intellectual climate whose most "advanced" members no longer believe that bourgeois society is something that ultimately needs to be overcome. This is not to say that the opinions of progressive intellectuals in Western countries are not deeply pathological in any number of ways. But those who believe that the future must inevitably be socialist tend to be very old, or very marginal to the real political discourse of their societies.

One may argue that the socialist alternative was never terribly plausible for the North Atlantic world, and was sustained for the last several decades primarily by its success outside of this region. But it is precisely in the non-European world that one is most struck by the occurrence of major ideological transformations. Surely the most remarkable changes have occurred in Asia. Due to the strength and adaptability of the indigenous cultures there, Asia became a battleground for a variety of imported Western ideologies early in this century. Liberalism in Asia was a very weak reed in the period after World War I; it is easy today to forget how gloomy Asia's political future looked as recently as ten or fifteen years ago. It is easy to forget as well how momentous the outcome of Asian ideological struggles seemed for world political development as a whole.

The first Asian alternative to liberalism to be decisively defeated was the fascist one represented by Imperial Japan. Japanese fascism (like its German version) was defeated by the force of American arms in the Pacific war, and liberal democracy was imposed on Japan by a victorious United States. Western capitalism and political liberalism when transplanted to Japan were adapted and transformed by the Japanese in such a way as to be scarcely recognizable.[12] Many Americans are now aware that Japanese industrial organization is very different from that prevailing in the United States or Europe, and it is questionable what relationship the factional maneuvering that takes place with the governing Liberal Democratic Party bears to democracy. Nonetheless, the very fact that the essential elements of economic and political liberalism have been so successfully grafted onto uniquely Japanese traditions and institutions guarantees their survival in the long run. More important is the contribution that Japan has made in turn to world history by following in the footsteps of the United States to create a truly universal consumer culture that has become both a symbol and an underpinning of the universal homogenous state. V. S. Naipaul travelling in Khomeini's Iran shortly after the evolution noted the omnipresent signs advertising the products of Sony, Hitachi, and JVC, whose appeal remained virtually irresistible and gave the lie to the regime's pretensions of restoring a state based on the rule of the *Shariah*. Desire for access to the consumer culture, created in large measure by Japan, has played a crucial role in fostering the spread of economic liberalism throughout Asia, and hence in promoting political liberalism as well.

The economic success of the other newly industrialized countries (NICs) in Asia following on the example of Japan is by now a familiar story. What is important from a Hegelian standpoint is that political liberalism has been following economic liberalism, more slowly than many had hoped but with seeming inevitability. Here again we see the victory of the idea of the universal homogenous state. South Korea had developed into a modern, urbanized society with an increasingly large and well-educated middle class that could not possibly be isolated from the larger democratic trends around them. Under these circumstances it seemed intolerable to a large part of this population that it should be ruled by an anachronistic military regime while Japan, only a decade or so ahead in economic terms, had parliamentary institutions for over forty years. Even the former socialist regime in Burma, which for so many decades existed in dismal isolation from the larger trends dominating Asia, was buffeted in the past year by pressures to liberalize both its economy and political system. It is said that unhappiness with strongman Ne Win began when a senior Burmese officer went to Singapore for medical treatment and broke down crying when he saw how far socialist Burma had been left behind by its ASEAN neighbors.

But the power of the liberal idea would seem much less impressive if it had not infected the largest and oldest culture in Asia, China. The simple existence of communist China created an alternative pole of ideological attraction, and as such constituted a threat to liberalism. But the past fifteen years have seen an almost total discrediting of Marxism-Leninism as an economic system. Beginning with the famous third plenum of the Tenth Central Committee in 1978, the Chinese Communist party set about decollectivizing agriculture for the 800 million Chinese who still lived in the countryside. The role of the state in agriculture was reduced to that of a tax collector, while production of consumer goods was sharply increased in order to give peasants a taste of the universal homogenous state and thereby an incentive to work. The reform doubled Chinese grain output in only five years, and in the process created for Deng Xiao-ping a solid political base from which he was able to extend the reform to other parts of the economy. Economic statistics do not begin to describe the dynamism, initiative, and openness evident in China since the reform began.

China could not now be described in any way as a liberal democracy. At present, no more than 20 percent of its economy has been marketized, and most importantly it continues to be ruled by a self-appointed Communist party which has given no hint of wanting to devolve power. Deng has made none of Gorbachev's promises regarding democratization of the political system and there is no Chinese equivalent of *glasnost*. The Chinese leadership has in fact been much more circumspect in criticizing Mao and Maoism than Gorbachev with respect to Brezhnev and Stalin, and the regime continues to pay lip service to Marxism-Leninism as its ideological underpinning. But anyone familiar with the outlook and behavior of the new technocratic elite now governing China knows that Marxism and ideological principle have become virtually irrelevant as guides to policy, and that bourgeois consumerism has a real meaning in that country for the first time since the revolution. The various slowdowns in the pace of reform, the campaigns against "spiritual pollution" and crackdowns on political dissent are more properly seen as tactical adjustments made in the process of managing what is an extraordinarily difficult political transition. By ducking the question of political reform while putting the economy on a new footing,

Deng has managed to avoid the breakdown of authority that has accompanied Gorbachev's *perestroika*. Yet the pull of the liberal idea continues to be very strong as economic power devolves and the economy becomes more open to the outside world. There are currently over 20,000 Chinese students studying in the U.S. and other Western countries, almost all of them the children of the Chinese elite. It is hard to believe that when they return home to run the country they will be content for China to be the only country in Asia unaffected by the larger democratizing trend. The student demonstrations in Beijing that broke out first in December 1986 and recurred recently on the occasion of Hu Yao-bang's death were only the beginning of what will inevitably by mounting pressure for change in the political system as well.

What is important about China from the standpoint of world history is not the present state of the reform or even its future prospects. The central issue is the fact that the People's Republic of China can no longer act as a beacon for illiberal forces around the world, whether they be guerrillas in some Asian jungle or middle class students in Paris. Maoism, rather than being the pattern for Asia's future, became an anachronism, and it was the mainland Chinese who in fact were decisively influenced by the prosperity and dynamism of their overseas co-ethnics—the ironic ultimate victory of Taiwan.

Important as these changes in China have been, however, it is developments in the Soviet Union—the original "homeland of the world proletariat"—that have put the final nail in the coffin of the Marxist-Leninist alternative to liberal democracy. It should be clear that in terms of formal institutions, not much has changed in the four years since Gorbachev has come to power: free markets and the cooperative movement represent only a small part of the Soviet economy, which remains centrally planned; the political system is still dominated by the Communist party, which has only begun to democratize internally and to share power with other groups; the regime continues to assert that it is seeking only to modernize socialism and that its ideological basis remains Marxism-Leninism; and, finally, Gorbachev faces a potentially powerful conservative opposition that could undo many of the changes that have taken place to date. Moreover, it is hard to be too sanguine about the chances for success of Gorbachev's proposed reforms, either in the sphere of economics or politics. But my purpose here is not to analyze events in the short-term, or to make predictions for policy purposes, but to look at underlying trends in the sphere of ideology and consciousness. And in that respect, it is clear that an astounding transformation has occurred.

Emigres from the Soviet Union have been reporting for at least the last generation now that virtually nobody in that country truly believed in Marxism-Leninism any longer, and that this was nowhere more true than in the Soviet elite, which continued to mouth Marxist slogans out of sheer cynicism. The corruption and decadence of the late Brezhnev-era Soviet state seemed to matter little, however, for as long as the state itself refused to throw into question any of the fundamental principles underlying Soviet society, the system was capable of functioning adequately out of sheer inertia and could even muster some dynamism in the realm of foreign and defense policy. Marxism-Leninism was like a magical incantation which, however absurd and devoid of meaning, was the only common basis on which the elite could agree to rule Soviet society.

What has happened in the four years since Gorbachev's coming to power is a revolutionary assault on the most fundamental institutions and principles of Stalinism, and their replacement by other principles which do not amount to liberalism *per se* but whose only connecting thread is liberalism. This is most evident in the economic sphere, where the reform economists around Gorbachev have become steadily more radical in their support for free markets, to the point where some like Nikolai Shmelev do not mind being compared in public to Milton Friedman. There is a virtual consensus among the currently dominant school of Soviet economists now that central planning and the command system of allocation are the root cause of economic inefficiency, and that if the Soviet system is ever to heal itself, it must permit free and decentralized decision-making with respect to investment, labor, and prices. After a couple of initial years of ideological confusion, these principles have finally been incorporated into policy with the promulgation of new laws on enterprise autonomy, cooperatives, and finally in 1988 on lease arrangements and family farming. There are, of course, a number of fatal flaws in the current implementation of the reform, most notably the absence of a thoroughgoing price reform. But the problem is no longer a *conceptual* one. Gorbachev and his lieutenants seem to understand the economic logic of marketization well enough, but like the leaders of a Third World country facing the IMF, are afraid of the social consequences of ending consumer subsidies and other forms of dependence on the state sector.

In the political sphere, the proposed changes to the Soviet constitution, legal system, and party rules amount to much less than the establishment of a liberal state. Gorbachev has spoken of democratization primarily in the sphere of internal party affairs, and has shown little intention of ending the Communist party's monopoly of power; indeed, the political reform seeks to legitimize and therefore strengthen the CPSU's rule.[13] Nonetheless, the general principles underlying many of the reforms—that the people should be truly responsible for their own affairs, that higher political bodies should be answerable to lower ones, and not vice versa, that the rule of law should prevail over arbitrary police actions, with separation of powers and an independent judiciary, that there should be legal protection for property rights, the need for open discussion of public issues and the right of public dissent, the empowering of the Soviets as a forum in which the whole Soviet people can participate, and of a political culture that is more tolerant and pluralistic—come from a source fundamentally alien to the USSR's Marxist-Leninist tradition, even if they are incompletely articulated and poorly implemented in practice.

Gorbachev's repeated assertions that he is doing no more than trying to restore the original meaning of Leninism are themselves a kind of Orwellian doublespeak. Gorbachev and his allies have consistently maintained that intraparty democracy was somehow the essence of Leninism, and that the various liberal practices of open debate, secret ballot elections, and rule of law were all part of the Leninist heritage, corrupted only later by Stalin. While almost anyone would look good compared to Stalin, drawing so sharp a line between Lenin and his successor is questionable. The essence of Lenin's democratic centralism was centralism, not democracy; that is, the absolutely rigid, monolithic, and disciplined dictatorship of a hierarchically organized vanguard Communist party, speaking in the name of the *demos*. All of Lenin's vicious polemics against Karl Kautsky, Rosa Luxemburg, and various other

Menshevik and Social Democratic rivals, not to mention his contempt for "bourgeois legality" and freedoms, centered around his profound conviction that a revolution could not be successfully made by a democratically run organization.

Gorbachev's claim that he is seeking to return to the true Lenin is perfectly easy to understand: having fostered a thorough denunciation of Stalinism and Brezhnevism as the root of the USSR's present predicament, he needs some point in Soviet history on which to anchor the legitimacy of the CPSU's continued rule. But Gorbachev's tactical requirements should not blind us to the fact that the democratizing and decentralizing principles which he has enunciated in both the economic and political spheres are highly subversive of some of the most fundamental precepts of both Marxism and Leninism. Indeed, if the bulk of the present economic reform proposals were put into effect, it is hard to know how the Soviet economy would be more socialist than those of other Western countries with large public sectors.

The Soviet Union could in no way be described as a liberal or democratic country now, nor do I think that it is terribly likely that *perestroika* will succeed such that the label will be thinkable any time in the near future. But at the end of history it is not necessary that all societies become successful liberal societies, merely that they end their ideological pretensions of representing different and higher forms of human society. And in this respect I believe that something very important has happened in the Soviet Union in the past few years: the criticisms of the Soviet system sanctioned by Gorbachev have been so thorough and devastating that there is very little chance of going back to either Stalinism or Brezhnevism in any simple way. Gorbachev has finally permitted people to say what they had privately understood for many years, namely, that the magical incantations of Marxism-Leninism were nonsense, that Soviet socialism was not superior to the West in any respect but was in fact a monumental failure. The conservative opposition in the USSR, consisting both of simple workers afraid of unemployment and inflation and of party officials fearful of losing their jobs and privileges, is outspoken and may be strong enough to force Gorbachev's ouster in the next few years. But what both groups desire is tradition, order, and authority; they manifest no deep commitment to Marxism-Leninism, except insofar as they have invested much of their own lives in it.[14] For authority to be restored in the Soviet Union after Gorbachev's demolition work, it must be on the basis of some new and vigorous ideology which has not yet appeared on the horizon.

If we admit for the moment that the fascist and communist challenges to liberalism are dead, are there any other ideological competitors left? Or put another way, are there contradictions in liberal society beyond that of class that are not resolvable? Two possibilities suggest themselves, those of religion and nationalism.

The rise of religious fundamentalism in recent years within the Christian, Jewish, and Muslim traditions has been widely noted. One is inclined to say that the revival of religion in some way attests to a broad unhappiness with the impersonality and spiritual vacuity of liberal consumerist societies. Yet while the emptiness at the core of liberalism is most certainly a defect in the ideology—indeed, a flaw that one does not need the perspective of religion to recognize[15]—it is not at all clear that it is remediable through politics. Modern liberalism itself was historically a consequence of the weakness of religiously-based societies which, failing to agree on the nature of the good life, could not provide even the minimal preconditions of peace and stability. In the contemporary world only Islam has offered a theocratic state as a political alternative to both liberalism and communism. But the doctrine has little appeal for non-Muslims, and it is hard to believe that the movement will take on any universal significance. Other less organized religious impulses have been successfully satisfied within the sphere of personal life that is permitted in liberal societies.

The other major "contradiction" potentially unresolvable by liberalism is the one posed by nationalism and other forms of racial and ethnic consciousness. It is certainly true that a very large degree of conflict since the Battle of Jena has had its roots in nationalism. Two cataclysmic world wars in this century have been spawned by the nationalism of the developed world in various guises, and if those passions have been muted to a certain extent in postwar Europe, they are still extremely powerful in the Third World. Nationalism has been a threat to liberalism historically in Germany, and continues to be one in isolated parts of "post-historical" Europe like Northern Ireland.

But it is not clear that nationalism represents an irreconcilable contradiction in the heart of liberalism. In the first place, nationalism is not one single phenomenon but several, ranging from mild cultural nostalgia to the highly organized and elaborately articulated doctrine of National Socialism. Only systematic nationalisms of the latter sort can qualify as a formal ideology on the level of liberalism or communism. The vast majority of the world's nationalist movements do not have a political program beyond the negative desire of independence *from* some other group or people, and do not offer anything like a comprehensive agenda for socio-economic organization. As such, they are compatible with doctrines and ideologies that do offer such agendas. While they may constitute a source of conflict for liberal societies, this conflict does not arise from liberalism itself so much as from the fact that the liberalism in question is incomplete. Certainly a great deal of the world's ethnic and nationalist tension can be explained in terms of peoples who are forced to live in unrepresentative political systems that they have not chosen.

While it is impossible to rule out the sudden appearance of new ideologies or previously unrecognized contradictions in liberal societies, then, the present world seems to confirm that the fundamental principles of socio-political organization have not advanced terribly far since 1806. Many of the wars and revolutions fought since that time have been undertaken in the name of ideologies which claimed to be more advanced than liberalism, but whose pretensions were ultimately unmasked by history. In the meantime, they have helped to spread the universal homogenous state to the point where it could have a significant effect on the overall character of international relations.

IV

What are the implications of the end of history for international relations? Clearly, the vast bulk of the Third World remains very much mired in history, and will be a terrain of conflict for many years to come. But let us focus for the time being on the larger and more developed states of the world who after all account for the greater part of world politics. Russia and China are not likely to join the developed nations of the West as liberal societies any time in the foreseeable future, but suppose for a moment that Marxism-Leninism ceases to be a factor driving the foreign policies of these states—a prospect which, if not yet here, the last few years have made a real possibility. How will the overall characteristics of a de-ideologized world differ from those of the one with which we are familiar at such a hypothetical juncture?

The most common answer is—not very much. For there is a very widespread belief among many observers of international relations that underneath the skin of ideology is a hard core of great power national interest that guarantees a fairly high level of competition and conflict between nations. Indeed, according to one academically popular school of international relations theory, conflict inheres in the international system as such, and to understand the prospects for conflict one must look at the shape of the system—for example, whether it is bipolar or multipolar—rather than at the specific character of the nations and regimes that constitute it. This school in effect applies a Hobbesian view of politics to international relations, and assumes that aggression and insecurity are universal characteristics of human societies rather than the product of specific historical circumstances.

Believers in this line of thought take the relations that existed between the participants in the classical nineteenth century European balance of power as a model for what a de-ideologized contemporary world would look like. Charles Krauthammer, for example, recently explained that if as a result of Gorbachev's reforms the USSR is shorn of Marxist-Leninist ideology, its behavior will revert to that of nineteenth century imperial Russia.[16] While he finds this more reassuring than the threat posed by a communist Russia, he implies that there will still be a substantial degree of competition and conflict in the international system, just as there was say between Russia and Britain or Wilhelmine Germany in the last century. This is, of course, a convenient point of view for people who want to admit that something major is changing in the Soviet Union, but do not want to accept responsibility for recommending the radical policy redirection implicit in such a view. But is it true?

In fact, the notion that ideology is a superstructure imposed on a substratum of permanent great power interest is a highly questionable proposition. For the way in which any state defines its national interest is not universal but rests on some kind of prior ideological basis, just as we saw that economic behavior is determined by a prior state of consciousness. In this century, states have adopted highly articulated doctrines with explicit foreign policy agendas legitimizing expansionism, like Marxism-Leninism or National Socialism.

The Expansionist and competitive behavior of nineteenth-century European states rested on no less ideal a basis; it just so happened that the ideology driving it was less explicit than the doctrines of the twentieth century. For one thing, most liberal European societies were illiberal insofar as they believed in the legitimacy of imperialism, that is, the right of one nation to rule over other nations without regard for the wishes of the ruled. The justifications for imperialism varied from nation to nation, from a crude belief in the legitimacy of force, particularly when applied to non-Europeans, to the White Man's Burden and Europe's Christianizing mission, to the desire to give people of color access to the culture of Rabelais and Moliere. But whatever the particular ideological basis, every "developed" country believed in the acceptability of higher civilizations ruling lower ones—including, incidentally, the United States with regard to the Philippines. This led to a drive for pure territorial aggrandizement in the latter half of the century and played no small role in causing the Great War.

The radical and deformed outgrowth of nineteenth-century imperialism was German fascism, an ideology which justified Germany's right not only to rule over non-European peoples, but over *all* non-German ones. But in retrospect it seems that Hitler represented a diseased bypath in the general course of European development, and since his fiery defeat, the legitimacy of any kind of territorial aggrandizement has been thoroughly discredited.[17] Since the Second World War, European nationalism has been defanged and shorn of any real relevance to foreign policy, with the consequence that the nineteenth-century model of great power behavior has become a serious anachronism. The most extreme form of nationalism that any Western European state has mustered since 1945 has been Gaullism, whose self-assertion has been confined largely to the realm of nuisance politics and culture. International life for the part of the world that has reached the end of history is far more preoccupied with economics than with politics or strategy.

The developed states of the West do maintain defense establishments and in the post-war period have competed vigorously for influence to meet a worldwide communist threat. This behavior has been driven, however, by an external threat from states that possess overtly expansionist ideologies, and would not exist in their absence. To take the "neo-realist" theory seriously, one would have to believe that "natural" competitive behavior would reassert itself among the OECD states were Russia and China to disappear from the face of the earth. That is, West Germany and France would arm themselves against each other as they did in the 1930s, Australia and New Zealand would send military advisers to block each others' advances in Africa, and the U.S.-Canadian border would become fortified. Such a prospect is, of course, ludicrous: minus Marxist-Leninist ideology, we are far more likely to see the "Common Marketization" of world politics than the disintegration of the EEC into nineteenth-century competitiveness. Indeed, as our experience in dealing with Europe on matters such as terrorism or Libya prove, they are much further gone than we down the road that denies the legitimacy of the use of force in international politics, even in self-defense.

The automatic assumption that Russia shorn of its expansionist communist ideology should pick up where the czars left off just prior to the Bolshevik Revolution is therefore a curious one. It assumes that the evolution of human consciousness has stood still in the meantime, and that the Soviets, while picking up currently fashionable ideas in the realm of economics, will return to foreign policy views a century out of date in the rest of Europe. This is certainly not what happened to China after it began its reform process. Chinese competitiveness and expansionism on the world scene have virtually disappeared: Beijing no longer sponsors Maoist insurgencies or tries to cultivate influence in distant African countries as it did in the 1960s. This is not to say that there are not troublesome aspects to contemporary Chinese foreign policy, such as the reckless sale of ballistic missile technology in the Middle East; and the PRC continues to manifest traditional great power behavior in the sponsorship of the Khmer Rouge against Vietnam. But the former is explained by commercial motives and the latter is a vestige of earlier ideologically-based rivalries. The new China far more resembles Gaullist France than pre-World War I Germany.

The real question for the future, however, is the degree to which Soviet elites have assimilated the consciousness of the universal homogenous state that is post-Hitler Europe. From their writings and from my own personal contacts with them, there is no question in my mind that the liberal Soviet intelligentsia rallying around Gorbachev has arrived at the end-of-history view in a remarkably short time, due in no small measure to the contacts they have had since the Brezhnev era with the largest European civilization around them. "New political thinking," the general rubric for their views, describes a world dominated by economic concerns, in which there are no ideological grounds for major conflict between nations, and in which, consequently, the use of military force becomes less legitimate. As Foreign Minister Shevardnadze put it in mid-1988:

> The struggle between two opposing systems is no longer a determining tendency of the present-day era. At the modern stage, the ability to build up material wealth at an accelerated rate on the basis of front-ranking science and high-level techniques and technology, and to distribute it fairly, and through joint efforts to restore and protect the resources necessary for mankind's survival acquires decisive importance.[18]

The post-historical consciousness represented by "new thinking" is only one possible future for the Soviet Union, however. There has always been a very strong current of great Russian chauvinism in the Soviet Union, which has found freer expression since the advent of *glasnost*. It may be possible to return to traditional Marxism-Leninism for a while as a simple rallying point for those who want to restore the authority that Gorbachev has dissipated. But as in Poland, Marxism-Leninism is dead as a mobilizing ideology: under its banner people cannot be made to work harder, and its adherents have lost confidence in themselves. Unlike the propagators of traditional Marxism-Leninism, however, ultranationalists in the USSR believe in their Slavophile cause passionately, and one gets the sense that the fascist alternative is not one that has played itself out entirely there.

The Soviet Union, then, is at a fork in the road: it can start down the path that was staked out by Western Europe over forty-five years ago, a path that most of Asia has followed, or it can realize its own uniqueness and remain stuck in history. The choice it makes will be highly important for us, given the Soviet Union's size and military strength, for that power will continue to preoccupy us and slow our realization that we have already emerged on the other side of history.

V

The passing of Marxism-Leninism first from China and then from the Soviet Union will mean its death as a living ideology of world historical significance. For while there may be some isolated true believers left in places like Managua, Pyongyang, or Cambridge, Massachusetts, the fact that there is not a single large state in which it is a going concern undermines completely its pretensions to being in the vanguard of human history. And the death of this ideology means the growing "Common Marketization" of international relations, and the diminution of the likelihood of large-scale conflict between states.

This does not by any means imply the end of international conflict *per se*. For the world at that point would be divided between a part that was historical and a part that was post-historical. Conflict between states still in history, and between those states and those at the end of history, would still be possible. There would still be a high and perhaps rising level of ethnic and nationalist violence, since those are impulses incompletely played out, even in parts of the post-historical world. Palestinians and Kurds, Sikhs and Tamils, Irish Catholics and Walloons, Armenians and Azeris, will continue to have their unresolved grievances. This implies that terrorism and wars of national liberation will continue to be an important item on the international agenda. But large-scale conflict must involve large states still caught in the grip of history, and they are what appear to be passing from the scene.

The end of history will be a very sad time. The struggle for recognition, the willingness to risk one's life for a purely abstract goal, the worldwide ideological struggle that called forth daring, courage, imagination, and idealism, will be replaced by economic calculation, the endless solving of technical problems, environmental concerns, and the satisfaction of sophisticated consumer demands. In the post-historical period there will be neither art nor philosophy, just the perpetual caretaking of the museum of human history. I can feel in myself, and see in others around me, a powerful nostalgia for the time when history existed. Such nostalgia, in fact, will continue to fuel competition and conflict even in the post-historical world for some time to come. Even though I recognize its inevitability, I have the most ambivalent feelings for the civilization that has been created in Europe since 1945, with its north Atlantic and Asian offshoots. Perhaps this very prospect of centuries of boredom at the end of history will serve to get history started once again.

Notes

1. Kojève's best-known work is his *Introduction à la lecture de Hegel* (Paris: Editions Gallimard, 1947), which is a transcript of the *Ecole Practique* lectures from the 1930s. This book is available in English entitled *Introduction to the Reading of Hegel* arranged by Raymond Queneau, edited by Allan Bloom, and translated by James Nichols (New York: Basic Books, 1969).

2. In this respect Kojève stands in sharp contrast to contemporary German interpreters of Hegel like Herbert Marcuse who, being more sympathetic to Marx, regarded Hegel ultimately as an historically bound and incomplete philosopher.

3. Kojève alternatively identified the end of history with the postwar "American way of life," toward which he thought the Soviet Union was moving as well.

4. This notion was expressed in the famous aphorism from the preface to the *Philosophy of History* to the effect that "everything that is rational is real, and everything that is real is rational."

5. Indeed, for Hegel the very dichotomy between the ideal and material worlds was itself only an apparent one that was ultimately overcome by the self-conscious subject; in his system, the material world is itself only an aspect of mind.

6. In fact, modern economists, recognizing that man does not always behave as a *profit*-maximizer, posit a "utility" function, utility being either income or some other good that can be maximized: leisure, sexual satisfaction, or the pleasure of philosophizing. That profit must be replaced with a value like utility indicates the cogency of the idealist perspective.

7. One need look no further than the recent performance of Vietnamese immigrants in the U.S. school system when compared to their black or Hispanic classmates to realize that culture and consciousness are absolutely crucial to explain not only economic behavior but virtually every other important aspect of life as well.

8. I understand that a full explanation of the origins of the reform movements in China and Russia is a good deal more complicated than this simple formula would suggest. The Soviet reform, for example, was motivated in good measure by Moscow's sense of *insecurity* in the technological-military realm. Nonetheless, neither country on the eve of its reforms was in such a state of *material* crisis that one could have predicted the surprising reform paths ultimately taken.

9. It is still not clear whether the Soviet peoples are as "Protestant" as Gorbachev and will follow him down that path.

10. The internal politics of the Byzantine Empire at the time of Justinian revolved around a conflict between the so-called monophysites and monothelites, who believed that the unity of the Holy Trinity was alternatively one of nature or of will. This conflict corresponded to some extent to one between proponents of different racing teams in the Hippodrome in Byzantium and led to a not insignificant level of political violence. Modern historians would tend to seek the roots of such conflicts in antagonisms between social classes or some other modern economic category, being unwilling to believe that men would kill each other over the nature of the Trinity.

11. I am not using the term "fascism" here in its most precise sense, fully aware of the frequent misuse of this term to denounce anyone to the right of the user. "Fascism" here denotes any organized ultra-nationalist movement with universalistic pretensions—not universalistic with regard to its nationalism, of course, since the latter is exclusive by definition, but with regard to the movement's belief in its right to rule other people. Hence Imperial Japan would qualify as fascist while former strongman Stoessner's Paraguay or Pinochet's Chile would not. Obviously fascist ideologies cannot be universalistic in the sense of Marxism or liberalism, but the structure of the doctrine can be transferred from country to country.

12. I use the example of Japan with some caution, since Kojève late in his life came to conclude that Japan, with its culture based on purely formal arts, proved that the universal homogenous state was not victorious and that history had perhaps not ended. See the long note at the end of the second edition of *Introduction à la Lecture de Hegel*, 462–3.

13. This is not true in Poland and Hungary, however, whose Communist parties have taken moves toward true power-sharing and pluralism.

14. This is particularly true of the leading Soviet conservative, former Second Secretary Yegor Ligachev, who has publicly recognized many of the deep defects of the Brezhnev period.

15. I am thinking particularly of Rousseau and the Western philosophical tradition that flows from him that was highly critical of Lockean or Hobbesian liberalism, though one could criticize liberalism from the standpoint of classical political philosophy as well.

16. See his article, "Beyond the Cold War," *New Republic*, December 19, 1988.

17. It took European colonial powers like France several years after the war to admit the illegitimacy of their empires, but decolonialization was an inevitable consequence of the Allied victory which had been based on the promise of a restoration of democratic freedoms.

18. *Vestnik Ministerstva Inostrannikh Del SSSR* no. 15 (August 1988), 27–46. "New thinking" does of course serve a propagandistic purpose in persuading Western audiences of Soviet good intentions. But the fact that it is good propaganda does not mean that its formulators do not take many of its ideas seriously.

Concerning Violence

Frantz Fanon

National liberation, national renaissance, the restoration of nationhood to the people, commonwealth: whatever maybe the headings used or the new formulas introduced, decolonization is always a violent phenomenon. At whatever level we study it—relationships between individuals, new names for sports clubs, the human admixture at cocktail parties, in the police, on the directing boards of national or private banks—decolonization is quite simply the replacing of a certain "species" of men by another "species" of men. Without any period of transition, there is a total, complete, and absolute substitution. It is true that we could equally well stress the rise of a new nation, the setting up of a new state, its diplomatic relations, and its economic and political trends. But we have precisely chosen to speak of that kind of tabula rasa which characterizes at the outset all decolonization. Its unusual importance is that it constitutes, from the very first day, the minimum demands of the colonized. To tell the truth, the proof of success lies in a whole social structure being changed from the bottom up. The extraordinary importance of this change is that it is willed, called for, demanded. The need for this change exists in its crude state, impetuous and compelling, in the consciousness and in the lives of the men and women who are colonized. But the possibility of this change is equally experienced in the form of a terrifying future in the consciousness of another "species" of men and women: the colonizers.

Decolonization, which sets out to change the order of the world, is, obviously, a program of complete disorder. But it cannot come as a result of magical practices, nor of a natural shock, nor of a friendly understanding. Decolonization, as we know, is a historical process: that is to say that it cannot be understood, it cannot become intelligible nor clear to itself except in the exact measure that we can discern the movements which give it historical form and content. Decolonization is the meeting of two forces, opposed to each other by their very nature, which in fact owe their originality to that sort of substantification which results from and is nourished by the situation in the colonies. Their first encounter was marked by violence and their existence together—that is to say the exploitation of the native by the settler—was carried on by dint of a great array of bayonets and cannons. The settler and the native are old acquaintances. In fact, the settler is right when he speaks of knowing "them" well. For it is the settler who has brought the native into existence and who perpetuates his existence. The settler owes the fact of his very existence, that is to say, his property, to the colonial system.

Decolonization never takes place unnoticed, for it influences individuals and modifies them fundamentally. It transforms spectators crushed with their inessentiality into privileged actors, with the grandiose glare of history's floodlights upon them. It brings a natural rhythm into existence, introduced by new men, and with it a new language and a new humanity. Decolonization is the veritable creation of new men. But this creation owes nothing of its legitimacy to any supernatural power; the "thing" which has been colonized becomes man during the same process by which it frees itself.

In decolonization, there is therefore the need of a complete calling in question of the colonial situation. If we wish to describe it precisely, we might find it in the well-known words: "The last shall be first and the first last." Decolonization is the putting into practice of this sentence. That is why, if we try to describe it, all decolonization is successful.

The naked truth of decolonization evokes for us the searing bullets and bloodstained knives which emanate from it. For if the last shall be first, this will only come to pass after a murderous and decisive struggle between the two protagonists. That affirmed intention to place the last at the head of things, and to make them climb at a pace (too quickly, some say) the well-known steps which characterize an organized society, can only triumph if we use all means to turn the scale, including, of course, that of violence.

You do not turn any society, however primitive it may be, upside down with such a program if you have not decided from the very beginning, that is to say from the actual formulation of that program, to overcome all the obstacles that you will come across in so doing. The native who decides to put the program into practice, and to become its moving force, is ready for violence at all times. From birth it is clear to him that this narrow world, strewn with prohibitions, can only be called in question by absolute violence.

The colonial world is a world divided into compartments. It is probably unnecessary to recall the existence of native quarters and European quarters, of schools for natives and schools for Europeans; in the same way we need not recall apartheid in South Africa. Yet, if we examine closely this system of compartments, we will at least be able to reveal the lines of force it implies. This approach to the colonial world, its ordering and its geographical layout will allow us to mark out the lines on which a decolonized society will be reorganized.

The colonial world is a world cut in two. The dividing line, the frontiers are shown by barracks and police stations. In the colonies it is the policeman and the soldier who are the official, instituted go-betweens, the spokesmen of the settler and his rule of oppression. In capitalist societies the educational system, whether lay or clerical, the structure of moral reflexes handed down from father to son, the exemplary honesty of workers who are given a medal after fifty years of good and loyal service, and the affection which springs from harmonious relations and good behavior—all these aesthetic expressions of respect for the established order serve to create around the exploited person an atmosphere of submission and of inhibition which lightens the task of policing considerably. In the capitalist countries a multitude of moral teachers, counselors and "bewilderers" separate the exploited from those in power. In the colonial countries, on the contrary, the policeman and the soldier, by their immediate presence and their frequent and direct action maintain contact with the native and advise him by means of rifle butts and napalm not to budge. It is obvious here that the agents of government speak the language of pure force. The intermediary does not lighten the oppression, nor seek to hide the domination; he shows them up and puts them into practice with the clear conscience of an upholder of the peace; yet he is the bringer of violence into the home and into the mind of the native.

The zone where the natives live is not complementary to the zone inhabited by the settlers. The two zones are opposed, but not in the service of a higher unity. Obedient to the rules of pure Aristotelian logic, they both follow the principle of reciprocal exclusivity. No conciliation is possible, for of the two terms, one is superfluous. The settlers' town is a strongly built town; all made of stone and steel. It is a brightly lit town; the streets are covered with asphalt, and the garbage cans swallow all the leavings, unseen, unknown and hardly thought about. The settler's feet are never visible, except perhaps in the sea; but there you're never close enough to see them. His feet are protected by strong shoes although the streets of his town are clean and even, with no holes or stones. The settler's town is a well-fed town, an easygoing town; its belly is always full of good things. The settlers' town is a town of white people, of foreigners.

The town belonging to the colonized people, or at least the native town, the Negro village, the medina, the reservation, is a place of ill fame, peopled by men of evil repute. They are born there, it matters little where or how; they die there, it matters not where, nor how. It is a world without spaciousness; men live there on top of each other, and their huts are built one on top of the other. The native town is a hungry town, starved of bread, of meat, of shoes, of coal, of light. The native town is a crouching village, a town on its knees, a town wallowing in the mire. It is a town of niggers and dirty Arabs. The look that the native turns on the settler's town is a look of lust, a look of envy; it expresses his dreams of possession—all manner of possession: to sit at the settler's table, to sleep in the settler's bed, with his wife if possible. The colonized man is an envious man. And this the settler knows very well; when their glances meet he ascertains bitterly, always on the defensive, "They want to take our place." It is true, for there is no native who does not dream at least once a day of setting himself up in the settler's place.

This world divided into compartments, this world cut in two is inhabited by two different species. The originality of the colonial context is that economic reality, inequality, and the immense difference of ways of life never come to mask the human realities. When you examine at close quarters the colonial context, it is evident that what parcels out the world is to begin with the fact of belonging to or not belonging to a given race, a given species. In the colonies the economic substructure is also a superstructure. The cause is the consequence; you are rich because you are white, you are white because you are rich. This is why Marxist analysis should always be slightly stretched every time we have to do with the colonial problem.

Everything up to and including the very nature of pre-capitalist society, so well explained by Marx, must here be thought out again. The serf is in essence different from the knight, but a reference to divine right is necessary to legitimize this statutory difference. In the colonies, the foreigner coming from another country imposed his rule by means of guns and machines. In defiance of his successful transplantation, in spite of his appropriation, the settler still remains a foreigner. It is neither the act of owning factories, nor estates, nor a bank balance which distinguishes the governing classes. The governing race is first and foremost those who come from elsewhere, those who are unlike the original inhabitants, "the others."

The violence which has ruled over the ordering of the colonial world, which has ceaselessly drummed the rhythm for the destruction of native social forms and broken up without reserve the systems of reference of the economy, the customs of dress and external life, that same violence will be claimed and taken over by the native at the moment when, deciding to embody history in his own person, he surges into the forbidden quarters. To wreck the colonial world is henceforward a mental picture of action which is very clear, very easy to understand and which may be assumed by each one of the individuals which constitute the colonized people. To break up the colonial world does not mean that after the frontiers have been abolished lines of communication will be set up between the two zones. The destruction of the colonial world is no more and no less that the abolition of one zone, its burial in the depths of the earth or its expulsion from the county.

The Conquest of Violence

Mohandas K. Gandhi

Satyagraha is a word coined during the movement of Indian resistance in South Africa to the Asiatic Law Amendment Ordinance introduced into the Transvaal Legislative Council in 1906. Gandhi explains that he first called the movement "passive resistance," but as the struggle continued he became aware that "some new principle had come into being." He then announced through the pages of his newspaper, *Indian Opinion*, that a prize would be given for the best name invented to designate the movement. One competitor suggested the word "sadagraha," meaning "firmness in a good cause."

> I liked the word, but it did not fully represent the whole idea I wished it to connote. I therefore corrected it to "Satyagraha." Truth (Satya) implies love and firmness (Agraha) engenders and therefore serves as a synonym for force. I thus began to call the Indian movement "Satyagraha," that is to say, the Force which is born of Truth and Love or non-violence, and gave up the use of the phrase "passive resistance"…

Satyagraha allows for several stages of winning over an opponent. The first stage is characterized by persuasion through reason. The subsequent stages enter the realm of persuasion through suffering wherein the satyagrahi attempts to dramatize the issues at stake and to get through to the opponent's unprejudiced judgment so that he may willingly come again onto a level where he may be persuaded through rational argument. Finally, if persuasion by reason or by suffering does not succeed, the satyagrahi may resort to non-violent coercion characterized by such tools as non-cooperation or civil disobedience.

Steps in a Satyagraha Campaign

The outline below is applicable to a movement growing out of grievances against an established political order. These steps could be adapted to other conflict situations.

(1) *Negotiation and arbitration.* Every effort to resolve the conflict or redress the grievance through established channels must be exhausted before the further steps are undertaken.

(2) *Preparation of the group for direct action.* Immediately upon recognizing the existence of a conflict situation which might lead to direct action, motives are to be carefully examined, exercises in self-discipline initiated, and the fullest discussion launched within the group regarding issues at stake, appropriate procedures to be undertaken, the circumstance of the opponents, the climate of public opinion, etc. This step often included, for Indian satyagrahis, purificatory fasting.

(3) *Agitation.* This step includes an active propaganda campaign together with such demonstrations as mass-meetings, parades, slogan-shouting.

(4) *Issuing of an ultimatum.* A final strong appeal to the opponent should be made explaining what further steps will be taken if no agreement can be reached. The wording and manner of presentation of the ultimatum should offer the widest scope for agreement, allowing for face-saving on the part of the opponent, and should present a constructive solution to the problem.

(5) *Economic boycott and forms of strike.* Picketing may be widely employed, together with continued demonstrations and education of the public. Sitting dharna (a form of sit-down strike) may be employed, as well as non-violent labor strike, and attempts to organize a general strike.

(6) *Non-cooperation.* Depending upon the nature of the issues at stake, such action as non-payment of taxes, boycott of schools and other public institutions, ostracism, or even voluntary exile may be initiated.

(7) *Civil disobedience.* Great care should be exercised in the selection of laws to be contravened. Such laws could be either central to the grievance, or symbolic.

(8) *Usurping of the functions of government.* Shridharani calls this "assertive satyagraha." Fullest preparations are necessary to make this step effective.

(9) *Parallel government.* The establishment of parallel functions should grow out of step (8), and these should be strengthened in such a way that the greatest possible cooperation from the public can be obtained…

The Salt Satyagraha

Note: The Salt Satyagraha was part of the year-long Civil Disobedience movement of 1930-31. The following outline touches upon the entire movement, although many of the details of that extensive struggle have been omitted.

Dates, Duration, and Locale

(1) March 1930-March 1931.

(2) In its extended form, civil disobedience continued for about one year.

(3) A national movement, with headquarters in Bombay. Satyagraha activities were launched in every province.

Objectives

(1) *Immediate:* Removal of the Salt Acts. These statutes provided for a government monopoly of salt. Revenue realized from the Salt Tax amounted at this time to $25,000,000 out of a total revenue of about $800,000,000. These laws were held to work a hardship on the people, especially the poor, and to constitute the taxation of a necessity.

(2) *Long-range:* The Salt Acts were chosen by Gandhi for contravention in a general civil disobedience movement because they not only appeared to be basically unjust in themselves, but also because they symbolized an unpopular, unrepresentative, and alien government. British official sources described the object of the satyagraha as "nothing less than to cause a complete paralysis of the administrative machinery...." The ultimate objective of civil disobedience was complete independence...

Organization and Constructive Program

(1) *Role of the Indian National Congress:* This campaign was conducted as part of an over-all political movement for independence. It was a program adopted by the largest political opposition party in India and so was planned in the light of the organization and constitutional make-up of the Party. The Congress Party delegated to Gandhi full power and responsibility for organizing and leading the campaign (by resolution, 21 March 1930).

(2) *Succession of leadership:* Extensive powers were given to the president of the Congress (then Jawaharlal Nehru) to act on behalf of the executive committee in case it could not meet. The president was empowered to nominate a successor in the event of his removal from action, the successor, in turn, was to have the same power of appointment of a successor. Similar powers were given to provincial and local Congress chiefs.

(3) *Khadi:* The wearing of hand-spun cloth was imperative for all satyagrahis—it became the uniform of the Congress and the movement.

(4) *Other aspects of constructive work:* Welfare and self-sufficiency work was considered one of the ways in which the cause could be promoted. A satyagrahi should "find himself in one of the following states," Gandhi instructed: "1. In prison or in an analogous state, or 2. Engaged in Civil Disobedience, or 3. Under orders at the spinning wheel, or at some constructive work advancing Swaraj."

Preparation for Action

(1) *Public opinion on swaraj:* Prior to the launching of this campaign, the sentiment for full independence was developed through discussion and the deliberation of the Congress Party. On 26 January the Congress, meeting in Lahore, had pledged its members to "carry out the Congress instructions issued from time to time for the purpose of establishing Purna Swaraj" (full independence).

(2) *Training courses:* Volunteers for satyagraha undertook courses of training for direct action, especially in methods of controlling large crowds. Satyagrahis drilled regularly, though they did so without arms.

(3) *Planning for civil disobedience:* The salt laws were selected for contravention. Gandhi planned to lead a march to the sea where satyagrahis would, in violation of the salt monopoly, prepare salt from sea water. Vallabhbhai Patel was chosen to prepare the way for the proposed march. He proceeded along the route to be taken, advising the people of the objectives of the movement, and instructing them in the principles of satyagraha. They were urged to undertake constructive work, to abstain from intoxicants, and to overcome untouchability. (On 7 March Patel was arrested.)

(4) *The Satyagraha Pledge:* The All-India Congress Committee, meeting at Ahmedabad on 21 March 1930, drew up the following pledge to be taken by those volunteering for satyagraha:

1. I desire to join the civil resistance campaign for the Independence of India undertaken by the National Congress.

2. I accept the Creed of the National Congress, that is, the attainment of Purna Swaraj (complete independence) by the people of India by all peaceful and legitimate means.

3. I am ready and willing to go to jail and undergo all other sufferings and penalties that may be inflicted on me in this campaign.

4. In case I am sent to jail, I shall not seek any monetary help for my family from the Congress funds.

5. I shall implicitly obey the orders of those who are in charge of the campaign.

Preliminary Action

(1) *Notice of civil disobedience:* Through the Congress independence resolution adopted at Lahore, subsequently advertised and discussed widely, the intention of the Congress Party to agitate for independence, if necessary through civil disobedience, was made known.

(2) *Gandhi's letter to Lord Irwin, the Viceroy:* On 2 March 1930, Gandhi apprised the Viceroy of the satyagraha plan and reviewed the grievances of the people. Non-violence, he wrote, could be "an intensely active force." It was his purpose, he told the Viceroy, "to set in motion that force, as well against the organised violent force of the British rule as the unorganised violent force of the growing party of violence….The non-violence will be expressed through Civil Disobedience, for the moment confined to the inmates of the Satyagraha Ashram, but ultimately designed to cover all those who choose to join the movement with its obvious limitations."

(3) *The ultimatum:* In his letter, Gandhi urged a negotiated settlement, barring which, he would lead a satyagraha movement. He further stated the exact day upon which he would proceed, with co-workers, to disregard the provisions of the Salt Acts. "It is, I know, open to you," he told the Viceroy, "to frustrate my

design by arresting me. I hope that there will be tens of thousands ready, in a disciplined manner, to take up the work after me, and, in the act of disobeying the Salt Act, to lay themselves open to the penalties of a Law that should never have disfigured the Statute Book." He would, Gandhi said, welcome further discussion, and his letter was in no way a threat but a "simple and sacred duty peremptory on a civil resister." A young Englishman (Reginald Reynolds) who had joined the ashram was selected to deliver the letter.

Action

(1) *The march to the sea:* On 12 March, Gandhi and his co-satyagrahis left Ahmedabad for Dandi on the sea coast. He urged villagers along the way to pursue constructive work, to remain non-violent, and to participate in the civil disobedience following the initial breach of the law at Dandi. The march was considered a form of penance and discipline for the beginning of civil disobedience. It also dramatized the issues and attracted nationwide attention.

(2) *The opening of civil disobedience:* The satyagrahis reached Dandi on 5 April. The following morning, after prayers, they proceeded to the beach where they prepared salt from sea water, thus technically breaking the salt laws.

(3) *Gandhi's statement to the press:* Upon breaking the law, Gandhi declared that it was then open to anyone who would take the risk of prosecution to manufacture salt wherever he wished. Villagers were to be instructed concerning the meaning of the salt tax and directed in methods of preparing salt.

(4) *Issuing of leaflets:* Instructions concerning the manufacture of salt were published in the various parts of the country.

(5) *Response from the people:* "It seemed as though a spring had been suddenly released, "Nehru wrote. Everywhere people began to make salt. They collected "pots and pans and ultimately succeeded in producing some unwholesome stuff, which we waved about in triumph, and often auctioned for fancy prices." The main thing, Nehru continued, was to commit a breach of the "obnoxious Salt Law….As we saw the abounding enthusiasm of the people and the way salt-making was spreading like a prairie fire, we felt a little abashed and ashamed for having questioned the efficacy of this method when it was first proposed by Gandhiji. And we marveled at the amazing knack of the man to impress the multitude and make it act in an organised way."

(6) *Hartal:* Throughout the country shops closed in response to arrests of satyagraha leaders.

(7) *Resignation of offices:* Headsmen in villages and subordinate officers resigned in large numbers in sympathy with satyagraha.

(8) *Symbolic acts:* In many parts of India dramatic demonstrations were conducted. In Bombay an "effigy" of the Salt Acts was thrown into the sea as a symbol that British law was dead in the land.

(9) *Succession in leadership:* Jawaharlal Nehru was arrested on 14 April and was succeeded by his father, Motilal Nehru. In other places, leaders of the

satyagraha were replaced by appointment following the arrest of the initial leadership. Gandhi, arrested 5 May, was replaced by Abbas Tyabji.

(10) *Non-payment of taxes:* In some areas, as in Bardoli, a program of non-payment of taxes was undertaken.

(11) *Action to control rioting:* Leaders attempted to preserve the non-violent character of satyagraha. In response to the outbreak of riots in Karachi and Calcutta, Gandhi announced: "If non-violence has to fight the people's violence in addition to the violence of the Government it must still perform its arduous task at any cost." (17 April.) Gandhi later (26 April) announced that if satyagrahis who followed him did not fulfill the basic conditions, he himself would practice satyagraha against them.

(12) *Gandhi's second letter to Viceroy:* The Government, in a sort of non-cooperation of its own, refused to arrest Gandhi early in the campaign. The first week of May he explained in a second letter his next move—he would set out for Dharsana where the Government operated a large salt works. There he would demand possession of these works. It would be possible, he said, for the Viceroy to prevent this "raid" in one of the following three ways:

1. by removing the salt tax;
2. by arresting me and my party unless the country can, as I hope it will, replace every one taken away;
3. by sheer goondaism [hooliganism] unless every head broken is replaced as I hope it will be.

(13) *Raids on the salt works:* Following Gandhi's arrest on 5 May (just after midnight), volunteers, led by Congress notables, marched to occupy the salt depots. Fresh volunteers stepped in as others were struck down by the police. Organized first-aid units worked to revive victims.

(14) *Non-violent persuasion of the police:* Throughout the attack upon the satyagraha raiders, volunteers refrained from striking back or even from deflecting blows. They rushed onto the salt pans, wave upon wave. Where they could, they pleaded with the police to join them. Incidents were reported of policemen refusing to continue the assault. An American journalist, Negley Farson, recorded an incident in which a Sikh, blood-soaked from the assault of a police sergeant, fell under a heavy blow. Congress first-aid volunteers rushed up to rub his face with ice. "…he gave us a bloody grin and stood up to receive some more…." The police sergeant was "so sweaty from his exertions that his Sam Browne had stained his white tunic. I watched him with my heart in my mouth. He drew back his arm for a final swing—and then he dropped his hands down by his sides. 'It's no use,' he said, turning to me with half an apologetic grin, 'You can't hit a bugger when he stands up to you like that!' He gave the Sikh a mock salute and walked off."

(15) *Economic boycott:* When raids on salt works were halted upon the advent of the monsoon, civil disobedience took other forms including boycott of foreign-made products, especially cloth. Both cloth and liquor shops were persistently picketed.

(16) *Disobedience of ordinances:* As the campaign proceeded, special ordinances designed to suppress publicity and control assembly were promulgated by the Government. These were consistently disobeyed in a general movement to the jails.

(17) *Continuing activities:* The extensive campaign continued throughout the year and involved many manifestations of non-cooperation and civil disobedience.

(18) *Culmination of the movement:* A settlement was reached following talks between Gandhi and the Viceroy, and the Gandhi-Irwin Agreement was published on 5 March 1931.

Results

(1) *Modification of salt regulations:* The immediate objective of the salt satyagraha which opened the overall civil disobedience movement was, to a large extent, realized. The salt laws were not repealed, but a new official interpretation was effected in the settlement agreed to by Gandhi and Lord Irwin. That interpretation specified that "For the sake...of giving relief to certain of the poorer classes," the Government would "extend their administrative provisions, on lines already prevailing in certain places, in order to permit local residents in villages, immediately adjoining areas where salt can be collected or made, to collect or make salt for domestic consumption or sale within such villages, but not for sale to, or trading with, individuals living outside them..."

Summary Analysis of the Salt Satyagraha

During 1930-31, satyagraha was employed throughout India to advance the cause of Indian independence. Thousands of localized campaigns in the over-all civil disobedience movement involved hundreds of thousands of persons, many of whom adopted satyagraha as a temporary expedient without fully understanding its basic philosophy. Nevertheless, the movement remained, for the most part, non-violent. The opening campaign led by Gandhi in the march to the sea provided a model of adherence to basic principles and brilliance of strategy. An outstanding characteristic of the other campaigns during these months was the assertion of strong and effective leadership by hundreds of provincial and local Congressmen.

As for the elements of true satyagraha, all are to be found in the salt satyagraha. The immediate objective was the removal of laws which worked a hardship upon the poor. The Salt Acts, establishing a government monopoly over a food necessity, symbolized the further injustice—the subjugation of India by a foreign power. It therefore became the duty of the satyagrahi to disobey the unjust salt laws and to cling to the truth understood to be the right of the Indian people to manufacture salt as they chose. The further truth implications were understood to lie in a people's right to self-government.

The volunteer satyagrahis who initiated the salt campaign rigorously abided by the principle of non-violence. During the later raids on the salt pans, some satyagrahis destroyed property by cutting wire an otherwise pulling down the fences surrounding the salt works. Gandhi himself did not lead the raids in which property was destroyed, and he might well have restrained property destruction or considered it a weakness in that phase of the campaign. Some satyagrahis justified the destruction of fences to gain access to the salt pans by arguing that the salt works were public property and should be made available to all citizens. There is no evidence, however, that any physical injury was inflicted by satyagrahis upon their opponents. Violence was, indeed, at work in the successive raids on the salt pans—but it was violence inflicted by police forces upon satyagrahis, many of whom sustained grave and agonizing injury. Wave upon wave of satyagrahis responded to the attack, their action remaining non-violent but nonetheless aggressive. They retaliated, not with non-violence, but with the several persuasive tactics at their command.

Self-reliance characterized the conduct of the satyagrahis. They signed a pledge to offer civil resistance without expectation of material help for themselves or their families. Again, organized propaganda was published and distributed in the form of bulletins and leaflets, and publicity was further supplied by the press throughout the country in detailed reporting of satyagraha activities. Suppression of satyagraha propaganda and censorship of the press served to extend the opportunities for contravention of the law…

This satyagraha proceeded through the early steps of attempted negotiation, of agitation and demonstration, and the issuing of an ultimatum. The opponent was kept informed of intention and procedure. When the settlement was finally effected, following discussions between Gandhi and the Viceroy, the immediate objective—redress of grievances arising from the Salt Acts—was to a substantial degree realized even though the Acts themselves were not abolished. The long-term objective of Swaraj (independence) was, of course, not at once achieved. However, the Gandhi-Irwin Agreement provided that the Congress should participate in the second Round Table Conference to consider constitutional questions involved in the advancement of India along the road towards full independence…

Why Can't People Feed Themselves?

Frances Moore Lappé and Joseph Collins

Question: You have said that the hunger problem is not the result of overpopulation. But you have not answered the most basic and simple question of all: Why can't people feed themselves? As Senator Daniel P. Moynihan put it bluntly, when addressing himself to the Third World, "Food growing is the first thing you do when you come down out of the trees. The question is, how come the United States can grow food and you can't?"

Our Response: In the very first speech I, Frances, ever gave after writing Diet for a Small Planet, I tried to take my audience along the path that I had taken in attempting to understand why so many are hungry in this world. Here is the gist of that talk that was, in truth, a turning point in my life:

When I started I saw a world divided into two parts: a minority of nations that had "taken off" through their agricultural and industrial revolutions to reach a level of unparalleled material abundance and a majority that remained behind in a primitive, traditional, undeveloped state. This lagging behind of the majority of the world's peoples must be due, I thought, to some internal deficiency or even to several of them. It seemed obvious that the underdeveloped countries must be deficient in natural resources—particularly good land and climate—and in cultural development, including modern attitudes conducive to work and progress.

But when looking for the historical roots of the predicament, I learned that my picture of these two separate worlds was quite false. My "two separate worlds" were really just different sides of the same coin. One side was on top largely because the other side was on the bottom. Could this be true? How were these separate worlds related?

Colonialism appeared to me to be the link. Colonialism destroyed the cultural patterns of production and exchange by which traditional societies in "underdeveloped" countries previously had met the needs of the people. Many precolonial social structures, while dominated by exploitative elites, had evolved a system of mutual obligations among the classes that helped to ensure at least a minimal diet for all. A friend of mine once said: "Precolonial village existence in subsistence agriculture was a limited life indeed, but its certainly not Calcutta." The misery of starvation in the streets of Calcutta can only be understood as the end-point of a long historical process—one that has destroyed a traditional social system.

"Underdeveloped," instead of being an adjective that evokes the picture of a static society, became for me a verb (to "underdevelop") meaning the *process* by which the minority of the world has transformed—indeed often robbed and degraded—the majority.

That was in 1972. I clearly recall my thoughts on my return home. I had stated publicly for the first time a world view that had taken me years of study to grasp. The sense of relief was tremendous. For me the breakthrough lay in realizing that today's "hunger crisis" could not be described in static, descriptive terms. Hunger and underdevelopment must always be thought of as a *process*.

To answer the question "why hunger?" it is counterproductive to simply *describe* the conditions in an underdeveloped country today. For these conditions, whether they be the degree of malnutrition, the levels of agricultural production, or even the country's ecological endowment, are not static factors—they are not "givens." They are rather the *results* of an ongoing historical process. As we dug ever deeper into that historical process for the preparation of this book, we began to discover the existence of scarcity-creating mechanisms that we had only vaguely intuited before.

We have gotten great satisfaction from probing into the past since we recognized it is the only way to approach a solution to hunger today. We have come to see that it is the *force* creating the condition, not the condition itself, that must be the target of change. Otherwise we might change the condition today, only to find tomorrow that it has been recreated—with a vengeance.

Asking the question "Why can't people feed themselves?" carries a sense of bewilderment that there are so many people in the world not able to feed themselves adequately. What astonished us, however, is that there are not more people in the world who are hungry—considering the weight of the centuries of effort by the few to undermine the capacity of the majority to feed themselves. No, we are not crying "conspiracy!" If these forces were entirely conspiratorial, they would be easier to detect and many more people would by now have risen up to resist. We are talking about something more subtle and insidious; a heritage of colonial order in which people with the advantage of considerable power sought their own self-interest, often arrogantly believing they were acting in the interest of the people whose lives they were destroying.

The Colonial Mind

The colonizer viewed agriculture in the subjugated lands as primitive and backward. Yet such a view contrasts sharply with the documents from the colonial period now coming to light. For example, A. J. Voelker, a British agricultural scientist assigned to India during the 1890s, wrote:

Nowhere would one find better instances of keeping land scrupulously clean from weeds, of ingenuity in device of water-raising appliances, of knowledge of soils and their capabilities, as well as of the exact time to sow and reap, as one would find in Indian agriculture. It is wonderful, too, how much is known of rotation, the system of "mixed crops" and of fallowing.

. . . I, at least, have never seen a more perfect picture of cultivation."[1]

None the less, viewing the agriculture of the vanquished as primitive and backward reinforced the colonizer's rationale for destroying it. To the colonizers of Africa, Asia, and Latin America, agriculture became merely a means to extract wealth—much as gold from a mine—on behalf of the colonizing power. Agriculture was no longer seen as a source of food for the local population, nor even as their livelihood. Indeed the English economist John Stuart Mill reasoned that colonies should not be thought of as civilizations or countries at all but as "agricultural establishments" whose sole purpose was to supply the "larger community to which they belong." The colonized society's agriculture was only a subdivision of the agricultural system of the metropolitan country. As Mill acknowledged, "Our West India colonies, for example, cannot be regarded as countries . . . The West Indies are the place where England *finds it convenient* to carry on the production of sugar, coffee and a few other tropical commodities."[2]

Prior to European intervention, Africans practiced a diversified agriculture that included the introduction of new food plants of Asian or American origin. But colonial rule simplified this diversified production to single cash crops—often to the exclusion of staple foods—and in the process sowed the seeds of famine.[3]

Rice farming once had been common in Gambia. But with colonial rule so much of the best land was taken over by peanuts (grown for the European market) that rice had to be imported to counter the mounting prospect of famine. Northern Ghana, once famous for its yams and other foodstuffs, was forced to concentrate solely on cocoa. Most of the Gold Coast thus became dependent on cocoa. Liberia was turned into a virtual plantation subsidiary of Firestone Tire and Rubber. Food production in Dahomey and southeast Nigeria was all but abandoned in favor of palm oil; Tanganyika (now Tanzania) was forced to focus on sisal and Uganda on cotton.

The same happened in Indochina. About the time of the American Civil War the French decided that the Mekong Delta in Vietnam would be ideal for producing rice for export. Through a production system based on enriching the large landowners, Vietnam became the world's third largest exporter of rice by the 1930s; yet many landless Vietnamese went hungry.[4]

Rather than helping the peasants, colonialism's public works programs only reinforced export crop production. British irrigation works built in nineteenth-century India did help increase production, but the expansion was for spring export crops at the expense of millets and legumes grown in the fall as the basic local food crops.

Because people living on the land do not easily go against their natural and adaptive drive to grow food for themselves, colonial powers had to force the production of cash crops. The first strategy was to use physical or economic force to get the local population to grow cash crops instead of food on their own plots and then turn them over to the colonizer for export. The second strategy was the direct takeover of the land by large-scale plantations growing crops for export.

Forced Peasant Production

As Walter Rodney recounts in *How Europe Underdeveloped Africa*, cash crops were often grown literally under threat of guns and whips.[5] One visitor to the Sahel commented in 1928: "Cotton is an artificial crop and one the value of which is not entirely clear to the natives. . ." He wryly noted the "enforced enthusiasm with which the natives . . . have thrown themselves into . . . planting cotton."[6] The forced cultivation of cotton was a major grievance leading to the Maji Maji wars in Tanzania (then Tanganyika) and behind the nationalist revolt in Angola as late as 1960.[7]

Although raw force was used, taxation was the preferred colonial technique to force Africans to grow cash crops. The colonial administrations simply levied taxes on cattle, land, houses, and even the people themselves. Since the tax had to be paid in the coin of the realm, the peasants had either to grow crops to sell or to work on the plantations or in the mines of the Europeans.[8] Taxation was both an effective tool to "stimulate" cash cropping and a source of revenue that the colonial bureaucracy needed to enforce the system. To expand their production of export crops to pay the mounting taxes, peasant producers were forced to neglect the farming of food crops. In 1830, the Dutch administration in Java made the peasants an offer they could not refuse; if they would grow government-owned export crops on one fifth of their land, the Dutch would remit their land taxes.[9] If they refused and thus could not pay the taxes, they lost their land.

Marketing boards emerged in Africa in the 1930s as another technique for getting the profit from cash crop production by native producers into the hands of the colonial government and international firms. Purchases by the marketing boards were well below the world market price. Peanuts bought by the boards from peasant cultivators in West Africa were sold in Britain for more than *seven times* what the peasants received.[10]

The marketing board concept was born with the "cocoa hold-up" in the Gold Coast in 1937. Small cocoa farmers refused to sell to the large cocoa concerns like United Africa Company (a subsidiary Anglo-Dutch firm, Unilever—which we know as Lever Brothers) and Cadbury until they got a higher price. When the British government stepped in and agreed to buy the cocoa directly in place of the big business concerns, the smallholders must have thought they had scored atleast a minor victory. But had they really? The following year the British formally set up the West African Cocoa Control Board. Theoretically, its purpose was to pay the peasants a reasonable price for their crops. In practice, however, the board, as sole purchaser, was able hold down the prices paid the peasants for their crops when the world prices were rising. Rodney sums up the real "victory":

None of the benefits went to Africans, but rather to the British government itself and to the private companies . . . Big companies like the United African Company and John Holt were given . . . quotas to fulfill on behalf of the boards. As agents of the government, they were no longer exposed to direct attack, and their profits were secure.[11]

These marketing boards, set up for most export crops, were actually controlled by the companies. The chairman of the Cocoa Board was none other than John Cadbury of Cadbury Brothers (ever had a Cadbury chocolate bar?) who was part of a buying pool exploiting West African cocoa farmers.

The marketing boards funneled part of the profits from the exploitation of peasant producers indirectly into the royal treasury. While the Cocoa Board sold to the British Food Ministry at low prices, the ministry upped the price for British manufacturers, thus netting a profit as high as 11 million pounds in some years.[12]

These marketing boards of Africa were only the institutionalized rendition of what is the essence of colonialism—the extraction of wealth. While profits continued to accrue to foreign interests and local elites, prices received by those actually growing the commodities remained low.

Plantations

A second approach was direct takeover of the land either by the colonizing government or by private foreign interests. Previously self-provisioning farmers were forced to cultivate the plantation fields through either enslavement or economic coercion.

After the conquest of the Kandyan Kingdom (in present day Sri Lanka), in 1815, the British designated all the vast central part of the island as crown land. When it was determined that coffee, a profitable export crop, could be grown there, the Kandyan lands were sold off to British investors and planters at a mere five shillings per acre, the government even defraying the cost of surveying and road building.[13]

Java is also a prime example of a colonial government seizing territory and then putting it into private foreign hands. In 1870, the Dutch declared all uncultivated land—called waste land—property of the state for lease to Dutch plantation enterprises. In addition, the Agrarian Land Law of 1870 authorized foreign companies to lease village-owned land. The peasants, in chronic need of ready cash for taxes and foreign consumer goods, were only too willing to lease their land to the foreign companies for very modest sums and under terms dictated by the firms. Where land was still held communally, the village headman was tempted by high cash commissions offered by plantation companies. He would lease the village land even more cheaply than would the individual peasant or, as was frequently the case, sell out the entire village to the company.[14]

The introduction of the plantation meant the divorce of agriculture from nourishment, as the notion of food value was lost to the overriding claim of "market value" in international trade. Crops such as sugar, tobacco, and coffee were selected, not on the basis of how well they feed people, but for their high price value relative to their weight and bulk so that profit margins could be maintained even after the costs of shipping to Europe.

Suppressing Peasant Farming

The stagnation and impoverishment of the peasant food-producing sector was not the mere by-product of benign neglect, that is, the unintended consequence of an overemphasis on export production. Plantations—just like modern "agro-industrial complexes"—needed an abundant and readily available supply of low-wage agricultural workers. Colonial administrations thus devised a variety of tactics, all to undercut self-provisioning agriculture and thus make rural populations dependent on plantation wages. Government services and even the most minimal infrastructure (access to water, roads, seeds, credit, pest and disease control information, and so on) were systematically denied. Plantations usurped most of the good land, either making much of the rural population landless or pushing them onto marginal soils. (Yet the plantations have often held much of their land idle simply to prevent the peasants from using it—even to this day. Del Monte owns 57,000 acres of Guatemala but plants only 9000. The rest lies idle except for a few thousand head of grazing cattle.)[15]

In some cases a colonial administration would go even further to guarantee itself a labor supply. In at least twelve countries in the eastern and southern parts of Africa the exploitation of mineral wealth (gold, diamonds, and copper) and the establishment of cash-crop plantations demanded a continuous supply of low-cost labor. To assure this labor supply, colonial administrations simply expropriated the land of the African communities by violence and drove the people into small reserves.[16] With neither adequate land for their traditional slash-and-burn methods nor access to the means—tools, water, and fertilizer—to make continuous farming of such limited areas viable, the indigenous population could scarcely meet subsistence needs, much less produce surplus to sell in order to cover the colonial taxes. Hundreds of thousands of Africans were forced to become the cheap labor source so "needed" by the colonial plantations. Only by laboring on plantations and in the mines could they hope to pay the colonial taxes.

The tax scheme to produce reserves of cheap plantation and mining labor was particularly effective when the Great Depression hit and the bottom dropped out of cash crop economies. In 1929 the cotton market collapsed, leaving peasant cotton producers, such as those in Upper Volta, unable to pay their colonial taxes. More and more young people, in some years as many as 80,000, were thus forced to migrate to the Gold Coast to compete with each other for low-wage jobs on cocoa plantations.[17]

The forced migration of Africa's most able—bodied workers—stripping village food farming of needed hands—was a recurring feature of colonialism. As late as 1973 the Portuguese "exported" 400,000 Mozambican peasants to work in South Africa in exchange for gold deposited in the Lisbon treasury.

The many techniques of colonialism to undercut self-provisioning agriculture in order to ensure a cheap labor supply are no better illustrated than by the story of how, in the mid-nineteenth century, sugar plantation owners in British Guiana coped with the double blow of the emancipation of slaves and the crash in the world sugar market. The story is graphically recounted by Alan Adamson in *Sugar Without Slaves.*[18]

Would the ex-slaves be allowed to take over the plantation land and grow the food they needed? The planters, many ruined by the sugar slump, were determined they would not. The planter-dominated government devised several schemes for thwarting food self-sufficiency. The price of crown land was kept artificially high, and the purchase of land in parcels smaller than 100 acres was outlawed—two measures guaranteeing that newly organized ex-slave cooperatives could not hope to gain access to much land. The government also prohibited cultivation on as much as 400,000 acres—on the grounds of "uncertain property titles."

Moreover, although many planters held part of their land out of sugar production due to the depressed world price, they would not allow any alternative production on them. They feared that once the ex-slaves started growing food it would be difficult to return them to sugar production when world market prices began to recover. In addition, the government taxed peasant production, then turned around and used the funds to subsidize the immigration of laborers from India and Malaysia to replace the freed slaves, thereby making sugar production again profitable for the planters. Finally, the government neglected the infrastructure for subsistence agriculture and denied credit for small farmers.

Perhaps the most insidious tactic to "lure" the peasant away from food production—and the one with profound historical consequences—was a policy of keeping the price of imported food low through the removal of tariffs and subsidies. The policy was double-edged: first, peasants were told they need not grow food because they could always buy it cheaply with their plantation wages; second, cheap food imports destroyed the market for domestic food and thereby impoverished local food producers.

Adamson relates how both the Governor of British Guiana and the Secretary for the Colonies Earl Grey favored low duties on imports in order to erode local food production and thereby release labor for the plantations. In 1851 the governor rushed through a reduction of the duty on cereals in order to "divert" labor to the sugar estates. As Adamson comments, "Without realizing it, he [the governor] had put his finger on the most mordant feature of monoculture: . . . its convulsive need to destroy any other sector of the economy which might compete for 'its' labor."[19]

Many colonial governments succeeded in establishing dependence on imported foodstuffs. In 1647 an observer in the West Indies wrote to Governor Winthrop of Massachusetts: "Men are so intent upon planting sugar that they had rather buy foode at very deare rates than produce it by labour, so infinite is the profitt of sugar workes . . ."[20] By 1770, the West Indies were importing most of the continental colonies' exports of dried fish, grain, beans, and vegetables. A dependence on imported food made the West Indian colonies vulnerable to any disruption in supply. This dependence on imported food stuffs spelled disaster when the thirteen continental colonies gained independence and food exports from the continent to the West Indies were interrupted. With no diversified food system to fall back on, 15,000 plantation workers died of famine between 1780 and 1787 in Jamaica alone.[21] The dependence of the West Indies on imported food persists to this day.

Suppressing Peasant Competition

We have talked about the techniques by which indigenous populations were forced to cultivate cash crops. In some countries with large plantations, however, colonial governments found it necessary to *prevent* peasants from independently growing cash crops not out of concern for their welfare, but so that they would not compete with colonial interests growing the same crop. For peasant farmers, given a modicum of opportunity, proved themselves capable of outproducing the large plantations not only in terms of output per unit of land but, more important, in terms of capital cost per unit produced.

In the Dutch East Indies (Indonesia and Dutch New Guinea) colonial policy in the middle of the nineteenth century forbade the sugar refineries to buy sugar cane from indigenous growers and imposed a discriminatory tax on rubber produced by native smallholders.[22]

A recent unpublished United Nations study of agricultural development in Africa concluded that large-scale agricultural operations owned and controlled by foreign commercial interests (such as the rubber plantations of Liberia, the sisal estates of Tanganyika [Tanzania], and the coffee estates of Angola) only survived the competition of peasant producers because "the authorities actively supported them by suppressing indigenous rural development."[23]

The suppression of indigenous agricultural development served the interests of the colonizing powers in two ways. Not only did it prevent direct competition from more efficient native producers of the same crops, but it also guaranteed a labor force to work on foreign-owned estates. Planters and foreign investors were not unaware that peasants who could survive economically by their own production would be under less pressure to sell their labor cheaply to the large estates.

The answer to the question, then, "Why can't people feed themselves?" must begin with an understanding of how colonialism actively prevented people from doing just that.

Colonialism

- forced peasants to replace food crops with cash crops that were then expropriated at very low rates;
- took over the best agricultural land for export crop plantations and then forced the most able-bodied workers to leave the village fields to work as slaves or for very low wages on plantations;
- encouraged a dependence on imported food;
- blocked native peasant cash crop production from competing with cash crops produced by settlers or foreign firms.

These are concrete examples of the development of underdevelopment that we should have perceived as such even as we read our history schoolbooks. Why didn't we? Somehow our schoolbooks always seemed to make the flow of history appear to have its own logic—as if it could not have been any other way. I, Frances, recall, in particular, a grade-school, social studies pamphlet on the idyllic life of Pedro, a nine-year-old boy on a coffee plantation in South America. The drawings of lush vegetation and "exotic" huts made his life seem romantic indeed. Wasn't it natural and proper that South America should have plantations to supply my mother and father with coffee? Isn't that the way it was *meant* to be?

Notes

1. Radha Sinha, *Food and Poverty* (New York: Holmes and Meier, 1976), p. 26.
2. John Stuart Mill, *Political Economy*, Book 3, Chapter 25 (emphasis added).
3. Peter Feldman and David Lawrence, "Social and Economic Implications of the Large-Scale Introduction of New Varieties of Foodgrains," Africa Report, preliminary draft (Geneva: UNRISD, 1975), pp.107–108.
4. Edgar Owens, *Right Side of History*, unpublished manuscript, 1976.
5. Walter Rodney, *How Europe Underdeveloped Africa* (London: Bogle-L'Ouverture Publications, 1972), pp. 171–172.
6. Ferdinand Ossendowski, *Slaves of the Sun* (New York: Dutton, 1928), p. 276.
7. Rodney, *How Europe Underdeveloped Africa*, pp. 171–172.
8. Ibid., p. 181.
9. Clifford Geertz, *Agricultural Involution* (Berkeley and Los Angeles: University of California Press, 1963), pp. 52–53.
10. Rodney, *How Europe Underdeveloped Africa*, p. 185.
11. Ibid., p. 184.
12. Ibid., p. 186.
13. George L. Beckford, *Persistent Poverty: Underdevelopment in Plantation Economies of the Third World* (New York: Oxford University Press, 1972), p. 99.
14. Ibid., p. 99, quoting from Erich Jacoby, *Agrarian Unrest in Southeast Asia* (New York: Asia Publishing House, 1961), p. 66.
15. Pat Flynn and Roger Burbach, North American Congress on Latin America, Berkeley, California, recent investigation.
16. Feldman and Lawrence, "Social and Economic Implications," p. 103.
17. Special Sahelian Office Report, Food and Agriculture Organization, March 28,1974, pp. 88–89.
18. Alan Adamson, *Sugar Without Slaves:The Political Economy of British Guiana*, 1838–1904 (New Haven and London: Yale University Press, 1972).

Globalization and Social Change

John McGrath

During the late twentieth century, and especially since the end of the Cold War, the term "**globalization**" began to appear frequently in connection with all sorts of issues and developments. By the 1990s, observers were noting that world societies were becoming linked in so many different ways that it seemed as if the world was shrinking: diffusion and acculturation were taking place so regularly and rapidly that national borders had less and less relevance to the events taking place within them. Even before the end of the century, it was clear that the era of globalization had arrived.

In one sense, globalization represents the logical culmination of processes that began deep in the historical record, when separate societies first began to interact, resulting in both direct and indirect exchanges of goods and ideas. Obviously, some societies engaged in cross-cultural exchange more than others, but even five hundred years ago, all but the most isolated societies in the world were being significantly affected by some other society in one way or another. This often took place gradually, but sometimes it happened with an awesome suddenness and force that transformed or even destroyed existing societies.

The modernization of Western society contributed in a major way to this process. Though Western Europeans were not the first to engage in trans-oceanic trade, the trade links and colonial systems that they began to create in the sixteenth century formed and maintained lasting connections among many previously isolated societies, and this intensified over the course of the Early Modern period. The Industrial Revolution enabled European nation-states to develop formal empires, as growing industrial economies created both a demand for far-flung resources and the technological means to communicate, travel, and conquer. By the late nineteenth and early twentieth centuries, energized by political competition and nationalist ideologies, European nations were absorbing some of the remotest corners of the world into dependent parts of their colonial networks. Even after the Second World War, this process of international interconnection continued, despite the independence of many former colonies. The Cold War collision between capitalism and communism only encouraged the two superpowers to expand their "spheres of influence" over societies throughout the world, through what has sometimes been called neoimperialism. Meanwhile, further advances in transportation and communication continued to permit more frequent contact among different world societies.

While the rate of diffusion and acculturation unquestionably accelerated throughout the course of the last century, it did not amount to what most would call "globalization" until late in the twentieth century. Only then did certain key developments transform the ongoing process of internationalization into something qualitatively, not just quantitatively, different. Globalization has become both a process and a consequence of social change, on an international scale, that has gained in momentum over time. And while we can clearly see globalization as a product of modernization, globalization has also become the chief means by which modernization is now taking place around the world.

Globalization as Economic Change

It is difficult to come up with a precise definition of what globalization is, because it has become a thorough process of systemic change that affects all aspects of societies. Many who study it focus on the economic aspects, while others look at how globalization affects politics, social organization, and culture.[1] Most observers would point to the primacy of economic forces, broadly defined, as being the essential motors of the process, and examining these helps both to define globalization and to understand its dynamics. What we can consider to be globalization, as a distinctive phenomenon, is the result of significant changes in the international economy that first became pronounced around the end of the Cold War era. By then—the decade of the 1990s—it displayed certain prominent, mutually reinforcing characteristics, all of which have been made possible by modernization.

The first, and perhaps most obvious, is an **increased volume of trade**, as economic, technological, and political developments have all allowed and encouraged it to grow exponentially. Since 1950, as world economic output has tripled, international trade has expanded by a factor of twenty-seven. More societies have become active participants, and they are exchanging a widening spectrum of goods and services.[2]

One important reason for this expansion of trade is the tremendous **advances in transportation and communication** that have linked different parts of the world ever more closely, and this constitutes another defining element of globalization. In today's world physical distances have less and less relevance, as labor and raw materials can travel the globe in a day, while information and capital can be transmitted within seconds. As opposed to earlier eras, the movement of goods, people, capital, and ideas is both faster and less expensive, and this has an enormous impact on the way that different societies relate to one another.

Such logistical advances have both contributed to and been enabled by a third characteristic, which is greatly **expanded capital investment**. Due largely to the research and development and specialized technology demanded in today's economy, the proportion of fixed costs to variable costs has steadily increased, and this means that initial startup costs require access to large amounts of capital, a point made by Marx over a century ago, who regarded it as inevitable in an investment-driven economic system. When only larger businesses that can operate with an economy of scale can compete in today's global marketplace, this presents a "barrier to entry" that interferes with the ability of producers to enter and leave the marketplace freely. A growing proportion of fixed costs leads unavoidably to the domination of the largest business enterprises, and less true business competition.

This in turn has contributed to another defining element of globalization: the **emergence of transnational corporations**. Also referred to as "multinational corporations," such entities are able to conduct their planning and production processes in many separate nations, often simultaneously, while their scale of operations makes transportation costs relatively minor as a proportion of cost. Thus the physical location of their business activities can be adjusted according to the most favorable current conditions, such as access to natural resources, labor availability, tax rates, or access to transportation. Even their financial operations are conducted internationally, as the capital upon which their operations depend can and often must move quickly back and forth across national boundaries. While the largest of such companies have revenues and expenditures that exceed those of many independent nations, at the same time, they operate largely independently of national allegiances.

What these factors add up to is the last major characteristic of globalization. In the last two decades we have seen, for the first time, a true internationalization of economic *production*, as distinct from the international *distribution* that had defined international trade for thousands of years. This means that separate elements of the production process can be carried out in many different places, and a **global division of labor** has emerged that is based on the principle of comparative advantage. While this increases overall efficiency, it also makes the nations of the world economically dependent upon each other. The age of globalization means that even highly developed nations with abundant natural and human resources, such as the United States, no longer enjoy true economic self-sufficiency.

The global economy takes the advantages demonstrated by Adam Smith's pin factory to an entirely new level. In the pin factory, a division of labor enables an exponential increase in output by dividing the stages of the pin-making process among individual workers, each responsible for only a single operation. Yet even with this advantageous division of labor, Smith's pinmakers all performed their tasks under the same roof.[3] In contrast, global production, with the costs of transport and communication steadily declining as elements of cost, now takes place in multiple locations often thousands of miles apart.

For example, the manufacture of a single automobile often takes place in literally dozens of nations. The various parts of a car—headlights, carburetors, tires, dashboards, GPS systems, and many other components of the finished product—may be produced in a number of separate countries, using parts and materials that themselves have been imported from other nations. While the final "assembly" of the automobile may occur in a single factory, it has become common for even this stage of production to take place in a different nation than the one in which the corporate headquarters is located. In this way, literally dozens of different nations can take part in the manufacture of a single automobile. Admittedly, many other economic activities—agriculture, insurance, or education, for instance—may not be as complicated as manufacturing is in terms of benefiting from different tasks being performed in many different places. Yet even these economic sectors are becoming dominated by large transnational corporations, and increasingly rely upon new technologies, greater economies of scale, and global divisions of labor.

Of course, the forces of change unleashed by globalization have had an impact that goes far beyond just the economic realm. Globalization has affected and continues to affect politics, culture, social organization, and even the natural landscape. Any process this powerful is bound to provoke controversy, and globalization has attracted both critics and defenders who represent a wide variety of perspectives. Let us now turn our attention to the ways in which globalization contributes to social change.

Growth and Inequality

Perhaps the most evident impact of globalization has been economic, and the economic results have provided globalization advocates with their most persuasive evidence that globalization has been, on the whole, a force of positive change. It is a fairly undeniable fact that in the last two decades, overall economic growth worldwide has increased, and most economists would agree that the globalization of the economy is the major reason for this.[4] For the reasons outlined above, the global economy has made it possible to produce more goods and services for less cost. The direct result has been greater overall productivity, that is, economic growth, and this economic growth has translated into a higher average standard of living around the world over the last twenty years. Economic data also support the conclusion that even many less developed countries have increased their average wealth during this time period.[5]

The cause and effect comes right out of Adam Smith and classical economic theory: given an opportunity for profit, people and businesses will compete in the marketplace, and competition fosters innovation and higher productivity. This stimulates both demand and investment, which in the long run, leads to higher employment and higher wages. While some groups may do better than others, the resulting creation of wealth ultimately benefits all sectors of the economy. If economic growth is the goal, and if globalization creates economic growth, then it is logical that globalization should be promoted and that restraints on the process are counterproductive. It is a compelling argument, made all the more persuasive by the dismal economic performances of the societies that have participated least in the global economy in the last two decades, such as Cuba, Myanmar, and North Korea.

Yet other economists criticize the way that globalization has contributed to wealth creation. Some point out that statistics about economic growth can be deceptive, because they measure long-term averages and fail to acknowledge the uneven and inconsistent distribution of benefits.[6] Critics of globalization have pointed out that that in the last two decades increases in wealth have been concentrated among certain groups: specifically, the most developed nations, and, in societies at all levels of development, the social groups who are already the most well-off. The wealthiest fifth of the world's nations—mostly located in Western Europe, North America, and East Asia—have vastly increased their relative wealth compared to the rest over the last fifty years. In contrast, average standards of living have stagnated or declined in the poorest quarter of the world's countries. Meanwhile, within all nations, modernized or not, the last two decades have seen a growing concentration of wealth and power in the hands of fewer people, whose often remarkable gains significantly distort the overall averages. It is argued that the era of globalization has actually made most people throughout the world either no better off or worse off in terms of wealth and income.

In other words, while overall and even average wealth has increased, so has economic inequality, and this inequality operates on two levels. First, critics argue, the gap between the most developed societies and the still-developing nations has grown in recent years. In particular, the poorest nations, including most nations in sub-Saharan Africa, have seen their economic fortunes decline in both real and relative terms. Second, it has been noted that the wealth differential between well-off groups and poor groups within individual societies, both developed and less developed, has also widened.[7] Both sorts of inequality have historically been destabilizing social factors, as observers from Marx and Durkheim right up to the present have pointed out, especially when combined with some of the less-quantifiable consequences discussed below.

Power & Authority in an Era of Globalization

While even firm economic statistics can be open to interpretation, other effects of globalization are difficult if not impossible to describe with objective data. One area where this is especially true is in the political realm: one of globalization's most important impacts has been on the way power and authority work in the modern world, especially in developing societies.

In the modern world, it has become an accepted dictum that a nation that wishes to raise the standard of living of its citizens needs to attract capital investment to create jobs and infrastructure. In the developing parts of the world, almost by definition, this means that development is reliant upon foreign investment. Most sources of foreign investment are in the private sector, such as transnational corporations, or are guided from international entities such as the World Bank or the International Monetary Fund that rely on private investment. To invest in a developing nation, the potential source of investment must believe that there is a reasonable prospect of profit, and in practice, what this means is that national governments are under pressure to create a "positive investment climate" where profit seems more likely. Yet, obviously, investment capital is not infinite, which means that the governments of developing nations must compete to attract it.

Most often, the creation of such an investment climate has pressured national governments into changing and restricting their roles in their national economies. Certain related conditions that contribute to the "liberalization" or "**restructuring**" of national economies are typically required to attract foreign investment.[8] These include such elements as deregulation, lower corporate taxes, and less protection of domestic industries, and together they amount to the reduction of the role of government in the economy. Increasingly, the International Monetary Fund and the World Bank insist on such restructuring for client states to qualify for debt relief and the procurement of loans.[9] Moreover, if a given government refuses to conform to such requirements, it is likely that some other nation, one even more desperate for investment capital, will conform to them, and will thus be a better candidate for investment. What this often means is that if the government of a particular nation does not liberalize enough, that nation will get little investment capital, and find it difficult or impossible to create or sustain economic growth.

While these conditions are usually justified on the basis of economic efficiency, they undermine national sovereignty by restricting the role of government in national affairs. Less government power does not automatically translate into more productivity and efficiency. In fact, classical liberal economic theory notes that the efficient operation of a free market system works best when there is a balance of power between private and public interests, because economic competition needs a legal and infra-structural framework within which it can take place lawfully and openly. Early proponents of market economies, such as Smith and John Stuart Mill, explained that governments, acting on behalf of the public interest, must play the role of "referee" to ensure an orderly and stable "playing field." One evident effect of globalization is that this balance is upset, because the demands of investment capital, in the view of some critics, hold governments "hostage" to the demands of large transnational businesses and the international organizations that represent their interests. This has meant that governments in the era of globalization have had to accept a smaller role and less authority in economic matters. At the same time, international businesses, through mergers and acquisitions, have become larger and fewer, which has diminished the amount of true competition in the marketplace, as Marx had foreseen.

Of course, one may argue that larger economic enterprises are more efficient, and that globalization has not undermined competition enough to allow monopolistic behavior; some in fact contend that a freer flow of investment stimulates competition. Yet even if this is so, a highly problematic structural problem remains. This has to do with incentives: while national governments exist for the explicit purpose of protecting the public welfare, private businesses do not. In fact, the primary—some might argue the only—responsibility of a private business is to its stockholders, by expanding market share and providing a return on investment. Corporate directors, if they have to choose between profitability and public interest, have a clear and obvious choice.

It is largely for this reason that much contemporary criticism of globalization focuses on the way that private gains are frequently achieved by businesses in direct opposition to the public interest.[10] In particular, market incentives can do little to solve major social crises like famines, epidemics, or rampant inflation, or to deal with long-term problems such as environmental damage or the exhaustion of natural resources. Conforming to the requirements of capital investment often erodes governments' ability to carry out their primary responsibility of "protective security," which can have ominous results throughout the society in question. As one recent critic noted,

> Some of the fundamental responsibilities of the state in a market economy—responsibilities first recognized, described, and discussed by Adam Smith over two hundred years ago—are not now being discharged by anyone. At the heart of the international political economy, there is a vacuum . . . the diffusion of authority away from national governments has left a yawning hole of non-authority, ungovernance it might be called.[11]

Economic Volatility

Of course, one can easily see that government's definition of the "public interest" can be problematic, and one critical lesson of the twentieth century is certainly that expanded government power is not always benign. The careers of such leaders as Stalin, Hitler, and Pol Pot demonstrate how dictators and warlords can employ the fruits of modernization—technological, military, and bureaucratic—to oppress, persecute, and even enslave their own citizens. Yet it is a logical fallacy to conclude that less government power automatically increases individual liberties. Increasingly, globalization has shown a distinct tendency to put people at the mercy of different types of power, ones that are not only beyond their control, but even beyond their understanding. As public power declines, the net result is not always more freedom for the individual.

Over a century ago, observers like Durkheim, Marx and Weber warned of the vulnerability of societies to the effects of powerful economic forces that come with a modern capitalist economy.[12] One reason is that when investors rapidly move their capital from one investment to another it results in dramatic swings both in economic sectors and throughout the economy as a whole. This phenomenon is known as **market volatility**. Especially at the higher levels of finance, markets tend to rise and fall according to perceived future values that may or may not have any grounding in economic reality. In the age of the world-wide web, when financial transactions can take place almost instantaneously, the prices of such investments as stocks, bonds, and national currencies are determined by the behavior of the "electronic herd," instead of reflecting whatever objective material value they may have originally represented.[13]

Because of this, one of the most serious consequences of globalization is that nations, industries, regions, and even individuals lose control over their economic destinies. As buying and selling takes place in international financial markets, the flows of capital that fuel the modern economy affect interest rates, prices, employment rates, and the value of money, which have direct impacts on the livelihoods of citizens. Quite literally, decisions that are made in corporate boardrooms or in stock exchanges halfway around the world can have more real impact on the lives of individuals than anything their national or local governments can do. Globalization has meant that this new sort of power has reduced the abilities of most people to control their own welfare.[14] The result has been that the global era of "economic freedom" hardly resembles what classical liberals had in mind when they promoted the virtues of independence and self-reliance.

Today, the problem of volatility is a critical issue in developing nations. The rapidly shifting flows of capital upon which today's global economy depends seldom allow for the type of steady and reliable investment that is necessary for long-term economic development. This is even true when investment is managed by international organizations. For instance, one former World Bank official notes that the policies of this organization actually discourage investment and increase the tax burdens on the middle class and working classes. They also lead to high interest rates and do little to encourage job creation, even though two of the most serious economic problems in developing nations are the scarcity of capital and high unemployment rates.[15]

The **Asian Financial Crisis of 1997** demonstrates the sorts of havoc that economic volatility can create in widely different parts of the world.[16] While the 1980s and early 1990s had seen steady and occasionally spectacular economic growth in Southeast Asia, worries about the financial stability of certain governments had emerged in financial markets. In July of 1997, actions taken by the government of Thailand caused international investors to suddenly lose confidence in the value of that country's currency, and in just a few days, the Thai *baht* lost more than 80% of its value on international markets. As a result, Thailand's government was essentially bankrupted, and a spillover affect in neighboring economies encouraged private and public investors alike to quickly "dump" their investments in Asian governments and stock markets. The result was a financial collapse that within weeks paralyzed the economies of not just Thailand but Indonesia and South Korea, while severely affecting the Philippines, Malaysia, Hong Kong, and other East Asian nations. Over the course of the summer, financial panic contributed to a variety of economic ills in the region that ranged from massive unemployment, to corporate bankruptcies, to roaring inflation, to rioting in the streets, and even to the collapse of the Indonesian government. It also affected many private firms and national governments throughout the world that had significant financial involvements in the countries directly affected.

In retrospect, the primary cause of this crisis was financial overspeculation by investors seeking to profit from fluctuations in world financial markets. When confidence suddenly evaporated, the "electronic herd" panicked, as investors all over the world scrambled madly pull their money out of areas perceived as risky. These financial decisions, made by executives and government officials, victimized literally millions of people who had no influence whatsoever over this chain reaction of investment and disinvestment; these included business owners, individual investors, workers, farmers, consumers, and, perhaps especially, the desperately poor in the nations affected. Almost all of these groups were harmed for no reason that had anything to do with their own actions or choices. Vulnerable to huge, incomprehensible market forces over which they had no control whatsoever, people suffered unemployment, poverty, hunger, homelessness, and even violent death because of the volatility of the global marketplace.

Despite the purported benefits of such economic freedom, globalization and the economic dependency it promotes undermines peoples' abilities to control their lives. For many, the determinants of their success in life are not hard work or wise choices or being good citizens. Instead, sweeping economic forces resulting from business decisions made in New York, Shanghai, and London have become the factors most responsible for whether many people today, and their children, will enjoy a promising future—or, in some cases, whether they will enjoy any sort of future at all. Weber, Marx and Durkheim were only among the first to explain the social destruction that happens when individuals lose control over their own destinies.

Those of us living in more fortunate situations may think, as our ancestors have done, that while life is often unfair, the misfortunes of others don't really affect our own lives. However, in a global world in which the world's societies are ever more interconnected in all sorts of ways, the misfortunes of others are becoming less distant, and more relevant to our own welfare, every day.

Urbanization and the Environment

Recent demographic trends reveal another troubling element that is intimately connected with globalization: as the world population has grown over the last century from about one billion in 1900 to almost seven billion today, most of the growth has taken place in the developing world.[17] The reasons for this are clear and logical. Since the Industrial Revolution, wealthier and more developed societies have lowered their birth rates, and this has meant that even while average lifespans have increased, population levels have been largely steady. In contrast, in most developing parts of the globe, modernization has brought advances in health care and food production, without a corresponding decline in birthrates. Hence, the demographic balance between developed and less developed nations has shifted in both real and relative terms. Should this trend continue, in another fifty years, about 10% of the world's population will control as much as 80% of the total wealth, while accounting for more than 90% of the consumption of the world's resources.[18]

While this is unsettling in and of itself, it is compounded by another key demographic feature of the modern age, which is steadily growing urbanization. Undoubtedly globalization has contributed to this trend by creating far more jobs in cities than in the countryside.[19] One reason why this is a problem is that urban growth in the developing world contributes to environmental change and degradation, which is perhaps the most serious threat affecting the world today. The continued growth of cities contributes to global warming, ozone depletion, the disruption of hydrologic processes threatening water supplies, erosion, the loss of biodiversity, and a shrinking supply of key resources such as clean water and fossil fuels.[20] Since the coming of the Industrial Revolution, half the world's wetlands have been destroyed and two-thirds of the world's farmlands have been designated as either "somewhat degraded" or "strongly degraded."[21]

Solutions to such problems are difficult in the global era. As noted above, globalization has made national governments, especially those in the developing world, less able to prevent or repair such damage, because the need for capital investment discourages governments from enacting more stringent environmental restrictions. Meanwhile, it is difficult to expect the private enterprises that are both directly and indirectly contributing to such environmental damage to help in more than a symbolic way. For corporations whose responsibility is to shareholders, the need to operate profitably is a higher priority than long-term environmental interests. The latter is irrelevant to input and production decisions, except as scarcity affects costs; at most, corporations may adopt more environmentally friendly policies to enhance their corporate image for marketing purposes. In the words of one observer, "In modernity, nature has come to be considered as a 'resource' to be used instrumentally to fulfill human desires."[22]

Even when they do intervene in the public interest, governments of developing countries often find that their choices are quite difficult. A good example of the dilemma faced can be seen in the case of the Brazilian Amazon, where hundreds of acres of environmentally critical rainforest are cleared every day. It is largely a misperception that large transnational corporations are responsible for this; instead, these practices are mostly being carried out by common Brazilians who are trying to make a living in the region by clearing areas where they can establish farms and ranches. If their government prevents them from doing this, as some environmental groups insist, such people will remain in Brazil's overcrowded cities, where there is already significant unemployment.[23]

In the era of globalization, it is the people living in the developing world who are paying most of the environmental price tag for the global economy. In exchange for jobs and tax revenues, they get toxic chemicals in their air and water, have less good farmland to grow food, and a shortage of needed natural resources for their own people. While affluent nations can often afford the added costs that come with environment protection and recovery, poorer nations usually cannot. It is places like Indonesia, India, Brazil, and China, where swelling urban populations are putting unsustainable pressure on nature, where the environmental costs of globalization become brutally clear.

Globalization and Cultural Backlash

As a complex and far-reaching process, globalization can affect every aspect of a society. In many cases, it forces change on people whose societies have been functioning successfully for many generations, by disrupting traditional types of authority, ways of doing business, and patterns of social interaction. Some societies are able to absorb the social change it puts into motion better than others, while within a given society, some groups usually benefit more than others.[24]

What this means is that today most people experience a different kind of poverty than the poor of a century ago. While their more rural ancestors were isolated, traditional, uneducated, and more concerned with local issues, the vast majority of today's poor are living in cities where traditional cultures have been disrupted by rapid social change. One commonality that globalization brings is an emphasis on money transactions. In the global world of economic dependency and specialization, nearly everybody needs money in order meet basic needs such as food, clothing, and housing, yet money economies are more compatible with some cultures than others, and can disrupt kinship, social, and political relationships. In fact, some have argued that globalization is driven by the immense power of modern media to manipulate tastes and preferences, consciously forcing a consumer-oriented culture upon traditional world societies.[25]

In 1944, in the midst of the most destructive war in human history, the economist Karl Polanyi linked the rise of European militarism and totalitarianism to the uncertainties of the global free market economy that had emerged out of the Industrial Revolution.[26] In Polanyi's view, both the First World War and the economic chaos that followed were consequences of rapid modernization that made many political states helpless to protect the interests of their citizens, while tearing apart the social fabric that held communities together. By the 1930s, socialism and fascism appeared to many as reasonable solutions to the collapse of civil society. Sociologically, these phenomena represented a backlash against rapid social change and modernization, and legitimately or not, opportunistic leaders gained popular support by demonizing "free market" economic policies. While Lenin and Stalin denounced worldwide capitalist exploitation, the Nazis promised to create a "*volksge-meinschaft*" that would give alienated Germans a sense of belonging and purpose.

The trends of the more recent age of globalization offer a frightening parallel. An increasing proportion of the world's population can be found in overcrowded urban areas that feature damaged ecosystems and few opportunities to earn the money necessary to maintain a reasonable standard of living. Poverty, of course, is nothing new, but today's poverty takes place in a far more combustible environment. While in past ages the world's poor tended to be rural and ignorant, this is no longer the case. Today's poor not only share urban space with the wealthy, but they have access to all sorts of media, from television to billboards to the internet, that make them keenly aware of their own disadvantages. The bombardment of images of "the good life" made possible by global consumerism forces them to compare their situations to that of wealthier neighbors and wealthier societies elsewhere, and wonder, "why do they have what we can't have?" A seemingly inescapable result of the modernization of the world is that today's poor are far more conscious of global inequality than ever before, and it should surprise no one that resentment and anger are reaching new levels as well.

One may well ask whether globalization is really the cause of these people's helplessness and misery, as well as whether the Western world, especially the United States, should be held accountable for it. Persuasive cases can be made either way, because globalization is obviously a complicated process. But whether blame is justified isn't really the issue; instead what does matter is that a growing number of people, primarily outside the Western world, increasingly *believe* that globalization is responsible. The actual accuracy of this belief is far less relevant than the potential consequences of the belief.

This is why it may be helpful to view **terrorism** not as an element in and of itself, but as a symptom of a larger phenomenon. In many respects, terrorism is an expression of growing frustration and resentment against the huge, incomprehensible global forces that have come to dominate so many people's lives. Charismatic leaders, positioning themselves as defenders of traditional values, offer the helpless and dispossessed the opportunity to defend themselves and their cultures against outside enemies.

Perhaps the attacks on September 11, 2001 may attain a deeper significance to future historians. Thus far in the twenty-first century, only certain groups, such as Al-Qaeda, have had both the means and the ideology to justify violence in the name of what they see as "self-defense," and have been able to carry out terrorist attacks effectively. It may be just a matter of time before other frustrated societies start to take the same path.

"Gift from the West" or "Western Curse"?

As the Nobel Prize-winning economist Amartya Sen points out, there is currently a tendency to see globalization as one of two extremes, either as a "gift from the West to the world" or else as a "Western curse."[27] Those who agree with the first view naturally conclude that globalization should continue without restraint, while those who agree with the second idea work to prevent or reverse it.

Neither viewpoint is especially helpful. The conclusion that globalization is an unalloyed blessing leads to a denial of its role in the problems that face world civilization today. This clearly undermines our ability to understand and solve such problems. The second view is equally shortsighted, since it encourages a backlash that can create even more problems, such as quasi-fascist states or terrorism.[28] Instead, what is needed is an understanding of how globalization works, so that we can take advantage of the opportunities it presents while being aware of the challenges it creates. In all likelihood, as modernization proceeds in the coming decades, the world's communities will become even more interdependent, and we will need to deal with this continuing process in a constructive and thoughtful way.

References and Suggested Readings:

Blustein, Paul. *The Chastening: Inside the Crisis that Rocked the Global Financial System and Humbled the IMF.* New York: Public Affairs, 2001.

Friedman, Thomas. *The Lexus and the Olive Tree.* New York: Anchor. 2000.

Imazon: Amazon Institute of People and the Environment. Website. http:// www.imazon.org.br (accessed August 10, 2010).

International Forum on Globalization. "A Better World is Possible!" 2002. http://www.ifg.org/alt_eng.pdf (accessed August 10, 2010).

Lechner, Frank J., and John Boli, *The Globalization Reader*, 3rd Ed., New York: Wiley-Blackwell, 2007.

Marcotullio, Peter, and Gordon McGranahan. *Scaling Urban Environmental Challenges.* New York: International Institute for Environment and Development and United Nations University/Institute for Advanced Studies, 2007.

Margulis, Sergio *Causes of Deforestation of the Brazilian Amazon.* Washington D.C.: The World Bank. Working Paper No. 22 2004.

Marx, Karl. *Wage Labour and Capital,* "Effect of Capitalist Competition on the Capitalist Class, the Middle Class and the Working Class" (1847) http://www.marxists.org/archive/marx/works/ (accessed August 10, 2010).

Ohmae, Kenichi. *The End of the Nation State and the Rise of Regional Economies.* New York: Simon & Schuster, 1995.

Sachs, Jeffrey D. *Common Wealth: Economics for a Crowded Planet.* New York: Penguin, 2008.

Sen, Amartya. "How to Judge Globalism" Frank J. Lechner and John Boli, eds. *The Globalization Reader*, 3rd Edition. Oxford: Blackwell 2008.

_____. *Development as Freedom.* New York: Anchor Books, 1999.

Smith, Adam. *An Inquiry into the Nature and Causes of the Wealth of Nations* (1776), Edwin Cannan, ed. New York: Modern Library 1937.

Steger, Manfred B. *Globalization: A Very Short Introduction* (London: Oxford University Press, 2009.

Strange, Susan. *The Retreat of the State.* Cambridge: Cambridge University Press, 1996.

Stiglitz, Joseph. "Globalism's Discontents." *The Globalization Reader*, 3rd Edition. Frank J. Lechner and John Boli, eds., Oxford Blackwell 2008.

Torrey, Barbara Boyle. "Urbanization: An Environmental Force to Be Reckoned With" Population Reference Bureau website. April 2004. http://www.prb.org/Articles/2004/ (accessed August 10, 2010).

United Nations. *World Urbanization Prospects: The 2003 Revision* (New York: UN, 2004).

_____. *2007 Human Development Report,* "A Safe City is a Just City" http://hdr.undp.org/en/nhdr/monitoring/news/2007/title,4456,en.html (accessed August 10, 2010).

Wade, Robert Hunter. "Is Globalization Reducing Poverty and Inequality?" *World Development*, 32:4, 2004, p. 567-589.

Weber, Max. *Readings and Commentary on Modernity*, Stephen Kalberg, Ed. (Oxford: Oxford University Press, 2005).

Wolf, Martin. *Why Globalization Works* (New Haven: Yale University Press, 2004).

World Trade Organization. "The GATT/WTO at 60: WTO World Trade Report examines six decades of multilateralism in trade" Dec. 4 2007 http://www.wto.org/english/news_e/ (accessed August 10, 2010).

Notes

1. For a spectrum of definitions, see Manfred B. Steger, *Globalization: A Very Short Introduction* (London: Oxford University Press, 2009), p. 13.

2. World Trade Organization, Dec. 4, 2007 www.wto.org/english/news_e/ (accessed August 10, 2010).

3. Adam Smith, *An Inquiry into the Nature and Causes of the Wealth of Nations,* Book 1, Chapter 1 (New York: Modern Library, 1937), pp. 3-12

4. The connection between globalization and increased economic growth has been noted by many, including Thomas Friedman, *The World is Flat: A Brief History of the Twenty-First Century*, (New York: Farrar, Straus & Giroux, 2007); and Martin Wolf, *Why Globalization Works* (New Haven: Yale University Press, 2004).

5. Wolf, *Why Globalization Works*, pp. 140-144.

6. Steger, *Globalization*, p. 106-111; Amartya Sen, "How to Judge Globalism," *The American Prospect* 13:1 (Jan. 2002), p. 19-24.

7. In addition to the sources cited in note 6, see Joseph Stiglitz, "Globalism's Discontents," eds. Lechner and Boli, *The Globalization Reader*, 3rd Ed., p. 210-212; Robert Hunter Wade, "Is Globalization Reducing Poverty and Inequality?" *World Development*, 32:4 (2004), p. 567-589.

8. International Forum on Globalization website. "A Better World is Possible!" (2002) http://www.ifg.org/alt_eng.pdf (accessed August 10, 2010); Kenichi Ohmae, *The End of the Nation State and the Rise of Regional Economies* (New York: Free Press, 1995), p. 11-16.

9. Some of the problems created by such conditions are discussed in Stiglitz, "Globalism's Discontents," p. 208-215; Sen, "How to Judge Globalism," p. 19-24; Steger, *Globalization*, p. 54-57.

10. Sen, *Development as Freedom* (New York: Anchor Books, 1999), p. 123-129, 183-188.

11. Susan Strange, *The Retreat of the State* (Cambridge: Cambridge University Press, 1996), p. 14.

12. Marx, *Capital*, 1887, Vol. I, Section One, Ch. 25; vol III, Part One Ch 6 ; Marx, *Wage Labour and Capital*, "Effect of Capitalist Competition on the Capitalist Class, the Middle Class and the Working Class" (1847) http://www.marxists.org/archive/marx/works/ (accessed August 10, 2010); Weber, "The Antagonism of the Economy and Political Domains to Ethical Action," Ch. 18, Max Weber, *Readings and Commentary on Modernity*, Stephen Kalberg, Ed. (Oxford, 2005), p. 251-254; the concept is an essential foundation of Durkheim's *Division of Labor and Suicide.*

13. The term "electronic herd" was coined by Thomas Friedman in *The Lexus and the Olive Tree* (New York: Anchor, 2000).

14. Steger, *Globalization*, 101-106; Stiglitz, "Globalism's Discontents," p. 211-212.

15. Stiglitz, "Globalism's Discontents," p. 210-212.

16. On the 1997 Asian financial crisis, see Paul Blustein, *The Chastening: Inside the Crisis that Rocked the Global Financial System and Humbled the IMF* (New York: Public Affairs, 2001).

17. Jeffrey D. Sachs, *Common Wealth: Economics for a Crowded Planet* (New York: Penguin, 2008), p. 26-46; United Nations, *World Urbanization Prospects: The 2003 Revision* (New York: United Nations, 2004), p. 1-35. http://www.un.org/esa/population/publications/wup2003/WUP2003Report.pdf (accessed August 10, 2010).

18. United Nations, *World Urbanization Prospects*, p. 1-8.

19. Sachs, *Common Wealth*, p. 25-28.

20. Peter Marcotullio and Gordon McGranahan "Scaling the Urban Environmental Challenge," in *Scaling Urban Environmental Challenges*. ed. Marcotullio and McGranahan (New York, International Institute for Environment and Development and United Nations University/Institute for Advanced Studies 2007) p. 1-17; Barbara Boyle Torrey, "Urbanization: An Environmental Force to Be Reckoned With" Population Reference Bureau website. April 2004. http://www.prb.org/Articles/2004/ (accessed August 10, 2010).

21. Steger, *Globalization*, p. 87; Sachs, *Common Wealth*, p. 39-41.

22. Steger, *Globalization*, p. 84.

23. Margulis, Sergio. *Causes of Deforestation of the Brazilian Amazon.* (Washington DC: World Bank, 2004); Imazon: Amazon Institute of People and the Environment website http://www.imazon.org.br (accessed August 10, 2010).

24. Sen, *Development as Freedom*, p. 240-242.

25. Leslie Sklair, *Globalism: Capitalism and its Alternatives*, 3rd ed. (London, 2002), p. 62-69; Steger, *Globalization*, p. 70-80.

26. Polanyi, *The Great Transformation: The Political and Economic Origins of Our Time* (New York, 1944). His argument has been elaborated and expanded by more recent observers, including Susan Strange, *The Retreat of the State.*

27. Sen, "How to Judge Globalism," p. 1.

28. *Ibid.*, p. 1.

Can Any Good Come of Radical Islam?

A Modernizing Force? Maybe.

Francis Fukuyama and Nadav Samin

Thursday, September 12, 2002 12:01 a.m.

What is going on in the Muslim world? Why does it produce suicide hijackers on the one hand and, on the other, lethargic and haphazardly capitalist societies that have delivered neither economic development nor democracy? A good if partial answer to these questions—partial because it is limited to the Arab region of that world—can be found in a United Nations "development report" issued in July. As the U.N. assessment concludes, the entire Arab sector, with all its oil wealth, is "richer than it is developed." Its economies are stagnant, illiteracy is widespread, political freedom is hardly to be found, and its inhabitants, especially its women, are denied the basic "capabilities" and "opportunities" of the modern world.

The U.N. report—written significantly, by a group of Arab intellectuals—was commissioned well before last fall's attacks on the U.S. But its pertinence to those attacks has seemed clear enough to commentators. Thomas Friedman of the *New York Times* called it the key to understanding "the milieu that produced bin Ladenism, and will reproduce it if nothing changes." An editorial in *The Wall Street Journal* found "little wonder" in the fact that "such an isolated culture became a breeding ground for the Islamic fundamentalism that spawned September 11."

The Islamism of Osama bin Laden and his followers is indeed inseparable from the developmental failures of the world's Arab societies. All the same, however, it would be a mistake to conceive of the Islamist movement as nothing more than an expression of those failures. The phenomenon of radical Islam is more complicated than that, and in all sorts of surprising ways its long-term effect on the entire orbit of Islamic society may turn out to be more complicated still.

Last September's attacks against the United States were carried out by a group of Muslims led by a gaunt, bearded ascetic sitting in a cave in Afghanistan and spouting unfathomable rhetoric. So all-consuming was the hijackers' hatred of America that they were willing to blow *themselves* up for their cause—something that set them apart from earlier generations of terrorists. Where did this zeal, so foreign to the modern democratic temperament, come from?

On the part of many observers, the immediate impulse was to attribute it to deep cultural factors, and in particular to the teachings of fundamentalist Islam. And of course there was, and is, much to be said for this view. In particular, the fact that, far from repudiating bin Laden, Muslims and Westerners tended to line up on opposite sides in their interpretation of the events of September 11 gave credence to the paradigm of the Harvard political scientist Samuel Huntington, who predicted a number of years ago that the post-Cold War world would give rise to a "clash of civilizations."

Still, foolish as it would be to downplay the role of religious or "civilizational" factors, it will not do simply to call Osama bin Laden an Islamic fundamentalist. For the Islamism of which he is a symbol and a spokesman is not a movement aimed at restoring some archaic or pristine form of Islamic practice. As several observers have argued, including most recently the Iranian scholars Ladan and Roya Boroumand in the *Journal of Democracy*, it is best understood not as a traditional movement but as a very modern one.

Groups like al Qaeda, the Boroumands write, owe an explicit debt to 20th-century European doctrines of the extreme right and left. One stream of influence can be traced to Hassan al-Banna, the schoolteacher who founded the Muslim Brotherhood in Egypt in 1928. From Italy's Fascists, al-Banna borrowed the idea of unquestioning loyalty to a charismatic leader, modeling the slogan of his paramilitary organization—"action, obedience, silence"—on Mussolini's injunction to "believe, obey, fight." Taking a cue from the Nazis, he placed great emphasis on the Muslim Brotherhood's youth wing and on the marriage of the physical and the spiritual, of Islam with activism. Unsurprisingly, al-Banna also taught his followers to expect not encouragement but repression from traditional Islamic authorities.

A second European source of Islamism can be traced to Maulana Mawdudi, who founded the Jamaat-e-Islami movement in Pakistan in the early 1940s. A journalist well-versed in Marxist thought, Mawdudi advocated struggle by an Islamic "revolutionary vanguard" against both the West *and* traditional Islam. As the Boroumands observe, he was perhaps the first to attach "the adjective 'Islamic' to such distinctively Western terms as 'revolution,' 'state,' and 'ideology.'"

These strands of the radical right and left eventually came together in the person of Sayyid Qutb, the Egyptian who became the Muslim Brotherhood's chief ideologist after World War II. In his most important work, "Signposts Along the Road," Qutb called for a monolithic state led by an Islamic party, advocating the use of every violent means necessary to achieve that end. The society he envisioned would be classless, one in which the "selfish individual" of liberal societies would be abolished and the "exploitation of man by man" would end. This, as the Boroumands point out, was "Leninism in an Islamist dress," and it is the creed embraced by most present-day Islamists.

Though developed among Sunnis, this virulent ideological mix reached the Shiite world as well, most notably through its influence on Ayatollah Khomeini in Iran. Indeed, the Iranian revolution of 1979 conferred on Islamism a degree of religious respectability that it had never before possessed. But the fact that the movement could so easily bridge the bitter Shiite-Sunni divide also suggests just how sharply divorced it is from Islamic history and custom. As the Boroumands conclude, the key attributes of Islamism—"the aestheticization of death, the glorification of armed force, the worship of martyrdom, and 'faith in the propaganda of the deed'"—have little precedent in Islam but have been defining features of modern totalitarianism. The seeming rigor of Osama bin Laden's theology belies the reality of his highly heterodox beliefs.

So much for the ideological side of things. On the sociological side, there is still another close parallel between Islamism and the rise of European fascism. Though Hitler was a great entrepreneur of ideas, the roots of his movement, as described in classic analyses like Fritz Stern's "The Politics of Cultural Despair" (1974), lay in the rapid industrialization of central Europe. In the course of a single generation, millions of peasants had moved from tightly knit village communities to large, impersonal cities, losing in the process a range of familiar cultural norms and signposts.

This rapid transition—captured in Ferdinand Toennies's famous distinction between *Gemeinschaft* (community) and *Gesellschaft* (society)—was perhaps the most powerful impetus behind modern nationalism. Deprived of local sources of identity, displaced villagers found new social bonds in language, in ethnicity and—ultimately—in the mythopoetic propaganda of Europe's extreme right. Though the various right-wing parties pretended to revive ancient traditions—pre-Christian Germanic ones in the case of Nazism, Roman ones in the case of the Italian Fascists—their doctrines were really a syncretic mishmash, old symbols and new ideas brought together by the most up-to-date forms of communications technology.

Islamism, as the late Ernest Geliner was among the first to note, has followed a similar path. Over the last several decades, most Muslim societies have undergone a social transformation not unlike that of Europe in the late 19th century. Large numbers of villagers and tribesmen have moved to the vast urban slums of Cairo, Algiers and Amman, leaving behind the variegated, often preliterate Islam of the countryside. Islamism has filled the void, offering a new identity based on a puritanical, homogenized creed. Syncretist in the manner of fascism, it unites traditional religious symbols and rhetoric with the ideology of revolutionary action.

Some observers, especially after September 11, have suggested that the real engine of Islamism's growth is poverty, but this is not the case. According to the recent U.N. report, for example, the Arab world actually compares favorably to other developing regions when it comes to preventing abject want. Rather, like European fascism before it, Islamism is bred by rapid social dislocation. More often than not, its leaders and propagandists are newcomers to the middle or upper classes. Islamism introduces these educated but often lonely and alienated individuals to a larger *umma* (community) of believers, from Tangier to Jakarta to London. Through the magic of the cassette tape recorder (in Khomeini's case) or video (for bin Laden), they become members of a vibrant, if dangerous and destructive, international community.

Seeing Islamism for what it really is goes beyond correct taxonomy. It also points us in the direction of an important, if seemingly perverse, question: Could it, like both fascism and communism before it, serve inadvertently as a modernizing force, preparing the way for Muslim societies that can respond not destructively but constructively to the challenge of the West?

The question is not as absurd as it may sound. Comparisons are especially tricky here, but the Bolsheviks succeeded in creating an industrialized, urbanized Russia, and Hitler managed to get rid of the Junkers and much of the class stratification that had characterized prewar Germany. Through a tortuous and immensely costly path, both of these "isms" cleared away some of the premodern underbrush that had obstructed the growth of liberal democracy. There are, of course, much safer and more peaceful routes toward modernization, such as those taken by countries like South Korea or Britain or the United States, and less expensive paths to modernity were surely available to Russia and Germany. But one has to deal with what one has, and in Islamic cultures, in any case, there is arguably much more underbrush to be cleared away. If Islamism is directed as much against traditional forms of Islam as against the West, could it, too, be a source of such creative destruction?

There are myriad ways in which not only Islamic practice but the rigid legal framework within which it is encased has obstructed change. The economic historian Timur Kuran has documented in painstaking detail a series of traditional Islamic institutions whose inflexibility and legalism have served as immense barriers to development. Interest rates are fixed by religious authorities, schooling focuses on rote learning of religious texts and discourages critical thinking, women are kept out of political and economic life, and so on. Even an institution like the *waqf*, or traditional Islamic charity, which could serve as a bulwark of civil society in a reformed Islamic order, fixes the bequests of wealthy individuals in perpetuity, with no opportunity for adaptation to changing circumstances.

Many of these same constraints existed historically in the Judeo-Christian West, and were eliminated or ameliorated only after long struggle. All of them continue to exist in the Islamic present, and can only be removed through the exercise of political power. Islamism has already demonstrated the capability of doing this, and even of accommodating Western norms when it has to. Though Khomeini brought back the chador, or veil, for women, he also reluctantly sanctioned women's right to vote in Iranian elections, a practice (won under the shah) that he had once likened to prostitution.

In Egypt, the Muslim Brotherhood as well as other, even more radical Islamist organizations have created a layer of voluntary associations standing between the family and the state. It was, for example, Islamist charities that stepped into the breach at the time of the 1992 Cairo earthquake, providing important social services unavailable from the inept and corrupt Egyptian state. The Islamists clearly hope to reunite religion and political power one day, which would be a disaster. But they are learning—and inculcating—habits of association and independent action that, if somehow divorced from their radical ideology, might yet help lay the groundwork of a true civil society.

There is another area in which the reactionary ideas of the Islamists may play a potentially progressive role, and this has to do with the fundamental sources of authority and legitimacy in the Islamic world.

The traditional system of Islamic jurisprudence—with its rigid rules and hierarchies—has been under attack, in one way or another, since at least the 19th century. The most important early figures in this effort were modernizers, like the Iranian Jamal al-din al-Afghani (1839–97) and his student, the Egyptian reformer Muhammad Abduh (1849–1905). Abduh was among the first to depart from the rigidly textual form of interpretation that had characterized the Sunni world since the earliest caliphates. In his view, human reason was the only appropriate tool for applying the fundamental truths of the Koran and the Sunna (the traditions of the Prophet). Appointed mufti of Egypt toward the end of his life, Abduh issued rulings reflecting, in the words of one scholar, his desire "to render the religion of Islam entirely adaptable to the requirements of modern civilization."

The implications of this turn were profound. Though the institutional base of orthodox Sunni Islam remained intact, the long-sealed gates of doctrinal explication were unhinged. Like a Muslim Luther, Abduh shook up the clerical establishment by reviving, under the influence of his mentor al-Afghani, the possibility of independent legal interpretation. His example gave unprecedented latitude to all subsequent construers of Islamic tradition, whether saints or demagogues—the latter including anti-Western radicals like the Muslim Brotherhood's Sayyid Qutb and, eventually, Osama bin Laden.

In the battle for interpretative power, it is no coincidence that the primary breeding ground for Islamism has been the brittle oligarchies of Saudi Arabia and Egypt. Both regimes have co-opted the traditional clergy, forcing the populist current of Islam into back alleys and storefront mosques and turning it into an ideological guerrilla movement. Detached from the moorings of tradition, the Islamists have proved adept at manipulating the symbols of faith and appropriating them for their own revolutionary purposes.

Osama bin Laden's famous 1998 *fatwa*, in which he declared jihad on the United States and any American fair game for his followers, is a case in point. Though the content of this declaration is itself contrary to traditional Islamic moral teachings—as the eminent Middle East scholar Bernard Lewis has observed, "At no point do the basic texts of Islam enjoin terrorism and murder"—the most notably radical thing about it is the identity of its author. Osama bin Laden has no credentials as a religious authority and no right, under traditional Islamic practice, to issue a fatwa. It is a bit like Hitler issuing a papal encyclical, or Lenin a decree in the name of the Russian Orthodox church. The mere fact that bin Laden was willing to cross this line shows the extent to which Islamism has undermined traditional Islamic legal authority. But a line crossed in the name of waging all-out war against the West may yet be crossed in the name of healthier purposes.

We should not kid ourselves. The modernization of Islam is hardly imminent, and it will not occur without enormous struggle. There are several deeply imbedded obstacles in Islamic society, not least the often-noted lack of a tradition of secular politics. To many Muslims, what may simply seem more "natural" is a totalizing ideology that seeks to unite society and the state within a single revolutionary whole. Nor is it clear, despite the UN's recent report, that the Muslim world is capable of the realistic self-appraisal necessary for a modernizing shift to occur.

The West: Unique, Not Universal

Samuel P. Huntington

Samuel P. Huntington is the Albert J. Weatherhead III University Professor at Harvard University, where he is also director of the John M. Olin Institute for Strategic Studies and chairman of the Harvard Academy for International and Area Studies. This article is drawn from his book The Clash of Civilizations and the Remaking of World Order.

Modernity Is Not Enough

In recent years Westerners have reassured themselves and irritated others by expounding the notion that the culture of the West is and ought to be the culture of the world. This conceit takes two forms. One is the Coca-colonization thesis. Its proponents claim that Western, and more specifically American, popular culture is enveloping the world: American food, clothing, pop music, movies, and consumer goods are more and more enthusiastically embraced by people on every continent. The other has to do with modernization. It claims not only that the West has led the world to modern society, but that as people in other civilizations modernize they also westernize, abandoning their traditional values, institutions, and customs and adopting those that prevail in the West. Both theses project the image of an emerging homogeneous, universally Western world—and both are to varying degrees misguided, arrogant, false, and dangerous.

Advocates of the Coca-colonization thesis identify culture with the consumption of material goods. The heart of a culture, however, involves language, religion, values, traditions, and customs. Drinking Coca-Cola does not make Russians think like Americans any more than eating sushi makes Americans think like Japanese. Throughout human history, fads and material goods have spread from one society to another without significantly altering the basic culture of the recipient society. Enthusiasms for various items of Chinese, Hindu, and other cultures have periodically swept the Western world, with no discernible lasting spillover. The argument that the spread of pop culture and consumer goods around the world represents the triumph of Western civilization depreciates the strength of other cultures while trivializing Western culture by identifying it with fatty foods, faded pants, and fizzy drinks. The essence of Western culture is the Magna Carta, not the Magna Mac.

The modernization argument is intellectually more serious than the Coca-colonization thesis, but equally flawed. The tremendous expansion of scientific and engineering knowledge that occurred in the nineteenth century allowed humans to control and shape their environment in unprecedented ways. Modernization involves industrialization; urbanization; increasing levels of literacy, education, wealth, and social mobilization; and more complex and diverse occupational structures. It is a revolutionary process comparable to the shift from primitive to civilized societies that began in the valleys of the Tigris and Euphrates, the Nile, and the Indus about 5000 B.C. The attitudes, values, knowledge, and culture of people in a modern society differ greatly from those in a traditional society As the first civilization to modernize, the West is the first to have fully acquired the culture of modernity. As other societies take on similar patterns of education, work, wealth, and class structure, the modernization argument runs, this Western culture will become the universal culture of the world.

That there are significant differences between modern and traditional cultures is beyond dispute. A world in which some societies are highly modern and others still traditional will obviously be less homogeneous than a world in which all societies are comparably modern. It does not necessarily follow, however, that societies with modern cultures should be any more similar than are societies with traditional cultures. Only a few hundred years ago all societies were traditional. Was that world any less homogeneous than a future world of universal modernity is likely to be? Probably not. "Ming China . . . was assuredly closer to the France of the Valois," Fernand Braudel observes, "than the China of Mao Tse-tung is to the France of the Fifth Republic."[1] Modern societies have much in common, but they do not necessarily merge into homogeneity. The argument that they do rests on the assumption that modern society must approximate a single type, the Western type; that modern civilization is Western civilization, and Western civilization is modern civilization. This, however, is a false identification. Virtually all scholars of civilization agree that Western civilization emerged in the eighth and ninth centuries and developed its distinctive characteristics in the centuries that followed. It did not begin to modernize until the eighteenth century. The West, in short, was Western long before it was modern.

What Makes the West Western?

What were the distinguishing characteristics of Western civilization during the hundreds of years before it modernized? The various scholars who have answered this question differ on some specifics but agree on a number of institutions, practices, and beliefs that may be legitimately identified as the core of Western civilization. They include:

The Classical legacy. As a third-generation civilization, the West inherited much from earlier civilizations, including most notably Classical civilization. Classical legacies in Western civilization are many, and include Greek philosophy and rationalism, Roman law, Latin, and Christianity. Islamic and Orthodox civilizations also inherited from Classical civilization, but to nowhere near the same degree as the West.

Western Christianity. Western Christianity, first Catholicism and then Protestantism, is the single most important historical characteristic of Western civilization. Indeed, during most of its first millennium, what is now known as Western civilization was called Western Christendom. There was a well-developed sense of community among Western Christian peoples, one that made them feel distinct from Turks, Moors, Byzantines, and others. When Westerners went out to conquer the world in the sixteenth century, they did so for God as well as gold. The Reformation and Counter Reformation and the division of Western Christendom into Protestantism and Catholicism—and the political and intellectual consequences of that rift—are also distinctive features of Western history, totally absent from Eastern Orthodoxy and removed from the Latin American experience.

European languages. Language is second only to religion as a factor distinguishing people of one culture from those of another. The West differs from most other civilizations in its multiplicity of languages. Japanese, Hindi, Mandarin, Russian, and even Arabic are recognized as the core languages of other civilizations. The West inherited Latin, but a variety of nations emerged in the West, and with them developed national languages grouped loosely into the broad categories of Romance and Germanic. By the sixteenth century these languages had generally assumed their contemporary forms. Latin gave way to French as a common international language for the West, and in the twentieth century French succumbed to English.

Separation of spiritual and temporal authority. Throughout Western history, first the Church and then many churches existed separate from the state. God and Caesar, church and state, spiritual authority and temporal authority had been a prevailing dualism in Western culture. Only in Hindu civilization were religion and politics as clearly separated. In Islam, God is caesar; in China and Japan, caesar is God; in Orthodoxy, God is caesar's junior partner. The separation and recur between church and state that typify Western civilization have occurred in no other civilization. This division of authority contributed immeasurably to the development of freedom in the West.

Rule of law. The concept of the centrality of law to civilized existence was inherited from the Romans. Medieval thinkers elaborated the idea of natural law, according to which monarchs were supposed to exercise their power, and a common law tradition developed in England. During the phase of absolutism in the sixteenth and seventeenth centuries, the rule of law was observed more in the breach than in practice, but the idea of subordinating human power to some external restraint persisted: *Non sub homine sed sub Deo et lege.* The tradition of the rule of law laid the basis for constitutionalism and the protection of human rights, including property rights, against the arbitrary exercise of power. In other civilizations law has been a much less important factor in shaping thought and behavior.

Social pluralism and civil society. Western society historically has been highly pluralistic. What is distinctive about the West, as Karl Deutsch noted, "is the rise and persistence of diverse autonomous groups not based on blood relationship or marriage."[2] Beginning in the sixth and seventh centuries these groups initially included monasteries, monastic orders, and guilds, but afterwards expanded in many areas of Europe to include a variety of other associations and societies. For more than a millennium, the West has had a civil society that distinguished it from other civilizations.

Associational pluralism was supplemented by class pluralism. Most Western European societies included a relatively strong and autonomous aristocracy, a substantial peasantry, and a small but significant class of merchants and traders. The strength of the feudal aristocracy was particularly important in limiting absolutism's ability to take firm root in most European nations. This European pluralism contrasts sharply with the poverty of civil society, the weakness of the aristocracy, and the strength of the centralized bureaucratic empires that existed during the same time periods in Russia, China, the Ottoman lands, and other non-Western societies.

Representative bodies. Social pluralism gave rise at an early date to estates, parliaments, and other institutions that represented the interests of the aristocracy, clergy, merchants, and other groups. These bodies provided forms of representation that in the course of modernization evolved into the institutions of modern democracy. In some instances during the era of absolutism they were abolished or their powers greatly limited. But even when that happened, they could, as in France, be resurrected as a vehicle for expanded political participation. No other civilization today has a comparable heritage of representative bodies stretching back a millennium. Movements for self-government also developed at the local level, beginning in the ninth century in the cities of Italy and then spreading northward, wresting power from bishops and nobles and finally, in the thirteenth century, leading to such confederations of "strong and independent cities" as the Hanseatic League.[3] Representation at the national level was thus supplemented by a measure of autonomy at the local level not seen in other regions of the world.

Individualism. Many of the above features of Western civilization contributed to the emergence of a sense of individualism and a tradition of individual rights and liberties unique among civilized societies. Individualism developed in the fourteenth and fifteenth centuries, and acceptance of the right of individual choice, which Deutsch terms "the Romeo and Juliet revolution," prevailed in the West by the seventeenth century. Even claims for equal rights for all—"the poorest he in England has a life to live as much as the richest he"—were articulated if not universally accepted. Individualism remains a distinguishing feature of the West in twentieth-century civilizations. In one analysis involving similar population groups from 50 countries, the 20 countries scoring highest on the individualism index included 19 of the 20 Western countries in the sample. Another cross-cultural survey of individualism and collectivism similarly highlighted the dominance of individualism in the West compared with the prevalence of collectivism elsewhere, concluding that "the values that are most important in the West are least important worldwide."[4] Again and again both Westerners and non-Westerners point to individualism as the central distinguishing mark of the West.

The above list is not an exhaustive enumeration of the distinctive characteristics of Western civilization. Nor is it meant to imply that those characteristics were always and everywhere present in Western society They obviously were not: the many despots in Western history regularly ignored the rule of law and suspended representative bodies. Nor is it meant to suggest that none of these characteristics have appeared in other civilizations. They obviously have: the Koran and the sharia constitute basic law for Islamic societies; Japan and India had class systems paralleling that of the West (and perhaps as a result are the only two major non-Western societies to sustain democratic governments for any length of time). Individually, almost none of these factors is unique to the West. But the combination of them is, and has given the West its distinctive quality. These concepts, practices, and institutions have been far more prevalent in the West than in other civilizations. They form the essential continuing core of Western civilization. They are what is Western, but not modern, about the West.

They also generated the commitment to individual freedom that now distinguishes the West from other civilizations. Europe, as Arthur M. Schlesinger, Jr., has said, is "the source—the *unique* source" of the "ideas of individual liberty, political democracy, the rule of law, human rights, and cultural freedom . . . These are *European* ideas, not Asian, nor African, nor Middle Eastern ideas, except by adoption. . . ."[5] These concepts and characteristics are also in large part the factors that enabled the West to take the lead in modernizing itself and the world. They make Western civilization unique, and Western civilization is precious not because it is universal but because it is unique.

Can the Rest Copy the West?

To modernize, must non-Western societies abandon their own cultures and adopt the core elements of Western culture? From time to time leaders of such societies have thought it necessary. Peter the Great and Mustafa Kemal Ataturk were determined to modernize their countries and convinced that doing so meant adopting Western culture, even to the point of replacing traditional headgear with its Western equivalent. In the process, they created "torn" countries, unsure of their cultural identity. Nor did Western cultural imports significantly help them in their pursuit of modernization. More often, leaders of non-Western societies have pursued modernization and rejected westernization. Their goal is summed up in the phrases *ti-yong* (Chinese learning for the fundamental principles, Western learning for practical use) and *woken, yosei* (Japanese spirit, Western technique), articulated by Chinese and Japanese reformers of a century ago, and in Saudi Arabia's Prince Bandar bin Sultan's comment in 1944 that "'foreign imports' are nice as shiny or high-tech 'things.' But intangible social and political institutions imported from elsewhere can be deadly—ask the Shah of Iran . . . Islam is for us not just a religion but a way of life. We Saudis want to modernize but not necessarily westernize." Japan, Singapore, Taiwan, Saudi Arabia, and, to a lesser degree, Iran have become modern societies without becoming Western societies. China is clearly modernizing, but certainly not westernizing.

Interaction and borrowing between civilizations have always taken place, and with modern means of transportation and communication they are much more extensive. Most of the world's great civilizations, however, have existed for at least one millennium and in some cases for several. These civilizations have a demonstrated record of borrowing from other civilizations in ways that enhance their own chances of survival. China's absorption of Buddhism from India, scholars agree, failed to produce the "Indianization" of China; it instead caused the Sinification of Buddhism. The Chinese adapted Buddhism to their purposes and needs. The Chinese have to date consistently defeated intense Western efforts to Christianize them. If at some point they do import Christianity, it is more than likely that it will be absorbed and adapted in such a manner as to strengthen the continuing core of Chinese culture.

Similarly, in past centuries Muslim Arabs received, valued, and used their "Hellenic inheritance for essentially utilitarian reasons. Being mostly interested in borrowing certain external forms or technical aspects, they knew how to disregard all elements in the Greek body of thought that would conflict with 'the truth' as established in their fundamental Koranic norms and precepts." Japan followed the same pattern. In the seventh century Japan imported Chinese culture and made the "transformation on its own initiative, free from economic and military pressures," to high civilization. "During the centuries that followed, periods of relative isolation from continental influences during which previous borrowings were sorted out and the useful ones assimilated would alternate with periods of renewed contact and cultural borrowing." In similar fashion, Japan and other non-Western societies today are absorbing selected elements of Western culture and using them to strengthen their own cultural identity. It would, as Braudel argues, almost "be childish" to think that the "triumph of civilization in the singular" would lead to the end of the plurality of cultures embodied for centuries in the world's great civilizations.[6]

Cultural Backlash

Modernization and economic development neither require nor produce cultural westernization. To the contrary, they promote a resurgence of, and renewed commitment to, indigenous cultures. At the individual level, the movement of people into unfamiliar cities, social settings, and occupations breaks their traditional local bonds, generates feelings of alienation and anomie, and creates crises of identity to which religion frequently provides an answer. At the societal level, modernization enhances the economic wealth and military power of the country as a whole and encourages people to have confidence in their heritage and to become culturally assertive. As a result, many non-Western societies have seen a return to indigenous cultures. It often takes a religious form, and the global revival of religion is a direct consequence of modernization. In non-Western societies this revival almost necessarily assumes an anti-Western cast, in some cases rejecting Western culture because it is Christian and subversive, in others because it is secular and degenerate. The return to the indigenous is most marked in Muslim and Asian societies. The Islamic Resurgence has manifested itself in every Muslim country; in almost all it has become a major social, cultural, and intellectual movement, and in most it has had a deep impact on politics. In 1996 virtually every Muslim country except Iran was more Islamic and more Islamist in its outlook, practices, and institutions than it was 15 years earlier. In the countries where Islamist political forces do not shape the government, they invariably dominate and often monopolize the opposition to the government. Throughout the Muslim world people are reacting against the "Westoxification" of their societies.

East Asian societies have gone through a parallel rediscovery of indigenous values and have increasingly drawn unflattering comparisons between their culture and Western culture. For several centuries they, along with other non-Western peoples, envied the economic prosperity, technological sophistication, military power, and political cohesion of Western societies. They sought the secret of this success in Western practices and customs, and when they identified what they thought might be the key they attempted to apply it in their own societies. Now, however, a fundamental change has occurred. Today East Asians attribute their dramatic economic development not to their import of Western culture but to their adherence to their own culture. They have succeeded, they argue, not because they became like the West, but because they have remained different from the West. In somewhat similar fashion, when non-Western societies felt weak in relation to the West, many of their leaders invoked Western values of self-determination, liberalism, democracy, and freedom to justify their opposition to Western global domination. Now that they are no longer weak but instead increasingly powerful, they denounce as "human rights imperialism" the same values they previously invoked to promote their interests. As Western power recedes, so too does the appeal of Western values and culture, and the West faces the need to accommodate itself to its declining ability to impose its values on non-Western societies. In fundamental ways, much of the world is becoming more modern and less Western.

One manifestation of this trend is what Ronald Dore has termed the "second-generation indigenization phenomenon." Both in former Western colonies and in continuously independent, non-Western countries, "the first 'modernizer' or 'post-independence' generation has often received its training in foreign (Western) universities in a Western cosmopolitan language. Partly because they first go abroad as impressionable teenagers, their absorption of Western values and lifestyles may well be profound." Most members of the much larger second generation, in contrast, receive their education at home in universities the first generation established, where the local language, rather than its colonial replacement, is used for instruction. These universities "provide a much more diluted contact with metropolitan world culture" and "knowledge is indigenized by means of translations—usually of limited range and of poor quality." Graduates of these universities resent the dominance of the earlier Western-trained generation and thus often "succumb to the appeals of nativist opposition movements."[7] As Western influence recedes, young and aspiring leaders cannot look to the West to provide them with power and wealth. They have to find the means of success within their own society and hence accommodate the values and culture of that society.

Indigenization is furthered by the democracy paradox: when non-Western societies adopt Western-style elections, democracy encourages and often brings to power nativist and anti-Western political movements. In the 1960s and 1970s westernized and pro-Western governments in developing countries were threatened by coups and revolutions; in the 1980s and 1990s they have been increasingly in danger of being ousted in elections. Democracy tends to make a society more parochial, not more cosmopolitan. Politicians in non-Western societies do not win elections by demonstrating how Western they are. Electoral competition stimulates them to fashion what they believe will be the most popular appeals, and those are usually ethnic, nationalist, and religious in character. The result is popular mobilization against Western-oriented elites and the West in general. This process, which began in Sri Lanka in the 1950s, has spread from country to country in Asia, Africa, and the Middle East, and is manifest in the victories of religiously oriented parties in India, Turkey, Bosnia, and Israel in elections in 1995 and 1996. Democratization is thus at odds with westernization.

The powerful currents of indigenization at work in the world make a mockery of Western expectations that Western culture will become the world's culture. The two central elements of any culture are language and religion. English, it has been asserted, is becoming the world's language. It clearly has become the lingua franca for communication in multinational business, diplomacy, international institutions, tourism, and aviation. This use of English for intercultural communication, however, presupposes the existence of different cultures; like translation and interpretation, it is a way of coping with those differences, not eliminating them. In fact, the proportion of the world's population speaking English is small and declining. According to the most reliable data, compiled by Sidney S. Culbert, a professor at the University of Washington, in 1958 roughly 9.8 percent of human beings spoke English as a first or second language; in 1992, 7.6 percent did. A language foreign to 92 percent of the world's population is not the world's language. Similarly, in 1958, 24 percent of humans spoke one of the five major Western languages; in 1992, less than 21 percent did. The situation is similar for religion. Western Christians now make up perhaps 30 percent of the world's population, but the proportion is declining steadily, and at some point in the next decade or so the number of Muslims will exceed the number of Christians. With respect to the two central elements of culture, language and religion, the West is in retreat. As Michael Howard has observed, the "common Western assumption that cultural diversity is a historical curiosity being rapidly eroded by the growth of a common, Western-oriented, Anglophone world culture, shaping our basic values . . . is simply not true."[8]

As indigenization spreads and the appeal of Western culture fades, the central problem in relations between the West and the rest is the gap between the West's, particularly America's, efforts to promote Western culture as the universal culture and its declining ability to do so. The collapse of communism exacerbated this disparity by reinforcing the view in the West that its ideology of democratic liberalism had triumphed globally and was thus universally valid. The West—and especially the United States, which has always been a missionary nation—believes that the non-Western peoples should commit themselves to the Western values of democracy, free markets, limited government, separation of church and state, human rights, individualism, and the rule of law, and should embody these values in their institutions. Minorities in other civilizations embrace and promote these values, but the dominant attitudes toward them in non-Western cultures range from skepticism to intense opposition. What is universalism to the West is imperialism to the rest.

Non-Westerners do not hesitate to point to the gaps between Western principle and Western practice. Hypocrisy and double standards are the price of universalist pretensions. Democracy is promoted, but not if it brings Islamic fundamentalists to power; nonproliferation is preached for Iran and Iraq, but not for Israel; free trade is the elixir of economic growth, but not for agriculture; human rights are an issue with China, but not with Saudi Arabia; aggression against oil-owning Kuwaitis is repulsed with massive force, but not so aggression against oil-less Bosnians.

The belief that non-Western peoples should adopt Western values, institutions, and culture is, if taken seriously, immoral in its implications. The almost universal reach of European power in the late nineteenth century and the global dominance of the United States in the latter half of the twentieth century spread many aspects of

Western civilization across the world. But European globalism is no more, and American hegemony is receding, if only because it is no longer needed to protect the United States against a Cold War Soviet threat. Culture follows power. If non-Western societies are once again shaped by Western culture, it will happen only as a result of the expansion and deployment of Western power. Imperialism is the necessary, logical consequence of universalism, yet few proponents of universalism support the militarization and brutal coercion that would be necessary to achieve their goal. Furthermore, as a maturing civilization, the West no longer has the economic or demographic dynamism required to impose its will on other societies. Any effort to do so also runs contrary to Western values of self-determination and democracy. This March, Prime Minister Mahathir of Malaysia told the assembled heads of European governments: "European values are European values; Asian values are universal values." As Asian and Muslim civilizations begin to assert the universal relevance of their cultures, Westerners will come to appreciate the connection between universalism and imperialism and to see the virtues of a pluralistic world.

Shoring Up the West

The time has come for the West to abandon the illusion of universality and to promote the strength, coherence, and vitality of its civilization in a world of civilizations. The interests of the West are not served by promiscuous intervention into the disputes of other peoples. In the era that is dawning, primary responsibility for containing and resolving regional conflicts must rest with the leading states of the civilizations dominant in those regions. "All politics is local politics," Thomas P. "Tip" O'Neill, the former Speaker of the House, observed, and the corollary to that truth is "All power is local power." Neither the United Nations nor the United States can impose on local conflicts long-lasting solutions that deviate from the realities of local power. As anyone knowledgeable about crime knows, local law and order are best insured by a cop walking the beat, not by the potential appearance over the horizon of a squad of motorized police. In a multipolar, multicivilizational world, the West's responsibility is to secure its own interests, not to promote those of other peoples nor to attempt to settle conflicts between other peoples when those conflicts are of little or no consequence to the West.

The future of the West depends in large part on the unity of the West. Scholars of civilizations see them evolving through times of trouble and a period of warring states, eventually leading to a universal state for the civilization that may be either a source of renewal or a prelude to decay and disintegration. Western civilization has moved beyond its warring states phase and is heading toward its universal state phase. That phase is still incomplete, with the nation-states of the West cohering into two semi-universal states in Europe and North America. These two entities and their constituent units are, however, bound together by an extraordinarily complex network of formal and informal institutional ties. The universal states of previous civilizations were empires. Since democracy is the political form of Western civilization, the emerging universal state of Western civilization is not an empire but rather a compound of federations, confederations, and international regimes.

The problem for the West, in this situation, is to maintain its dynamism and to promote its coherence. Western unity depends more on events in the United States than on those in Europe. At present the United States is pulled in three directions. It is pulled south by the continuing immigration of Latin Americans and the growing size and power of its Hispanic population; by the incorporation of Mexico into the North American Free Trade Agreement and the possibility of extending NAFTA to other western hemisphere countries; and by the political, economic, and cultural changes in Latin America that make it more like the United States. At the same time, the United States is pulled westward by the increasing wealth and influence of East Asian societies; by the ongoing efforts to develop a Pacific community, epitomized in the Asia-Pacific Economic Cooperation (APEC) forum; and by migration from Asian societies. If democracy, free markets, the rule of law, civil society, individualism, and Protestantism take firm root in Latin America, that continent, whose culture has always been closely related to that of the West, will merge with the West and become the third pillar of Western civilization. No such convergence is possible with Asian societies. Asia is instead likely to pose continuing economic and political challenges to the United States specifically and the West more generally. The third pull, toward Europe, is the most important. Shared values, institutions, history, and culture dictate the continuing close association of the United States and Europe. Both necessary and desirable is the further development of institutional ties across the Atlantic, including negotiation of a European-American free trade agreement and creation of a North Atlantic economic organization as a counterpart to NATO.

The major current differences between Europe and America arise not from direct conflicts of interest with each other, but from their policies toward third parties. Among other questions, these include the provision of support to a Muslim-dominated Bosnia, the priority of Israeli security needs in Middle Eastern policy, U.S. efforts to penalize foreign companies that do business with Iran and Cuba, the maintenance of full economic sanctions against Iraq, and the part human rights and weapons proliferation concerns should play in dealing with China. Non-Western powers, especially China, have actively attempted to exploit these differences and play one Western country off against another. The differences themselves arise largely from different geopolitical perspectives and domestic political and economic interests. Maintaining the unity of the West, however, is essential to slowing the decline of Western influence in world affairs. Western peoples have far more in common with each other than they have with Asian, Middle Eastern, or African peoples. The leaders of Western countries have institutionalized patterns of trust and cooperation among themselves that, with rare exceptions, they do not have with the leaders of other societies. United, the West will remain a formidable presence on the international scene; divided, it will be prey to the efforts of non-Western states to exploit its internal differences by offering short-term gains to some Western countries at the price of long-term losses for all Western countries. The peoples of the West, in Benjamin Franklin's phrase, must hang together, or most assuredly they will hang separately.

Promoting the coherence of the West means both preserving Western culture within the West and defining the limits of the West. The former requires, among other things, controlling immigration from non-Western societies, as every major European country has done and as the United States is beginning to do, and ensuring the assimilation into Western culture of the immigrants who are admitted. It also means recognizing that in the post–Cold War world, NATO is the security organization of Western civilization and that its primary purpose is to defend and preserve that civilization. Hence states that are Western in their history, religion, and culture should, if they desire, be able to join NATO. Practically speaking, NATO membership would be open to the Visegrad states, the Baltic states, Slovenia, and Croatia, but not countries that have historically been primarily Muslim or Orthodox. While recent debate has focused entirely on the expansion rather than the contraction of NATO, it is also necessary to recognize that as NATO's mission changes, Turkish and Greek ties to NATO will weaken and their membership could either come to an end or become meaningless. Withdrawal from nato is the declared goal of the Welfare Party in Turkey, and Greece is becoming as much an ally of Russia as it is a member of NATO.

The West went through a European phase of development and expansion that lasted several centuries and an American phase that has dominated this century. If North America and Europe renew their moral life, build on their cultural commonality, and develop closer forms of economic and political integration to supplement their security collaboration in NATO, they could generate a third Euroamerican phase of Western affluence and political influence. Meaningful political integration would in some measure counter the relative decline in the West's share of the world's people, economic product, and military capabilities and revive the West's power in the eyes of the leaders of other civilizations. The principal responsibility of Western leaders is not to attempt to reshape other civilizations in the image of the West—which is increasingly beyond their ability—but to preserve and renew the unique qualities of Western civilization. That responsibility falls overwhelmingly on the most powerful Western country, the United States of America. Neither globalism nor isolationism, neither multilateralism nor unilateralism will best serve American interests. Its interests will be most effectively advanced if the United States eschews those extremes and instead adopts an Atlanticist policy of close cooperation with its European partners, one that will protect and promote the interests, values, and culture of the precious and unique civilization they share.

Notes

1. Fernand Braudel, *On History,* Chicago: University of Chicago Press, 1980, p. 213.

2. Karl Deutsch, "On Nationalism, World Regions, and the Nature of the West," in Per Torvik, ed., *Mobilization, Center-Periphery Structures and Nation-Building,* Bergen: Universitetsforlaget, 1981, p. 77.

3. Stein Rokkan, "Dimensions of State Formation and Nation-Building," in Charles Tilly, ed., *The Formation of Nation-States in Western Europe,* Princeton: Princeton University Press, 1975, p. 576.

4. Geert Hofstede, "National Cultures in Four Dimensions," *International Studies of Management and Organization,* 1983, Vol. 13, p. 53; Harry C. Triandis, "Cross-Cultural Studies of Individualism and Collectivism," *Nebraska Symposium on Motivation 1989,* Lincoln: University of Nebraska

Press, 1990, pp. 44–133, quoted in Daniel Coleman, "The Group and the Self: New Focus on a Cultural Rift," *The New York Times,* December 25, 1990, p. 41.

5. Arthur M. Schlesinger, Jr., *The Disunity of America,* New York: W.W. Norton, 1992, p. 127.

6. Adda B. Bozeman, "Civilizations under Stress," *Virginia Quarterly Review,* Winter 1975, p. 7; William E. Naff, "Reflections on the Question of 'East and West' from the Point of View of Japan," *Comparative Civilizations Review,* Fall 1985–Spring 1986, p. 222; Braudel, *On History,* pp. 212–213.

7. Ronald Dore, "Unity and Diversity in Contemporary World Culture," in Hedley Bull and Adam Watson, eds., *Expansion of International Society,* Oxford: Oxford University Press, 1984, pp. 420–21.

8. Michael Howard, *America and the World* (Annual Lewin Lecture), St. Louis: Washington University, 1984, p. 6.

Globalizing Hate

Amy Chua

This article appeared in World on Fire: How Exporting Free Market Democracy Breeds Ethnic Hatred and Global Instability (2003).

One beautiful blue morning in 1994, my mother phoned me from California. In a hushed voice, she told me that my Aunt Leona, my father's twin sister, had been murdered in her home in the Philippines, her throat slit by her chauffeur. My mother broke the news in our native Hokkien Chinese dialect. But "murder" she said in English, as if to wall off the act from the family through language.

The murder of a relative is horrible for anyone, anywhere. My father's grief was impenetrable; to this day, he has not broken his silence on the subject. For the rest of the family, though, there was added disgrace. For traditional Chinese, luck is a moral attribute, and a lucky person would never be murdered. Like having a birth defect, or marrying a non-Chinese, being murdered is shameful.

My three younger sisters and I were very fond of Aunt Leona, who was petite and quirky and had never married. Like many wealthy Filipino Chinese, she had all kinds of bank accounts in Honolulu, San Francisco, and Chicago. She visited us in the United States regularly. She and my father—Leona and Leone—were close, as only twins can be. Having no children of her own, she doted on her nieces and showered us with trinkets. As we grew older, the trinkets became treasures. On my tenth birthday, she gave me ten small diamonds, wrapped in toilet paper. My aunt loved diamonds and bought them up by the dozen, concealing them in empty Elizabeth Arden face moisturizer jars, some right on her bathroom shelf. She liked accumulating things. When we ate at McDonald's, she stuffed her Gucci purse with free ketchups.

According to the police report, my Aunt Leona, "a 58-year-old single woman," was killed in her living room with "a butcher's knife" at approximately 8 P.M. Two of her maids who were questioned confessed that Nilo Abique, my aunt's chauffeur, had planned and executed the murder with their knowledge and assistance.

"A few hours before the actual killing, respondent was seen sharpening the knife allegedly used in the crime." After the killing, "respondent [Abique] joined the two witnesses and told them that their employer was dead. At that time, he was wearing a pair of bloodied white gloves and was still holding a knife, also with traces of blood." But Abique, the report went on to say, had "disappeared" with the warrant for his arrest outstanding. The two maids were released.

After the funeral, I asked one of my uncles whether there had been any further developments in the murder investigation. He replied tersely that the killer had not been found. His wife explained that the Manila police had essentially closed the case. Why were they not more shocked that my aunt had been killed by people who worked for her, lived with her? Or that the maids had been released? When I pressed my uncle, he was brusque. "That's the way things are here," he said. "This is the Philippines—not America."

My uncle was not simply being callous. As it turns out, my aunt's death is part of a common pattern. Hundreds of Chinese in the Philippines are kidnapped every year, almost invariably by ethnic Filipinos. Many victims, often children, are brutally murdered, even after ransom is paid. Other Chinese, like my aunt, are killed without a kidnapping, usually in connection with a robbery.

Nor is it unusual that my aunt's killer was never apprehended. Police in the Philippines, all poor ethnic Filipino themselves, are notoriously unmotivated in these cases. Asked by a Western journalist why it is so frequently the Chinese who are targeted, one grinning Filipino policeman explained, "They have more money."

My family is part of the Philippines' tiny but entrepreneurial, economically powerful Chinese minority. Just 1 percent of the population, Chinese Filipinos control as much as 60 percent of the private economy, including the country's four major airlines and almost all its banks, hotels, shopping malls, and conglomerates. My own relatives in Manila, who run a plastics conglomerate, are only "third-tier" Chinese tycoons. Still, they own swaths of prime real estate and several vacation homes. They also have safe deposit boxes full of gold bars, each the size of a Snickers bar. My Aunt Leona FedExed me a similar bar as a law school graduation present.

Since my aunt's murder, one childhood memory keeps haunting me. I was eight, visiting from the United States, and staying at my family's splendid hacienda-style house in Manila. It was before dawn, still dark when I went to the kitchen for a drink. But I must have gone down an extra flight of stairs because I literally stumbled onto six male bodies.

I had found the male servants' quarters. My family's house-boys, gardeners, and chauffeurs—I sometimes imagine that Nilo Abique was among them—were sleeping on mats on a dirt floor. The place stank of sweat and urine. I was horrified.

Later that day, I mentioned the incident to my Aunt Leona, who laughed affectionately and explained that the servants—there were perhaps 20 living on the premises, all ethnic Filipino—were fortunate to be working for our family. If not for their positions, they would be living among rats and open sewers, without even a roof over their heads. A Filipino maid then walked in with a bowl of food for my aunt's Pekingese dog. The Filipinos, my aunt continued—in Chinese, but not caring whether the maid understood—were lazy and unintelligent, and didn't really want to do much else. If they didn't like working for us, they were free to leave any time. After all, they were employees, not slaves.

According to the World Bank, UNICEF, and official statistics of the Philippines, nearly two-thirds of the Philippines' 80 million ethnic Filipinos live on less than $2 a day, 40 percent spent their entire lives in temporary shelters, and 70 percent of all rural Filipinos own no land. Almost a third have no access to sanitation.

But that is not the worst of it. Poverty alone never is. Poverty by itself does not make people kill. To poverty must be added indignity, hopelessness, and grievance.

In the Philippines, millions of ethnic Filipinos work for Chinese; almost no Chinese work for Filipinos. The Chinese dominate industry and commerce at every level of society. Global markets intensify this dominance: When foreign investors do business in the Philippines, they deal almost exclusively with Chinese. Apart from a handful of corrupt politicians and a few aristocratic Spanish mestizo families, all of the Philippines' billionaires are Chinese. By contrast, all menial jobs in the Philippines are filled by Filipinos. All peasants, domestic servants, and squatters are Filipinos. Outside Manila, thousands of ethnic Filipinos lived on or around the Payatas garbage dump: a 12-block-wide mountain of fermenting refuse known as The Promised Land. By scavenging through rotting food and animal carcasses, squatters eked out a living. In July 2000, as a result of accumulating methane gas, the garbage mountain imploded and collapsed, smothering more than 100 people, many of them young children.

When I asked an uncle about the Payatas explosion, he was annoyed. "Why does everyone wanted to talk about that? It's the worst thing for foreign investment."

I wasn't surprised. My relatives live literally walled off from the Filipino masses, in a posh, all-Chinese residential enclave, on streets named Harvard, Yale, and Princeton. Armed, private security forces guard every entry point.

Each time I think of Nilo Abique—he was 6'2" and my aunt was 4'11"—I well up with a hatred and revulsion so intense, it is actually consoling. But over time, I have also had glimpses of how the Chinese must look to the vast majority of Filipinos, to someone like Abique: as exploiters, as foreign intruders, their wealth inexplicable, their superiority intolerable. I will never forget the entry in the police report for Abique's "motive for murder": not robbery, despite the jewels and money the chauffeur was said to have taken, but just one word: "Revenge."

There is a connection between my aunt's killing and the waves of global violence and mass murder that we read about with mounting frequency. It lies in the relationship—and increasingly the explosive collision—among the three most powerful forces operating in the world today: markets, democracy, and ethnic hatred.

After the fall of the Berlin Wall, a common economic and political consensus emerged, not only in the West, but to a considerable extent around the world. Markets and democracy, working hand in hand, would transform the world into a community of modernized, peace-loving nations. In the process, ethnic hatred, religious zealotry, and other "backward" aspects of underdevelopment would be swept away. The sobering lesson of the last 20 years, however, is that the global spread of free-market democracy—at least in its current, raw, for-export form—has been a principal aggravating cause of ethnic violence throughout the non-Western world.

The reason has to do with a phenomenon—pervasive outside the West, yet rarely acknowledged—indeed often viewed as taboo—that turns free-market democracy into an engine of ethnic conflagration. The phenomenon is that of *market-dominant minorities*: ethnic minorities who—for widely varying reasons ranging from entrepreneurialism to a history of apartheid or colonial oppression—can be expected under market conditions to economically dominate the "indigenous" majorities around them, at least in the near to mid-term future.

Examples of market-dominant minorities include the Chinese, not just in the Philippines, but throughout Southeast Asia. Most recently, in Myanmar, ethnic Chinese have literally taken over the economies of Mandalay and Yangon. Whites are a market-dominant minority in South Africa and Zimbabwe—and, in a more complicated sense in Bolivia, Ecuador, Guatemala, and much of Latin America. Indians are a market-dominant minority in East Africa, Fiji, and parts of the Caribbean, as are Lebanese in West Africa and Jews in post-Communist Russia. Ibo are a market-dominant minority in Nigeria as were Croats in the former Yugoslavia and Tutsi in pre-genocide Rwanda.

In countries with a market-dominate minority, markets and democracy will tend to favor not just different people or different classes, but different ethnic groups. Markets magnify the often astounding wealth of the market-dominant minority while democracy increases the political power of the impoverished "indigenous" majority.

In such circumstances, where the rich aren't just rich—but belong to a resented, "outsider" ethnic group—the pursuit of free-market democracy often becomes an engine of catastrophic ethno-nationalism, pitting a poor "indigenous" majority, easily aroused and manipulated by opportunistic politicians, against a hated ethnic minority.

Consider Indonesia: Free-market policies in the 1980s and 1990s led to a situation in which the country's 3 percent Chinese minority controlled 70 percent of the country's private economy. The introduction of democracy in 1998—hailed with euphoria in the United States—produced a violent backlash against both the Chinese and markets. Some 5,000 shops and homes of ethnic Chinese were burned and looted, 2,000 people died, and 150 Chinese women were gang-raped. Free and fair elections in the midst of all this gave rise to ethnic scapegoating by demagogic politicians, along with calls for confiscation of Chinese assets and a "People's Economy" that would return Indonesia's wealth to the country's "true owners," the *pribumi* (indigenous Indonesian) majority. The wealthiest Chinese left the country, along with $40 billion to $100 billion of Chinese-controlled capital, plunging the country into an economic crisis from which it has still not recovered.

Indonesia is part of a much larger global problem: Whenever free-market democracy is pursued in the presence of a market-dominant minority, the result is not peace and prosperity but tremendous instability and some form of backlash—even mass slaughter. Sept. 11 brought this same dynamic home to the United States.

While Americans are not an ethnic minority, the world now sees us as a kind of global market-dominant minority, wielding outrageously disproportionate economic power relative to our numbers. With just 4 percent of the world's population, the U.S is the principal engine and beneficiary of global capitalism. We are also seen as "almighty," "exploitative," and "able to control the world" by the world's poor, whether through military power or through the IMF-implemented austerity measures forced on developing populations. As a result, the United States has become the object of the same kind of mass popular, demagogue-fueled resentment that afflicts so many other market-dominant minorities around the world.

For the last 20 years, the United States has been promoting throughout the non-Western world a bare-knuckled, laissez-faire brand of capitalism abandoned by every Western nation—including the United States—long ago. At the same time, it has been using most of the developing world, with the conspicuous exception of the Middle East, to hold immediate majority-rule elections—"overnight democracy"—whereas Western democracies evolved much more gradually.

The U.S. attempt now underway in Iraq to install free-market democracy raises grave concerns. Like the former Yugoslavia, Iraq's ethnic dynamics are extremely complex—including long-suppressed hatreds among Kurds, Shiites, and Sunnis—and cross-cutting desires for revenge, especially against the brutal Baathist regime and its allies. Post-invasion chaos has made predictions impossible, but many fear that overnight elections could create a fundamentalist Islamic state that is opposed to free markets, to Washington, and to individual liberties, especially for women.

Moreover, because the U.S. is the world's most powerful and resented market-dominant minority, every move it makes with respect to Iraq will be scrutinized by hostile eyes. The best strategy for the U.S. may be the same one that market-dominant minorities everywhere would be well-advised to pursue: cooperate openly and fairly to advance a broad public interest, and support a government that ensures that the country's resources and wealth—in the Iraqi case, oil—benefit *all* the people.